# Losing Face

This book is a study of shame in English society in the two centuries between c.1550 and c.1750, demonstrating the ubiquity and powerful hold it had on contemporaries over the entire era. Using insights drawn from the social sciences, the book investigates multiple meanings and manifestations of shame in everyday lives and across private and public domains, exploring the practice and experience of shame in devotional life and family relations, amid social networks, and in communities or the public at large. The book pays close attention to variations and distinctive forms of shame, while also uncovering recurring patterns, a spectrum ranging from punitive, exclusionary and coercive shame through more conciliatory, lenient and inclusive forms. Placing these divergent forms in the context of the momentous social and cultural shifts that unfolded over the course of the era, the book challenges perceptions of the waning of shame in the transition from early modern to modern times, arguing instead that whereas some modes of shame diminished or disappeared, others remained vital, were reformulated and vastly enhanced.

**Ilana Krausman Ben-Amos** is Professor (emerita) of History at the Department of History, Ben-Gurion University of the Negev. Her publications include *Adolescence and Youth in Early Modern England* (1994), and *The Culture of Giving: Informal Support and Gift-Exchange in Early Modern England* (2008).

# Routledge Research in Early Modern History

**Diplomatic Cultures at the Ottoman Court, c.1500–1630**
*Edited by Tracey A. Sowerby and Christopher Markiewicz*

**William the Silent and the Dutch Revolt**
Comparative Starting Points and Triggering of Insurgencies
*Nick Ridley*

**Seventeenth Century Practical Mathematics**
Navigation by Greenvill Collins
*Paul Hughes*

**Religion and the Early Modern British Marketplace**
*Edited by Kristin M.S. Bezio and Scott Oldenburg*

**Deposing Monarchs**
Domestic Conflict and State Formation, 1500–1700
*Cathleen Sarti*

**The Politics of Obscenity in the Age of the Gutenberg Revolution**
Obscene Means in Early Modern French and European Print Culture and Literature
*Edited by Peter Frei and Nelly Labère*

**The Early Modern State: Drivers, Beneficiaries and Discontents**
Essays in Honour of Prof. Dr. Marjolein 't Hart
*Edited by Pepijn Brandon, Lex Heerma van Voss, and Griet Vermeesch*

**Losing Face**
Shame, Society and the Self in Early Modern England
*Ilana Krausman Ben-Amos*

For more information about this series, please visit: https://www.routledge.com/Routledge-Research-in-Early-Modern-History/book-series/RREMH

# Losing Face
Shame, Society and the Self in Early Modern England

Ilana Krausman Ben-Amos

LONDON AND NEW YORK

First published 2022
by Routledge
4 Park Square, Milton Park, Abingdon, Oxon OX14 4RN

and by Routledge
605 Third Avenue, New York, NY 10158

*Routledge is an imprint of the Taylor & Francis Group, an informa business*

© 2022 Ilana Krausman Ben-Amos

The right of Ilana Krausman Ben-Amos to be identified as author of this work has been asserted in accordance with sections 77 and 78 of the Copyright, Designs and Patents Act 1988.

All rights reserved. No part of this book may be reprinted or reproduced or utilised in any form or by any electronic, mechanical, or other means, now known or hereafter invented, including photocopying and recording, or in any information storage or retrieval system, without permission in writing from the publishers.

*Trademark notice*: Product or corporate names may be trademarks or registered trademarks, and are used only for identification and explanation without intent to infringe.

*British Library Cataloguing-in-Publication Data*
A catalogue record for this book is available from the British Library

*Library of Congress Cataloging-in-Publication Data*
A catalog record has been requested for this book

ISBN: 978-1-032-12925-9 (hbk)
ISBN: 978-1-032-12927-3 (pbk)
ISBN: 978-1-003-22687-1 (ebk)

DOI: 10.4324/9781003226871

Typeset in Sabon
by SPi Technologies India Pvt Ltd (Straive)

# Contents

*Acknowledgements* vii

Introduction 1
*Approaches to shame* 5
*Shame and attendant emotions* 6
*Structure and themes* 10

1 Constructions of shame 15
 *Manners, honour, morality* 16
 *Civility, courage, and masculinity* 24
 *Body constitution and gender* 27
 *Shame on the stage* 32
 *Sin and salvation* 37
 *Conclusion* 42

2 Puritans and the experience of shame 50
 *All-consuming punitive shame* 51
 *Strategies of mitigation* 57
 *Oscillating between punitive and redemptive shame* 60
 *Benign shame, inward light* 66
 *Conclusion* 70

3 Family, networks, and shame 77
 *Childhood memories of humiliation and shame* 78
 *Model letters, polite shame* 81
 *Parental shaming and the family bond* 84
 *Honour, bonding, and interpersonal ties* 88
 *Women's letters and shame* 96
 *Conclusion* 99

## 4 Commercial enterprise and exchange — 105
*Damaged reputations* 106
*Honour, morality, proficiency* 111
*Friendship and the personalization of shame* 118
*Shame and formal litigation* 124
*Merchant shame, Protestant shame* 127
*Signals of trust* 129
*Conclusion* 131

## 5 Communities as sites of shame — 137
*Communal shaming* 138
*Inferiors shaming superiors* 143
*The shamed poor* 147
*The penal system and shame* 155
*Conclusion* 160

## 6 Crime narratives and shame — 167
*The amplification of punitive shame* 168
*Repentance and redemptive shame* 173
*Defiance of shame* 178
*Bounded shame, inclusion, self-respect* 181
*Conclusion* 189

## 7 Transformations of shame — 194
*Shameful incivility, class, race* 195
*Sin, sexuality, enlightened shame* 199
*Print, satire, and public shame* 205
*Honour, pride, and shame* 212
*Conclusion* 217

Conclusion: early modern and modern shame — 226

*Bibliography* — 235
*Index* — 250

# Acknowledgements

Research for the book was conducted at the British Library and London Metropolitan Archives, and I am grateful to the staff for their assistance. The research was made possible thanks to the generous support of the Israeli Science Foundation (grant no. 258/11). Ideas and themes were presented in conferences and workshops at the Hebrew University of Jerusalem, the Israeli Forum for Early Modern History, and the Women Historians' Forum at the Haifa Feminist Research Institute. I thank the participants for their feedback and advice.

I owe many thanks to colleagues and friends for their encouragement and support along the way: Iris Agmon, Gadi Algazi, Miri Eliav-Feldon, Itzik Gilead, Ruti Ginio, Hagai Goren, Iris Goren, Hana Kaufman, Yaacov Kaufman, Avner Offer, Yulia Ustinova, and Hillay Zmora. A meeting and exchanges with Eviatar Zerubavel offered insightful and stimulating ideas on 'specifics' and 'generalities' in the history of shame, and much else. I am especially indebted to Lea Freilich and Iris Parush, for their unfailing support and for numerous discussions that improved my thinking on the ever-elusive topic of shame.

Paul Seaver encouraged the project in its inception. He had been a guide and source of inspiration ever since my early days at Stanford University many years ago. He died last year, leaving those who knew him with sadness and grief. I'll always cherish him as a mentor, scholar, friend, and one of the most decent human beings I had the fortune to have known.

My deepest gratitude goes to my family. Avner's support was unwavering and his advice and companionship sustained me over the many years of writing the book. Ory, Noa and Omri, Alma, Yuval and Lotem, all offered love and affection that filled my heart with joy and meant the whole world to me. The book is dedicated to them all.

# Introduction

> When a man is overwhelm'd with Shame, he observes a Sinking of Spirits; the heart feels cold and condensed, and the blood flies from it to the Circumstance of the Body; the Face glows, the Neck and part of the Breast partake of the Fire: He is heavy as Lead; the Head is hung down; and the Eyes through a Mist of Confusion are fix'd on the Ground: No injuries can move him; he is weary of his Being, and heartily wishes he could make himself invisible.
>
> Bernard Mandeville, *An Enquiry into the Origin of honour* (1732)[1]

In his keen description of the physical symptoms and outward manifestations of shame, Bernard Mandeville drew on a long-standing Western tradition that went back to classical authors and Christian morality. Discussion of shame figured prominently in the writings of Socrates, Plato, and Aristotle, who located shame in the cheeks and associated it with the act of covering the face. In late medieval commentary and literature, shame was thought to be expressed by blushing and a downturned face, or mediated through the face and the eyes; in Renaissance paintings, dramatic scenes of the expulsion from the Garden of Eden were conveyed in images of the first sinners ashamed of their nakedness and sin, Eve covering her breasts and loins and Adam desiring to hide by covering the eyes. Early modern writers on human passions also singled out the 'sweat and blushing for shame, which causeth heate to ascend into the face'.[2] These authors, like their ancient predecessors, commented not only on the physiological features of shame but also on its additional facets as an emotion or 'passion', as it was referred to. They discussed the circumstances under which shame arose, its benefits and drawbacks, its links to morality, shyness, and modesty, and to honour, pride, or self-esteem. Mandeville's reference to shame's physical and mental symptoms, set within his analysis of honour and pride as innate elements of human existence, indicates that interest in the emotion and its distinctive qualities by no means diminished or faded away.

This book is about shame in English society in the two centuries before Mandeville wrote his treatise. It presents a history of shame that goes beyond these theoretical discussions of what shame was about, seeking to delineate and understand the force and role of shame in society at large. It

DOI: 10.4324/9781003226871-1

2  *Introduction*

explores the sources and meanings of early modern shame; when it arose and how it was applied, the manner in which it was constructed, the values within which it was embedded, the practices and experiences associated with it. The book also examines the changing contours of shame in an era that witnessed momentous changes in religion, society, and culture, observing the transformations it underwent as these changes unfolded across time.

Early modern historians have long been aware of shame's presence in the rural communities of the pre-modern past. Two issues drew the historians' attention; the centrality of honour and shame among the landed elite, and the role of public shaming in enforcing order and norms in the small, tight-knit peasant communities of late medieval times. Inspired by anthropological studies arguing that notions of honour and shame typically flourished in cultures where society was rural, highly stratified, and lacking central authority, historical accounts of elite culture and politics resonated with honour-related shame. In his study of aristocratic culture in the Tudor North, Mervin James presented a 'lineage society' governed by a code of honour that was rooted in a long-established military and chivalric tradition. The code typically invoked competitive assertiveness and a resort to violence and retribution when honour was transgressed: 'blot, discredit, shame [being] keywords in the vocabulary of honour'. As James also argued, by 1600 this culture of honour and shame receded under the impact of new forces and beliefs associated with Christian humanism and service to the state, as well as the diffusion of the Protestant religion.[3] A similar perspective dominated historical accounts of peasant communities of late medieval times. In these 'closed corporate communities', public shaming acted as an informal mechanism of regulation and control, with gossip and slander serving to maintain conformity to inward-oriented community norms. Like elite honour, community shaming dissipated in the face of developments entailed in the expansion of markets, social atomization, and the breakdown of small communities, with informal control mechanisms being replaced by a sophisticated system of central and local courts. Ideas associated with Renaissance humanism and the Protestant notion of sin, which was attuned to feelings of guilt instead of public practices of shame, also contributed to the view of the diminishing force of shame.[4]

Research in recent decades has eroded central tenets of this view of the diminishing force of shame on the threshold of early modern times. Studies point to the continued role of the concept of honour among the elite and the persisting susceptibility of its members to insults and assaults on their honour. The research has also broadened our understanding of elite honour, indicating the set of values and assets underpinning it and their indispensability to the power and status of the ruling elite well into the late seventeenth century.[5] Among the populace at large, public shaming persevered as well. As a large body of research on crime has shown, in its attempt at controlling and supervising communities, the state and its expanding legal system inflicted harsh shaming penalties well into the mid-seventeenth century and beyond. Studies have also demonstrated the paramount role of ritual and verbal shaming in exacting conformity from community members, with gossip, insult, and slander coming to a peak in the decades between the late sixteenth and mid-seventeenth century, when they began to gradually decline.[6]

The single most important formulation of shame's progressive ascent – rather than its demise – in the early modern past was Norbert Elias' seminal study *The Civilizing Process*.[7] Taking its cue from sociological and psychological insights, Elias identified shame as relating neither to aggressive responses to honour nor solely to the gaze of the public. Instead, he posited a more refined shame that was related to internal instincts and inhibitions, through which an innate tendency to aggressive behaviour and uncontrolled emotions were tamed. Acquired through education and socialization from a young age, shame acted as an internal mechanism of control, predisposing a person to emotional restraint, with the compulsion being experienced as originating internally rather than enforced externally. Shame was central to the process of 'civilizing' individuals, that is, the prolonged shift from medieval society, in which individuals were prone to impulsive and violent action, to a modern society, where individuals came to guard their emotions, maintaining self-restraint and control over impulses, feeling ashamed when violating norms of conduct and exhibiting poor manners, or when observing others act similarly.

Critics have long exposed major historiographical and methodological flaws in Elias' grand narrative. Historians pointed to the limits of his sources, especially his reliance on etiquette and advice manuals rather than on actual practice. His theory of the domestication of the aristocracy is questionable in light of developments in our understanding of aristocratic politics and culture in late medieval and early modern times, in England as well as on the continent. Historians critiqued the linearity and progression of the process he described, with medievalists pointing to Elias' overemphasis on the violence of medieval people, and modern historians indicating his neglect of persisting patterns of aggression well into modern times. Sociologists, too, raised issues regarding Elias' analysis of social change in the transition to modernity.[8] Historical research has also shown the roots of civility and manners in a long medieval tradition of injunctions for polite behaviour among the elite and other groups, and the coarse image of an emotional state of an entire epoch, both medieval and early modern, is no longer sustainable.[9] Elias' assumptions regarding the emotion of shame as an affect or a drive, which was based on a Freudian interpretation of basic human instincts, raised critical responses as well. With its tendency to reduce emotional states to innate drives, such an interpretation loses sight of the role of culture and values in shaping emotional states and their complexity. Elias' emphasis on shame as an internal mechanism of control that becomes a sort of 'superego' ignored the potential for an active self that espoused beliefs, convictions, and a measure of reflective judgement beyond inhibitions and semi-automatic responses.[10]

For all the critique, some of Elias' ideas remain pertinent, especially for a proper rendering of the history of shame in the early modern past. Elias was the first to address the history of shame as an emotion on its own, shame being central to his research agenda rather than deriving from, or incidental to, other topics of inquiry. Instead of associating shame with traditional rural society and small tight-knit communities, he addressed shame's contribution to modernizing processes, not only state formation and the rise of court society but also – a point not always sufficiently emphasized – to social relations and interactions, amid 'chains of dependence' in which individuals were bound 'more and more closely' and the 'mutual observation of people increases'.[11] His insightful argument that in a society increasingly governed by greater labour division, expanding markets and interdependencies, shame was critical for monitoring and regulating interactions among groups and classes below the elite, still resonates. This perspective, which places greater emphasis on subtle and moderate forms of control, and on a more constructive component of shame, will be emphasized and explored in this book.

All in all, historical accounts of early modern shame, Elias' as well as others, remain partial and leave many issues regarding the meanings of shame unexplored. The kind of refined shame Elias described – subtle, internal, pervading everyday practice and involving the threat or anticipation of shame – deserves closer investigation, examining a wider range of documents beyond, or alongside, the manuals on which he relied, and in groups and classes below the elite. Additional facets and sources of shame need be accounted for, including honour-related shame as well as public shaming, the latter involving brutal penalties far removed from the type of refined shame Elias had described. Other practices and experiences of shame need to be considered; from Protestant ideas regarding sin and the shameful experience they induced, through experiences of shame in families and across genders, or the shame that was associated with inferior social status, the lower classes and the poor. Arguably, early modern shame – and its contours of change over time – cannot be fully assessed through the prism of a specific practice or emotional state, but rather its meanings and manifestations need to be explored across classes and in different public and private settings, as well as across time.

The present study investigates early modern shame amid varied settings and social interactions, arguing that the emotion was ubiquitous and remained potent throughout the entire era. This argument is pursued along three major strands. First, shame was grounded in, and buttressed by, a host of beliefs and processes that marked the era and affected varied domains of life across social classes and genders. These beliefs and processes included not only an emerging civility code and notions of honour, but also Protestant understanding of sin and immorality, perceptions of patriarchy and community relations, a burgeoning print market along with growing religious and social divisions, an expansive state apparatus and networks of exchange. Secondly, shame varied in meanings, content, and form. While contextualizing shame and paying close attention to variations and distinctive uses or experiences, the book uncovers recurring patterns, a spectrum ranging from punitive, exclusionary, and coercive shame through more lenient and inclusive forms. These divergent modes, it is argued, offer a key to understanding shame's powerful hold on contemporaries, and the potent role it played in the lives of individuals and in social interactions throughout.

Lastly, the book revisits notions of change over time. It rejects arguments about the decline of shame over the course of the seventeenth century, while also resisting a model of the progressive ascendency of shame into modern times. It captures a more complex transition, involving several, and at times contrasting, trajectories of shame, evident especially from the mid-seventeenth century through the mid-eighteenth century and beyond.

## Approaches to shame

Modern scholarly interest in shame has been marked, and there is today an abundance of theoretical literature on shame in a wide range of disciplines, from the life sciences through social, linguistic, legal, and human studies. In some disciplines shame may be considered an innate human, or evolutionary, affect, while in others it is identified as socially and culturally constructed. In some analyses, both the cultural and universal dimensions of shame are emphasized. A study of emotions across languages and cultures identifies shame as belonging to 'complex and culture-specific' emotions that are not translatable nor have corresponding terms in other languages; nevertheless, in most languages shame has equivalents, that is, words linking feelings with other people's disapproval, hence a 'universal core meaning' of shame can be observed.[12]

Most theoretical approaches do not focus on words and precise definitions, but rather analyse the sources and circumstances under which shame arises. These approaches are diverse and somewhat disparate. Some theorists, for example, conceptualize shame as a reaction to criticism, disapproval, and rejection, usually when a breach of norms occurs. Others conceive of shame as resulting from a sense of personal failure; failure to live up to one's ideals or some desired ideal state, or of having one's weaknesses or inadequacies exposed, leading to negative self-evaluation in comparison to others. Still other scholars elaborate on shame as a 'moral emotion', which is linked to an awareness by others, as well as by oneself, of a moral infringement. This may occur when others become aware that one has committed a moral infraction and the actor concurs with this judgement, or when a person is afraid others will become aware of the infringement at some future point.[13]

These varied conceptions of shame need not always apply to past societies nor to the historical circumstances that will be discussed in this book. Nevertheless, the social science literature opens up ways of thinking about shame that inform this book and its approach to examining the historical sources at hand. The literature alerts us to the sheer breadth of meanings, manifestations, and sources of shame. It underlines the embeddedness of shame in everyday relationships and social interactions, while also pointing to its entanglement in issues of self-awareness or consciousness, self-assessment or self-esteem. Shame may be intimately linked to an external, relational self, as well as to internal sources of the self.

Sociological accounts that build on the type of analysis offered by Elias also alert us to dispositions and habits of shame connected to social relations across classes and the gender divide. They point to shame's role in applying stigma and the marking of individuals and groups as disgraced, or else in buttressing the boundaries between social groups, classes, genders and race.[14] Some theories, also drawing on Elias, bring into sharper focus the ubiquity of hidden shame; that is, the shame that goes unmentioned, unspoken or is invisible; the shame of feeling ashamed.[15] In an early modern context, for example, while words of shame and cognate terms – shaming, shameful, shame – abound in Shakespeare's plays, scenes implying hidden shame also recur, with the protagonists remaining speechless and their shame being left for the audience to imagine or guess; 'the silence of the shamed repentance that cannot speak', as a dramatic moment in *The Tempest*, when the usurping brother (Antonio) did not respond to his sibling's (Prospero) proclamation of forgiveness, was described.[16] The shame that went unmentioned and unspoken – the shamed child, for example – are among the themes that will be considered in this book. And while overall searching outright expressions of shame words, the book explores forms of shame that were insinuated, expressed tacitly or indirectly, or through emotions closely related to shame. The rhetoric, vocabulary, and imagery associated with shame are brought to light throughout.

Theories and conceptualizations of shame also alert us to broader patterns and modes of shame and shaming that are particularly relevant for probing early modern shame. Two major approaches are pertinent. The first approach views shame as a painful state, an emotional reaction to denigration, humiliation, and exclusion, causing fear, anxiety, or an impairment to the personality; the shame stigmatizes people for their weaknesses, failures, or being 'spoiled'. The second perception of shame points to its integrative potential, a signal in human relations that is essential for human bonds. The shame could be constructive; feeling ashamed about the negligence of human obligations or the lack of regard to others, which may prompt empathy, solidarity, and connectedness, or else encourage self-examination that promotes reform. In criminology studies, these modes of shame are conceptualized as, respectively, a shame that is punitive, stigmatic, and exclusionary, and a shame that is re-integrative. While the former makes the shamed criminal an outcast whose evil deed defines the totality of his character, the latter focuses on a specific transgression rather than viewing the offender as irremediably evil, with the shame invariably bringing in its wake regret, apologies or forgiveness.[17]

## Shame and attendant emotions

Shame spills into other emotions. Lucien Febvre, who pioneered the study of emotions in the past, had long noted the difficulty of distinguishing one emotion from another, and identifying emotions that are often ambivalent, nuanced, layered, or constantly 'hide and reveal' one another. Present-day historians of emotions are particularly aware of these emotional alignments, insisting that emotions be studied as emotional 'regimes', 'communities', or 'sequences', or through the clusters of values connecting them.[18] In the case of shame, scholars underline its related emotions, referring to shame and attendant emotions, shame and its 'relatives', or denoting shame as part of 'self-conscious emotions' and emotions of 'self-assessment'.[19]

The emotions most frequently associated with shame are pride, guilt, embarrassment, humiliation, and, to a lesser extent, anger or shame-driven rage. In the historical literature, honour is considered alongside, or in place of, pride. Since these emotions are referred to and recur in this book, it is appropriate to briefly consider their distinctive qualities and their affinities with shame, so as to clarify the manner in which these terms indicating emotion are used and their overall relevance to the study of early modern shame.

## Shame, honour, pride

Historians and anthropologists have long associated dishonour and shame with honour and pride, the twin set of emotions being linked as binary opposites. Assault to honour brings dishonour, hurt pride brings shame. In a culture of honour, dishonour is imminent; 'with every engagement of honour came the opportunity for dishonour', as king Henry VIII cautioned upon assuming his new functions as king of Ireland.[20]

Anthropologist Frank Henderson Stewart argued that shame is not exactly the opposite of honour, but rather of pride. This perspective considers shame and pride to be emotions; honour is not an emotion but a right to respect, with dishonour rather than shame being regarded as its opposite. Shame in this view is also broader than dishonour.[21] As the abovementioned assertion of Henri VIII suggests, in his view dishonour, and not shame, was the obvious opposite of honour, and to this extent Stewart's distinction is valid. In the literature on emotions in modern society, shame is considered the mirror-image of pride rather than of honour, with the latter presumed to have collapsed or lost its appeal in modern times.[22]

Nevertheless, a distinction between dishonour and shame in past societies need not be drawn too far or considered as significant. Some historians have argued that in the pre-modern past honour itself was an emotion or an 'emotional disposition', which, when violated, caused individuals disgrace and shame in the eyes of an audience of peers. Even if honour is regarded as a right or an entitlement, arguably the loss of that right may inflict shame. Recent research on honour in ancient Greek culture and among the elite of early modern England has demonstrated the diversity of notions of honour in these societies, and the plurality of claims to honour these notions generated. Violation of any one of these claims would be considered dishonour and could bring shame in its wake. Shame would be felt even if actual dishonour did not occur; threatened honour, the fear of losing honour or even picturing oneself losing honour could all trigger feelings of being ashamed.[23] When referring to honour in this book, these intimate links between dishonour and shame will be emphasized.

## Shame and guilt

One of the most well-known distinctions related to shame is the distinction between shame and guilt. Shame is related to an external opinion and the judgement of others, while guilt is oriented inwardly, to internalized values and one's conscience. The classic statement of this antithesis is anthropologist Ruth Benedict's influential study on shame and guilt cultures; whereas the former relied on shame and on external sanctions to achieve conformity, the latter were governed by guilt, which responded to internal sanctions and standards. This conception was grounded in assumptions regarding the Protestant (and Judeo-Christian) notion of sin, which, so it was presumed, invoked internalized values and an introspective self rather than externally-enforced norms. In some historical accounts, the distinction was related to the transition to modern society; in his study on early New England, John Demos observed a shift from a society governed by shame and the preoccupation with the opinion of others, to one in which guilt and internal morality came to prevail.[24]

Theorists of shame overwhelmingly reject this distinction between externally-oriented shame and internal guilt, arguing that both shame and guilt possess an internalized component. Norbert Elias had indeed been innovative in discarding the distinction between shame and guilt, emphasizing instead the inward and outward dimensions of shame, with shame being experienced both internally and as a response to the observation or regard of others. As many have argued, since shame is an emotion of self-assessment and concerns matters that may touch innermost facets of the self, it may arise whether the world is looking or not; it may be experienced regardless of the view of others.[25]

Alternative definitions of shame vs guilt have also been proposed. Shame is broader than guilt; it is concerned with the self as a whole (one's wishes, traits, shortcomings), whereas guilt relates only to one's actions as an agent. In some formulations, the emphasis is on guilt being triggered when actions have specific consequences, that is, something bad happens to others that was caused by the agent's actions, even if unintended.[26] This approach is more productive, and will also inform the discussion in this book. Still, even if the distinction is sustained, it need not be stretched too far; in practice, the differences are too slight or even not particularly important. There are 'grey areas', as people may feel not only guilt but also shame with regards to some aspects of their personality or specific actions, whether or not these had consequences. Guilt may lead to shame or be entangled in it, and the two are often complementary.[27] Early modern Protestants used the word guilt to describe specific acts (the 'guilt of our sins'), but also to denote a broader moral sense (the 'guilt of our conscience'). For the most part, they used 'shame' to describe both, first and foremost the emotion that engulfs the believer following self-reflection and the recognition of sin, making no apparent distinction between shame and guilt.[28]

Throughout this book, guilt as an emotion that relates to acts and consequences will be indicated at some points. For the most part, though, the differences will not be emphasized; guilt will be considered as complementary, and closely related, to shame.

*Shame and embarrassment*

Shame is often linked to embarrassment. The word itself was not used in English before the eighteenth century, and some studies point to its emergence as an emotional concept and a 'unique cultural artefact' in modern times.[29] Definitions of embarrassment vary, but several features are commonly identified. In embarrassment, issues of exposure and self-presentation are critical, even more than in shame; there is no embarrassment without an audience. Like shame, the emotion focuses on a breach of norms, but the norms relate to manners rather than morals, causing a sense of awkwardness, social discomfort or unease rather than exclusion or outright rejection. Scholars emphasize the lighter features of embarrassment, considering it usually more short-lived or inconsequential; only rarely is it deliberately inflicted.[30]

All this implies that embarrassment is a more specific, subtle, or softer variant of shame. It need not necessarily exclude shame and could be linked to it, and in many contexts it is difficult to differentiate between the two. More important still, these features of embarrassment would have been recognized and experienced by early modern contemporaries. That is, the absence of a vocabulary did not preclude an experience of embarrassment or feeling embarrassed in circumstances involving exposure to others. For Norbert Elias, shame by no means excluded embarrassment, and the German term he used ('Scham') denoted something between shame, embarrassment, and a sense of awkwardness or unease.[31] Early modern literature on manners is suffused with situations that would cause embarrassment rather than, or alongside with, shame, focusing on self-presentation more than on morals (or focusing on both). As we shall also see, in some configurations involving interpersonal relations, embarrassment could be experienced in response to rebuke and certain types of more lenient shaming. While exploring shame in this book, embarrassment as a subtle variant of shame will be considered and observed.

*Shame and humiliation*

Alongside embarrassment, humiliation is viewed as a subset within the 'large domain' of shame. Humiliation may be viewed as the active, harsher face of shame, or as an extreme case of insult touching on the intrinsic value, self-esteem, or self-perception of individuals or groups. It is caused by something being actually done to a person, or through conditions that are the result of actions (or omissions) by others. It often involves a deep sense of helplessness, vulnerability, or the fear of lacking or losing control.[32]

Shame need not always imply humiliation, especially if it is not too severe or harsh, or where it is considered humbling and reformative. On the other hand, someone who is humiliated is also shamed, and to humiliate someone is to expose them to shame. Moreover, under certain circumstances and configurations, shame may still cause humiliation, as in the case of the person who is ashamed of a feature of themselves deriving from their belonging to a group that might expose them to feelings of humiliation (e.g., inferior status, religious or ethnic minority), even if actual shaming is not involved.[33] These and other possible entanglements of shame in varied forms of humiliation, harsher as well as less severe, are of vital importance for the study of early modern shame, and will be observed and emphasized in this book.

The above comments on shame's emotional affinities suggest that these emotions are linked to shame either as variants – soft or harsh – of the emotion, or else they are complementary to shame, precede it, or emerge in its wake. These feelings often reflect on, or may conceal, shame, indicating its presence when it is not directly invoked or talked about. They all may offer important clues and insights on shame and will be considered as an integral part of this study of early modern shame.

## Structure and themes

The book is divided into several chapters, each investigating facets of shame in a specific context or social setting, using different sets of documents. Chapter 1 sets the stage by tracing constructions of shame in varied early modern discourses and literary sources, using selected publications of different genres, including books of manners, educational and scientific treatises, drama, and devotional literature. The chapter unravels divergent and richly invoked constructions, while also uncovering overlapping patterns and modes of shame that run throughout. Chapter 2 focuses more closely on the Protestant message on shame in sin, exploring the responses and experiences it induced. It is based on spiritual autobiographies and diaries written by puritans of varied orientations, moderate, non-conforming and radicals, and uncovers a set of intensely internalized experiences, ranging from a devastating experience of self-inflicted shame to more mitigated and redeeming shame oriented towards sanctification. By the mid- and late seventeenth century, an altogether radical defiance of shame, in which a sense of sin and shame was replaced with an inward experience of God, can be observed.

The next two chapters shift to shame and shaming amid personal interactions and social networks. The chapters rely on autobiographies and correspondences, focusing on detailed cases among the elite and especially among the professional and middling classes. Chapter 3 offers a child's perspective of shame, while also exploring parental shaming and the shame applied amid networks of kin, patronage, and friends. It also reveals shared experiences of shame among women. Chapter 4 looks closely into the shame that surfaces in merchant correspondence, demonstrating its role in inflicting penalties and undermining reputations of merchants who defaulted on their obligations, but also, more importantly, its function in reinforcing trust and cementing traders' ties and loyalties to one another. Both chapters indicate the role of punitive shame as a form of threat or punishment that could undermine ties, at time irrevocably; both also identify distinctive patterns of 'network shame', especially the pervasive use of rebukes and personalized shame, that is, the shame that invoked bonding and personal ties of exchange. Shame's role in the regulation of interpersonal relations, monitoring and cementing bonds and obligations is highlighted.

Chapters 5 and 6 turn the focus to the public domain. These chapters build on the findings of a large body of research on penal practice and community regulation, as well as on a close reading of reports on crime, including ballads, news reports and published confessions of criminals condemned to death. The chapters address different facets and manifestations of shame; from community rituals, gossip and slander, through public shame penalties inflicted by the courts and the shame wreaked on the poor by an emerging system of the Poor Laws. Both chapters highlight the pivotal role of punitive and stigmatic shame, which brought humiliation and marked individuals as totally sinful or flawed, the punitive stigma being broadcast and enhanced through publications and reports on crime. Yet the chapters also outline different, at times contrasting, forms of moderate or mitigated shame, which could generate conciliation, re-integration or empathy among community members and crowds. The chapters overall pay close attention to the voices of ordinary people and the shamed themselves – the criminals, the poor, and the social outcasts. They point to patterns of resistance and defiance of shame, evident in the appropriation of a shame vocabulary to critique superiors or the authorities, or in an emerging distinctive form of 'bounded shame'. Here, convicted criminals admitted their shame or guilt, but still resisted their castigation as outcasts, advancing broadly shared notions of justice, mitigating circumstances and pardonable crimes through which they carved and regained for themselves a measure of self-esteem and respect.

Whereas each of the chapters focuses on specific experiences and settings, overall they demonstrate the pervasiveness of shame in everyday interactions in virtually all domains of life, both private and public. They indicate recurring patterns and modes of shame across all settings; a spectrum between harsh, punitive, and humiliating shame through varied forms of subtle, mitigated, or redeeming and more rehabilitative forms, pointing also to the contrasting implications they had for social relations and a sense of an internal and a relational self. The chapters indicate the embeddedness of these contrasting shame patterns in broader ideological, social, and gender divisions that came to mark the decades from the mid-sixteenth century onwards. They also show the ways in which these varied forms of shame were amplified through the growing print market, expanding social and commercial networks, as well as the mounting force of state institutions and a penal system through which individuals and communities were regulated and surveilled.

In the final chapter, these processes are pursued over time, across the decades from the mid-seventeenth century and through the early and mid-eighteenth, probing their effect on the changing contours of shame. The chapter underscores several major shifts; the enhanced diffusion of notions of civility and incivility in English society and its increased encounters with foreign peoples and races across the seas; new practices in penal practice and culture that entailed a decline in public shame penalties; and novel enlightenment ideas regarding sin and sexuality, education and penal reform. The chapter highlights the explosion of the print market and a vastly expanding public sphere, where the shaming of groups and individuals among all classes took a new and vigorous role. While shaming and shame experiences gradually mutated, the change was neither linear nor homogenous; some practices, notably public shame rituals and penalties, diminished or faded, whereas others were transformed, reformulated, and vastly enhanced. As the concluding chapter points out, these different trajectories of shame persisted into the nineteenth century and beyond, suggesting a renewed and vigorous role for shame in modernity and modern life.

## Notes

1 *An Enquiry into the Origin of Honour, and The Usefulness of Christianity in War. By the Author of Fable of the Bees [B. de Mandeville]* (London, 1732), 11–12.
2 Aristotle, *On Rhetoric: A Theory of Civic Discourse*, trans. George A. Kennedy (Oxford, 1991), Book 2, Chap. 6, 143–9, esp. 148–9; Peter N. Stearns, *Shame: A Brief History* (Urbana and Chicago, 2017), 19–21; Werner L. Gundersheimer, 'Concepts of shame and Pocaterra's Dialoghi Della Vergogna', *Renaissance Quarterly*, 47 (1994), 34–56, esp. 36–40; Martha Hollander, 'Losses of Face: Rembrandt, Masaccio, and the Drama of Shame', *Social Research*, 70 (2003), 1327–50; Pierre de la Primaudaye, *The French academie wherein is discoursed the institution of manners ... by precepts of doctrine, and examples of the lives of ancient sages and famous men.* Trans. T.B. (London, 1594), STC2 15235, 243.
3 J.G. Peristiany (ed.), *Honour and Shame: The Values of Mediterranean Society* (London, 1965); Mervyn James, 'English Politics and the Concept of Honour, 1485–1642', in his *Society, Politics and Culture: Studies in Early Modern England* (Cambridge, 1986), 308–415, quotation on 342. See also, Lawrence Stone, *The Crisis of the Aristocracy, 1558–1641* (Oxford, 1965).
4 Lawrence Stone, *The Family, Sex and Marriage in England 1500– 1800* (New York, 1977), 142–50. For an analysis of the earlier historiography on the breakdown of medieval village communities, see Richard M. Smith, '"Modernization" and the Corporate Medieval Village Community in England: Some Skeptical Reflections', in A.H.R. Baker and Derek Gregory (eds.), *Explorations in Historical Geography* (Cambridge, 1984), 140–245, esp. 148–9.
5 Major studies include Markku Peltonen, *The Duel in Early Modern England: Civility, Politeness and Honour* (Cambridge, 2003); Linda A. Pollock 'Honor, Gender, and Reconciliation in Elite Culture, 1570–1700', *Journal of British Studies*, 46 (2007), 3–29; Brendan Kane, *The Politics and Culture of Honour in Britain and Ireland, 1541–1641* (Cambridge, 2010); Keith Thomas, *The Ends of Life: Roads to Fulfilment in Early Modern England* (Oxford, 2009), esp. 174–9, 44–50; Courtney Erin Thomas, *If I Lose Mine Honour, I Lose Myself: Honour among the Early Modern English Elite* (Toronto, 2017).
6 Major recent studies include Simon Devereaux and Paul Griffiths (eds.), *Penal Practice and Culture, 1500– 1900: Punishing the English* (Basingstoke, 2004); David Nash and Anne-Marie Kilday, *Cultures of Shame: Exploring Crime and Morality in Britain, 1600– 1900* (Basingstoke, 2010); Martin Ingram, *Carnal*

*Knowledge: Regulating Sex in England, 1470–1600* (Cambridge, 2017), esp. 75–7; Bernard Capp, *When Gossips Meet: Women, Family and Neighbourhood in Early Modern England* (Oxford, 2003); Bernard Capp, *England's Culture Wars: Puritan Reformation and Its Enemies in the Interregnum, 1649–1660* (Oxford, 2012); Robert Shoemaker, 'The Decline of Public Insult in London 1660–1800', *Past and Present*, 169 (2000), 97–131.

7 Norbert Elias, *The Civilizing Process: The History of Manners and State Formation and Civilization* (1939), trans. Edmund Jephcott (Oxford, 1969, new edition 1994).

8 Giora Sternberg, *Status Interaction during the Reign of Louis XIV* (Oxford, 2014), 4–5; Barbara H. Rosenwein, 'Worrying about Emotions in History', *American Historical Review*, 107 (2002), 821–45, esp. 826–8, 834–42; Richard E. Evans, *Rituals of Retribution: Capital Punishment in Germany, 1660–1987* (Oxford, 1996), 891–9; Ute Frevert et al., *Emotional Lexicons: Continuity and Change in the Vocabulary of Feeling 1700–2000* (Oxford, 2014), 3–4; Robert van Krieken, 'Norbert Elias and Emotions in History', in David Lemmings and Ann Brooks (eds.), *Emotions and Social Change: Historical and Sociological Perspectives* (New York and Abingdon, 2014), 19–42.

9 Keith Thomas, *In Pursuit of Civility: Manners and Civilization in Early Modern England* (Massachusetts, 2018), 15–7; Jan Plamper, *The History of Emotions: An Introduction* (Oxford, 2015), 70–1.

10 Frevert, *Emotional Lexicons*, 3–4; Rosenwein, 'Worrying about Emotions', 834–42; Plamper, *The History of Emotions*, 50–1; Linda A. Pollock, 'The Practice of Kindness in Early Modern Elite Society', *Past and Present*, 211 (2011), 122–5, 149–58. For reflective judgement that sometimes takes place 'on a less than conscious level', see Jerrold Seigel, *The Idea of the Self: Thought and Experience in Western Europe since the Seventeenth Century* (Cambridge, 2005), 17–32.

11 Elias, *The Civilizing Process*, 496. For a positive assessment of this aspect (and others) of Elias' work, see van Krieken, 'Norbert Elias and Emotions in History', 37–8.

12 Anna Wierzbicka, *Emotions Across Languages and Cultures: Diversity and Universals* (Cambridge, 1999), 7–9, 109–12, 286–9. For a broad perspective on emotions in historical studies and in the social and life sciences, see Plamper, *The History of Emotions*.

13 For an overview of approaches, see Eliza Ahmed, Nathan Harris, John Braithwaite and Valerie Braithwaite (eds.), *Shame Management through Reintegration* (Cambridge, 2001), 78–93. And see also Wierzbicka, *Emotions Across Languages*, 109–12.

14 Erving Goffman, *Stigma: Notes on the Management of Spoiled Identity* (New Jersey, 1963); Pierre Bourdieu, *Outline of a Theory of Practice*, trans. Richard Nice (Cambridge, 1977), 43–52; Martha C. Nussbaum, *Hiding from Humanity: Disgust, Shame and the Law* (Princeton, 2004), 172–221.

15 Thomas J. Scheff, 'The Ubiquity of Hidden Shame in Modernity', *Cultural Sociology*, 8 (2014), 129–41.

16 Gundersheimer, 'Concepts of shame', 36–7; Emma Smith, *The Cambridge Shakespeare Guide* (Cambridge, 2012), 179. See also Ewan Fernie, *Shame in Shakespeare* (London, 2002), and Chap. 1 below.

17 Nussbaum, *Hiding from Humanity*, 241–7; Thomas J. Scheff, 'Shame and the Social Bond: A Sociological Theory', *Sociological Theory*, 18 (2000), 84–99, esp. 98; John Braithwaite, 'Shame and Modernity', *British Journal of Criminology*, 33 (1993), 2–3.

18 Lucien Febvre, 'Sensibility and History: How to Reconstitute the Emotional Life of the Past', in Peter Burke (ed.), *A New Kind of History and Other Essays*, trans. K. Folca (New York, 1973), 12–26, esp. 18, 23; Plamper, *The History of Emotions*, 41, 67–74; Barbara Rosenwein, *Generations of Feeling: A History of Emotions, 600–1700* (Cambridge, 2016), 3–10; Pollock, 'The Practice of Kindness', 153.

## 14  Introduction

19 Michael Lewis, 'Self-Conscious Emotions: Embarrassment, Pride, Shame and Guilt', in Michael Lewis, Jeannette M. Haviland-Jones, and Lisa Feldman Barrett (eds.), *Handbook of Emotions* (London, 2008), 742–56; Nussbaum, *Hiding from Humanity*, 203–10; Wierzbicka, *Emotions Across Languages*, 108–22; Scheff, *Shame and the Social Bond*, 96. See also the editor's introduction to an issue of *Social Research* devoted to 'shame', *Social Research*, 70 (2003), 1015.
20 Brenan Kane, *The Politics and Culture of Honour*, 3.
21 Frank Henderson Stewart, *Honor* (Chicago, 1994), 128–9.
22 Wierzbicka, *Emotions across Languages*, 116–7; Thomas Scheff, 'Pride and Shame: The Master Emotions', in *Bloody Revenge: Emotions, Nationalism and War* (Boulder, 1994), 39–55.
23 Ute Frevert, *Emotions in History – Lost and Found* (Budapest, 2011), 40–8; Kwame Anthony Appiah, *The Honor Code: How Moral Revolutions Happen* (New York, 2010), 12–8; Douglas L. Cairns, *Aidos: The Psychology and Ethics of Honour and Shame in Ancient Greek Literature* (Oxford, 1993), 12–4; Douglas L. Cairns, 'Honour and Shame: Modern Controversies and Ancient Values', *Critical Quarterly*, 53 (2011), 23–41, esp. 28–39; Thomas, *If I Lose Mine Honour*.
24 Ruth Benedict, *The Chrysanthemum and the Sword: Patterns of Japanese Culture* (Boston, 1946); Cairns, *Aidos: The Psychology and Ethics*, 27–45; John Demos, 'Shame and Guilt in Early New England', in C.Z. Stearns and P.N. Stearns (eds.), *Emotions and Social Change: Toward a New Psychohistory* (New York, 1988), 69–86. See also Stephen Pattison, *Shame: Theory, Therapy, Theology* (Cambridge, 2000), 137–9. For applications of the distinction between shame and guilt cultures, in classical studies, see Cairns, *Aidos: The Psychology and Ethics*, 27, note. 59.
25 Elias, *The Civilizing Process*, 493; Ahmed et al. (eds.) *Shame Management*, 84; Cairns, *Aidos: The Psychology and Ethics*, 14–7; Nussbaum, *Hiding from Humanity*, 205.
26 Lewis, 'Self-Conscious Emotions', 748–9; Cairns, *Aidos: The Psychology and Ethics*, 18–23; Nussbaum, *Hiding from Humanity*, 207–8; Wierzbicka, *Emotions Across Languages*, 119–21.
27 Cairns, *Aidos: The Psychology and Ethics*, 22–5; Ahmed et al (eds.), *Shame Management*, 123–4. See also Pattison, *Shame: Theory, Therapy, Theology*, 43–5.
28 See also Chap. 2 below. For the argument that Christianity 'innovated less by replacing shame with guilt than by embracing shame shamelessly', see also Virginia Burrus, *Saving Shame: Martyrs, Saints, and Other Abject Subjects* (Philadelphia, 2008), 7.
29 Peter N. Stearns, 'History of Emotions: Issues of Change and Impact', in Lewis et al. (eds.), *Handbook of Emotions*, 17–32, esp. 25; Wierzbicka, *Emotions Across Languages*, 112.
30 Ibid., 112–6; Nussbaum, *Hiding from Humanity*, 204–6; Ahmed et al. (eds.), *Shame Management*, 124–6; Scheff, 'Shame and the Social Bond', 93, note 5.
31 Wierzbicka, *Emotions Across Languages*, 112. For the close affinity between shame and embarrassment, see also Thomas J. Scheff, 'Elias, Freud and Goffman: Shame as the Master Emotion', in Steven Loyal and Stephen Quilley (eds.), *The Sociology of Norbert Elias* (Cambridge, 2004), 229–42, esp. 235–8.
32 Ian William Miller, *Humiliation: And Other Essays on Honor, Social Discomfort, and Violence* (Ithaca, 1993), esp. 12; Nussbaum, *Hiding from Humanity*, 203–4; Avishai Margalit, *The Decent Society* (Cambridge, Massachusetts, 1998), 9–10, 119–21.
33 Nussbaum, *Hiding from Humanity*, 203–4; Frevert, *Emotions in History* 5–6; Margalit, *The Decent Society*, 130–3.

# 1 Constructions of shame

Early modern writers on the subject of the 'humane passions' accorded shame a central role. Drawing on a long tradition of thought that dated back to ancient authorities and Christian theology, these authors pointed to the external manifestations and signs of shame – the blushing, downturned or covered face, the averted gaze. Yet first and foremost, they elaborated on shame as a passion that resonated with moral qualities. Citing Cicero and Plato, the author of *The French Academie* (1586) described shame as 'the guardian of all the vertues … [which] deserveth great commendation … as that which fashioneseth [life] according to the paterne of decencie and honestie'. Other authors drew attention to the moral benefits of shame as a deterrent against 'loose affections' and producing a 'bridle on vice', pointing as well to its moral drawbacks. In his *A Table of Humane Passions* (1621), Nicolas Coeffeteau warned that the shame that induced humans to 'decline from wickednesse' could also produce moral laxity: 'sometimes shee diverts them from commendable and vertuous actions, by apprehension of an imaginary dishonour'. In Robert Burton's *The Anatomy of Melancholy* (1621), the shame that came from the loss of honour – 'the apprehension of some crosses, which may make man infamous' – could bring in its wake despair, mental anguish and disease, even death.[1]

These discussions of shame as a passion, with their emphasis on immorality and dishonour as the sources of shame, convey important and enduring dimensions of early modern shame. Yet they do not indicate shame's many divergent, rich and compelling constructions. An array of discourses and beliefs that marked the era from the mid-sixteenth century onwards resonate with implications for shaming and shame; the discourse on civility and honour, humanist notions of virtue and morality, beliefs regarding gender, sexuality and the human body, Protestant notions of sin and salvation – all these invariably implied sources and inducements for shaming and shame. As the print market expanded substantially over the course of the era, the shame that was intrinsic to these discourses was communicated in numerous publications, including books on manners and conduct manuals, scientific treatises, and literary and devotional works of varied genres and sorts.

This chapter examines the shame that was conveyed in a selected set of these writings and genres. The aim is to probe contemporary ways of

DOI: 10.4324/9781003226871-2

thinking about, and communicating, shame; the values and belief systems that gave rise to shame, its varied constructions and meanings, the rhetorical means, vocabulary, and imagery through which the shame was evoked. The chapter unravels great variations within and between the different writings and genres, each with its purported aim and audience; yet it also identifies overlapping themes and recurring constructions. It indicates not only diverse meanings of shame and the powerful hold it had on the contemporary mind, but also the major forms in which it could be experienced and applied in society at large.

## Manners, honour, morality

Early modern constructions of shame were profoundly affected by an emerging code of civility designed to regulate the manners of an educated elite. The codification of rules for proper conduct dated back to medieval traditions of injunctions for polite behaviour and to fifteenth-century courtesy poems intended to advise on the upbringing and education of aristocratic youth. Over the ensuing centuries, the literature on manners expanded, greatly enhanced by works imported from the Continent and increasingly aiming at wider audiences beyond the courtly aristocracy. Writers gradually came to replace 'courtesy' with 'civility' in denoting the forms of conduct and set of moral values that were the distinguishing mark of an educated elite.[2] At the core of the code were rules regarding the care and control of the body and its processes, followed by detailed directions for communication in speech and writing, ceremonial proceedings and social interactions. All the rules were designed to produce a mode of conduct typically marked by emotional control, moderation, and the accommodation of the self to the expectations of others. Francis Seager's *The schoole of virtue*, an early manual that remained popular throughout the sixteenth century and beyond, detailed instructions that were carefully structured around the daily routine of a young man, from the early morning 'when thou risest', until dusk. Beginning with rules for bodily care – washing, dressing, taking care of every body part, including the nose ('thy nose to cleanse, from all filthiness',) nails, ears, and teeth – the book proceeded with instructions on behaviour 'in going by the streets', at school, during meals ('How to behaue thy selfe in sitting at the Table'), and when attending church. Separate chapters were devoted to the merit of learning and moral conduct, while the two central chapters offered guidelines on communication – 'how to behave thy selfe in talking with any man'. Here detailed instructions were presented regarding rhetorical skill, bodily position and tone of voice during conversations, all of which were intended to project control of the body and sobriety: 'thy words duly place, with countenance sober and body upright, thy feet just together, thy hands in like plight … in an audible voyce thy words plainly utter … nor high, nor too low since both exceed measure'.[3] Similar rules and principles were repeated and elaborated upon in numerous manuals that appeared during the sixteenth and seventeenth centuries, with the publications, both translated and indigenous, becoming increasingly bulky, and the rules outlined in them ever more numerous, refined and stringent.[4]

A strong sense of shame was built into this highly elaborate edifice of detailed and intricate rules, for the art of 'delivering things well' – as Antoine de Courtin referred to moderate and precise manners performed under the guise of effortlessness and a 'pleasing appearance' – was the defining mark of elite status. It not only denoted a person's superior position, but also earned him the right to respect and the honour accorded by inferiors and among peers. Immense social meanings and values were hence inscribed in every act, speech, or bodily signal, with minute deviations presented as having grave consequences and 'provoking or disobliging', causing 'injury, disesteem, offence'. While good breeding and training from a young age were deemed indispensable for mastering the art of manners, skill, and resourcefulness were still required to accomplish it, and the risk of transgression lingered. One could stumble in the display of a specific act or speech, gestures could have unintended outcomes, the gestures of others could be misinterpreted or their treatment could be perceived as deficient. As the rules became stricter and more elaborate, so the stakes became higher; 'Do *nothing* [emphasis mine] which may be unpleasant, and offensive their senses', as one writer summed the challenge of decorum and the stakes that were entailed.[5] With every single aberration being construed as liable to offend, the opportunity for shaming and shame – showing inconsiderateness and disrespect or being afflicted by these – was imminent.

Conduct manuals habitually constructed this type of shame through the detailed elaboration of those gestures and acts considered to cause disesteem or offence. Rather than focus strictly on the postures judged appropriate and hence rewarded with honour and esteem, they devoted large sections of their work to the kind of impropriety that a person should avoid, and it is through these that shame was elicited and greatly enhanced. Already in the fifteenth century, courtesy poems described poor table manners with the pejorative reference to serfs and peasants, warning against the spectre of humiliation and shame: 'Kutte nouht[e] youre mete ... as it were felde men ... leste th[ou] be callyd ... both cherle or gloton'.[6] Similarly, sixteenth-century conduct books not only set the rules for proper manners but also went on to offer negative formulations and prohibitions that were rife with particularly offensive notions of punitive and exclusionary shaming and shame. Indecent manners were considered the mark of inferior status, as displayed by the servants, the uneducated, artisans, and common people. Since civility was increasingly depicted as the product of the human urge to distance oneself from brute nature, bad manners were more pronouncedly associated with beasts, and inappropriate manners minutely and graphically conjured up as the epitome of brutishness and savagery.[7] In his discussion of table manners, Seager began with instructions on proper table arrangements and manners, but then moved to negative constructions and prohibitions in which every faulty manner was singled out as 'rude' or described as beastly. 'And rudeness it is thy pottage to sup or speak to any his nose in the cup'... 'thy mouth fill not full ... not smacking thy lips as commonly do dogs ... nor gnowing of bones as doe dunghill dogs, such rudeness abhor, such beastliness flie'. His injunctions to avoid over-talking, picking ones' teeth and spitting were followed with the denigrating caveat, 'this rudeness in youth is naught at a word', while habits of 'filthy talk' were labelled as an indecent abuse of the tongue, 'like a beast'. In the late seventeenth century, Antoine de Courtin devoted a special chapter in *The Rules of Civility* to the issue of how to distinguish 'things decent from things indecent', pointing out that 'the farther we keep from the practice of Beasts, the nearer we come to that perfection to which nature directs'. Acts involving bodily needs, which humans shared with animals (eating, drinking, sneezing), should be performed 'with much decency and as little conformity with the beasts as is possible'. Elsewhere in his list of prohibitions, Courtin used the beastly metaphor to invoke utter disdain. 'You must ... cut out your meat into small pieces, and not put great Gobbets into your mouth that may bunch out your cheeks like a monkey'.[8]

A rich and increasingly expansive vocabulary describing the shame of incivility appeared in the pages of many manuals, marked by the use of numerous synonyms, elaborate phrases, and an exaggerated style that greatly enhanced the shame and disgrace entailed in the lack of manners. Courtin's chapter on the rules of conversation was structured entirely by referencing improper conduct – what to avoid rather than how a person should speak – with each instance highlighting impropriety through repetitive and synonymous phrases:

> It is unmannerly to make comparison with the person to whom you are speaking ... It is unhandsome ... to add the surname or quality of a person to whom you speak ... It is unhandsome likewise ... to say rudely, you are mistaken Sir... tis indiscretion to make use of the person to whom you speak; it is not discreet for a man to express ... it is not decent to Fly out in the praise ...

'It is not civil' 'nor is comely', 'it is not mannerly', 'it would be want of respect' to intrude yourself; – 'indecent', 'disobliging', 'disrespectful', 'ungraceful', 'disagreeable', 'not becoming', 'rude', 'very ill breeding', 'ridiculous' – these are but a few examples of the entire vocabulary used in a single chapter to denote the impropriety and shame of unmannerly speech.[9]

Other chapters in Courtin's work were not as packed with shame phrases, but were still prone to amplification and exaggeration that raised the spectre of ridicule and disgrace ever higher, not only repeatedly referring to 'those repugnancies', but exaggerating their effects. 'Nothing is more indecent' than to touch any liquor ... or syrup with our fingers'; '[it] is the worst way and the most uncomely' to wipe or lick your finger; while blowing the nose, wiping off sweat, belching, hawking, and tearing 'anything up from the bottom of your stomach', are things 'so intolerably sordid, they are sufficient to make a man vomit to behold them'. Courtin also discussed forms of speech and eloquent style, using particularly damning rhetoric and an utterly disdainful tone: 'That which is oppos'd to this (i.e., plain style), is the flate and dull style, made up of mean and low expressions that favour wholly of the vulgar, and many times consisting of improper, if not barbarous terms'. In a similar vein, Seager's early manual contained comments on stuttering which not only associated it with vulgarity but also crime, connoting a particularly harsh and punitive shame: 'thy words plainly utter, smoothly pronounce them without stop or stutter ... To stutter and stammer is a foule crime'.[10]

Above all, the shame of incivility was invoked through repeated references to the reactions of others; 'lest it turne afterwards to rebuke and shame', as Seagar explained when referring to the consequences of deviating from the precise tone of moderate speech.[11] Elsewhere he raised the spectre of shame by using terms associated with disrespect, disdain, mocking, or ridicule. In discussing 'how to behave thy selfe in going by the streets', he contrasted mannerly conduct that 'must sound to your great prayse', with shouting and screaming, which 'men in hearing deride ... with mockes'. Talking with haste might bring an interlocutor to 'iudge in thee little wit', while casting the eyes 'on every side' or betraying a laugh or smile would trigger disdain: 'Such folly forsake thou, and count it but vile'. Courtin also tended to ridicule inapt manners. In his advice on proper attire, readers were urged to follow moderation and favour rules of proportion over impulsive conformity with fashion, citing the case of a small man who wore a large hat: if 'the man would be drawned (in the hat) ... it would be as ridiculous to the Eye' as the painter who erred in the rules of proportion by drawing 'a large arm to a little man'. In table manners and recreations, 'we must have a care of odd and ridiculous postures with our Bodies ... lest we be laught at for our pains', while at the ball one must avoid dancing if 'your ear be Bad', for 'it renders a man ridiculous to see him out in his time [i.e., in his steps]'. When finally summing up the manner young men should adopt towards their superiors, Seagar resorted again to the beastly metaphor, exclaiming: 'And indeed what a monstrous thing it is to see a Nobleman without civility! Every body shuns him, every body despises him, no body pays him respect'.[12]

The shame that was construed as emanating from the observation of others and linked to outward appearances and decorum was thus overwhelmingly punitive and exclusionary. Impoliteness was 'of all vices, that which makes a Man most despisable', as one author claimed.[13] Lack of manners was not simply the result of an occasional lapse and failure to abide by the rules, but bespoke of social degradation and beastly dispositions; hence all forms of transgression, be they grave or small, incurred punitive shame that involved a diminished status and loss of honour and even implied exclusion from humanity at large. It was the spectre of this kind of absolute and total disgrace that could produce, as some authors observed, constant fear and anxiety while interacting with one's peers or when facing superiors; 'shame and fear make us respectful', as Courtin expressed the effectiveness of the anxiety about one's performance in producing the appropriate civility and

20   *Constructions of shame*

deference towards superiors.[14] This totality of shame and its attendant anxiety were powerfully evoked in the discourse on duels, which from the late sixteenth century advanced a set of justifications in its defence. The central supposition of writers who advocated the practice of duelling was that in the face of incivility that threatened one's honour, a response was obligatory if one was to avenge the shame and restore their status. It was not only that impolite speech implied insult, dishonour, or disrespect, but that it was better to die than withstand the shame that such disrespect incurred. A man of honour ought to prefer death rather than suffer the shame of refusing to accept a challenge to a duel, or even of avoiding to offer such a challenge when himself faced with dishonour or disgrace. As Richard Brathwaite elucidated the outright totality of this type of punitive shame; 'is there any punishment so grievous as shame?', retorting 'yea were it not better for a man who is eminent in the eye of the world, to die right out, than still live in reproach and shame?'[15]

Yet alongside the construction of an absolute shame, thoroughly grounded in outward appearances and the opinion of others, the civility code also conveyed a shame that effected internal dispositions. In fifteenth-century courtesy poems, the rules regarding cleanliness and table manners were in some instances set against an assumed moral and religious background, especially when addressing the misconduct of girls and women.[16] Major conduct books in the ensuing decades espoused the view that manners impinged on character and inner worth rather than solely on one's reputation and good standing, a view particularly pronounced in Erasmian humanism, which placed special emphasis on virtue and an inner self over and above outward appearances and the opinion of others.[17] For Erasmus, the 'principall point' and very purpose of instructing civility to children was that the 'tender sprite and mynde may be seasoned with virtue', with the additional and more practical targets – learning the liberal arts and acquiring the behaviour 'the which this lyfe requyreeth' – being second to this first and overall moral aim. In his *De Civitate*, Erasmus described lack of manners as 'indecent', 'uncivil', or 'uncomely', connoting it with beastly inclinations and rudeness, mocking and ridicule, with gestures like scratching the head, picking one's teeth or spitting tantamount to 'rustical shame and behaviour'. Yet above all, Erasmus presented civility as the epitome of honesty; proper table manners were considered 'honest gestures', while indecent habits like biting the lips, drinking at meals or putting a hand on the dish were 'scarcely honest'. Manners were grounded in and reflected moral character and integrity, while incivility denoted immoral, shameful dispositions – pride or cruelty, hypocrisy, vileness, slothfulness and dishonesty.[18]

Seager's manual likewise devoted several chapters to moral conduct and character, referring to the shame of misconduct and immorality in tandem and as intimately linked, and warning children to shy away from games like dicing and carding no less than from other indecent manners, all of which brought 'many one to shame'. His injunctions 'against the vice of lying', alluded to shame as 'the reward that to lying is due', the value of telling the

## Constructions of shame    21

truth being elevated as a duty towards God; 'Speak Truth however stand the case, so shalt thou find more favour and grace', while the shame of dishonesty ultimately signalled the death of the 'soul' – 'Trust to the truth, and speak that is plaine, for the death of the soule in lyes doth remaine'. His chapter 'against anger and malice' also presented wrath as a vice that 'leads shame in a leash', that is, it prevented the positive aspect of shame, as influencing one's conscience and capacity to do good. Like many others, Seager highlighted the moral qualities of shame; rather than indicating exclusion and social degradation, shame was presented as an internal sensation that performed as the 'guardian of virtue'.[19] Other authors emphasized the morality implied in bodily gestures, with the external sources of shame – what others perceive – being inextricably linked to internal dispositions of a vile, corrupt, and shameful self. Obadiah Walker associated some postures of the eyes – fixed eyes, staring, wondering looks or winking – with, respectively, impudence, foolishness, madness, light-headedness and an evil nature.[20]

Not all writers upheld this understanding of civility and internal morality as inextricably linked. They pointed instead to the tension and even incongruity between a civility code that focused on appearances, and an inner morality emanating from faith or civic virtue, boldly rejecting the former in favour of the latter. Protestant writers, while overall acknowledging the merit of civility, were still prone to pronounce the discrepancy between the code's focus on appearances or ceremony and practices rooted in religious devotion and spirituality. 'Good manners are a hindrance to grace' – as William Gough, the puritan divine, put it. Protestants also voiced strong objections to the theory (and practice) of duelling, which was perceived as utterly belying Christian views and morality.[21] Others offered a critique of the entire theory of civil courtesy, contesting that the preoccupation with decorum was 'imports from the Continent' and alien to English customs, the latter being presented as rooted in 'the puritie of Religion'. Following classical humanist tradition, they expounded a theory of civic life and communication within which virtue and morality were central. Others acceded that outward behaviour could reflect inner virtue, but still insisted that the former was more often no more than a mask of deformity and lack of virtue. Francis Bacon, for example, depicted manners as suggesting superficiality, excessive formalities, inflated notions of virility, lack of patience and addiction to petty insults or other 'dishonourable affections'. All these attributes, for Bacon, implied dishonour, shame and disgrace.[22]

Despite this critique, which pointed to the discrepancy between honour and morality – shame being used by critics of the code to denigrate the civility code and its implications – writers on civility, for the most part, presented outward decorum and internal morality as reinforcing, rather than opposing, one another. Even writers who followed the tradition associated with continental authors, such as Castiglione and Dela Casa, who stressed the priority of courtesy and outward appearances, still acknowledged the links between manners and morality, voicing moral concerns and viewing external and internal sources of shame as inherently aligned, regardless of the potential for conflict between them.[23] Antoine de Courtin, who, as noted above, strongly advocated the ridicule and disgrace entailed in shameful manners, acknowledged the role of morality and habitually quoted the shame of incivility as the consequence of belying inner morality. As he stated when offering his definition of politeness, 'To please the corporal Eye, is no great matter ... we must labour for something more solid, that may shew the good disposition within, as well as the graceful comeliness without'. In some sections of his work, he was adamant in his preference for the integrity of body and mind over the sheer art of behaving well, as in his statement that the art of rhetoric was marginal to the contents of speech itself, or his insistence that apparel and the 'neatness of property of our cloathes' reflected virtue and discretion. As for the display of pleasantness and wit, these, in his view, were unwarranted unless morally and justly applied – 'our wit must be present and just' – the connotation being that immoral qualities, rather than an incapacity to display wit, were to be seen as shameful and a disgrace.[24]

At the heart of these constructions of the integrity of body and mind was a preoccupation with the issue of authenticity and hypocrisy. While some authors insisted on the prominence of outward gestures, arguing that it was imperative to control and suppress 'true feelings', and that sincerity was a hindrance to proper interactions between men of honour, most writers deplored all signs of a discrepancy, construing hypocrisy and dishonesty as inevitably leading to derision and shame. 'We blush when wee praise any one above his merit ... to the end that wee may obtain some favour, some present, or some assistance from him ... for all these are insupportable signs of flattery'.[25] The shame – and the blushing – reflected self-awareness and the recognition of one's failure to display internal standards through proper manners. Civil conduct, in this sense, was rooted in 'true' character and 'genuine merit'; it demanded that one constantly evaluate their internal standards – 'the good disposition within' – along with the quality of one's speech, gestures and appearances.[26] These internal dispositions, moreover, reflected not only on moral values acquired through education and training, but also on 'certain innate principles of Civility naturally imprinted in us', and on the 'talents that she [i.e., nature] has given us'. These natural gifts could imply, for example, special wit, excellence in learning, and 'greatness of mind'. The ability to show wit and pleasant speech was construed by Courtin as designed not simply to induce jesting or laughter, but 'to bring forth something that is new, smart, or sublime'.[27]

Morality and authenticity, genuine merit and capabilities, self-awareness – all these resonated with implications for shame as an experience of failure and a threat to an internal self. In this respect, the manuals examined here emphasized the external along with the internal sources of shame; alongside the shame that resulted from being judged by others, inflicting dishonour, degradation or loss of status, shame was perceived as a sense of failure in internal standards and accomplishments. This form of shame could denote a subtle experience, involving an unpleasant sensation of unease, a 'shamefastness' or blushing that indicated a sense of inadequacy or embarrassment. It did not necessarily require the view or perception of others.[28] It could also entail an anticipation of shame and disgrace, prompting internal inhibitions and an aversion to acting in certain ways, which, as Norbert Elias had pointed out, acted as an internal mechanism of controlling behaviour. Moreover, under certain circumstances, internal shame could imply a harsh and more devastating experience, which, in a process of self-evaluation, might damage one's sense of an interior self. It could undermine a sense of personal merit and self-esteem, reflecting on an inner morality or standards of excellence rather than solely on one's social standing and reputation.

A harsh and devastating experience of shame that was the outcome of external claims and judgements while simultaneously being rooted in internal reflection and a negative evaluation of the self was potently captured in Robert Burton's *The Anatomy of Melancholy*, mentioned at the outset of this chapter. In his discussion of the 'passions and perturbations of the mind', Burton articulated the centrality of shame to civility, viewing shame as the very mark of polite, honourable, and superior status. 'I know there be many base, impudent, brazenfaced rogues, that will take no infamy or disgrace to heart, ... what care they?' In contrast, he opined,

> a modest man, one that hath grace, a generous spirit, tender of his reputation, will be deeply wounded, and so grievously affected with it, that he had rather give myriads of crowns, lose his life, than suffer the least defamation of honour, or blot in his good name.

While fully accepting that the experience of shame was the result of dishonour and the negative opinion of others, Burton nevertheless conceived the emotion as emanating from the internal and personal dispositions of the civilized person – modesty, 'grace' and a 'generous spirit'. Many of the examples he cites suggested an experience of shame related less to the gaze of others or even the loss of good name, but rather indicating deep agony and sense of failure in personal standards of excellence, especially intellectual and creative capabilities. So, for example, Aristotle drowned himself 'for grief and shame' because he could not understand the ebb and flow of the Euripus strait; Homerus 'was swallowed up with this passion of shame' because he failed to figure out the fisherman's riddle, while Sophocles killed himself 'for that a tragedy of his was hissed off the stage'. Apollonius Rhodius also banished himself 'because he was out in reciting his poems'. In all these examples the experience of shame, while within the purview of the reaction of others, still entailed a deep sense of failure in accomplishments, leading to the damage of one's self-worth. In the wake of a process of negative self-evaluation, the shame brought internal suffering, despair, and melancholy that ended with self-inflicted death. 'And if so be ... [he] dies for shame ... languisheth and pineth away in the anguish of his spirit'.[29]

## Civility, courage, and masculinity

The shame that implied a threat to honour, morality, and personhood was inextricably linked to a masculine self. Early courtesy books occasionally addressed themselves to 'every gentilman or woman', and the conduct literature overall depicted gentlewomen as participants in a world of courtesy by virtue of their class and upbringing. Yet the entire edifice of manners that developed over the sixteenth and seventeenth centuries was written with a male audience in mind, typically, and at times specifically, addressing males.[30] The central defining tenets of civility – self-restraint and pleasing appearances, honour, the excellence that comes with a mannerly demeanour in conversation and speech – were overly and essentially male, with varied instructions regarding the acceptable manner of dressing, cleanliness, walking in the streets or going to school considered the corollary of manliness, at times even designated as 'manly'.[31] While writers would allude to the female capacity to be 'temperate in her appetites', demanding self-control and moderate manners in women as well, the literature overall presented women as the passive objects or receivers of the civility offered by males. Thus Courtin warned his audience that it was 'not becoming to handle them [i.e., Ladies] roughly', advising against putting 'hands in their necks, or their bosoms', or kissing them 'by surprise'. When approaching women, he further urged the use of compliments and moderate flattery, with the 'respect to Ladies' being identified as the 'essential … part of good breeding, that to be defective in it, is not only uncivil but brutish'. These manly gestures of respect, moreover, reflected specific female qualities, as Courtin typically advised his male readers to focus their compliments on female beauty (the 'excellence of her parts'), her 'unusual modesty', education, 'sweetness' and 'goodness'.[32]

A woman's manners and exemplary virtue resided in her beauty, morality, and modesty, the latter often designated the 'shamefastness' that was typically feminine. When Thomas Elyot described the female qualities manifested in a woman's manner of dancing (the 'good order' of dancing), he asserted that 'The good nature of a woman is to be milde, timerous, tractable, benigne, of sure remembrance and shamfast'. Richard Brathwaite likewise considered shamefastness as the 'choicest beauty maiden bashfulnesse', the property of the 'Matron, Wife or Virgin', which distinguished her from 'common and base whores'.[33] When present in males, however, shamefastness risked degenerating into immoderate bashfulness, which was no less grave than the absence of shame or shameless manners themselves. According to Pierre de la Primaudaye, alongside virtuous and honest shame, which was commendable in men, there was the shame that expressed 'cowardliness of mind', the 'feare to displease the greatest', the fear of being blamed, reproved, or disliked, which disposed men to 'bow and bend to another man's becke against right and equity', and commonly entailed neglect of duty and naiveté in 'not being able to distrust those who they take for their friends'. The latter disposition was particularly evident in those who had a lengthy experience of living under 'governors, magistrates and Judges'. For

James Cleland, shamefastness in men was childish and foolish: 'blushing everie light word, which maketh him [ie the child] astonished at everie grave countenance and sharp word that is spoken'. The words used by Primaudaye to express the disgrace involved in overindulged shame and timidity in a man were unambiguous – 'hurtful', 'naughty', 'foolish'; 'we must shun all evil, excessive and pernitious shame ... insomuch that of itself it is able to procure unto us losse, dishonour, and infamie'.[34]

Underlying this preoccupation with effeminate shame or shamefastness was a notion of civility that was defined not only in terms of moderate passions and refinement, but also by the strength of body and mind, courage, and 'valour', cowardice being the defining mark of man's shame. Keith Thomas has shown the persistence of the chivalric ideal among the aristocracy well into the mid-seventeenth century; the centrality of physical courage as the supreme proof of manhood, and the identification of virtue with military prowess and courage.[35] What we wish to emphasize here is the construction of male courage and strength in humanist educational schemes, which, while not endorsing military prowess for its own sake, still encouraged physical skill along with strength of body and of mind. 'A man in his naturall perfection is fiers, hardy, stronge in opinion, couaitous of glorie, desirous of knowledge', as Thomas Elyot described it. While a woman in her dancing moved with delicateness and mildness that exemplified the 'Constance Shamfastnes ... whiche is a meane betwene Chastilie and inordinate luste', the man showed vehemence, which 'signifienge the courage and strenthe that oughte to be in a man', his movements perfectly demonstrating his audacity, wilful opinion and 'glory'.[36] To display overindulged shame was indeed foolish, for it 'makes a man coward', as Primaudaye explained. It undermined a man's good judgement, livelihood and domestic responsibilities, hence reflecting a lack of virtue and cowardice: 'I will not heer stand to speake of those which saie they are ashamed to ask their due ... they have neither virtue, hart, nor courage'. Like other effeminate habits perceived as over-refined manners – walking too tenderly, riding too 'softly', using perfumes, being 'delicately and effeminately appareled', using tooth powder 'in the manner of maidens' – shamefastness displayed tenderness and fragility that connoted the ultimate negation of male robustness, courage and strength.[37]

The notion of male courage and strength was particularly pronounced in the role these educational initiatives accorded to physical exercises and recreations. Following Erasmus and Vives, in his *The book Named Governour* Thomas Elyot offered an extended treatment 'Of sondry fourmes of exercise necessary for euery gentilman', arguing that learning without physical exercises exhausted the 'vital spirits ... wherby mannes body is the soner corrupted and brought in to diuers sickenesis'. While drawing on Galenic medicine in his discussion of the benefit of physical exercises (see more below), Elyot's central concern was with the effects of such exercises on physical development and intellectual aptitude; 'it maketh the spirites of a man more strong and valiant', physical exercises being 'apt to the furniture of a gentilmannes personage, adapting his body to hardnesse, strength, and agilitie'. He recommended beginning physical education at the age of nine, 'in whiche tyme strength with courage increaseth', and stressed wrestling and running, which he deemed were the daily exercises practiced by 'Epaminondas the valiant capitayne of Thebanes, who as well in vertue and prowesse as in lerninge surmounted all noble men of his tyme'. Elyot also recommended swimming, fencing, and horse riding – 'the most honorable exercise … to ryde suerly and clene on a great horse … whiche undoubtedly … importeth a maiestie and drede to inferiour persones'. Additional exercises he encouraged were traditional aristocratic sports such as hawking and hunting, along with recreations like dancing. Except for the latter, in which he envisioned the female as the counterpart of the male ('a concorde of all the saide dualities'), the physical exercises he proposed for the future governor were a mix of traditional military and aristocratic sports as well as recreational activities, all thoroughly associated with men.[38]

Other humanist educators followed in Elyot's footsteps. Richard Mulcaster, who wrote one of the well-known educational treatises of the late sixteenth century, devoted about a third of his book to physical training. He divided the exercises into 'athletical for games', 'martiall for the fielde' and 'physical for health', and he also embraced 'loud speaking' and singing, laughing and even weeping as exercises, commending these for their efficacy in 'the purging of some parts' and for 'moving the blood'. Focusing above all on wrestling, fencing, walking, running, and leaping, and recommending swimming, horse riding, hunting, shooting, and dancing, he presented these as 'gentlemanly exercises' that 'beseeme a gentlamnly minde'. Mulcaster was also an advocate of the education of women, and he devoted a special chapter to the training of young girls, in which he stressed the female intellectual and creative capabilities, recommending they be taught reading, writing, and music. This learning program was set wholly within what he perceived as the female future place and role in governing her household; 'the bringing up of young maidens in any kind of learning', he presumed, 'is but an accessory' to this role. As for physical exercise, noting the greater weakness of the female body, Mulcaster fleetingly recommended physical exercises for women as a 'preservative to the body'. The skills designed to instil courage, strength, and governance overall remained a masculine preserve, conceived as inappropriate in the case of women.[39]

Physical skills and the cultivation of bodily strength remained part of the ideal formation of the gentleman throughout the seventeenth century, with many books on manners advising a mix of martial and recreational activities, while at the same time invoking and warning of the shame entailed in their neglect. James Cleland, for example, advised on appropriate manners alongside a set of physical exercises (riding, hunting and shooting, wrestling and handling of arms), subsequently moving to discuss 'valour in general'. While cautioning against a gentleman vaingloriously hazarding himself unto danger and warning against associating courage with violence, he unambiguously promoted valour as an essential attribute of the gentleman. Bravery was 'the accomplisher of all virtue', a 'habitude of mind' without which all learning and physical exercises were 'not worthy to be esteemed'.[40] Even other writers, who devoted less attention than Cleland to physical exercises, still stressed the value of martial training and physical accomplishments. In a section on recreational activities, Richard Brathwaite applauded their benefit as 'a refresher of the minde and enabler of the body', specifically endorsing hawking, hunting, fishing, swimming, running ('a recreation famously ancient'), his rhetoric accentuating the masculine quality of these activities as enabling a gentleman to perform his tasks and 'offices', his model being ancient 'emperors' who excelled in their recreations and martial activities. While proclaiming the risks of immoderate recreations, his injunctions regarding moderate exercises were laced with references to the bodily shame and disgrace that ensued when one neglected to engage in them. Pointing out 'those who were nayled to their Deske and admit no time for recreations', he exclaimed: 'See how pale and meager they looke, how sickly and infirme in the state of their bodies, how weak and defective in their constitution?'[41]

The presentation of male shame as residing in a man's feeble character and physique was reinforced by the emphasis on the gendered dimension of recreational skills. Richard Brathwaite, who noted that the ancient 'Amazonites' were expert in shooting, still depicted the gentlewoman as a passive observer of male exercises and courageous skills, adept solely in specific types of feminine recreations. Fencing was deemed 'the strongest and soveraignest exercise against death and grief', with tournaments being practised 'amongst our ancient Knights' for the purpose of 'gaining the favour of such Ladies as they loved as also for the honour of their country'. While female civility was demonstrated by her proficiency in music, playing, and painting, these arts, admirable in their own right (also in a male), were all too clearly inferior 'soft and effeminate recreations' when set against courageous male exercises and skills.[42] While elaborating on the misdeeds and attributes deemed offensive to men and women, Courtin distinguished between the genders. In the case of women, he opined, her strongest offence and shame resided in being designated foolish, immodest or else 'to be said to be no gentlewoman'. In the case of the man, the shame would be triggered by being reproached for folly, corruption, and especially cowardice; 'some Men would be less offended to be counted Fools, or debauch'd, then Cowards', as he put it.[43]

## Body constitution and gender

Focusing on bodily gestures and postures, the literature on manners envisioned a shame that was overwhelmingly located in the human body. Whether triggered by the reaction of others or through an internal feeling that related to one's sense of impropriety or shortcoming, the shame of incivility centred around a body that invariably appeared exposed or indecent, awkward or feeble, indulgent, menacing or unrestrained. Virtuous shame, which exemplified female modesty and shamefastness, was no less attuned to the body in its distinctive concealments and controls, its gestures and delicate movements, its silences, facial expressions and especially the blushing – the quintessential physical manifestation of shame.

A set of ideas regarding the physiological features of the human body potently bolstered this construction of the body as a site of shame. Medical knowledge throughout the sixteenth and seventeenth centuries encompassed varied strands of thought and ideas, both inherited and new, which were disseminated and increasingly popularized through a wide range of learned textbooks along with almanacs and books of advice. Especially influential was the renewed interest in Galenic medicine, according to which the body consisted of four fluids (blood, yellow bile, black bile, and phlegm), each displaying a distinctive blend of qualities of hot, cold, moist, and dry, all linked to the human complexion and temperaments or dispositions (sanguine, choleric, melancholic, and phlegmatic).[44] The theory, along with its presumed links between the corporeal body and human temperament, permeated numerous publications, and writers habitually appropriated humoral medicine as an explanatory framework for elaborating ideas and arguments in physiology, anatomy, education, and manners. Following Galen, Pierre de la Primaudaye identified the physiological symptoms of shame as typically located in the cheeks, while educational reformers cited Galen – the 'prince of physicians', as he was referred to – in their discussion of the efficacy of physical education. As Mulcaster explained, exercises increased the 'naturall heate' through which the body is 'augmented … and all thinges superfluous be expelled, and the conduits of the body clensed'.[45]

This appropriation of humoral knowledge underlined the tacit, yet salient association of the theory with broader beliefs and values relating to religion, civility and social rank.[46] Especially conducive in this regard was the Galenic perception of health and disease, health being conceived in terms of the balance between the four bodily fluids, illness as the product of deficient or superfluous fluids and the concomitant imbalance of bodily heat and moist. More important still, while health indicated perfect balance and harmony, illness was associated with imperfections and deficiencies, which could be implicitly or more directly aligned with a range of shortcomings, from deteriorated mental capacities to unrestrained passions and immoral dispositions:

> Now let every man consider with himselfe, how miserable and how wearisome also it is to have a body … martyred with sicknesse and sores, and (reason being mastered, banished and oppressed) to have the minde defiled, and utterly with inward vices polluted.[47]

'Disease' could connote not only specific illnesses but also a wide variety of bodily states dominated by specific fluids and blends that deviated, in one degree or another, from the perfect balance. While disease was governed in each human being by an individual and peculiar imbalance of humours, certain groups and social categories shared particular humoral imbalances. Female body imbalance (excessively moist and cold) was the least balanced and associated with a range of moral and mental faults and weaknesses. Children, young and old people, social inferiors and other individuals were also dominated by a particular disequilibrium that could create a host of physical, moral, and mental deficiencies. Even mature males, generally perceived as the epitome of the perfect temperate body, would, under certain circumstances, be presented as governed by immoderate fluids and imbalances. As Mulcaster explained when discussing the value of physical training, human bodies reached

> the perfectest degree ... [only] seldom, as any saw, bycause of great frailty, and britleness in our nature: it never continueth in one estate, but altereth still, and runnes to ruyne, ... Heat burnes, cold chilles, in excess both to much, in defect both to little, and both causes to decaie.[48]

The implications of these physiological cum moral and mental constructions for conveying bodily shame were clear. If nearly all bodily states presented a deviation from perfect balance and health, a whole range of bodily states was deemed deficient and hence liable to be considered with reproach or disdain, ridicule and shame. Humoral pathology offered a particularly florid and affective language for amplifying these body states as sites of shame; the central role assigned to moistness and heat, the variations and hierarchies of bodily blends of fluids – all offered potent images and metaphors for delineating the shame of individuals as well as gendered, age, and social groupings. The moistness that typified the female body was enhanced to invoke weakness, irrationality, and vice, and excessive moisture – blood, urine, menstruation – exemplified the female inability to control sexual lust and rationality. It marked her body as a potent source not only of inferiority, but also of embarrassment, denigration, and shame.[49] Moisture was also overly present in children's bodies, where it connoted, alongside warmth, softness, and weaknesses, lack of reason, selfishness, rashness, and a host of other sins. The qualities of heat and cold offered yet another source of moral judgement and shaming images. Increasingly dominating bodies of children as they grew up, the 'boyling' blood of youth produced 'nimble and active' temperaments, along with a host of selfish and shameful dispositions, including wantonness, immodesty, pride, lack of wit. Heat, which in mature men was a source of perfection and balance, when unbridled and excessive could still turn them into immoral and shameful characters: 'crafty coozeners, slye make-shifts, nimble conveiers ... unconstant, wavering, fraudulent ... untrusty and factious'.[50] Diminished heat and coldness produced a particularly derogatory vocabulary and gruesome descriptions of the physical, mental, and virile debilitations typical of cold bodies and especially of old age. Cold constitutions invariably symbolized effeminacy and fearfulness, feeble faculties, ill memory, 'blockish wit', 'doltishe mind', sleepiness, or idleness. The diminished heat of old age – featuring the 'dry and wrinkled skin, hard flesh, weak digestion, dry bowles, trembling nerves' – ultimately connoted imperfect bodies at their utmost, stripped of human dignity and utterly full of shame.[51]

Complex variations and hierarchies of bodily fluids also produced rich images and a vocabulary that conveyed and amplified the shame of varied bodily states and conditions, especially of the lower classes. A sanguine constitution (hot and dry) was generally associated with male rationality and sharpness of mind, yet when present in the body of common people it hinted at foolishness and indiscretion, the excess sanguinity producing impulsive and unruly behaviour that resembled 'other beasts'. Individuals who were dominated by choleric humour – the 'choleric types' – could be construed as 'unconstant', 'crafty', 'cogging', or devious, their character and untrustworthiness being imagined and caricatured as having 'no more hold then is of wet Eele by the Tayle'. Individuals dominated by a phlegmatic complexion (moist and cold) were depicted as 'voide of reason, foolish, block-headed, doltish, dull and doting', the phlegmatic temperament dominating women along with inferior orders – common people, servants, and vagabonds. Fluids and their tempers were also associated with specific body organs, which in Galenic medicine governed the bodily hierarchy of functions (the heart, liver and brain heading this hierarchy) producing a set of metaphors that yet again could be used to raise the spectre of derision and ridicule of inferiors and the majority of common people. As the prominent anatomist Helkiah Crooke put it, while some humans had the 'the heart of the lyon', others had 'the temper of a dog, and an infinite number of as dull and blockish a temper as an Asse'.[52]

New medical ideas that emerged in the sixteenth century presented a challenge to humoral medicine and the construction of the human body as imperfect and full of shame. The new anatomy, associated with Andreas Vesalius, placed dissection and experimentation at the heart of the medical investigation, focusing on a corporeal body that was devoid of moral and religious meanings, hence stripped of the shameful connotations it assumed in humoral medicine. The rise of Paracelsian chemical medicine likewise challenged Galenic medical orthodoxy, stressing chemical processes rather than humoral imbalance as the cause of disease.[53] Yet neither anatomy nor even chemical medicine wholly undermined the construction of the body as essentially indecent and shameful. The humoral theory remained potent and influential throughout the period, and prominent anatomists continued to incorporate elements of the theory in their descriptions of the human body, especially the female body. Helkiah Crooke, who authored the comprehensive treatise on human anatomy and physiology *Mikrokosmographia, a Description of the Body of Man* (1616), offered a critique of traditional Aristotelian and Galenic medicine. Yet he continued to adhere to humoral theory, constructing the female body as inferior, weaker, and 'so much less perfect than a man', because 'her heat is less and weaker than his'. As much research has shown, the moralization and shaming of the humoral body of the female remained potent well into the late seventeenth and early eighteenth century.[54]

This presentation of the female body as shameful was further reinforced by the persistent reluctance of authors to discuss sexuality, indirectly deeming the female body, in its naked sexuality, as indecent and shameful. While increasingly and more openly presenting the human body in all its varied parts, medical textbooks and almanacs were reticent in delving into the subject of the female constitution and sexual organs. Underpinned by traditional religious inhibitions evident already in medieval medical literature, the reluctance to discuss sexuality was by the sixteenth century further reinforced through the language of civility and politeness. Thomas Elyot, in his popular medical guide *The Castel of Health*, still heavily relied on humoral medicine while discussing the manner in which 'superfluous blood' was expelled from the body, stopping short of elaborating on menstruation ('concerning other evacuations', as he referred to it). As he explained, 'in thys realme, it hath been accompted not honest, to declare them in the vulgare tongue, but only secretly'.[55] Even anatomists like Helkiah Crooke, whose book meticulously discussed the reproductive organs and included many woodcut illustrations (taken from Vesalius), still bolstered the depiction of female sexuality as full of shame. His discussion of the topic was introduced by a lengthy justification for writing on women's generative organs, an apologetic stance that was visually embodied in the title page of his book, with its illustration of the nude bodies of male and female. While the genitals of the male were exposed, the female genitals and breasts were covered by both her hands, in the ultimate gesture of biblical shame that symbolized original sin and the Fall.[56]

On another level, the new anatomy tacitly invoked representations of a failing body gradually descending into, and horribly exposed, at death. The new science that was based on the exposition and dissection of the human body implied an awareness of a body in its processes of morbidity – fragmented, deformed, ugly, and naked. According to Paracelsus, anatomy was indeed deplorable and useless, for it produced 'dead knowledge', that is, knowledge of dead rather than living bodies.[57] Echoing descriptions of the decrepitude and physical decay of old age, in which the line between life and death itself became faint, the dissected body of a human being could connote not only the frailty of life and reality of death, but a body exposed and no longer concealed under apparel and good manners, the nearness of death stripping a person of honour, rank and dignity, overwhelmingly consuming him or her with a sense of shame.

This sense of an undignified body going through a shameful process of decay was powerfully reflected by Thomas Browne, an author and physician trained in the new anatomy and sciences, whose book *Religio Medici* (1642), a mix of autobiography with a meditation on religion, science, and natural philosophy, quickly gained prominence in England and abroad.[58] In sections devoted to the issue of death, Browne proclaimed his acceptance of his mortality and expressed fearlessness, if not a desire to die as a Christian, making plain his adherence to the Protestant notions of death and the prospects of the afterlife,

> Were there not another life that I hope for, all the vanities of this world should not entreat a moment's breath for me; ... In expectation of a better [life], I can with patience embrace this life, yet in my best meditations do often desire death.

While for a pagan there were good motives 'to be in love with life', he announced, 'for a Christian to be amazed at death' implied that he was 'hopeless of the life to come'.[59]

Yet for all his avowed hope and courage in facing death, Browne still conveyed the infinite shame entailed in bodily decay and the process of dying, and here the voice of the anatomist was unambiguous:

> Not that I am insensible of the dread and horror [of death, which] ... by raking into the bowels of the deceased, continual sight of anatomies, skeletons, or cadaverous relics, like vespilloes, or grave-makers, I am become stupid [and full of] ... apprehension of mortality.

While ascertaining that he could overcome the apprehension of mortality, Browne still related the shocking degradation of the body and an inability to endure the sight of bodily exposure and disfigurement that signalled utmost humiliation and shame:

> I am not so much afraid of death, as ashamed thereof; tis the very disgrace and ignominy of our natures, that in a moment can so disfigure us that our nearest friends, wife, and children stand afraid and stare at us.[60]

## Shame on the stage

Some of the most potent images of shame were conveyed in imaginary literature and drama that emerged from the mid-sixteenth century onwards. In late medieval literature, shame acquired multiple connotations, most conspicuously in Dante's *Inferno*, where it was associated with moral shortcoming, military dishonour, an inferior and humiliating status, or distinctive facial and ocular expressions. By the sixteenth century, Humanist drama made abundant use of shame; in Thomas More's *Utopia*, an egalitarian world displayed social arrangements that were carefully designed to overcome and eliminate pride and shame. Other Humanist plays conveyed the moral virtue of shame and 'shamefastness' through a personified shame – a character who observed, reproached, and punished the protagonists. More elaborate forms of shame pervaded Elizabethan drama, with shame becoming the salient feature of many of Shakespeare's works as well as those of his contemporary playwrights and poets.[61]

Dramatic representations of shame evinced a particularly intense experience of the emotion, employing rich verbal and visual imagery in scenes of degradation and suffering designed to move, stir, and shock the beholder. At the heart of all Shakespearean tragedies was the theme of the fall and degradation of the hero, his shaming and shame brought to an utmost powerful impact on the stage. Scenes of humiliation of prominent powerful people abounded in many other plays, with noble men or women who were deplored, degraded, and disgraced, often in a public space, where they were watched by a mocking and contemptuous lower-class audience. In *Henry VI*, the Duke of Gloucester faces the shaming of his treasonous wife, Eleanor Cobham, Duchess of Gloucester, as he cries out to her and exclaims: 'The abject people gazing on thy face/With envious looks, laughing at thy shame'.[62] Other plays were rife with scenes of particularly brutal forms of shaming, presenting spectacles of disfigurement and mutilation in which the body became the site of utmost humiliation and disgrace, utterly stripping characters of their status and dignity as humans. In Christopher Marlowe's *Edward II*, the king is kept in the dungeon, his beard shaved and his body covered in sewage before he is savagely murdered in the presence of eyewitnesses (by means of anal penetration with a red-hot poker). In Ben Jonson's *The Alchemist*, a character is 'blindfolded, bound, pinched, robbed gagged with a piece of gingerbread and locked in a privy for two hours'; he is then visited by a whore and kisses her 'departing part' as instructed.[63] Brutal punishments, revenge, and the cruel degradation of the body were staple themes in Jacobean tragedies as well. In John Webster's *The Duchess of Malfi*, the duchess, having remarried, is agonized and tortured by her brothers, who also arrange for her to be strangled along with two of her children. Her twin brother Ferdinand is then filled with guilt and regret at the sight of his strangled sister's body: 'Cover her face; mine eyes dazzle … The wolf shall find her grave, and scrape it up,/ Not to devour the corpse, but to discover/The horrid murder'; he subsequently becomes deranged, punished and shamed in his lunacy. In John Ford's *'Tis Pity She's a Whore*, which boldly presents the theme of incest, Annabella is impregnated by her brother, Giovani, and both end up murdered. Annabella's shame and crude physical degradation are displayed in a chilling scene when her brother enters the stage with her heart skewered on a dagger; Giovani's own brutal murder follows, with one character concluding the play by announcing, 'thus long I lived …. /to see the effect of pride and lust at once/brought both to shameful ends'.[64]

Scholars have long pointed to the rich amalgam of ideas and meanings conveyed in these scenes, pointing first and foremost to the prominence of honour and dishonour, loss of status, and especially sexual and masculine dishonour as the sources of the protagonists' shame. Vicious honour codes that shamed and doomed the protagonists pervaded Shakespearean tragedies. Othello resolved to kill his wife Desdemona upon the first suspicion of adultery that threatened his masculinity; Hamlet vowed to avenge his father's dishonour, subsequently experiencing the shame of his own dishonour and cowardice in being unable to take revenge on his uncle. The shame of adultery featured numerous plays; husbands who feared the loss of control over their wives and whose jealousy became destructive to their own standing; cuckolds who became the target of ridicule and shame.[65] Women's indecency and sexual shame were the targets of particular degradation, with scenes invoking lurid images of female bodily shame. The shaming of the Duchess of Gloucester in *Henry VI* is presented through her vulnerable body; her tears and shudders of pain, along with her bruised and bleeding feet, her shaming becomes steeped in total exclusion and obliteration, when her husband and his friends appear on the stage in mourning garments. Anne Frankford, the adulterous wife in Thomas Heywood's *A Woman Killed with Kindness*, punishes herself by fasting and is stricken in her bed in agonizing pain, crying out 'Blush I not? ... Can you not read my fault in my cheeks? Is not my crime there?', subsequently calling her act a sin 'that with an angel's face / Conjured mine honour, till he sought my wrack'. Elsewhere, women's bodies were exposed and ridiculed in comic scenes of urinary incontinence, resonating with the humoral language of cold and moist that bolstered the image of the shameful female inability to control her bodily needs and temperaments.[66]

These images and representations of shame could be deeply immersed in notions of immorality, with characters agonizing not only over their humiliation, dishonour, or loss of status, but also over their corruption, vanity, and sin. Some scenes presented characters who experienced a deep sense of shame before God, overwhelmed with regret and feelings of guilt. In *Richard III*, the wicked and shameless king is engulfed with shame on the eve of the battle of Bosworth: 'O coward conscience, how dost thou afflict me! O, no, alas, I rather hate myself/... my conscience hath a several thousand tongues/... Perjury, perjury in the high'st degree ... crying all, 'Guilty, guilty!'. In *Hamlet*, the protagonist's agony is the product not only of the loss of his masculine honour, but also of deep religious convictions, as Hamlet experiences his mother's unfaithfulness as evil and a sign of sin. His inability to take revenge against his father's murderer, too, has strong Christian overtones, revealing a tension between the need to avenge the family honour and the Christian aversion to revenge and an avowed preference for modesty and humility.[67] In Thomas Heywood's *A Woman Killed with Kindness*, Anne's seducer, Master Wendoll, is painfully immersed in the shame and guilt of his adultery (and the betrayal of his friend): 'Pursued with horror of a guilty soul,/ And with the sharp scourge of repentance lashed,/ I fly from my own shadow. /... it strikes a terror like a lightning' flash'. Wendoll further describes his wish to hide and withdraw from the company of those he knew; 'Thus I, like the owl,/Ashamed of day, live in these shadowy woods,/Afraid of every leaf or murmu'ring blast', all conveyed through the imagery of the biblical punishment of Cain. 'And I must now go wander, like a Cain, /In foreign countries and remoted climes, /Where the report of my ingratitude /Cannot be heard'.[68]

In many plays, religious shame was construed as a form of reproach and exhortation, with plays projecting an overly moralizing stance, thoroughly exposing and condemning the sin and shame of characters – and of audiences themselves. Humanist morality plays presented the character of shame, whose role was to expose the sins and failures of protagonists; in *Nice Wanton* (1550) shame appears on the stage to expose the protagonist's (Xantippe) in her sins and failure as a mother, insisting that people will blame and scorn her, after which she faints and dies. Many Elizabethan and Jacobean plays, especially domestic drama, exhibited similar religious moralization. In Ben Jonson's *Every Man Out of his Humour*, Asper, 'the presenter' of the play, declares his intention to 'unmask public vice' and put a mirror to the audience, 'Where they shall see the time's deformity/ Anatomized in every nerve and sinew'. In Heywood's *A Woman Killed with Kindness*, Charles Montford, having killed Francis Acton and his two men, is overcome with guilt and regret. While trying to assuage his guilt by claiming that the act was the product of a rage beyond his control, he nevertheless takes full moral responsibility for his shameful act:

> My God, what have I done!... My rage hath plunged into a sea of blodd/In which my soul lies drowned ... When I would give this right hand, nay, this head,/To breathe in them new life whom I have slain!-/ Forgive me, God! .../It was not I, but rage, did this vile murder;/ Yet I, and not my rage, must answer it.

The main thrust of morality in the play lies with the adulterous Anne, who tells her husband she is willing to take upon herself the harshest punishment for her adultery, expressing profound shame that would not be redeemed: 'I would have my hand cut off, these my breasts seared;/ Be racked, strappadoed, put to any torment ... He cannot be so base as to forgive me,/Nor I so shameless to accept the pardon'. She then turns to the female audience with the moral of her shame: 'O women, women, you that yet have kept/ Your holy matrimonial vow unstained,/Make me your instance; when you read awry,/Your sins, like mine, will on your conscience lie'. Anne's shame finally leads to repentance and a plead for compassion: 'All you that have true feeling of my grief,/That know my loss, and have relenting hearts/Gird me about, and help me with your tears/To wash my spotted sins!'[69]

Some of these dramatic constructions of shame were embedded in an elaborate and enhanced understanding of the inner working of shame. Characters on the stage showed an awareness of shame as a private, profoundly intimate experience; 'My inward grief/ No tongue can utter', as Anne in *A Woman Killed with Kindness*, refers to it. Shame could be construed as an internal and agonizing experience that runs deep and becomes, alongside death itself, one of 'two of the ugliest shapes/that can confound a soul'. While relating an experience of shame under the watchful eyes of God, the experience was also presented as overly attuned towards an inner self, connoting a sense of unworthiness or inadequacy that undermined one's potential or moral standards, inducing negative self-assessment, self-reproach, disappointment, and a sense of ineptitude. An experience of deep humiliation resonated through Shakespeare's tragedies, leading the protagonists to internal torment that utterly devastated and shattered their selfhood, ultimately being linked to death itself. In *Hamlet*, the hero is engulfed with the shame of his unworthiness as a son and a prince, having failed to vindicate his father's and the family honour. Hamlet's shame then becomes the source of a tormented self that undergoes a psychological and spiritual crisis, being torn and divided, experiencing his shame as 'a sense of not being'. This inner distress infuses the entire play, ultimately replacing the shame of dishonour and the urge for revenge with the deep reflection on an inward self. Self-awareness and reflection resonated in the work of other dramatists and poets as well, notably in John Milton's poetic imagery of an agonizing shame experienced as an inflammation from within, which no medicine can relieve.[70]

The shame construed in its inner workings was not only brutally humiliating and degrading, but could also be presented as ameliorative and redemptive, leading the protagonist in a process of repentance and recognition of their faults, resulting in the restoration of the social order or ties, and ultimately the reconciliation with God. Hamlet's shame entails a torment and anguish that becomes a great spiritual force, enabling his awakening and liberation from selfish concerns and his move towards God. In *A woman Killed with Kindness*, Anne's shame is followed by repentance and self-afflicted punishment, leading in the final scene to forgiveness when her husband declares: 'Though thy rash offence/Divorced our bodies, thy repentant tears/Unite our soules'. Anne's own words upon her death express deep hope for redemption and release: 'Pardoned on earth, soul, thou in heaven art free;/Once more thy wife dies thus embracing thee'. Shame here is not only an experience of suffering and internal agony that culminates with the well-deserved destruction of a corrupt and mortal soul, but also leads to the restoration of the patriarchal order and unification with intimate relations and with God.[71]

An overwhelming shame that ultimately leads to the reconciliation of human bonding and ties is profoundly affected in the tragedy *King Lear*, which displays an infinitely intricate process of shaming and shame undergone by the protagonist Lear and all the actors. Lear's act of shaming his daughter with the love test and denial of her inheritance is portrayed as an act of vain pride that also reveals him in his 'dreadful insecurity about his inner worth' as a father. Lear himself then experiences a profound punitive shame inflicted through the cruelty of his daughters, compelling a prolonged and agonizing degradation that strips and reduces him to almost nothing. Yet this devastating experience also allows Lear to embark on his road to redemption. Recognizing the dreadful wrong he had done to Cordelia, he is transformed from a selfish and shamed person to a father who could feel and suffer intensely for his child, and so at last be reconciled to his daughter. Lear's redemption through his awakening, while exhibiting Christian overtones, nonetheless focuses on the parent–child bond and is presented less as a 'road to the absolute' and more as a process of moving through shame from selfishness towards human bonding and ties.[72]

## Sin and salvation

Early modern constructions of shame were ultimately suffused with the notion of shame before God. Deeply ingrained in the Christian tradition and the doctrine of original sin and the Fall, shame was vastly enhanced by the Protestant invocation of the wholeness of human depravity in the face of an omnipotent God.[73] In numerous sermons and works of devotion, Protestants depicted the initial encounter with sin as a harrowing experience of special ferocity and an intense sense of shame. As Arthur Dent, one of the most popular Protestant authors of the late sixteenth century, described it in the *Sermon of Repentance* (preached in 1582 and reprinted at least twenty-two times by 1638), the encounter with sin was like slipping into 'a deep pit and dangerous gulfe', or being burnt by fire from which one could barely recover. Using a mix of biblical allusions and metaphors, Dent invoked an intensely internal, self-inflicted, and utterly degrading experience of shame. Repentance was 'an inward sorrowing', with the sinner retiring 'into some corner or outspace', there proceeding 'to beate his owne Conscience' by deliberately enhancing the sense of sin through 'aggravation', 'exaggeration', and 'heaping up one thing to another', [so that] 'it is not enough to say, I have sinned: but to say I have most traiterously sinned, I have most obstinately, carelessly, and rebelliously sinned; … my own conscience doeth accuse mee of it'. The final result of the process was utter disgrace before God: '…And now (O Lord) Lord, what an ugly monster and wretched villaine am I; here I stand before thy presence, all naked, blind, wounded, poore, wretched and miserable, having deserved a thousand damnations'.[74]

Guides and works of practical divinity from the late sixteenth century onwards resonated with the shame of sin as an ongoing and foreboding experience, a 'continual mourning of the heart and conscience for sin' that called for the repentance 'not for some sinne, but for all sinne; not for an hour, but for ever; not for a day: but continually; not for a week, but as long as we live'.[75] The list of shameful sins registered in these works was expansive, and the vocabulary and rhetoric used – the repetition, dramatic build-up, the sheer detail – created poignant constructions of perpetual and daily potential for shame. A typical puritan book of instruction, Edward Elton's *A plaine and easy exposition of sixe of the commandments of God*, proceeded with an exposition of the Decalogue, enlisting for each of the commandments 'the negative part', that is, 'a threatening denounced against the breakers of [the commandment]', through which the shame of wrongdoing was referred to by invariably designating these acts pejoratively as 'foolish' and 'hainous' sins, or 'a light vain wicked and unseemely carriage', with sinners being described as lewd people who brought not only dishonour to God but also 'just disgrace and contempt on their owne persons'. The discussion of some commandments presented page after page of sinful acts, the build-up of numerous sins cumulatively bolstering a sense of continuous threat of shame. The account of deeds against the sixth commandment, for example, enhanced the sense of shameful sin by listing numerous acts that were only dimly related to the prohibition

38  Constructions of shame

to kill, a mixture of incivility and irreligiousness that included hatred, envy, or desire for revenge, through drunkenness, riot, idleness, unchastity, and careless neglect of the body, 'monstrous' pride, and, at last, varied acts of murder and the taking away of one's own life, 'out of horror of conscience, and despaire of God's mercie: or out of feare of wordly punishment or shame'.[76]

A sense of deep shame was likewise instilled through sermons and devotional works that invariably castigated audiences for their wickedness, warning them of the consequences of their shamelessness and sins. While styles of preaching varied, zealot puritans were prone to convey their sermons in an accusatory mood, using blatant rhetoric and dramatic gestures to stir up emotional responses. Stressing the gulf that existed between an ideal life and a reality of one's immorality and profanity, they induced a sense of imperfection and an inability to live without succumbing to sin, feeding on, and deepening, audience's feelings of shame and guilt. Calamities and natural disasters such as fire, epidemics, and drought offered occasions for warnings of providential retribution, with ministers denouncing their audiences for their abundant transgressions and offences – pride, lying, disobedience; fornication, adultery, usury, and more – imparting on them the burden of guilt and shame for triggering the wrath of God not only on themselves, but on others as well.[77]

Punitive shame also filled the pages of an increased array of popular publications – providential stories, news pamphlets, and ballads – with shame being construed less as an internal experience and more as the suffering and extreme degradation that was wreaked on sinners through the wrath of God. Blending traditional beliefs with more distinct Protestant assertions regarding an omnipotent and interventionist God, these stories were overly didactic and immersed with reproach and moral warnings of the penalties awaiting those succumbing to shameful sins and transgressions. Whether narrating the stories of women and men committing one of the seven deadly sins, or of those engaged with the devil or violating the Ten Commandments, the narratives conveyed shame in its utmost harsh and retributive mode, often taking the form of profound bodily shame and public degradation. Using graphic detail and imagery, providential stories depicted gruesome punishments and tortuous death; sinners dying with their bodies deformed, mutilated, and rotten; bodies consumed by rats, lice, or vermin, or by gangrenous decaying and revolting stench, often before a watching crowd. 'Such a multitude of lice … as maggots are wont to engender in a dead and rotten carrion', as described in one of the numerous stories in Thomas Beard's massive compilation of providential stories, where the sinner subsequently dies in the most inhuman and shameful death, 'like a mad beast', with audiences in close attendance.[78] The increased use of woodcut pictures added a visual dimension to the stories, bolstering utter disgust and disgrace. Bizarre and revolting punishments were meted on the female body with special force, as in the ballad on the lady who refused to offer alms to a poor woman and was punished by becoming pregnant with 'as many children at one birth, as there are daies in the yeare'. The ballad conveyed an extreme form of a disgraced pregnant body in shame:

And on my bodies pampred pride,/a fearfull judgement shoes. /My cheeks that were so lovely red,/of natures choicest dye;/Grew blacke and ugly to behould ... And in my wombe ... I sweld so big that I appeard, a strange and monstrous wight ... being made my countryes scorne, I wished I had in child-bed dyed.[79]

For all the centrality of these constructions of shame in its dreadfully retributive, brutal bodily form, Protestants also advanced alternative uses and meanings of shame, with shame being turned on its head in a gesture of defiance, or else fostering solidarity and compassion among spectators, ultimately leading to redemption through God's justifying grace. A major source for these representations of shame was John Foxe's *Actes and Monuments* (1563), the influential 'Book of Martyrs' as it came to be called, in which accounts of the persecution of Protestant martyrs reverberated with shaming and shame.[80] The shame was first and foremost directed against the Catholic church itself; that is, instead of inflicting shame on ordinary sinners, the torrent of shaming that emerged from the pages of the *Actes and Monuments* targeted the church itself, presenting not only a rebuttal of traditional beliefs and doctrines, but also harsh and defiant reproach and condemnation. Thus, in narrating the atmosphere that preceded the emergence of Martin Luther, Foxe invoked the pervasive hatred 'agaysnt the pompe and pryde of Rome', the 'disdayne' and 'contempt and derision ... against the pope', with a flood of publications and proverbs advertising the corruptions and tyranny of a church that 'ha[s] no shame'. Using an array of derogatory speech, Foxe's narratives invariably cited the 'bloody babylonical byshops', their 'abhominable false doctrine', their 'hipocricie, bloudthirst, whoredome, idleness, their pestilent life', all of which would bring the church 'to utter shame: rebuke, ruyne, decaye, and destruction'. In some stories, martyrs emerged from humiliating interrogations ('calling him heretic, spitting on him') praying to God to forgive their persecutors, defiantly proclaiming they 'will rather die than worship such a beast', designating the church as 'the very whoore of Babylon', which will eventually be exposed in its 'vtter confusion and shame'. In still other narratives, the martyrs shamed their interrogators with triumphant arguments, as was the case of Giles of Brusels, persecuted in Germany and brought to Louvain where, following days of disputations, the 'singularly witted' Giles forced his interrogators to go away 'many tymes wyth shame'.[81]

Foxe's *Actes and Monuments* also abounded with descriptions of the punishment and bodily shame meted on martyrs. Yet instead of inflicting utter degradation, bodily shame here connoted a desirable and elevated state that signalled the spread and triumph of Protestantism. The model for these representations was Christ's bodily suffering, which was conveyed in Foxe's narration of the early followers of Christ and their bodily suffering and disgrace: 'their hands cut off or otherwise dismembred, ... left naked to the open shame of the world'. Such disgrace, however, became the mark of true faith, with the description of bodily mutilation being replaced by varied metaphors that signified martyrdom and the power of a saving God.[82] The faggots that martyrs were forced to bear when led to their burning represented humility and Truth; the road to the stake was depicted as abounding with torment and misery that were ameliorated by an intervening, compassionate God, while the body of the burnt heretic itself became a sign of the divine. For example, the narrative of a preacher in Turin, Geffreye Varagle, typically recorded his apprehension, interrogation, and condemnation, as well as his prayers to God and offering of forgiveness to his executioner and audiences, with the description of his death ('he was first strangled, and then burned') lacking any graphic details of a disgraced body. Instead, it connoted innocence and divine inspiration, embodied by a dove flying over the body:

> Relation is made moreover, concerning the sayd Geffrey, that at the tyme of his burning, a dove was seene ... flying and fluttering divers times about the fire, testifying (as was thought) the innocency of theis holy martyr of the Lord.[83]

The martyrs' shame also fostered social integration. Rather than leading to the shunning of the heretic, the shame inflicted by the church generated compassion, transforming the hearts and minds of audiences and uniting them in ties of sentiment and solidarity. 'When his frends saw him so constaunt, and fully determined to go, they with weeping eyes commended him vnto God: and he within a day or two prepared himselfe to his iourney', as it was described in an account detailing the examination and burning in Norwich of Rowland Taylor. Compassion and integrative shame that bound the community in ties of unity were depicted as the quintessential mark of the life and deeds of many martyrs, who displayed forgiveness and delivered sinners from their shameless deeds. In an account of the early history of the church, the narrative presented the encounter of the apostle John with a man who was accused of theft; the apostle beseeched the man, who became engulfed with 'confusion and shame', to have no fear, and then promised hope for salvation, praying and comforting him, not going away 'from him ... before he had restored him to the congregation againe'. The account of the life of Martin Luther similarly recounted how he confronted sinners and 'willed the whole congregation to pray: and he himselfe ceased not with hys praiers to labour', allowing the sinner to reunite with the audience.[84]

Above all, the *Actes and Monuments* conveyed the transformative power of shame. For the suffering and shame of the heretics was not only a sign of truth or social integration, but also brought about the prospect of a journey towards God: 'We may be reproved, put to shame and rebuked, yea and finally be slaine and killed, but we will neither yield, nor be ouercome. And with great triumph will we reiyce in our father's doings'. Foxe's narratives were full of martyrs who fearlessly confronted the shame and condemnation inflicted by the church, and then transcended their shame by 'looking

Constructions of shame 41

vpon Christ ... which for the ioy that was set before hym, abode the Crosse and despised the shame'.[85] A typical account was the story of *'The trouble and persecution of Dalaber. Doctor Cotisford'*, who while imprisoned and put to the stocks encountered 'that most constant martyr of God, M. John Clarke', and was greatly affected by his preaching. Being cautioned by Clarke of the prospects of the persecution and shame awaiting him – 'Yea, you shall be called and iudged an heretike ... to your reproche and shame, to the great sorow of all your faithfull friendes and kinsfolke' – Dalaber was undeterred and placed his trust in God. Clarke then

> came to me, and toke me vp in his armes, kissed me, the teares trickling downe from his eyes, and sayd vnto me: The Lorde almighty grant you so to do, and from henceforth for euer take me for your father, and I will take you for my sonne in Christe.

Other speeches and extracts from martyrs' letters scattered in the *Actes and Monuments* exalted in the hope and potential for redemption wrought by the experience of shame.[86]

The shame experienced by martyrs could become a model and source of hope for others. For once they faced the shame entailed in their sins, all human beings could embark on a similar road, their shame being the first step in the long journey towards God's forgiveness and mercy. As it was proclaimed in the narrative of the examination and confession of William Thorpe,

> Whosoeuer wil shame and sorow hartely for their sinnes, knowledging them faithfully to God, amending them ... all such men and women may find, sufficient meanes to come to Gods mercy, and so to be cleane assoiled of all their sinnes.

The experience of shame by no means absolved the sinner, nor did it relieve their suffering, for without God's 'measurelesse vnspeakeable mercye and loue to saue vs', the sinner would be brought 'to euerlasting damnation, and death perpetuall'. Yet once a sinner recognized their misdeeds and was 'styrred up to a shamefastnes and blushing, because we are not as we should be', and when casting oneself 'wholly vpon him', and, above all, if God granted them forgiveness and assurance, then they would experience a different, new kind of shame. This newer sensation of shame was less burdensome, more tempered and full of hope; 'then shall your conscience be quieted ... then shal you be certayn that no man can touch one heare of your head further then shall please your good father, to your euerlasting ioye', as quotations from the 'godly letters' of John Bradford announced.[87]

In the ensuing decades following the publication of the *Actes and Monuments*, the transformative power of shame came to feature numerous devotional works, sermons, spiritual guides, and stories. In all these works, harsh punitive shame was intricately linked to a more ameliorative and ultimately redeeming shame. For a depraved human being could not truly repent and feel guilty or ashamed in her sins unless God already intervened; human conscience was, in this sense, '[a]sleepe until God awake it and call it to account'. With punitive shame itself already a signal of Godly intervention, a process of reconciliation to God could ensue. 'For where true repentance goeth before, there remission of sinnes must necessarily follow after; not that repentance deserveth remissions of sinnes, but because where God worketh repentance, there hee pardonneth sinnes because of his promise'.[88] Even popular stories of providential intervention, which recounted the misfortunes and natural calamities inflicted upon shameless sinners, depicted these horrible punishments as also acting to open the eyes of the blind, with repentance, acknowledgement of shame, and prayers leading to God potentially withdrawing his wrath. In all these works, while shame revealed one's depravity and overwhelming sin, it was also a critical initiating step that triggered a prolonged spiritual process, conceivably leading to rebirth and regeneration from which one's soul could emerge redeemed.[89]

## Conclusion

Early modern constructions of shame denoted an array of meanings and sources for shame – incivility and dishonour, sexual gendered transgression, bodily imperfection, sin, and immorality. The ideas and values underlying these sources of shame did not present a unified belief system, and the writings examined here varied greatly in their aim, audience, rhetoric, and literary style. Yet shaming and shame permeated all these diverse writings and genres, reflecting the sheer range of meanings of shame, and the potent means through which it was articulated, communicated and advanced.

For all the varied constructions and representations, several patterns of shame emerge. First and foremost was the preponderance of an overwhelmingly punitive and exclusionary shame. Whether in the form of harsh censure, ridicule, or denunciation, or brutal physical pain and abuse, the shame was construed as leading to public disgrace, estrangement from social ties, loss of status, damnation, or death. Varied writings negotiated this form of harsh shame using a rich vocabulary and rhetoric, augmented with verbal and visual imagery that evinced an immensely degrading and humiliating experience. Especially potent was the presentation of the human body as a site of shame, the visual aspect of shame being presented not only through blushing or an averted gaze but through the failing and disgraced body. In civic manuals the shame resided in the brute body – beastly, revolting, embarrassed, and undignified; in educational treatises, an effeminate body, and physical frailty were perceived as sources of masculine shame. Medical texts offered particularly potent images of bodily shame – imperfect and unbalanced bodies, feeble or uncontrolled, deficient or decaying, with images of females' shameful inability to control their bodily temperaments penetrating drama and the stage in scenes resonating with physical vulnerability and exclusion. Prominent above all was the Protestant perception of the body as utterly sinful and corrupt, with popular stories of providential punishments graphically and intensely focusing on sinners' bodies being cruelly mutilated, de-humanized and disgraced.

These constructions of exclusionary shame were prone to reflect on, and amplify, social, gender, and ideological divides that came to mark the era from the mid-sixteenth century onwards. Shaming and shame could demarcate the lower classes as uncivilized and incapable of experiencing shame, or enhance a perception of the insubordinate woman as justly receiving punishment and being shunned from human ties. Zealot puritans inflicted shame on those they perceived as sinners and profane, singling them out as deserving utter exclusion, damnation, and death; or they could expose the shame of their opponents' superficial manners, mocking and ridiculing them for their addiction to appearances and petty insults. Shame could also be turned upside down, deployed to defy superiors or church authorities, as in the case of the early Protestant martyrs who were presented as boldly shaming the traditional church and its corruptions. On the stage, shame could be construed as a critique of elite vice and oppressions, with images of the degradation and public disgrace of noble men and women at times consuming the dramatic unfolding of a scene.

A second construction permeating the works examined here evinced more lenient practices and experiences of shame. These modes of shame could be articulated directly or insinuated and more tacitly tied in with the dominant forms of punitive shame. Moderate shame could take varied forms; notions of moral shame as an internal sensation that warned a person of their vices, a 'shamefastness' that signalled inner morality and conscience prompting an averseness to act in certain ways regardless of the gaze and censure of others. Lenient modes of shame could entail an anticipation of shame rather than the actual experience of it, or be manifested in blushing that indicated unease or embarrassment rather than deep pain or the terror of exclusion. Erasmus exalted in this mode of shamefastness and moral shame as an agreeable sensation arising under the presence of 'the angels'. A century later, John Locke would refer to this mode of shaming as the 'softer ways of shame and commendation'.[90] Rather than implying division, ostracism, and exclusion, the shame invoked through these constructions was conciliatory, leading to the restoration of the social order and affirmation of family ties, or else to solidarity and compassion among audiences and crowds. In some Shakespearean tragedies, the demeaning and destructive shame of the protagonist was wholly superseded by a more lenient and integrative shame, generating empathy and responsiveness to others. Above all, there was the shame entailed in the recognition of sin and repentance. While initially bringing immense suffering, the shame could also offer a measure of solace, paving the way to a spiritual process marked by regeneration and the prospect of sanctification.

Lastly, the shame construed in these works was simultaneously inward-looking as well as strongly attuned to others and towards God. In many ways, these representations reflected on and enhanced what historians have identified as a newly recognized 'self-awareness', or sense of subjectivity.[91] Shame was evoked as reflecting on an internal self, invariably undermining an inner sense of worthiness and pride, of internal morality, virtue, and standards of excellence. A wide range of writings – civil manuals, drama, devotional works – portrayed shame as an intimate experience induced by negative self-assessment, leading to a sense of inadequacy and ineptitude, or anguish, guilt, and despair over the failure to comply with one's own internalized values.

Yet the shame construed in these works consistently pointed to the external dimension of shame, and to a self that was oriented outwardly. Both punitive and more moderate modes of shame resonated with implications for a relational self; a shame triggered by negative reactions and condemning attitudes of others – 'superiors', 'inferiors', or 'equals', as all conduct manuals were careful to denote. Even moderate constructions of an internalized sense of shame still indicated an acute sense of relations with others, the inner working of shame being prompted by the critique and judgement of others. The shame that was intrinsic to internalized values and standards of morality evinced regard for others, involving not only the fear of penalties or loss of respect, but also the damage to relations deemed essential among peers. Nor did the suffering that conjoined the recognition of sin remain private or end with interiority, rather it potentially – and ideally – led outwardly, with the inner working of shame pointing to relations with others as well as ultimately towards God.

In all these constructions and patterns of shame, the discourses and publications examined in this chapter open a window to, and reflect upon, actual practices and experiences in society at large, which the remainder of the chapters proceed to explore. As these chapters will also show, whereas the shame patterns uncovered here reverberated in the lives of women and men of all social strata, they were also expanded, elaborated, and reinvented over time, as contemporaries gave meanings to shame and applied it in their daily lives and interactions amid different social settings, both public and private.

## Notes

1 Pierre de la Primaudaye, *The French academie wherein is discoursed the institution of manners, ... by precepts of doctrine, and examples of the lives of ancient sages and famous men*. Trans. T.B. (1594), STC2 15235, 242; Thomas Wright, *The passions of the minde in generall in six books* (1601, 1621), STC2 26042, 17; Nicolas Coeffeteau, *A table of humane passions With their causes and effects* (1621), STC2 5473, 473, 495, 507; Edward Reynolds, *A treatise of the passions and faculties of the soule of man* (1640), STC2 20938, 311–12; Robert Burton, *The anatomy of melancholy* (1621), STC2 4159, 135. See also Werner L. Gundersheimer, 'Concepts of Shame and Pocaterra's Dialoghi Della Vergogna', *Renaissance Quarterly*, 47 (1994), 34–56. For the language of 'passions' in Christian theology and its roots in Greek philosophy, see Thomas Dixon, *From Passions to Emotions: The Creation of a Secular Psychological Category* (Cambridge, 2003), 26–61.

2 Merridee L. Bailey, *Socializing the Child in Late Medieval England c. 1400–1600* (Woodbridge, 2012), 11–42; Anna Bryson, *From Courtesy to Civility: Changing Codes of Conduct in Early Modern England* (Oxford, 1998), 43–74; Keith Thomas, *In Pursuit of Civility: Manners and Civilization in Early Modern England* (Waltham, Massachusetts, 2018), 11–19.
3 F[rancis] S[eager], *The schoole of vertue, and booke of good nurture teaching children and youth their duties* (1621), STC2 22137.7, no pages. quotation Chap. 7.
4 Bryson, *From Courtesy to Civility*, 105; Thomas, *In Pursuit of Civility*, 37–8.
5 Antoine de Courtin, *The rules of civility, or, Certain Ways of deportment observed in France amongst all persons of quality upon several occasions* (1671, 1678), Wing2 C6604, 275; Markku Peltonen, *The Duel in Early Modern England: Civility, Politeness and Honour* (Cambridge, 2003), 17–44; Bryson, *From Courtesy to Civility*, 110–11.
6 Bailey, *Socializing the Child*, 24.
7 Bryson, *From Courtesy to Civility*, 84–5, 105.
8 Seager, *The schoole of vertue*, Chaps. 3, 12 no pages; Courtin, *The Rules of Civility*, 11, 14–15, 132.
9 Courtin, *The Rules of Civility*, 26–56.
10 Ibid., 132, 137, 186; Seager, *The schoole of vertue*, Chap. 7. For the technique of amplification (fancy phrasing, use of synonyms) for the purpose of highlighting the importance of certain issues, see Peter Mack, *Elizabethan Rhetoric: Theory and Practice* (Cambridge, 2002), 42, 149.
11 Seager, *The schoole of vertue*, Chap. 2.
12 Ibid., Chap. 2; Courtin, *The rules of civility*, 84, 151, 155, 255.
13 Peltonen, *The Duel*, 168.
14 Courtin, *The rules of civility*, 257.
15 Peltonen, *The Duel*, 41–4.
16 Bailey, *Socializing the Child*, 28–32, 64.
17 Bryson, *From Courtesy to Civility*, 107–111. For the two separate traditions, one presented by Castiglione and De La Casa, and focusing on courtesy, the other associated with Christian Humanism, with its emphasis on the body as an 'outward reflection of the soul', see also Peltonen, *The Duel*, 30.
18 Desiderius Erasmus, *The ciuilitie of childehode with the discipline and institucion of children, distributed in small and compe[n]dious chapiters ... translated oute of French into Englysh, by Thomas Paynell* (1560), STC2 10470.3, Aiiii, Diii, Biii.
19 Seager, *The schoole of vertue*, Chaps. 6, 9, 13; Pierre de la Primaudaye, *The French academie*, 242.
20 Bryson, *From Courtesy to Civility*, 109.
21 For objections to civility and the duel, see Ibid., 191–242 (quotion from Gough, 197); Peltonen, *The Duel*, 80–145.
22 Peltonen, *The Duel*, 121–31. For the critique of the code see also, Thomas, *In Pursuit of Civility*, 219–35.
23 Bryson, *From Courtesy to Civility*, 198–9.
24 Courtin, *The rules of civility*, 2, 110, 178, 263.
25 Peltonen, *The Duel*, 1647; Coeffeteau, *A table of humane passions*, 477.
26 Courtin, *The rules of civility*, 264, 267.
27 Ibid., 13, 256, 263–4. For the interplay between nature and nurture in the discourse on 'sincerity', see John Martin, 'Inventing Sincerity, Refashioning Prudence: The Discovery of the Individual in Renaissance Europe', *The American Historical Review*, 102 (1997), 1309–42, esp. 1330, 1333, 1337.
28 As Erasmus put it in his discussion of the virtue of modesty, a boy should acquire the habit of covering his 'unhonest members' in private, so that he learnt 'to dooe it with a certayne decent shamefastness: ye and that he have no witnesse to see them. For the Aungels are always present unto whom shamefast company and keping

46  Constructions of shame

of chastity is very [a]greable'. Erasmus, *The ciuilitie of childehode*, Biiii. See also Bryson, *From Courtesy to Civility*, 101; Thomas, *In Pursuit of Civility*, 39–40.
29 Burton, *The anatomy of melancholy* (1621), 133–5.
30 See, for example, Richard Brathwaite, *The English gentleman: containing sundry excellent rules or exquisite observations, tending to direction of every gentleman, of selecter ranke and qualitie; how to demeane or accommodate himselfe in the manage of publike or private affaires* (1630), STC2 3563; *The English gentleman, and The English gentlevvoman both in one volume couched, and in one modell portrayed: to the living glory of their sexe, the lasting story of their worth* (1641) Wing2 B4262.
31 Brysson, *From Courtesy to Civility*, 270, 229. For self-control and moderation as quintessentially masculine, see also Alexandra Shepard, *Meanings of Manhood in Early Modern England* (Oxford, 2003), 28–31.
32 Courtin, *The rules of civility*, 44, 90, 97, 101, 103, 106–7. For the masculinity of the civil code, and for female civility, see also Sara Mendelson, 'The Civility of Women in Seventeenth-Century England', in Peter Burke, Brian Harrison and Paul Slack (eds.), *Civil Histories: Essays Presented to Sir Keith Thomas* (Oxford, 2000), 111–26, esp. 111–13.
33 Thomas Elyot, *The boke, named The gouernour deuised by Sir Thomas Elyot Knight* (1532, 1580), STC2 7642, 69. Brathwaite, *The English gentleman*, 169. See also, Bailey, *Socializing the Child*, 108, 131; Shepard, *Meanings of Manhood*, 32. For an extended treatment of female shamefastness and its centrality in the formation of female honour, in late medieval literature, see Mary C. Glannery, *Practising Shame: Female Honour in Later Medieval England* (Manchester, 2020).
34 Primaudaye, *The French academie* 242–3, 245, 247, 250; Bryson, *From Courtesy to Civility*, 228–29. For early courtesy poems portraying the benefits and drawbacks of meekness in young men, see Bailey, *Socializing the Child*, 19–20.
35 Keith Thomas, *The Ends of Life: Roads to Fulfilment in Early Modern England* (Oxford, 2009), 44–61.
36 Elyot, *The boke, named The gouernour*, 69.
37 Primaudaye, *The French academie*, 245, 247; Brysson, *From Courtesy to Civility*, 229; Shepard, *Meanings of Manhood*, 28–9.
38 Elyot, *The boke, named The gouernour*, 52–71. See also Gregory M. Colón Semenza, *Sport, Politics and Literature in the English Renaissance* (Newark, 2003), esp. 29–39.
39 Richard Mulcaster, *Positions Concerning the Training Up of Children* (1581), ed. William Barker (Toronto, 1994), 51–128; 169–99, quotations on 180, 178, 184, 197.
40 James Cleland, *Hero-paideia, or The Institution of a young noble Man* (1607), STC2 5393, 222–6, 230–1.
41 Brathwaite, *The English gentleman*, 165–76, quotations on 174.
42 Ibid., 166–7.
43 Courtin, *The rules of civility*, 266.
44 Lawrence I. Conrad, Michael Neve, Vivian Nutton, Roy Porter and Andrew Wear (eds.), *The Western Medical Tradition 800 BC to AD 1800* (Cambridge, 1994), 250–6; Mary Lindemann, *Medicine and Society in Early Modern Europe* (Cambridge, 1999), 69–70; Anthony Fletcher, *Gender, Sex and Subordination in England, 1500–1700* (New Haven and London, 1995), 30–3; Shepard, *Meanings of Manhood*, 50–1; Hannah Newton, *The Sick Child in Early Modern England* (Oxford, 2012), 32–3.
45 Primaudaye, *The French academie*, 243; Elyot, *The boke, named The gouernour*, 52; Mulcaster, *Positions*, 51–4.
46 For medieval learning, in which humoral theory provided the basis for a set of social and moral meanings, see Joan Cadden, *Meanings of Sex Difference in the Middle Ages: Medicine, Science, and Culture* (Cambridge, 1993), 170–227.

47 Levinus Lemnius, *The touchstone of complexions expedient and profitable for all such as bee desirous and carefull of their bodily health* (1633), STC2 15458, 4; Shepard, *Meanings of Manhood*, 52–3.
48 Lindemann, *Medicine and Society*, 88; Shepard, *Meanings of Manhood*, 47–69; Mulcaster, *Positions*, 54–5.
49 Gail Kern Paster, *The Body Embarrassed: Drama and the Discipline of Shame in Early Modern England* (Ithaca, NY, 1993), 1–22, 64–112; Shepard, *Meanings of Manhood*, 48 and note 5.
50 Newton, *The Sick Child*, 34–5; Shepard, *Meanings of Manhood*, 56, 61.
51 Ibid., 38–45, 57–9, quotation on 59.
52 Ibid., 61–2; Lindemann, *Medicine and Society*, 69.
53 Ibid., 70–77; Newton, *The Sick Child*, 32.
54 Lindemann, *Medicine and Society*, 70; Shepard, *Meanings of Manhood*, 47–8; Fletcher, *Gender, Sex and Subordination*, 44–59, quotation on 58.
55 Thomas Elyot, *The castel of health. Corrected and in some place augmented* (1561) STC2 7651, 64; Shepard, *Meanings of Manhood*, 47–8, note 4; Fletcher, *Gender, Sex and Subordination*, 35. For the medieval practice of beginning the discussions of sexual organs with an apologia, in an apparent need to establish respectability of the subject, see Cadden, *Meanings of Sexual difference*, 91.
56 Helkiah Crooke, *Mikrokosmographia a description of the body of man. Together with the controuersies thereto belonging (1615)*, title page, 197. Shepard, *Meanings of Manhood*, 48, note 4; Paster, *The Body Embarrassed*, 21, 24.
57 Lindemann, *Medicine and Society*, 75.
58 Thomas Browne, *Religio Medici* (1642) Wing2 B5166; Claire Preston, *Thomas Browne and the Writing of Early Modern Science* (Cambridge, 2009), 2.
59 Browne, *Religio Medici*, 73–4. For the Protestant ideal of good death, see Ralph Houlbrook, *Death, Religion and the Family in England, 1480–1750* (Oxford, 1998), 295–330.
60 Ibid., 76. See also Ewan Fernie, *Shame in Shakespeare* (London, 2002), 41, 43–4; Michael Neill, *Issues of Death: Mortality and Identity in English Renaissance Tragedy* (1997), Chap. 2. For body marks and scars as signs of imperfection and reminders of mortality, see Stephen Greenblatt, *Shakespeare's Freedom* (Chicago, 2011), 18–48.
61 Gundersheimer, 'Concepts of Shame', 35–6, 38–40; Fernie, *Shame in Shakespeare*, 44, 41–108. For his comments on the 'unique intensity' of the shame of the expulsion of Adam and Eve from the Garden of Eden, in John Milton's *Paradise Lost*, see 51–2.
62 Ibid., 75–7.
63 Ibid., 53, 50.
64 John Webster, *The Duchess of Malfi* (1623), Act 4, scene 2; John Ford, *'Tis Pity She's a Whore* (1633), Act 5, scene 6.
65 For the extensive literature on stage representations of sexual honour, see Elizabeth A Foyster, *Manhood in Early Modern England: Honour, Sex and Marriage* (London and New York, 1999), 93–4, 130–6.
66 Fernie, *Shame in Shakespeare*, 76–7; Thomas Heywood, *A Woman Killed with Kindness* (1603), Act IV, scene V; Act V, scene III; Paster, *The Body embarrassed*, 23–63, 84–112; Gail Kern Paster, 'The Unbearable Coldness of Female Being: Women's Imperfection and the Humoral Economy', *English Literary Renaissance*, 28 (1998), 416–40.
67 Fernie, *Shame in Shakespeare*, 70–3, 99–108, 114, 118–9, 125, quotation from *Richard III* on 102.
68 Heywood, *A Woman Killed with Kindness*, Act 5, scene 3.
69 Fernie, *Shame in Shakespeare*, 44, 50–1; Heywood, *A Woman Killed with Kindness*, Act I scene III, Act iv, scene v, Act v, scene iii. On Tudor and early Stuart domestic tragedy as a 'dramatised sermon' and commercial drama as

48   Constructions of shame

a 'vessel for Protestant ideas', see Alexandra Walsham, *Providence in Early Modern England* (Oxford, 1999), 112, notes 191, 193.
70 Heywood, *A Woman Killed with Kindness*, Act v, scene iii; Fernie, *Shame in Shakespeare*, 43, 53–6, 78–82, 108, 120–6.
71 Fernie, *Shame in Shakespeare*, 132–4; Heywood, *A Woman Killed with Kindness*, Act v, scene v.
72 Ibid.; Fernie, *Shame in Shakespeare*, 205–7.
73 For a recent analysis of the Protestant reconfigured conception of sin, see Jonathan Willis, *The Reformation of the Decalogue: Religious Identity and the Ten Commandments in England, c. 1485–1625* (Cambridge, 2017), 135–76.
74 Arthur Dent, *A sermon of repentance a very godly and profitable sermon preached at Lee in Essex* (1630), STC2 6666.4, 5, 8–9.
75 Ibid., 5–6.
76 Edward Elton, *A plaine and easy exposition of sixe of the commandments of God* (1619), STC2 7620, 18, 41, 113, 119–20, 125–36, quotation on 131. For the role of the Ten Commandments as a framework for understanding the depth and breadth of sin, see Willis, *The Reformation of the Decalogue*, 138–76.
77 Walsham, *Providence in Early Modern England*, 116–24; Arnold Hunt, *The Art of Hearing: English Preachers and their Audiences, 1590–1640* (Cambridge, 2010), 81–94, esp. 87–8; Susan C. Karant-Nunn, *The Reformation of Feeling: Shaping the Religious Emotions in Early Modern Germany* (Oxford, 2010), 107–31; Willis, *The Reformation of the Decalogue*, 138–63.
78 Walsham, *Providence in Early Modern England* (Oxford, 1999), 65–115; Thomas Beard, *The theatre of Gods judgements revised, and augmented: wherein is represented the admirable justice of God* (1631), STC2 1661.5, 93–4.
79 *The Lamenting Lady, Who for the Wrongs done by her to a poore woman, for having two children at one burthen, was by the hand of God most strangely punished*, in Hyder E. Rollins, *A Pepysian Garland: Black-Letter Broadside Ballads of the Years 1595–1639 Chiefly from the Collection of Samuel Pepys* (Cambridge, 1922, 2011), 121–30, quotation on 129–30.
80 John Foxe, *Actes and monuments of these latter and perillous dayes touching matters of the Church* (1563). The following quotations are from *The Unabridged Acts and Monuments Online or TAMO* (1583 edition) (HRI Online Publications, Sheffield, 2011), https://www.johnfoxe.org. See also John N. King, *Foxe's Book of Martyrs and Early Modern Print Culture* (Cambridge, 2006), esp. 1–8.
81 TAMO, Book 7, 866–7; Book 7, 925; Book 8, 1063; Book 11, 1516. For derogatory speech in Foxe's narrative, see King, *Foxe's Book of Martyrs*, 65–6, 68.
82 TAMO, Book 1, 57; Book 5, 559. For Foxe's focus on the martyrs' behavior instead of the mutilation of their bodies, see also Katherine Royer, 'Dead Men Talking: Truth, Texts and the Scaffold in Early Modern England', in Simon Devereaux and Paul Griffiths, *Penal Practice and Culture, 1500–1900: Punishing the English* (Basingstoke, 2004), 63–84.
83 TAMO, Book 8, 1040 ('This sorte of folkes they cal heretickes, these they burne, these they rage agaynst, put to open shame and make them beare Fagots'); Book 7, 947–9. For popular images of Luther, one of the most popular being Luther with a dove, attesting to divine inspiration, see Robert Scribner, 'Incombustible Luther: The Image of the Reformer in Early Modern Germany', *Past and Present* 110 (1986), 47.
84 TAMO, Book 11, 1544; Book 1, 59; Book 7, 888.
85 Ibid., Book 4, 214; Book 8, 1066.
86 Ibid., Book 8, 1220; book 10, 1445 ('He that will follow me, let him forsake hymselfe, and take vp his crosse and follow me. What crosse? the crosse of infamy and shame, of misery and pouerty, of affliction and persecution for his names sake. Let the oft falling of those heauenly showers, pearce thy stony hart … that thou mayest once againe forsake thy selfe and embrace Christ'.)

87 Ibid., Book 5, 564; Book 11, 1515; Book 11, 1663.
88 John Brinsley, *The true watch, and rule of life Or, a direction for the examination of our spirituall estate, and for the guiding of our whole course of life* (1632), STC2 3784, 22; Dent, *A sermon of repentance*, 10.
89 Walsham, *Providence in Early Modern England*, 124, 150–56; Alec Ryrie, *Being Protestant in Reformation Britain* (Oxford, 2013), esp. 59–62; Willis, *Reformation of the Decalogue*, 177–215. For the constructive and redeeming dimenstion of shame, see also Han Zhao, '"Holy shame shall warm my heart": Shame and Protestant Emotions in Early Modern Britain', *Cultural and Social History*, 18 (2021), 1–21, esp. 7–10. See also Chap. 2 below.
90 Erasmus, *The ciuilitie of childehode*, Biiii ('For the Aungels are always present unto whom shamefast company and keping of chastity is very [a]greable'); John Locke, *Some Thoughts Concerning Education* (1693), The Harvard Classics, www.bartleby.com, Vol. 37, Part 1, Section 86. For a discussion of shame in John Locke, see Chap. 7.
91 Fernie, *Shame in Shakespeare*, 53–61; Gundersheimer, 'Concepts of Shame'; Martin, 'Inventing Sincerity, Refashioning Prudence'.

# 2 Puritans and the experience of shame

In its adherence to an encompassing notion of the wholeness of sin, Protestantism perceived shame as the defining, most profound experience of the initial encounter of human beings with God. Based on an Augustinian understanding of the consequences of Adam's fall and the sin conveyed to humans by birth, Protestants reconfigured the traditional notion of sin, positing the total depravity of humans and their absolute helplessness in the face of an omnipotent God. The deeper the depravity, the greater the shame that drove man to 'runne from God like Adam', bringing in its wake the painfulness of 'sadness ... terrible feare ... despaire'. The shame entailed in recognizing one's depravity was overwhelmingly punitive; 'a hell in our consciences, the very entrance into the lake, that wee shall be as the raging Sea, casting out our own shame; the worme of conscience beginning to gnaw without hope of releefe or any ease'.[1]

As we saw in the previous chapter, alongside this type of total punitive shame, Protestantism also cultivated a distinctive version of more ameliorative, redemptive shame. In their sermons and devotional writings, Protestant authors moved from the presentation of shame in sin as a set of actions to be castigated and deplored, to a shame in sin as a situation from which one could be elevated; that is, one in which, following diligent self-scrutiny, repentance, and strict adherence to the Commandments and the creed, fierce hopes for God's justifying grace could emerge. The sin and shame were not wholly washed away or eradicated, yet as the believer moved in their self-scrutiny, prayer, and obedience to a regime of godly rule, a more soothing form of shame emerged, allowing the believer a measure of liberation from the agony and suffering of the initial shame. An early punitive shame that was an indispensable signal of awakening was followed by a shame that indicated prospects for redemption, a step forward in a process that potentially led to righteousness in the eyes of God, and to sanctification.[2]

How was this dual notion of shame experienced by those who listened to the message or followed it in devotional writings and guides? Some insight can be gleaned from the spiritual diaries and autobiographies that emerged as a distinctive genre of writing from the late sixteenth century onwards.[3] Written by a select group among the literate strata of society, diarists and autobiographers were a mixed group of men and women, clergy and laity, some even of more humble origins. In their religious stance, they embraced a wide range of mainstream and non-conforming beliefs, reflecting on an evolving theological message, which was not always consistent nor consensual; their writings echoed the debates, disagreements, and divisions that marked the Post-Reformation era and came to a peak during the mid-century Civil War and Revolution.[4] Prominent among these writers were the puritans, or the 'godly'. While not subscribing to a unified single doctrine or strand of thought, and including moderates, nonconformists, and radicals, the godly were distinguished by a synthesis of beliefs and a distinctive style of piety, in which an appeal to the inner world of the believer was central.[5]

In the chapter that follows we examine the experience of shame as it was conveyed in several godly diaries and autobiographies written over the course of the seventeenth century. We explore the manner in which these authors confronted and made sense of the Protestant message on shame; how they accommodated harsh punitive shame, experienced a more redeeming sense of shame, and managed the ambiguity inherent in the notion that the believer could be elevated and justified by God, while still remaining a shamed sinner. Paying close attention to the writers' style and rhetoric, we probe the effect which the act of writing itself had on distinctive individual experiences of shame. Two key points are made. First, major experiences ranged between an all-consuming, self-inflicted punitive shame, through a more mitigated, ameliorative, and redemptive experience. Repeated oscillations between an agonizing punitive shame and a redemptive mode were particularly marked. Secondly, this set of experiences arising from the theology of sin and shame was greatly enhanced through individual rhetoric and style, with authors variously intensifying, mitigating or surpassing their experience. By the mid- and late seventeenth century, distinctive modes of benign and moderate shame became more pronounced, as some non-conforming puritans and radicals focused more intently on a redeeming God, or on an inward experience of Christ.[6]

## All-consuming punitive shame

A prominent feature of godly diaries and autobiographies was the description of an intense and utterly degrading experience of shame. In examining themselves for their sins, authors used their writing to identify and record the wholeness of their sins, both current and past, fleshing out and heightening the punitive shame attendant on these. Inspired by sermons and spiritual guides on self-examination, authors were prone to produce daily, weekly, or annual lists in which they enumerated and multiplied the number of their offences, thereby accentuating their shame.[7] Samuel Ward, the late Elizabethan diarist, compiled such a list from 1595 to 1599 when he was a student at Cambridge. Prompted by a revered godly don in a lecture on how to lead a godly life and the necessity of the 'affliction in mind for sin', Ward produced a record of his sins, listing on some days dozen and more of his misdeeds.[8] Nehemiah Wallington's voluminous notebooks in the two decades following 1618 abounded with references to his sins; in 1629 he began to make a special list, reasoning that 'in spreading them [the sins] before the Lord I mite break my proud heart and so gete an humbel spirit'. In the ensuing two years, Wallington, a London turner, compiled no less than seventy-seven articles, covering all manner of actual and potential breaches of his spiritual duties and other negligence. For each and every one of these, he vowed to contribute to the poor box 'to punish myself for my corruptions'. Reflecting on the list later, he vastly augmented the scale of these corruptions: 'Not to know the number of them: for they were more in number then the sand on the seashore or the haires of mine heade'.[9] In other instances he used similar imagery that enlarged his shame by infinitely exaggerating the scope of his sins:

> In May 1623 I was troubled againe for I thought I had binne a reprobate ... and when I wente ... alone by the riverside and looking upon the grasse my conscince tolde me my sinnes ware more in number then the speares of grasse upon the earth.[10]

By listing their sins, diarists not only identified general tendencies and transgressions, but also produced detailed and personalized accounts – with dates, venues, names of close persons – which rendered the sense of shame and guilt intimate and more piercing still. Samuel Ward listed the sins he committed on a single day, 14 June 1595, 'being Sunday', from morning until dusk; his failures included not only hearing sermons without 'that sense which I should have had', but also more specifically 'not talking of good things at dinner', 'sleeping immediately after dinner', 'returning home and omitting the repetition of sermons by reason that my countryman Eubank was with me', failing 'to give the poor women somewhat at 7 o'clock', as well as 'my dulness in stirring of my brother to Christian meditations'. Wallington's diary, too, is replete with these types of references to specific acts, not only recounting his general inclinations for lust, anger, pride, infidelity, or idleness, as he recorded in the list cited above, but also offering longer accounts of far more specific wrongdoing. In January 1622 he recalled his habit of stealing in his younger years ('about sixteen yeere before'), and gave a detailed account of all the times and occasions on which he took money from his father's shop, the exact sums, how he had spent the money, the occasions in which he returned it to the box after feeling a momentary 'sick conscince', which soon dissipated. Reflecting now on his misdeeds, his 'conscience' began to 'accuse' and torment him, and so he decided to confess: 'at last ... I went into my chamber and poored out my soule to the Lord'. He then took the courage to express his shame and guilt, confessing his sin to his father, who consoled and forgave him.[11]

A principal source for enhancing shame and guilt was the Bible, with authors using biblical models, quotations, and imagery to elucidate and validate the gravity of their sins. First and foremost were the Ten Commandments, viewed by devotional guides as a primary tool of self-examination for sin, the Decalogue ensuring full coverage and scrutiny of offences, causing sin 'to surg and swell'.[12] Wallington's occasional lists of sins implicitly referred to the Ten Commandments, with his register of his offences in the years 1629–31 specifically intended to set down, as he explained, 'all things that are disagreable to the holy law of God'. Other writers also used the Decalogue, relying on its rhetoric to examine and augment their sense of sinful conduct.[13] They also made use of the Bible in numerous other ways, searching and applying it when referring to their sins. Wallington quoted the Bible profusely, using biblical stories, figures, imagery, and rhetoric to comment on and expand his sense of guilt and fear. So, for example, when noting how 'commonly after committing of sinne, conscience will not only cry out but terrify', he likened the shame to the guilt-ridden Cain following the killing of his brother: 'As it was with Cane after he had killed his brother Abel cryed out that everyone that meet him would Kill him (Genesis 4:13–14)'.[14] Wallington was exceptional in the sheer bulk of his quotations, but most other puritan authors, well versed in reading and searching the Bible for models for practical application, habitually used it to elaborate and stimulate their sense of shame and sin. Gervase Disney commented on how 'those scriptures stared me in the face' when quoting the Paulinian epistles regarding sin. Isaac Archer also referred to biblical stories and imagery, whether to warn and reproach himself for his misdeeds, describe and highlight his struggle to mend his ways or rid himself of 'evil thoughts' and corruptions.[15]

Such enhanced and amplified sense of sin and shame did not constitute a single momentary writing event, but was a lasting experience that could come to define a writer's life and their sense of self. Samuel Ward kept his record of the sins of his undergraduate days in a separate volume, to which he subsequently returned, adding the occasional note and reflecting on it. Mid-seventeenth-century guides to diary-writing explicitly recommended re-reading one's self-examination of sin so as to enhance a sense of shame and degradation; 'Oh! how will the serious survey of such a Journall abase the soul before the Lord!', as John Beadle put it.[16] Diarists read over their notebooks, cross-referenced their sins, and reviewed their notes time after time, commenting and amending earlier entries and nourishing a memory of their sin and shame throughout.[17] For Wallington, shame became an organizing principle of his entire oeuvres and spiritual life. In a notebook dated 1654, 'The Booke of all my writing books', he surveyed what by then had become a vast corpus of 46 notebooks, expressing in the preface 'to the Christian Reader' an especially expansive notion of shame that he feared would haunt him until after his death. Referring to the prophecy of Zechariah on the Judgement Day ('On that day Holy to the Lord will be inscribed on the bells of the horses') he wrote:

> And as it is in Zechariah 14:20[:] It shall be written upon the bridles of the horses holinesse unto the Lord, so may I with shame write upon the covers of my books unholines to the Lord. Upon some I may write vainity of childhood and youth, upon some infidility and desperation,

upon some breach of promisses and covenants, upon some selfe and Hipocricy and upon others discontent and unthankfulnes and upon others prid and vaine glory[.] ... For although the matter be good that I have written in them, yet if my life and conversation be not answerabl O then what an heavy account have I to give at the grat and dreadfull day of Judgement when All Books shall be opened and these my own handwriting shall be broght against mee.[18]

A deep sense of shame in sin was evident in autobiographical writing as well, whereby a life-cycle narrative offered a distinctive means of dramatizing and enlarging the experience of shame. Moving from their early childhood years through their youth and adult life, autobiographies conveyed a sense of growing sin and shame that climaxed at some point in the writers' youth and transition to adulthood. Richard Norwood, the mathematician and surveyor, described his early childhood, in Hertfordshire in the 1590s, as full of self-conceit, vanity, pride and an 'evil heart against piety'.[19] As he grew up and became an apprentice to a London fisherman, these childish sins expanded, now embracing sins typically associated with youth; disobedience to parental advice (in abandoning his apprenticeship), increasing lust and 'the corruption of my heart', which 'showed itself abundantly'. He also wrote of his growing affection for the 'Popish' religion, with his trip to Rome in search of the Truth becoming an epitome of an ever-deeper sin; 'My heart after this grew more hardened ... Now Satan was leading away in triumph'; for while 'Before I knew I did evil: now I had gotten ... false pretnses'.[20] Norwood then returned to England, pursued his studies of mathematics and became a teacher. Yet his sinful ways persisted with an ever-greater intensity; 'I became more his (Satan's) vassal than ever before', 'As I grew in years so my wretched heart grew more disaffected and alienated from [the fear of God]', 'as ... I grew more negligent and remiss, so did Satan the more prevail to carry me captive into several wicked practices'. By his mid-twenties, this route of mounting corruption reached its apogee:

> I was now near twenty-five years of age, marvelously captivated unto sin and Satan in all the faculties of my soul and body ... taken by lust of the flesh, with pride and self-conceitedness and with vanity and lying imaginations, that there was scarce room at any time for any good thought or consideration.[21]

This type of life-cycle narrative of escalating sins and an ever-deeper shame governed autobiographies written in the mid- and late seventeenth century as well. The presbyterian Gervase Disney described his childhood years, in the 1640s, with only a few references to his sinful habits; he then devoted a whole chapter to his youthful offences during his service as an apprentice to a London bookseller. Upon leaving his apprenticeship, as he narrated it, the shame that accompanied these offences only increased, for by now God's 'Work of Grace' began to affect him, and he became aware of the full burden of his sin:

'I could never enough bewail the Sins of my Youth'. He now not only deeply regretted his youthful misdeeds ('I would have given ten thousand worlds, I had never committed them'), but with every new offence he committed, shame burgeoned: 'Conscience now flew in my face, and was more than a thousand Witnesses against me'.[22] For George Trosse, a presbyterian minister, the time when he left his mother's home to become an apprentice, in the mid-1640s, was also the decisive point in a prolonged and agonizing descent into sin and shame; 'Hence I may date the Beginning and Occasion of my after-Sins and Calamities', as he described the departure. The narrative of his life from that point onward – his travels as an apprentice overseas, return to London and settlement in his native town of Exeter – was suffused with misdeeds, a thorough account of his shameful manner of speech, gestures, 'actions without', and 'impure fancies within'. Reflecting on how 'All these years I liv'd in so constant a Breach of all God's Commands', Trosse's narrative then shifted to an overview of his lifetime failure to obey the Ten Commandments, listing them one by one, meticulously documenting the transgressions that came to epitomize an all-consuming sense of shame.[23]

Some autobiographers accentuated their shame by singling out their distinctive inclinations to wrongdoing. They cited the good education they had obtained or the exemplary godly teachers whom they defied; they compared themselves negatively to others or mentioned the perspective of others who singled out their sinful habits when young. In his memoir of his early life, Isaac Archer maintained that 'though I had good and godly education ... and examples of my master and mistress, and some pious youths in that family who would pray', yet 'my heart was corrupt'.[24] Reflecting back on his habits, he also claimed that 'by observing school-boyes since, I thinke we were worse then any', than exclaiming, 'And Oh, what fruit have I of thees sinns whereof now I [am] ashamed!'. A particularly expansive idiom of shame was conveyed in John Bunyan's *Grace Abounding to the Chief of Sinners* (1666), where from the outset the author announced, 'I had but few equals ... both for cursing, swearing, lying and blaspheming the holy name of God'.[25] In one episode he recounted, he was standing at a neighbour's shop window 'and there cursing and swearing, and playing the Mad-man after my wonted manner'. The neighbour, who was herself 'also a very loose and ungodly Wretch', still told him

> that I was the ungodliest Fellow for swearing that ever she heard in all her life; and that I was thus doing, was able to spoil all the Youth in a whole Town, if they came but in my company.

Bunyan's sense of shame was now overwhelming:

> At this reproof I was silenced, and put to secret shame, and that too, as I thought, before the God of Heaven: wherefore while I there stood, and hanging down my head, I wished with all my heart that I might be a little childe again.[26]

Bunyan's autobiography was filled with such vignettes, written in a prosaic style that conveyed familiarity and ordinary life – 'One day I was sitting...', 'One day as I was meeting people ...', 'as I was going home...' – a style that rendered his experience of shame intimate and all the more palpable. This is how, for example, he narrated the effect of a sermon on Sabbath breaking on one occasion:

> Wherefore I fell in my conscience under his [the parson's] Sermon, thinking and believing that he made that Sermon on purpose to shew me my evil-doing; and at that time I felt what guilt was, though never before, that I can remember ... and so went home when the Sermon ended with a great burden on my spirit.[27]

Above all, there was the sheer depth of the emotional state that the shame of recognizing sin wrought, with writers using a host of idioms, images, and metaphors to convey their afflicted state. Wallington's notebooks were brimming with references to such emotions, reflecting on his sins and noting how these 'grive my heart and trouble my minde', causing 'much sorro[w] and humilliation' or wounding his 'soul'. He invariably referred to sadness, fear, a tormented conscience, 'heavy' or 'odious' heart, the sin being 'as lead in my bellie', or causing a profound sense of filth. He also recorded restless days and sleepless nights, when he was 'groning and cryings out many times, I am wearie, I am wearie of my life'.[28] He used images of beasts – a bear 'enraged', a 'mad dog' – to describe a state of 'conscience [being] awakened', which 'teares a man in pices, it falles upon him like some mighty tower, and crushes him to powder'. Admitting at times that the torments could not be expressed in words ('I cannot express the bitternesse and troubles of my tormented continence'), he ultimately likened it all to 'hell upon the Earth'.[29] Other writers referred to the terror and threat of hell, an experience of being 'at the brink of the pit, looking for nothing, but to be swallowed up'. Sleeplessness caused by 'apprehension of Devils and wicked spirits', alongside the fear of hell and despair over an inability to avoid sin, featured prominently in John Bunyan *Grace Abounding*: 'These things ... did so distress my Soul ... that ... I was often much cast down and afflicted in my mind therewith ... I was so overcome with despair of life and heaven'.[30]

In some cases, profound punitive shame became entangled with mental illness. Some of the authors referred to above may have suffered a mild depression or mental breakdown. In his youth, Wallington went through a period of mental disturbance and several suicide attempts; John Bunyan may also have experienced occasional bouts of depression. George Trosse experienced a more dramatic breakdown that involved hallucinations, visions, and bursts of violent behaviour. Trosse was also treated more drastically, confined at a specialist's madhouse near Glastonbury, to which he returned three times before eventually being cured.[31] Throughout the period, medical authorities were indeed likely to identify such mental afflictions as symptoms of 'melancholy', that is, a mental disease that ought to be distinguished from more ordinary suffering caused by an awakened conscience and the emotional weight of a sense of sin. But the distinction was not always clear-cut, and medical authors also posited some connection, or common grounds, between melancholy and religious anguish, referring increasingly to 'religious melancholy' when describing these afflictions. Well into the late seventeenth century and beyond, 'religious melancholy' was offered as an explanation for the kind of behaviour described in some puritan writings about the self.[32]

For writers themselves, moreover, such experience was altogether perceived in religious terms, an utmost punitive shame inflicted on them by God for their sins. In the late 1610s, Dionys Fitzherbert, a gentlewoman who had suffered a mental breakdown in her twenties, wrote a narrative of her life that was specifically intended to demonstrate – and convince those who thought otherwise – that what had happened to her was not madness but rather a spiritual affliction and a punishment for her sins.[33] Nehemiah Wallington also believed his episodes of mental disturbance were a punishment that worked through demonic forces, and that his suicide attempts were an affront to God for which he ought to be severely punished and shamed. George Trosse fiercely believed that his mental disorder was God's harsh punishment for his dreadful sinfulness and debauchery. As he summed it up in his narrative of progression from sin to madness and to regeneration, written several decades later when he was already a pastor: 'By my Sins and Sensualities I had brought my self into horrible Distractions and perfect Madness … I had fitted my self for, and merited, the most grievous and intolerable of all the Torments of Hell'.[34]

## Strategies of mitigation

In writing about their sin and shame, diarists and autobiographers found ways to mitigate and assuage their harsh experience. While conveying utmost sin and an all-consuming shame, they invariably insinuated, or directly referred to, the boundaries of their corruption and sin. Richard Norwood wrote about the positive influence of his upbringing, emphasizing his 'Christian parents', whose severity curbed his sinful inclinations, or the impact of a 'pious' schoolteacher and a 'good' minister, through whom God's mercies were bestowed and the seeds of 'religion and the fear of God' were implanted in him. While asserting that these influences were by no means the 'fruits of regeneration', in retrospect he still thought that they had kept him 'for many years thereafter from falling into … gross sins', remaining 'in some measure even to the time of my conversion … doubtless a special principle'. All this, moreover, left in him a 'sweet' memory 'many years after'.[35] Providential warnings and punishments that befell him in his childhood and youth could also produce restrained conduct and a more moderate sense of shame, for thereafter he 'usually observed it and feared it, which was a great means to restrain that corruption'.[36] On some occasions

Norwood pointed to the limits of his sins by noting his good conduct, referring to neighbours who had good hopes of him 'because I seemed, as they said, to be something of a sober and serious countenance and carriage'.[37] In other instances he directly specified his capacity to do good; his habits of praying or visiting the sick, the occasional slowing down of his sinful ways ('my heart did relent a little … so I might have the favor of God'), his reconciliation with his father, or his ability to resist the temptation to take a hazardous and potentially corrupting voyage to Persia.[38] Norwood also alleviated the burden of his responsibility to his shame by the occasional allusion to lack of proper models and insufficient instruction, or by attributing his misconduct to the bad company he encountered during his travels.[39]

Norwood was not altogether exceptional in his mitigation of the sense of his sin and shame by invoking providence and the working of God, or his more positive dispositions and habits. One of Nehemiah Wallington's notebooks (covering the years 1619–30) included a detailed account of the remedies he used in order to combat his sinful ways, and he occasionally noted a measure of gratification in prevailing over them: 'and so I have by the goodnesse of God … got some victorie over this sinne' (i.e., sleepiness at church).[40] Other authors did not directly refer to God's intervention, but nonetheless described a sense of moral compass and understanding they had already possessed in their childhood. Isaac Archer confessed to being 'very bad' during the time he spent at the Colchester school, but then also claimed 'yet sometimes my conscience did check mee and dogg mee, though young'. Richard Baxter, who began his autobiography (written intermittently since 1664) with a chapter on the 'sins of youth', recorded a list of eight major sins he had committed, but he was also careful to note that he was by no means an utter sinner: 'for I had … some love to the things and people which were good, and a restraint from other sins except those forementioned'. He also claimed that he seldom committed 'most of them', and that when he did, 'it was with great reluctancy'.[41] Even George Trosse, whose record of sin and shame was marked by particularly intense self-condemnation and extreme sense of punitive shame, still claimed that until he reached the age of 14 or 15, 'I was seemingly more Virtuous than others, not inclined to such Extravagancies and Rudenesses as other Lads of my age were, but was modest, civil and dutiful … to my Parents, and industrious in Learning'. During his time as an apprentice, he wrote, he had occasional bouts of shame and guilt over his numerous sins, while also being altogether restrained, 'by the good Providence of God', from 'all gross, compleat Acts of fornication'. John Bunyan, the self-proclaimed 'chief of sinners', described an early stage in his spiritual awakening, when he began to read the Bible with 'new eyes', still saying to himself, 'though I am convinced that I am an ignorant Sot … yet at a venture I will conclude I am not altogether faithless'.[42]

Puritan authors also managed to assuage their shame by distancing themselves from the unregenerate and identifying with the community of the godly. Diarists could rebuke themselves for their misdeeds while also reproaching others for their sins, assuming a certain moral authority over themselves as well as over others. In his college days in the 1590s, Samuel Ward strongly identified with the godly, dissociating himself from others – Catholics and all other sorts of 'wicked' people. In recording his sins, he at times assumed the role of the preacher, listening to his own confessions and responding in a didactic manner, exhorting and instructing himself to repent for his negligence, take care of his charges and 'Remember God's mercy toward thee'.[43] Nehemiah Wallington also identified as godly, his record of sinfulness itself becoming a sign that he belonged to those who brought glory to God: 'I am contented to shame myself [by recording my sins] to the world, so that I may bring glory to God'. He invariably distinguished himself from the ungodly, be they more moderate Calvinists, sectarians, or neighbours who were 'polluting' the Sabbath by 'buying and selling'. As he commented when referring to the latter, 'As St Peter saith ... if the Righteous scarcely be saved, where shall the ungodly and the sinner appear'.[44] He also intended his diary to provide a form of instruction. In a notebook entitled *Profitable and Comfortable Letters*, compiled in 1650, he copied dozens of letters, the aim of which was, as he opined, 'to instruct and advise ... to reprove and admonish'. The letters were addressed to his kin, neighbours, and others, including his parish minister, whom he admonished and shamed for his negligence and erroneous ways.[45]

In the case of diarists who were clergy, the perception of their distinctive position in inducing others to repent and feel shame was especially pronounced. Isaac archer described in his diary an episode in 1665, when, on his way back to his parish he met a man who was a drunkard 'more then any in the towne'. When Archer began to speak 'good things to him by degrees', the man told him that he had indeed frequented his sermons at the church, and that 'I [Archer] had lately said some things in my sermon which cut him to the heart', and that he consequently burst into tears and resolved 'to reforme his wicked courses'. Noting to himself that there were also 'other things he said to me which, in modesty, I shall not mention', Archer then looked 'up to God as the author of all', praying 'the Lord grant that I may be faithful in admonishing all such that goe astray'.[46]

Archer's diary also points to a more implicit form of mitigation that writers invoked – deliberately or inadvertently – through the overall construction of their narrative and the space they devoted in it to their record of sin and shame. Richard Norwood, who, as noted above, variably attenuated the sense of his childhood and youthful sins, devoted a great deal of his autobiography to his social and professional life; his education and family relations, his apprenticeship and travels abroad, his studies of navigation and work as a surveyor, mathematician and teacher in London and Bermuda. Structured by a sense of sin and his subsequent conversion in his mid-twenties, his narrative, packed with descriptions of events, social interactions and accomplishments, conveyed a more diffused sense of sin within which the burden of shame regarding his pre-conversion days was moderated. Archer, whose diary covers the years 1641–1700, with the early parts written as a memoir, devoted his record equally to his inner spiritual life, family relations (as a child and a married adult), and ministerial work. Large sections of the diary are dominated by Archer's troubled relations with his non-conformist father, whom he defied in his decision to conform to the church, and with whom his rapport remained tenuous and became even more strained as the father approached his death. All this by no means diminished his account of his sins and sense of shame, which persisted throughout his life. Yet as he weaved the record of these moments of shame amidst a broader account of his everyday dealings, preoccupations and emotional life, the sense of sin and shame was diluted. In adulthood and old age, as will also be pointed out below, the shame and guilt of his younger years were attenuated by greater solace and a far more assured sense of trust in God.

## Oscillating between punitive and redemptive shame

The single most distinctive feature of godly self-writing was the description of their conversion, with authors recording the spiritual regeneration they underwent through awakening, repentance, and the emergence of a renewed faith.[47] In some cases, the process was quite distinct or relatively focused on a certain time in their life. Richard Norwood described a conversion that occurred sometime in 1616–17, when he was in his mid-twenties and living in Bermuda. 'But not long after, the Lord in mercy was pleased to give me better hopes', manifesting mercy and compassion 'in me, the chief of all sinners'. Soon after a deep change transpired: 'I was as one that had found some inestimable treasure which none knew but myself'.[48] George Trosse could not identify the 'very time' when he began 'Seeking after God', but he still described a quite decisive event that came about during his mental illness and confinement. Somewhat reminiscent of Augustine's *Confessions*, his autobiography ends with the narrative of his conversion, the last several pages consisting of a summary comparing his life 'before' his conversion and thereafter:

> Thus, for the space of about 25 or 26 years, I liv'd in a State of Nature, in a Course of Sin and Folly ... But now, ever since, for the Space of about 37 or 38 Years ... I have kept on steadily in the ways of God.[49]

While sin was still a threat ('notwithstanding all Oppositions from without and more dangerous Discouragement from within'), the shift he perceived was marked, involving many different ways (he lists about a dozen) through which his older sinful self was transformed, becoming now 'bless'd, honourable and comfortable', or having a 'well-grounded Peace in my Conscience', and, thro' Grace, a comfortable Prospect of Eternal Life'. Above all, Trosse now became quite assured in his sanctification:

> But now, I hope, God hath given me Grace; has advanced me in the Excellent of the Earth; given me Desires to love and serve Him, and glorify his Name ... hath justify'd and adopted me, and at last will advance me to a state of Glory.[50]

Most seventeenth-century autobiographies, however, related a far less dichotomous and conclusive conversion. While often occurring during the period of youth and early adulthood, the conversion they recorded was more ambiguous, spreading over longer periods of time, sometimes involving a series of events and crises, or a prolonged and non-linear process.[51] This ambiguity was rooted in the tension inherent to the Protestant theology of sin and salvation, which claimed that human beings were incapable of escaping sin and could not abandon it irrevocably, while at the same time postulating that following repentance and the adoption of godly discipline, the believer would be steered towards justification and sanctification. As historian Jonathan Willis put it, from the outset there existed an inherent contradiction between a theology that insisted that the Ten Commandments were impossible to observe, while simultaneously viewing them as essential for regeneration. The believer was hence prompted to continually test their faith in God's grace, fully assured that it was difficult, if not impossible, to obtain, and sin remaining evident even in a potentially redeemed self. The difficulty in bridging these contradictory claims became acute among the second generation of Protestants, with many godly writers in subsequent decades going through the emotional processes of conversion recurrently, so as to test and strengthen their faith and their godly ways towards sanctification.[52]

The result of this was that godly writers tended to oscillate time and again between an overwhelming sense of punitive and exacting shame related to their sin, and an experience that was marked by a diminished and more hopeful and redeeming shame. The pace of these oscillations varied. Richard Rogers, the Essex clergyman, recommended in a treatise published in 1603 that the move from shame in sin to a more redeeming shame be practised on a daily basis; 'First, that everie day wee should be humbled for our sins', and secondly, 'That everie day we be raised up in assured hope of the forgiveness of them by the promises of God in Christ'. Rogers' own diary, which covered the years 1586/7–1590, indicated less consistent oscillations, with greater gaps of periodic and monthly accounts of shifting between the shame caused by 'those things which have fallen out' coupled with a 'sensible sorrow for mine unworthiness and wants', and the 'sweet peace that came' in the days after.[53] The fluctuations described in Nehemiah Wallington's diary show even greater volatility. Although he clearly identified himself at some point as belonging to the godly, the timing of his conversion is uncertain, and his diary is generally marked by an ebb and flow of punitive tortuous shame followed by more redeeming shame, sometimes within a short or even a momentary space of time, at other times over longer periods, well into late in his life. In May 1623, he recorded being 'troubled greatly' when reflecting that the number of his sins were like 'the speares of grasse upon the earth'. Almost at the same time, he also conceived that God 'of his wanted [wonted] mercies' put into his mind that 'his mercies were more in number then my sinnes'. Two decades later, in January 1643, he still described his vicissitudes, now lasting several days. During a night of torment, he was 'troubled with many vaine sinfull thoughts', but early in the morning 'the Lord ... eased my minde and gave me comfort in him'. Soon after, he again became 'something dead and dull ...[being] discontent in my mind for my God hid his face', which persisted 'for three days more'. Thereafter he alternated between being 'somewhat revived' but also 'grived', concluding that there was in all this 'a hid mercy that God doth give me'.[54]

Wallington's oscillations were intense not only in their rhythm but also in their emotional content. In a notebook he kept during the 1620s, he devoted a section to reflections on 'the off and on[e] of the gods' children', in which he noted the contrasting emotional states entailed in oscillating between shame in sin and being bestowed with God's mercy. On the one hand, there was 'distemper' or a perception of being cast down to the 'deepes of Hell', feelings of 'deadness and dejectedness', fear of death, being brought to a low ebb, or 'falling down'. On the other hand, was a far more elevated sense of relief and soothing shame, which sometimes involved a sense of being 'hoysed up to the very skies' or engulfed with 'an abundance of pure and heavenly meditations and consolations'. At times the godly would feel 'so comfortable, and courageous', that, like the biblical David walking in the valley of death, they feared 'none evill'. Elsewhere in his diary, Wallington described these moments of greater solace and relief, when shame diminished and could even be taken away.[55] These were moments when the 'goodness of God' began to show in him and he was strengthened in faith, when he overcame 'the greatest dangers', or otherwise was overwhelmed with 'peace of conscience', the 'sweet honey' of God's love, sheer joy.[56] There was above all a sense of intimacy with God, especially in times of meditation and prayers, when Wallington perceived he was 'going to my God', or 'walking and talking with God as a friend with a friend'. On January 1643 he recorded how the night before 'at three a cloke I did arise and made my complaint and moone unto my God and challenged him of his promise' (to relieve him from his 'heavy looden' and 'sinnefull thoughts'). 'And the Lord was intreated of mee and eased my minde and gave me comfort in him'.[57]

By the mid-seventeenth century, as conversion narratives appeared in an increased number and in print, the oscillation between shame in sin and a more redeemed sense of self remained pronounced.[58] In some diaries and autobiographies, these shifts marked the period of conversion in youth and early adulthood, but they subsequently subsided. Isaac Archer, who, as noted earlier conformed to the Restoration Church in 1660, dated the early signs of his spiritual change to the year 1655, when he 'began to have some serious thoughts God-wards' and 'God was pleased to worke a secret willingness in mee for the good of my soule'. He was then 15 years old and soon after began studying in Cambridge, where for several years he experienced acute swaying, being 'tossed to and fro', between praying 'heartily' and being 'dull and languid, frigid and senseless'; between being plagued by 'evil thoughts', a desire 'to be rid of that corrupt nature which [was] so strong in mee', and then becoming hopeful of 'a renewed mind'. In 1665, when he was a young minister in Chippenham (Cambs.), he still recorded similar shifts: 'I observed in my selfe that after I had bin melancholick, full of anguish and bitternes, then was I in the greatest calme, had most peace, and ravishing joy at my heart'.[59] Overall, though, in the following years these repeated oscillations appear to have become more restrained. Focusing more on his ministerial work and family life, the diary now documented moments of anguished shame and guilt, punctuated by spells of calm and relief, the latter prompted by a host of providences in delivering him and his family from sickness and near-death, which inspired in him renewed hopes for Grace and greater trust in God.[60] On 29 January 1672, he recorded 'a good searching sermon which affected mee, and shamed mee for my secret faults', but he then noted more assuredly, 'which I hope will not be sett in order before mee!' By the early 1690s, as his diary recordings became sparse, he still expressed shame, at this point over his handling of his son's affairs: 'I am ashamed that I should be so overseen in the disposal of my child, and cannot forgive myself'. He then promised himself to reform 'what is amisse', prayed for God, and was hopeful, more than ever before: 'I have had experience of God's deliverance formerly, in many instances; I will trust in him'.[61]

In other accounts written by non-conformists, the oscillations appear to have been even longer and more persistent, well after the process of conversion reached a certain climax. Disney Gervase related that he began to experience 'the work of Grace' towards the end of his apprenticeship, when 'the Lord first enabled me to set my face Heavenwards', and shortly after, 'when the Lord was pleased again to check and stop me in my Career of sin, to awaken my drousy Conscience'. His account of the following years points to a progressive development of growing hope and solace, reaching a certain peak when he moved to Nottingham, where he came into contact with the society of the godly, and where he 'did enjoy more of God in a few years than I had done perhaps all my life before'. The period of his persecution and short imprisonment also prompted in him a more elevated spirit and, once he was released, an assured sense of God's Grace: 'I have seen the Goodness of the Lord in the Land of the Living'.[62] Yet, his account subsequently points to ongoing oscillations, lasting many years and throughout his life until the late 1680s. Finding himself going through 'up's and down's', he moved through 'temptations and miscarriages', 'omissions' or 'shortcomings', followed by strict observance of godly discipline, which he also imposed on his family.[63] The diary he kept during these years, parts of which he copied to his memoir, shows daily notes of sins – or his success in avoiding them – followed by descriptions of providences that delivered him from varied misfortunes, which, like other diarists and autobiographers, he interpreted as signs of 'divine goodness', with the 'Lord's Goodness' being, at times, bestowed on him 'beyond expectation'. While the tone of his account was somewhat subdued, his experiences were ongoing; moving from sin and shame to strict observance of the Law, 'growing more secure' by it and hoping for mercies, followed again by relapses and negligence. The fear and threat of shame remained throughout: 'O! that my sins may not provoke the Lord to turn away his face!' he prayed following a day when he felt 'under some Dulness' and discouraged in his faith.[64]

Standing above many of these accounts was John Bunyan's *Grace Abounding*, which, in its sheer literary style and rhetoric, powerfully depicted the turbulence entailed in the oscillations between a degrading shame and an elevated spirit. The autobiography, written during Bunyan's imprisonment for preaching without a license, appeared in six editions during his lifetime (until 1688), remaining popular and a model for evangelical conversion narratives well into the following century.[65] Vividly recounting his spiritual life from childhood and early signs of conversion through his inner struggles and spiritual doubts, Bunyan's account was imbued with intense and repeated fluctuations, from the horror of shame and guilt to the blessing of God's grace. These shifts displayed a pattern of extended periods of sin and a deep sense of guilt that could last weeks, months, or even a year, followed by short spells – 'the space of two or three hours' or 'several days' – of hope and a more elevated sense of redemption.[66] At times, the pattern became more volatile and abrupt, with Bunyan moving between observing the Law 'some times' and breaking it 'now and then', feeling pain and guilt and then 'suddenly' being overtaken by greater hopes, being 'troubled and tossed' repeatedly; 'twenty time in an hour', 'exceeding conflicts for the space of seven or eight weeks', 'for many weeks sometimes comforted, and sometimes tormented'.[67] The oscillations could become so intense that an anguished sense of sin became wholly merged with hope and joy, affecting simultaneously a sense of being 'enlightened' and feeling 'though I had seen the Lord Jesus look down [upon me] from Heaven', which still 'sent me mourning home, [and] broke my heart', causing him to feel at once 'full of joy' and 'low as the dust', merging into a short spell of 'glory ... and refreshing comfort'. As Bunyan summed it up: 'my soul did hang as in a pair of Scales again, sometimes up, and sometimes down, now in peace and anon again in terrour'.[68]

These volatile swings entailed extreme emotional states, referred to repeatedly through the use of rich idiom and figures of speech. Going well beyond a simple enumeration of his sins, Bunyan recounted not only his repeated struggles with the Devil, affliction in mind and despair ('there were no such thing [God]; no love, nor peace, nor gracious disposition'), but also 'trembling in fear' and terror, 'sinking into a gulf', feeling like 'some Child that was fallen into a Millpit'.[69] There are descriptions of doubts and shameful heretical thoughts – 'these suggestions ... I may not, nor dare not utter, neither by word nor pen' – that inflicted 'such a seizure upon my spirit, and did so over-weigh my heart'. The sense of shame was physical and utterly morbid: 'This one consideration would always kill my heart', he writes when perceiving that his sin was 'point blank against my Saviour'.[70]

Such harrowing experiences served to highlight the contrasting state of being uplifted by God; the 'milk and honey' that replaced the 'wilderness' of shame and despair.[71] While the shift was never a conclusive event and was recurrently experienced, the distance between the two states could not have been farther apart: 'for whereas before I lay continually trembling at the mouth of Hell; now me thought I was got so far therefrom, that I could not, when I looked back, scarce discern it'.[72] These renewed states were variously described as a 'happy and blessed condition', 'great softness and tenderness of heart', 'the sinews of my delight', being 'inflamed with the sight, and joy, and communion of him'. There were also moments when he was filled with 'the love and affection that then did ... burn within to my Lord and Saviour'.[73] Especially powerful was Bunyan's narration of the physical and intimate presence of God, and of the word of God, in him. Like Nehemiah Wallington before him, he could describe himself going to 'seek the Lord' and refer to God as a 'friend', or imagine that 'When the Lord Jesus did speak these words, he then did think of me'. Following a period of sin, temptations, and guilt, he could sense the words 'Christ's love' beginning 'to kindle in my spirit, *Thou art my Love, Thou art my Love*, twenty times together ... they waxed stronger and warmer, and began to make me look up'. When quoting the Gospel, as he did throughout, Bunyan could hear 'heavenly' sentences and then feel that he was being embraced 'within the arms of Grace and Mercy'. Towards the end of his account, he sees the ultimate fruits of this Grace, when he envisions 'blessed things of heaven set within my view'.[74]

Throughout the turbulence of moving between extreme emotional states, shame and guilt loomed large. The sense of guilt was not only an essential condition for his regeneration, but remained integral to his oscillations and affected his sense of a redeemed self. 'Great sins do draw out great grace; and where guilt is most terrible and fierce, there the mercy of God in Christ, when shewed to the Soul, appears most high and mighty'.[75] Early on in his account, he described his attempts to prolong and deepen the sense of guilt: 'for I found that unless guilt of conscience was taken off the right way, that is, by the blood of Christ, a man grew rather worse'. At other points, he also wrote of the manner in which 'the blood of Christ did take it [the guilt] off again, and again, and again…'. In still other instances, he observed how 'sometimes I should lie under great guilt for sin, ... and then the Lord would ... sprinkle my Conscience with [Christ's] blood, that I ... would rest and abide the Peace and Love of God'.[76]

As shame and guilt were time and again submerged in this process of being uplifted towards God, so the prospect of the shame being washed away emerged: 'About Ten or eleven o'cloke one day, as I was walking under a Hedge, full of sorrow and guilt ... suddenly this sentence bolted in upon me, *The Blood of Christ remits all guilt*'. His sense of guilt subsequently diminished:

> At the same time also I had my sin and the Blood of Christ thus represented to me, [I saw] that my sin when compared to the Blood of Christ, was no more to it, than this little clot or stone before me, is to this vast and wide field that here I see: This gave me good encouragement for the space of two or three hours.[77]

66  *Puritans and the experience of shame*

Shame was hence vastly weakened and transformed. Yet it did not altogether dissipate, and the sense of relief was short-lived. Well after Bunyan began to preach his non-conformist convictions, displaying an unwavering acceptance of his persecution and being more assured of his election than ever before, he remained troubled by the spectre of guilt and shame. In his account of his ministerial calling ('Call to the Work of the Ministery'), which he attached to his autobiography, he professed certainty that 'God had counted me worthy to understand something of his Will in his holy and blessed word'. Despite this, he continued to refer to himself as the sinner; 'unworthy wretch that I am!' as he exclaimed at one point. And he also related how, when preaching to audiences about sin, he by no means felt absolved of his own sense of guilt: 'Now this part of my work [i.e., preaching about sin] I fulfilled with great sense, for the terrours of the Law, and guilt for my transgressions lay heavy on my Conscience. I preached what I felt'.[78]

## Benign shame, inward light

As spiritual autobiographies appeared in increased numbers from the mid-seventeenth century onwards, the experiences of shame they recorded became more diverse. The years of the Civil War and the Revolution witnessed a tremendous growth of the print industry, reflecting the debates, controversies, and fermenting of competing radical ideas that emerged during these years. Conversion narratives began to appear in collective volumes in the early 1650s, with the practice of writing spiritual autobiographies becoming widespread in the ensuing decades, embracing nonconformist moderate Presbyterians, members of independent congregations, and radical sectarians of varied persuasions.[79] As noted above, some of these nonconformist autobiographers – Gervase Disney, John Bunyan – related a spiritual experience and a conversion immersed in a profound sense of sin and shame, oscillating, with varying degrees of intensity, between deep shame and a more elevated sense of redemption. Yet, in other accounts divergent perceptions and experiences of sin and shame became pronounced.

A distinctly moderate account of shame in sin was conveyed in Richard Baxter's *Reliquiae Baxterianae*, the autobiography he began to write in 1664 (published posthumously in 1696). Having engaged in the Civil War and the Commonwealth as a nonconformist minister, Baxter came to promote moderate Presbyterianism, working by 1660 to reach a broad settlement, which he failed to achieve. He was ejected from the church and persecuted for several years, but thereafter remained active, writing and preaching his convictions. The autobiography, which offered a historical account of his engagement with national events from the 1630s onwards, reflected his nonconformist commitment to a reformed national church that accommodated religious diversity, yet fiercely rejected the radical sectarian challenge to it.[80] This proclaimed moderate stance was also reflected in his account of his spiritual progression, which he elaborated upon especially in sections devoted to 'sins of youth' and to 'self-analysis and life-review', and in which he conveyed a distinctive notion and experience of shame.

From the outset, Baxter's account invoked an adherence to the puritan notion of shame, beginning the narrative of his childhood with the list of conventionally conceived youthful sins and transgressions. In his subsequent reflections, he invariably referred to sin and shame, as in the case of the 'temptations to sinful compliances, worldliness or flesh-pleasing', considered by him to be worse than an 'invitation to the Stocks or Bedlam', and which he perceived as persisting throughout his mature life.[81] Age and experience garnered a more profound appreciation of sin and sense of shame, for while in his younger years he was worried 'about actual failings in thought, word or action', his older self was troubled by the even greater sin 'for inward defects ... weakness of belief ... want of greater love to God'. Well into his old age Baxter still acknowledged the sin of not being altogether 'loosened from this world', and his 'self-analysis' effectively ended with self-reproach over his growing distemper and impatience. The latter fault not only impaired his 'zeal in educating others', but also revealed him in his shame; 'I the more know that it is sinful in me', he comments, ending his self-analysis by imploring; 'O Lord ... be merciful to me a sinner, and forgive my known and unknown sins'.[82]

Yet Baxter's account and expressions of shame were more moderate and restrained than those expressed by some other nonconformists.[83] As noted above, his attitude towards his childhood sins was benign; claiming that he could not tell when 'sincere conversion' occurred, he reasoned that even as a child he seldom committed 'most of them' [i.e., his youthful sins]. Occasional references to his habitual eschewing of the sin of covetousness also emerged in his reflections.[84] The sins of youth, moreover, were counterbalanced by his virtues as a young minister; there was his vigour, affection for teaching and preaching, and his quick understanding and grasp of religious issues.[85] If anything, these qualities were also the source of his sin and shame, for they could turn into rashness and overconfidence, lack of understanding of 'the mind of adversaries', being inclined to 'run up in a multitude of controversies' revolving around 'formalities and niceties', and, above all, being drawn to 'the evil of schism'.[86] As he grew older, he became aware of the imperfections of human beings and the limits of their attempts to create the 'saints' Kingdom' upon earth, valuing above all the 'necessity of living upon the principles of religion which we are all agreed in unity', and being more conscious than ever of the harm of separatism: 'I am much more aware of the evil of schism ... and of gathering parties ... and making several sects in the church'.[87]

Baxter's narrative of his spiritual experience was hence less a matter of profound shame or fear of the wrath of God, nor did it convey repeated oscillations between punitive shame and an exalted hope for sanctification. Instead, it focused on a long process of transformation chiefly conceived in terms of growing sagacity and moderation that came with mature age. Rather than recording his inner struggles against inborn tendencies to corruption and the violation of the Ten Commandments, he referred repeatedly to the intellectual and psychological deficiencies of his younger years – his shallow thinking, unsubstantiated discourse or raw judgement.[88] These were ideological misperceptions and errors of judgement of which he was ashamed or came to regret, but which could also be amended and transformed. The experience and learning he acquired over the years taught him the value of nonconforming moderation, offering assurance and pride, if not a sense of gratification, that well surpassed deep shame or sense of guilt.

Such assurance was also reinforced by Baxter's intense sense of a redeeming shame. While acknowledging that some of his sins persisted, he proclaimed to have come to reflect less on 'poring either on my sins or wants, or examining my sincerity', focusing instead on the hope and prospects of elevation towards God. This response to his sin and shame involved neither an agonizing frustration nor a sense of contradiction: 'I would have one thought at home upon myself and sins, and many thoughts above upon the high and amiable and beatifying objects'. Reading and meditating, he now perceived 'that it is the object that altereth and elevateth the mind'; rather than looking inwardly to reveal shame in 'my own heart', he now looked forward to 'a higher work … upon Christ, and God, and heaven', where 'matter of delight and joy and love and peace itself' prevailed.[89]

Other spiritual accounts published in the wake of the revolutionary decades articulated a far more radical notion of shame in sin. Unlike Baxter or other nonconformists, these accounts were embedded in an array of radical religious ideas that came to challenge fundamentals of religion, positing a multifaceted, anti-formalist discourse in matters of sin and salvation. In its extreme variant, these ideas led to an utter rejection of outward 'forms' and practices, including outward worship, preaching, prayers, and the institution of the church itself. Instead of upholding the authority of scripture and the Law, adherents to such ideas held that true religion resided in an 'indwelling Christ', that is, an inward experience of Christ through which the believer achieved perfection and was – crucially for our discussion here – sinless.[90]

George Fox, the founder of 'The Society of Friends' (in 1648) whose early followers came from among these circles, wrote an account that reflected the effect such ideas had on his experience and understanding of sin and shame. Like many other accounts, Fox's autobiography (published in 1694), began with a narrative of his boyhood; yet unlike others, it endeavoured to show from the outset how 'the work of the Lord … carried on in me even from my childhood'. Born in 1624 in Leicestershire to a father 'who had a Seed of God' in him, and a mother who was 'an upright woman … of the stock of martyrs', Fox himself had, in his younger years, obtained 'a gravity and stayedness of mind and spirit not usual in children'. At the age of eleven he 'knew pureness and righteousness', acting faithfully 'to God, and outwardly, to man'. The account of his years as a shoemaker's apprentice is no less devoid of sins or sense of shame; 'I never wronged man or woman in all that time', for 'the Lord's power was with me and over me, to preserve me', with people around him having 'a love to me for my innocency and honesty'.[91]

When he reached the age of nineteen, Fox entered a period of emotional turbulence, encountering varied 'temptations', walking solitary and being troubled by 'something wrong' – he does not specify what – that he had done. While these temptations grew 'almost to despair', Satan's 'design' at enticing him to sin did not prevail.[92] Referring somewhat ambiguously to 'trouble and temptations', 'exercises and troubles', 'clouds' or the 'misery I was in', he portrayed himself as a sad, lonely, and estranged young man; a wandering spirit in search of Truth and 'heavenly wisdom'. It was during these years, moreover, that God first 'opened to me', revealing 'that He did not dwell in these temples which men had commanded and set up, but in people's hearts'. The revelation gave him a sense of relief – 'I Yet smiled in myself knowing what the Lord had opened in me' – but at this point his anxieties still persisted: 'yet great trouble and temptation came many times upon me'.[93]

This state of spiritual search and 'seeking' persisted, as Fox failed to find solace among people of diverse religious persuasions, nor in books and varied writings, including the Scriptures. Yet gradually, 'Christ ... opened the door of Light and Life unto me', and Fox now came to perceive that the believer was able to achieve perfection in this life, and could live without sin. As he propagated the message and encountered great opposition among those 'who could not endure to hear talk of perfection, and of a holy and sinless life', his own sense of despair became focused on grieving for the wicked minds of others and their blindness to the Truth.[94] By the years 1646–48, when he was able to turn more of these people 'from the darkness to the Light' so that 'the Lord's power broke forthe more and more wonderfully', Fox fully experienced the presence of Christ in himself, being overwhelmed with a sense of perfection and sinlessness:

> Now I was come up in spirit through the flaming sword, into the paradise of God ... I knew nothing but pureness, and innocency, and righteousness; being renewed into the image of God by Christ Jesus, to the state of Adam, which he was in before he fell.[95]

From this point on, Fox's narrative was wholly overtaken by an account of his travels in the 'Lord's service', spreading the 'word of wisdom' in the 'thorny wilderness', showing people their errors and how they might be reformed, persuading them of the power of the Living God.[96] As he continued to spread the message 'that all might come ... into the image of God',[97] being increasingly subject to antagonism and scorn, persecution and prolonged periods of imprisonment, his early experiences of 'temptations' and turbulence of mind utterly faded. Travelling ceaselessly throughout the country and beyond, speaking to 'Priests and professors, magistrates and people', warning them 'to repent their wickedness' and witness the Lord's power in 'opening' their minds,[98] Fox's sense of purity and perfection in coming into the image of God remained unreservedly firm. A radical rejection of shame in sin became an enduring feature of his life.

Fox's stance in denying sin and a sense of shame was to some extent unique, even among those who joined the Society of Friends. Their testimonies and spiritual journals, published increasingly from 1650 onwards, attest to a presumption that all believers were prone to sin and inevitably succumbed to 'temptations', with authors describing anxieties over youthful vanities, agonies or sadness in the process of regeneration, being lost from God and subject to moments of shame.[99] Yet there is no doubting the effect that the doctrine of perfectionism, and the antinomian notion that believers were inherently perfect and sinless, had on them. Many of these writers endorsed the notion of original innocence, denying that children were born into a state of perdition, arguing that 'the sin of our first parents is not imputed to us', but rather 'as their offspring, we are by nature prone to evil'. What truly mattered was the inward experience of Christ through which perfectionism was achieved; their spiritual accounts overall focused on the revelation and experience of the inward light.[100] By the early eighteenth century, some Quaker autobiographies followed more directly in the footsteps of Fox, producing narratives that showed few qualms over childhood sins, and did not invoke shame or guilt as they embraced the new faith and became convinced of the Truth. Travelling around the country to deliver their message, undergoing an ordeal of persecution and suffering as they repeatedly defied the authorities, they persisted in encouraging fellow Friends in their zeal and sense of righteousness and purity: 'that Love which Edifies the Body, and which thinks no Evil: but bears and endures all things'.[101]

## Conclusion

The godly diaries and autobiographies examined in this chapter point to several responses and modes of experience arising from the Protestant message regarding sin and shame.[102] First and foremost was an experience of shame that came with the recognition and awareness of sin. Harsh and overwhelming, the shame could consume the lives of writers, shaping an initial experience and persisting throughout the process of spiritual regeneration and beyond. It produced agony, a sense of degradation, and, in extreme cases, despair and mental affliction. Shame could sometimes come to define an author's perception of his entire life. Yet in facing this deep and all-consuming shame, authors variably (if at times inadvertently) found ways to soothe and mitigate their experience. They presented distinctive personal dispositions or circumstances through which they managed to avoid sin and thereby ease the burden of shame and guilt; they also cited parental guidance or exemplary teachers and ministers through whom the seeds of 'religion and the fear of God' were planted and the potential for ever greater sin was circumscribed. Providential signals, too, instilled fear, placing limits on their corruption or else raising hopes for forgiveness and a justifying grace. And as authors went through the process of taking upon themselves godly discipline, the perceived gulf that separated them from the unregenerate and the profane helped to soften and moderate an experience of the wholeness of shame.

A common, potent experience was related to the process of conversion and the ambiguity implied in a shift from shame in sin that was total and irrevocable, to a state from which one could be elevated towards justification, while remaining a sinner. In their diaries and memoirs, authors repeatedly recorded oscillations between these two modes; the deep agony and shame of recurring sins from which they could never fully escape, and more exalted hopes of being justified by God, when the shame might possibly be surpassed. Not all authors experienced such oscillations. In some cases, the conversion marked a more definite transition from the anguish and shame of their pre-conversion days, to an overall secure sense of election and justification, regardless of a lingering sense of sin and shame. Yet for most others, repeated oscillations marked their long period of conversion and beyond, with an experience of punitive shame punctuated by spells of an assured sense of a justifying grace persisting, in varying degrees of intensity, throughout their lives.

As the seventeenth century wore on and mainstream puritanism was challenged by non-conformists and radicals, the spectrum of responses to shame, especially more mitigated forms of shame, broadened. In Richard Baxter's autobiography we find a moderate sense of shame over the sins of his childhood and throughout his life. Lacking a strong sense of conversion, he conceived his spiritual progress in terms of growing wisdom and moderation, whereby he abandoned the habit of looking inwardly to reveal sin and shame, concentrating instead on looking outwardly towards God, where he found joy and peace. In the case of George Fox and other Quakers, shame in sin was altogether surpassed. While not denying the human tendency to wrongdoing and the power of Satan to distract and tempt, Fox found few blemishes in his childhood and youth, his sense of sinlessness being altogether confirmed when he found the indwelling light. Rooted in early forms of antinomian thinking that came to the fore during the 1640s, Fox's denial of original sin and his sense of sinlessness were reinforced by the persecution he experienced, which, as in the case of many of his followers, overwhelmed the narrative of his life.

Over and above the force of a theology that framed and inspired a set of responses and experiences, there was also the act of writing itself, through which authors gave distinctive individual meanings and shape to these experiences. All written narratives discussed here were structured by manuals for practical piety that encouraged self-scrutiny through the written record of their sin, offering detailed instructions on discipline and the stages of conversion. Authors also relied upon a host of external authorities or sources: scriptural models and quotations, sermons, and the writings of puritan divines. They took notes, copied, paraphrased, or reconstructed from memory. Yet by putting pen to paper and writing about their inner lives, they did not simply apply prescriptions and models for self-scrutiny, nor did they produce a straightforward record of events and moments in their experience of shame. Writers made choices regarding the available sources and authorities, selected biblical models, quotes and imagery, offered original and private meditations or reflections using distinctive individual rhetoric and style. Whether writing a diary or a memoir, they made decisions regarding the structure of their narrative, organizing their record of sin and shame as part of a broader narrative of their lives.

The result was many variations in the style, intensity, and tenor of the narration, as well as in the sheer detail and space authors devoted to exposing and exploring the varied modes of their shame. While some writers were prone to using the authority of others, copiously quoting sermons and other written works, others focused on a private and internalized style of piety, meditations, and devotion.[103] Some autobiographical narratives were besotted by sin and self-flagellation, focusing on self-examination, multiplying their sins and enhancing punitive shame or a tortuous process of regeneration. Many were brimming with fluctuations between a devastating shame and a more redeeming, even liberating, shame. These oscillations could vary in duration and their emotional depth. There were those, like Gervase Disney or Isaac Archer, whose experience of shame was subdued and more restrained, while others – Nehemiah Wallington, John Bunyan – conveyed extreme emotional shifts, highlighting an experience of exaltation that adjoined hopes for grace and sanctification; the 'milk and honey' that replaced the 'wilderness' of shame and despair, as Bunyan referred to it. Among the writers examined here were those who weaved their experience of shame into a narrative packed with information regarding their upbringing, relations with parents and others, and their training and professional life. Or else, as in the case of Richard Baxter, their progress was subsumed within a broader political and historical account. In both cases, the experience of sin and shame became duller and less acute.[104] In all these variations in emotional tenor, rhetorical skill, and narrative structure, these writers displayed distinctive individualized style, greatly expanding the set of shame experiences arising from the theology of sin. In the case of George Fox and others among his followers, the written narrative of their lives amplified a radical stance that undermined the very notion of the shame of original sin, focusing instead on the light they experienced from within.

## Notes

1. John Brinsley, *The true watch, and rule of life Or, a direction for the examination of our spirituall estate, and for the guiding of our whole course of life* (1632), STC2 3784, 22–3; Jonathan Willis, *The Reformation of the Decalogue: Religious Identity and the Ten Commandments in England, c. 1485–1625* (Cambridge, 2017), 135–76.
2. Brinsley, *The true watch*, esp. Chaps. 9–15; Willis, *Reformation of the Decalogue*, 177–92.
3. Owen C. Watkins, *The Puritan Experience: Studies in Spiritual Autobiography* (1972); Tom Webster, 'Writing to Redundancy: Approaches to Spiritual Journals and Early Modern Spirituality', *Historical Journal*, 39 (1996), 33–56; Alexandra Walsham, 'The Reformation of the Generations: Youth, Age and Religious Change in England, c. 1500–1700', *Transactions of the Royal Historical Society*, 21 (2011), 93–121; Alec Ryrie, *Being Protestant in Reformation Britain* (Oxford, 2013), 298–301.

*Puritans and the experience of shame* 73

4  Ibid., 298–306; Willis, *Reformation of the Decalogue*, 186–92, 212–14; Peter Lake and Isaac Stephens, *Scandal and Religious Identity in Early Stuart England: A Northamptonshire Maid's Tragedy* (Woodbridge, 2015), esp. Chaps. 4–6. For fundamental inconsistencies of the Protestant theology, in a single diary, see Margo Todd, 'Puritan Self-Fashioning: The Diary of Samuel Ward', *Journal of British Studies*, 31 (1992), 257–62. For tensions, ambiguities and the effect of different views of the salvific process on self-writing, see Webster, 'Writing to Redundancy', 42–3, 51–6.
5  For the historiography and the varied definitions of 'Puritanism', and for the puritan distinctive synthesis of beliefs and style of piety, see Willis, *Reformation of the Decalogue*, 220–4. For the godly being distinguished from conforming Calvinist co-religionists through the strict observance of the Ten Commandments, see Ibid, 264–5. And see also Watkins, *The Puritan Experience*.
6  For a recent account that emphasizes the 'spiritually-productive' aspects of Protestant shame, see Han Zhao, '"Holy shame shall warm my heart": Shame and Protestant Emotions in Early Modern Britain', *Cultural and Social History*, 18 (2021), 1–21. In the analysis offered here, the emphasis is on the dual conception of shame, and on both the punitive shame and the more positive, redemptive experience.
7  Willis, *Reformation of the Decalogue*, 255–65.
8  Todd, 'Puritan Self-Fashioning', 236, 241–4.
9  David Booy (ed.), *The Notebooks of Nehemiah Wallington, 1618–1654: A Selection* (Aldershot, 2007), 49–50; Willis, *Reformation of the Decalogue*, 257–60, and note 146, where it is suggested that the quoted image, which had biblical origins, was borrowed from William Perkins.
10 Booy (ed.), *The Notebooks of Nehemiah Wallington*, 38.
11 Todd, 'Puritan Self-Fashioning', 236; Booy (ed.), *The Notebooks of Nehemiah Wallington*, 38–9.
12 Willis, *Reformation of the Decalogue*, 233–45, quotation on 245.
13 Booy (ed.), *The Notebooks of Nehemiah Wallington*, 47; Willis *Reformation of the Decalogue*, 256–65.
14 Booy (ed.), *The Notebooks of Nehemiah Wallington*, 20, 291. The image is repeated on 33, 50–1. For Wallington's use of the Bible, and for an index of biblical books, figures and places used in the diaries, see also ibid., 20, 357–60.
15 Gervase Disney, *Some remarkable passages in the holy life and death of Gervase Disney, Esq.* (1692), Wing2 D1671A, 42; Matthew Storey (ed.), *Two East Anglian Diaries 1641–1729: Isaac Archer and William Coe* (Suffolk Record Society, Vol. XXXVI, Suffolk, 1994), 48, 98–9, 109–10. See also Todd, 'Puritan Self-Fashioning', 249–51. For habits of Bible reading, see Ryrie, *Being Protestant in Reformation Britain*, 270–81.
16 Todd, 'Puritan Self-Fashioning', 239–40; John Beadle, *The Journal or Diary of a Thankful Christian* (1656), quoted in Webster, 'Writing to Redundancy', 48.
17 Ibid., 47–8; Booy (ed.), *The Notebooks of Nehemiah Wallington*, 11; Ryrie, *Being Protestant in Reformation Britain*, 310–11.
18 Booy (ed.), *The Notebooks of Nehemiah Wallington*, 264.
19 Richard Norwood, *The Journal of Richard Norwood, Surveyor of Bermuda*, ed. W.F. Craven and W.B. Hayward (New York, 1945), 7, 13.
20 Ibid., 17, 22–24.
21 Ibid., 42, 44–5, 51, 69.
22 Disney, *Some remarkable passages*, 40–1.
23 George Trosse, *The Life of the Reverend Mr. George Trosse*, ed. A.W. Brink (Montreal and London, 1974), 49, 69–83.
24 Storey (ed.), *Two East Anglian Diaries*, 48.
25 John Bunyan, *Grace Abounding to the Chief of Sinners* (1666), Wing2 B5523,

2. For similar expressions that magnified his sense of sin, see, for example, 36, 44 ('O me thoughts, this sin was bigger than the sins of a Countrey, of a Kingdom or of the whole world, no one pardonable, nor all of them together, was able to equal mine'), 79.
26 Ibid., 8–9.
27 Ibid., 6. For Bunyan's literary realism and his invocation of 'banal normality', see Christopher Hill, 'Bunyan's Contemporary Reputation', in Anne Laurence, W.R. Owens and Stuart Sim (eds.), *John Bunyan and His England 1628–88* (London and Ronceverte, 1990), 14.
28 Booy (ed.), *The Notebooks of Nehemiah Wallington*, 39–40, 48–51, quotations on 48, 50.
29 Ibid., 30, 51.
30 Ryrie, *Being Protestant in Reformation Britain*, 36–9, quotation on 39; Bunyan, *Grace Abounding*, 3.
31 Booy (ed.), *The Notebooks of Nehemiah Wallington*, 2, 33–8; Trosse, *Life of the Reverend*, 83–11. See also Katharine Hodgkin, *Madness in Seventeenth-Century Autobiography* (Basingstoke, 2007), 17, 102–3, 114–15.
32 Ibid., 63–66, 75–81, 86–101; Ryrie, *Being Protestant in Reformation Britain*, 27–9.
33 Hodgkin, *Madness in Seventeenth-Century Autobiography*, 16; Katharine Hodgkin (ed.), *Women, Madness and Sin in Early Modern England: The Autobiographical Writings of Dionys Fitzherbert* (Farnahm, 2010).
34 Trosse, *Life of the Reverend*, 132–3.
35 Norwood, *The Journal of Richard Norwood*, 4, 8–11.
36 Ibid., 7, 22, 26, 27, 42, 46, 49, quotation on 7.
37 Ibid., 13.
38 Ibid., 10, 7, 27, 31–2, 68.
39 Ibid., 8, 12, 14, 68.
40 Booy (ed.), *The Notebooks of Nehemiah Wallington*, 41–7, quotation on 47.
41 Storey (ed.), *Two East Anglian Diaries*, 47; N.H. Keeble (ed.), *The Autobiography of Richard Baxter* (London and Melbourne, abridged edition, 1985), 5, 7.
42 Trosse, *Life of the Reverend*, 48, 54, 63; Bunyan, *Grace Abounding*, 10–13.
43 Todd, 'Puritan Self-Fashioning', 241, 252, 256–7, 259–60.
44 Booy (ed.), *The Notebooks of Nehemiah Wallington*, 21–2, 31, 87.
45 Booy (ed.), *The Notebooks of Nehemiah Wallington*, 10, 235. See also the letters of Gervase Disney, in his *Some remarkable passages in the Holy life*, 122–31.
46 Storey (ed.), *Two East Anglian Diaries*, 112. For similar references to encouragement from his preaching, see also 118, 121 ('I found my hearers increased daily, and had encouragement').
47 Ryrie, *Being Protestant in Reformation Britain*, 436.
48 Norwood, *The Journal of Richard Norwood*, 69, 83.
49 For the distinctive quality of Augustine's *Confessions*, which ends abruptly with his conversion, see Paula Fredricksen, 'The *Confessions* as Autobiography', in Mark Vessey (ed.), *A Companion to Augustine* (Oxford, 2012), 87–98.
50 Trosse, *Life of the Reverend*, 112, 113, 131–3.
51 Ryrie, *Being Protestant in Reformation Britain*, 440–1.
52 Willis, *Reformation of the Decalogue*, 213–4, 233–45. See also Todd, 'Puritan Self-Fashioning', 257–62; Webster, 'Writing to Redundancy', 42–3, 51–6.
53 Marshall Mason Knappen (ed.), *Two Elizabethan Diaries by Richard Rogers and Samuel Ward* (Chicago, 1933), 7, 54–5.
54 Booy (ed.), *The Notebooks of Nehemiah Wallington*, 25–6, 38, 180–1.
55 Ibid., 52, 30 ('… yea shame is the best fruit of sinne (Romans 6) … Neither is our shame increased by confessing our sinnes, but rather diminished and taken away').

56 Ibid., 52, 71–2, 74.
57 Ibid., 23–4, 76, 180.
58 D. Bruce Hindmarsh, *The Evangelical Conversion Narrative: Spiritual Autobiography in Early Modern England* (Oxford, 2005), 33–50.
59 Storey (ed.), *Two East Anglian Diaries*, 50, 57, 62, 98–9, 105.
60 Ibid., 58–9, 54–5, 63, 104–5, 118, 121, 126.
61 Ibid., 142, 179–80.
62 Disney, *Some remarkable passages in the holy life*, 36–39, 52–6, 57, 92.
63 Ibid., 59, 74–7, 98–100.
64 Ibid., 103–4, 132, 133, 134.
65 Hindmarsh, *The Evangelical Conversion Narrative*, 50–2, 107, 227, 284, 309–10.
66 Bunyan, *Grace Abounding*, 8, 24, 25, 29–30, 39, 50.
67 Ibid., 6, 9, 39, 49, 50, 54, 55.
68 Ibid., 55.
69 Ibid., 7, 28, 52, 54.
70 Ibid., 25, 44.
71 Ibid., A3.
72 Ibid., 36.
73 Ibid., 6, 11, 36, 50.
74 Ibid., 49, 50, 19, 24–5, 74–5.
75 Ibid., 71.
76 Ibid., 23, 35–6.
77 Ibid., 39.
78 Ibid., 76, 78–9, 94. Quotations on 76, 79.
79 Hindmarsh, *The Evangelical Conversion Narrative*, 43–52; Kathleen Lynch, *Protestant Autobiography in the Seventeenth-Century Anglophone World* (Oxford, 2012), esp. 27–30; Peter Lake, 'Reading Clarke's Lives in Political and Polemical Context', in Kevin Sharpe and Steven N. Zwicker (eds.), *Writing Lives: Biography and Textuality, Identity and Representation in Early Modern England* (Oxford, 2008), 293–318.
80 N.H. Keeble, 'Baxter, Richard', *Oxford Dictionary of National Biography*, online edition, https://www.oxforddnb.com; Lake, 'Reading Clarke's Lives', esp. 304–5; Lynch, *Protestant Autobiography in the Seventeenth-Century*, 258–64.
81 Keeble (ed.), *The Autobiography of Richard Baxter*, 110.
82 Ibid., 112, 124, 132.
83 For the view of Baxter's autobiography as 'a refusal to write a spiritual experience à la *Grace Abounding*', see Lynch, *Protestant Autobiography*, 29.
84 Keeble (ed.), *The Autobiography of Richard Baxter*, 124 ('I was never much tempted to the sin of covetousness').
85 Ibid., 103–4.
86 Ibid., 105, 107, 108, 116.
87 Ibid., 115, 121–2, 106, 116.
88 Ibid., 103–4.
89 Ibid., 111–12.
90 For the recent most comprehensive treatment of religious radicalism in the early and mid-1640s, and its links to religious radicalism during the Commonwealth and later decades, see David Como, *Radical Parliamentarians and the English Civil War* (Oxford, 2018), 215–56, 384–408. See also Hindmarsh, *The Evangelical Conversion Narrative*, 43–45; Rosemary Moore, *The Light in their Consciences: Early Quakers in Britain 1646–1666* (University Park, Pennsylvania, 2000).
91 George Fox, *An Autobiography*, ed. Rufus M. Jones (Philadelphia, 1909), https://archive.org/details/georgefoxautobio00foxg, 66–7.

92  Ibid., 69.
93  Ibid., 76–7.
94  Ibid., 83, 85, 86–7.
95  Ibid., 97.
96  Ibid., 98, 102. For the history of the Quakers in these years, see Moore, *The Light in their Consciences*.
97  Ibid., 108.
98  Ibid., 102, 126–7.
99  Mary Cochran Grimes, 'Saving Grace Among Puritans and Quakers: A Study of 17th and 18th Century Conversion Experiences', *Quaker History*, 72 (1983), 3–26.
100 Hindmarsh, *The Evangelical Conversion Narrative*, 44–5; Grimes, 'Saving Grace', 9.
101 Oliver Sansom, *An Account of many remarkable passages of the life of Oliver Sansom, etc.* [Written by himself] (London, 1710), quotation on 318. For Quaker literature of persecution, which goes back to the late Elizabethan period, see Alexandra Walsham, *Charitable Hatred: Tolerance and Intolerance in England, 1500–1700* (Manchester, 2006), 173.
102 For additional responses among Protestants, see Ryrie, *Being Protestant in Reformation Britain*, 409–16.
103 Lake and Stephens, *Scandal and Religious Identity*, Part II, Chaps. 4–6.
104 For the variety of literary styles in spiritual autobiographies, and for Bunyan's text as a precursor to the novel, while Baxter's narrative becoming a model of historical writing, see Lynch, *Protestant Autobiography in the Seventeenth-Century*, esp. Chaps. 4–5.

# 3 Family, networks, and shame

Beyond the shame that was experienced as internal suffering and an awareness of sin before God, shame was inextricably linked to the relations between the self and others. As we saw in Chapter 1, prescriptive and literary constructions of shame invoked an experience that resonated with implications for social interactions and the relational self. Shame was invariably construed as the outcome of criticism and disapproval, a reaction to condemnation of behaviour that was deemed immoral, impolite, or undermining prevailing assumptions about social and gender roles. The shame could inflict rejection or humiliation, exclusion and dishonour, or – in its more moderate forms – it could imply social inclusion and reconciliation between a degraded self and those inflicting the shame. Nor was the shame always public or triggered by the gaze of large audiences. In books of manners, the shame that resulted from external claims and judgements could also be aligned to an internal sense of wrongdoing. On the stage, dramatic scenes of utmost degradation before mocking crowds were presented alongside scenes that evinced a shame inflicted in the more closed settings of family and the ties governed by intimate, face-to-face relations and exchange.

In the chapters that follow we explore this type of interpersonal shame in domestic settings and amidst broader networks, probing more closely the actual expressions and uses of shame as they came to be articulated and recorded in personal documents, especially in autobiographies and private correspondence. As we saw in a previous chapter, spiritual autobiographies point to emotions of shame arising from the recognition of sin, indicating internal struggles and an introspective self facing her or his God. Yet these personal accounts also offer glimpses of the shame that was experienced in domestic settings, revealing more elusive forms of shame that emerged in the early life of a child and pointing to a shame triggered less by the purview of the almighty and more by the judgements of family members, kin, and other close ties. Private letters, too, reveal shaming and an experience of shame in interpersonal exchange and relationships.[1] Modelled to some extent on letter-writing manuals, letters expressed an expansive array of shame sentiments and uses that were applied among members of the elite and increasingly among the middle classes as well.

DOI: 10.4324/9781003226871-4

These personal documents point to a host of issues; the circumstances and tensions that gave rise to shame, the manner in which it was applied, the role it played in monitoring and negotiating ties, and the effect shame had on individuals and their interactions amid different classes and genders. The investigation here pursues these issues by focusing on childhood experiences of shame that are revealed in autobiographies, and on the shame communicated through letters, both model letters and actual letters dispatched amid networks of kin, friends, patrons, and clients. As will become apparent throughout, shame was habitually and profusely applied in the regulation of an array of interactions, taking harsh and punitive forms that could pose a threat to, or damage, relationships, along with far more subtle and moderate uses and applications. Importantly, whereas the shame was induced by reference to values and assumptions regarding civility and honour, sin, morality or patriarchal rule, reinforcing and bolstering status and social disparities, shame's potency ultimately resided in the distinctive personalized form it took. Letter-writing became constitutive of a form of shame that evoked attachments and commitments, through which interpersonal relations were not only monitored but also reconciled, cemented and enhanced.

## Childhood memories of humiliation and shame

Early modern autobiographies offer rare yet telling memories of a shame experience that could beset young people as they grew up and matured. The record of these memories is fleeting and evasive, for writers were reticent about the shame they might have endured, their emotional experience overall remaining concealed and unacknowledged for long. Projecting an adult perspective on their early lives and offering a narrative filtered through their Protestant convictions, they tended in retrospect to efface or even justify what in childhood would likely have been experienced as a painful and foreboding experience of shame. 'My father was justly angry and deservedly corrected mee for [my mischiefs]', was how Isaac Archer tried to make sense of the harsh parental discipline to which he was subjected.[2] In other cases the writer expressed only a dim recollection of a sense of unease and insult caused by parental condescension towards the intellectual limitations and impressionable character of the young. 'But they made me little answer (so far as I remember) but seemed rather to smile at my childishness', was how Richard Norwood remembered his parents' reaction to what they deemed an erroneous reading of his learning material. His memory of the shame caused by his performance at school was more intricate and potentially hurtful. When one of his schoolmasters came to dine with his father, young Norwood overheard the master telling his father that it 'would be in vain to bestow much upon me in learning, for I would not be fit or capable of it'. In narrating the occasion, Norwood recalled that he was 'standing by … [thinking] the same', a comment he subsequently crossed out, suggesting unease and ambivalence towards his emotional state at the time. The harsh judgement aired in the presence of his father may have indeed caused him great shame, an experience Norwood subsequently found hard to admit, even to himself.[3]

Some memoirs offer more direct evidence of painful experiences of humiliation and shame that involved a sense of being peculiar or awkward, rejected or unjustly discriminated. Richard Norwood, born and raised to a gentleman farmer in the 1590s in Hertfordshire, provided an exceptionally detailed account of an incident that allegedly changed the course of his life, leaving an indelible sense of insult and shame, 'the remembrance whereof is even an abhorring unto me to this day'.[4] As he recalled, when he was about 12 years of age and his family moved away (to Northamptonshire), he was forced to depart from the school he had attended, where the schoolmaster, although 'severe and demanding', nonetheless 'did affect me very tenderly', commending him for his 'aptness and readiness in versifying above the rest of my schoolfellows', and consequently arranging with the school's patroness to continue and maintain him as a boarder. Yet to his anger and shame, the patroness then opted for a less qualified but more privileged classmate (whose father 'prevailed over her') of his. 'When that dismal day came that I must depart I had sundry thoughts, as to hide myself in some corner near the school'. Fearing he would be sent away with 'disgrace', he 'departed with a most sorrowful heart, sprinkling the way with tears, and not without cause in respect of those many evils which were to ensue. From thenceforth I went no more to school to any purpose'.

Other accounts of the early childhood years were no less forthcoming in their description of the humiliation and shame triggered by experiences of dejection or the sense of injustice being inflicted on the writers, not only through lack of connections that hampered their careers, but first and foremost through the entrapping of family relationships and interactions. Isaac Archer, born in Suffolk in 1641, suffered from a speech impediment that marked his childhood with a deep sense of shame, with his father, a stern puritan preacher, becoming emotionally distanced and estranged; 'and stammering when I did read [the Bible] did tire out his patience', as he put it later on. Among his schoolmates, his handicap brought ridicule, and young Archer found himself outcast, praying and reading alone. When he grew up and desired to pursue learning, his father 'was unwilling as thinking mee unfit for the ministry because of my stammering', sending him instead to become an apprentice. The overall sense of estrangement and shame in his handicap was unbearable: 'I would daily pray to God, and that earnestly and with teares, that he would give mee perfectness of speech'.[5]

More traumatic experiences of parental deprivation are evinced in accounts of parental death and remarriage, when autobiographers harboured resentment, anger and an indelible sense of shame the remainder of their lives. Simon Forman described his mother not only as lacking affection – 'his mother ... never loved him' – but inciting his brothers against him and discriminating him: 'what faulte soever was committed by any of the reste, he was allwaies beaten for yt'. When his father died and the mother, 'grudged at his beinge at hom', sent him to keep sheep and do other drudgery, his sense of insult and isolation grew deeper. A child with 'reasonable wit and discretion ... apte at anything', as he put it, he decided to leave home, 'seeynge the hatred of his mother and of the reste of his brethren and sisters towards him'. Arise Evans, too, remembered the discrimination he suffered by a father who, upon his death, left him out of his will, causing him to feel not only anger at the blatant neglect of parental obligation, but also humiliation and shame at being betrayed by a beloved father. 'And many wondered at it, and pitied me ... it was impossible, but wrong was done me contrary to my father's mind'.[6]

Some autobiographies indicate painful memories of the shame entailed in corporal punishment. While the references here are again scant, these writers reveal the routine beatings to which they were subjected, betraying the fear and shame that the experience had wreaked. Simon Forman's bitter account of his childhood referred to being beaten for 'what faulte soever', while Richard Norwood recalled how he 'craved' to escape the punishment, making it clear that the experience, which he viewed as a typical preoccupation of the child, was foremost on his mind in his daily prayers. 'And my prayers were usually for childish things, as often on the Lord's day at night or Monday morning I prayed to escape beating that week'. Blunt pronouncements regarding the scars corporal punishment could leave on a child were made by critics of the practice, as in the case of Samuel Hartlib, who in his educational treatise (1654) offered a scathing critique of the use of the rod in schools, referring to the 'servile fear which boys get in schools' and to the memory that 'sticks by many all their life long'. While the whip may have been more commonly used by schoolmasters than by parents, who were less likely to resort to the rod, it is clear that the experience, whether encountered at school or at home, would fill a child with fear, humiliation and shame.[7] John Locke, the most articulate and innovative among those arguing for the impracticality of corporal punishment and the emotional damage it caused, still endorsed the use of the rod in extreme cases of children deemed disobedient and rebellious, taking it for granted that the fear of the rod was entangled with a deep sense of shame. Considering shame as the more productive and positive effect of the punishment, he recommended 'that the shame of the whipping, and not the pain, should be the greatest part of the punishment'.[8]

Evasive, and to some extent exceptional, as these memories of shame are, they offer an insight into the sources of shame in the life of an early modern child, suggesting that the experience of shame was embedded in family life and could beset children as they grew up and matured. For while some of the circumstances and familial practice described by authors as exacting great humiliation and shame were rare, as for example in the case of disinheritance, others were hardly unique and remained integral to the social, demographic and ideological underpinnings of the early modern family.[9] Parental death and remarriage, which in the case of the autobiographers produced estrangement and shame, were by no means exceptional, and the use of corporal punishment, while not advocated by educational theorists as the most preferred method of governing the young, was nevertheless considered an acceptable method of punishment and was by no means wholly censured, nor denied some efficacy.[10]

More important still, the shame that was communicated in these autobiographical accounts was deeply related to the dynamic of familial relations, which was governed by the parental obligation to nurture, educate, and set their children in the world, along with the children's obligation to obey and follow parental guidance and rule. What these accounts reveal is that the authors' shame was aligned to a sense of fissures and ruptures in the parent–child exchange. That is, over and above the shame entailed in violating widely shared beliefs concerning obedience, morality or sin before God, the shame was conceived and experienced as a fear of the loss of parental trust and regard, the consequence of the child's perception of their failing to meet the expectations of their parent. Alternatively, the shame could be perceived as the outcome of failed parental obligations; rather than being grounded in negative self-evaluation – a child's sense of their own failing or wrongdoing – the shame was experienced as a wrong unjustly inflicted by the parent on the child, an intense sense of being rejected, undesired, abandoned and shamefully betrayed; 'had my father forgot me his darling', as Evans Arise put it in his account of the rupture with his family in his young years.[11]

## Model letters, polite shame

While autobiographical accounts offer rare glimpses of an experience of shame written from the point of view of a child, letters and correspondences reveal pervasive uses of shaming and shame by parents and among adults. This centrality of shame emotions in letter-writing can be gleaned from the specialized genre of epistolary manuals, which emerged as part of the civility inculcated to the young from the sixteenth century onwards. Based on classical and medieval models (*ars dictaminis*) as well as Humanist rhetoric and ideals, these manuals offered precepts and models for use in written communication in a host of private interactions. Among these models, letters designed to convey shaming and shame loomed large. So, for example, an early influential manual, Angel Day's *The English Secretorie* (1586), offered model letters of 'praise', 'reconciliation', 'petition' and 'consolation', along with letters aimed at the 'dispraise of the deeds of men', and an epistle 'vituperatorie', the two latter conveying rebuke and strong condemnation of the character – the 'wicked and shameless life' – of the addressee. As one author would later explain, letters inflicting shame were designed to address 'such as have committed some fault, to cause them to acknowledge it, or induce them to make amends for it'. With epistolary guides being gradually modified to increasingly receptive gentry and urban audiences, the categories under which shaming letters were classified became, over the course of the era, more elaborate. Letters aimed to 'make amends' and impart shame, or else to express these sentiments, emerged under a host of categories, from letters of 'discontentment' and 'reprehension', to 'chiding letters', 'letters of remonstrance', 'complaint', 'reproof', 'apology', or 'excuse' – all of which remained integral to an ever-evolving epistolary taxonomy well into the mid-eighteenth century and beyond.[12]

The shame conveyed in these model letters focused, for the most part, on the sin, immorality or incivility of the addressee. In Day's 'vituperatorie letter', a friend is denounced for leading a 'shameful life' from childhood and through adult life, his childhood marked by 'malice', 'boldness' 'mischief', his youth by 'pride', and old age by 'briberie, extortion, wrong, ... mischief and all kind of villany'. The content of exemplary letters found in a mid-seventeenth-century manual, *The Secretaries studie Containing new familiar epistles*, were full of moralism of a similar kind, as in a letter from a 'lady to a gentleman' denouncing his greed in a particularly harsh language of shame:

> Alas, what do you gain by unmeasurable hoording up of wealth ... but a base report, and a ridiculous pointing at, even as you ride along. Nay you shall be compared to a barking dog at Cattle, feeding on hay.

Under 'chiding letters' and 'excusing letters', the manual presented a letter to 'a son reprehended for his disordered life' alongside letters 'against swearing and common oaths', 'against covetousnesse', or an array of apologies and expressions of shame that would be communicated among close contacts – families, kin or friends. By the late seventeenth century, John Hill's *The young secretary's guide* (1687), which became one of the most popular manuals in the ensuing decades, incorporated letters of 'complaint for neglect', 'reproof from an uncle to a nephew', 'excuse from an apprentice', 'a letter from one scholar to another to reprove him for a slander' and a letter from an elder brother to a younger, 'exhorting him to good behaviour, and seemly carriage'.[13]

Alongside the shame of sin and incivility, model letters brought to the fore the shame entailed in forsaking the bonds and personal ties between 'friends'. One of the letters in *A president for yong pen-men* (1638) elicited the shame of breaking personal bonds as a distinctly forceful mode that went beyond the shame of immorality: 'to abuse any man, is but the badge of an ill minde, but to wrong a friend is a proofe of a vile nature'. Another letter articulated the indispensable role of keeping promises in relations between friends, singling out the special burden of the shame resulting from breaking these bonds: 'If promise be not a kinde of debt, I understand not the nature of a friend; and if performance be put off with delayes, there lacketh somewhat in the heart, that should be answerable to the tongue'. Sheppard's manual also included letters denouncing covetousness and wickedness not only as a 'disease', but as a threat to and breach of 'the bond of true friendship'. He also introduced 'civil letters' and 'excusing letters'; the former including varied letters on the subject of friendship (on 'true friendship', 'friendly precepts') or on the breach of these ties. The latter consisted of a set of apologies and expressions of shame over incivilities and breach of obligations, variously addressed to a 'best friend', 'honourable friend', 'displeased friend', and meticulously detailing the shame of specific acts – e.g., 'not lending money', 'being importunate in the behalf of a friend' 'not forbearing a friend', 'presuming to disgrace another' 'not being surety to a friend' or failing to entertain a friend.[14]

In all these model letters – whether invoking immorality, incivility or breach of bonds – the shame was carefully construed through the use of a language of civility that fitted a social universe strictly divided between superiors and inferiors. As de la Serre made explicit when discussing 'letters of remonstrance', while blunt and exaggerated shame required little 'invention' and was directed at inferiors ('when we have any power over the Person which we reprove'), a far more sophisticated shame would be imparted when an addressee was a superior, or an equal, to the writer. In the latter case, the shame was quintessentially polite; moderate, cautious, and indirect, it avoided incurring the displeasure of the addressee and offered expressions of apology, deference, and humiliation. Above all, polite shaming signalled sincerity of intent rather than flattery. Instead of inflicting punitive shame aimed at humiliation and exclusion, polite shame signalled deep and authentic affection, hence acting as a reminder of the bonds that tied the writer to their addressee, thereby solidifying, rather than disrupting, their ties:

> But these letters require more Art, when we will reprove our friend's vices without incurring his displeasure. First, we must commend his laudable qualities, … Or if we esteem that to be too rough a proceeding, and that we dare not speak so freely to him, we may say, that his best friend judge so of him, being very sorry to see him given over to such lewed courses… Then we may add … that the love we bear to him obligeth us to reveal unto him, the evil reports which run abroad of him; … We may also desire him to use the same freedom towards us in the like case, assuring him, that we shall be much bound to him for it, if we may find the sincerity of his love by his not flattering us.[15]

This idiom of polite shame in addressing friends and intimate ties did not remain in the realm of prescriptive rules or epistolary models, but rather permeated the actual practice of letter-writing. Use of the letter-writing manual was part of grammar school education, and the rhetorical skills acquired through it invariably infiltrated and came to dominate a developing culture of writing among the educated classes, attesting to an increased dissemination of the style, content and values – civility, morality, friendship – embodied in these model letters. No less important, the manuals themselves were reshaped by the practice of letter-writing, making use of actual letters alongside fictitious and more traditional models; that is, model letters were both descriptive and prescriptive. While typically fashioned by the rule-bound character of a polite and decorous language of epistolary writing, guides became increasingly varied in their classification, subjects, sentiments, and styles, indicating a flexible use of models rather than the sheer reiteration of learned habits.[16]

It is amidst this developing tradition of letter-writing that a polite language of shame acquired its distinctive form, moving from model letters to written communication, where it was creatively and vigorously applied in addressing family members and a host of other ties.

## Parental shaming and the family bond

Some of the most pronounced forms of shaming were conveyed in letters addressed by parents to their offspring. The use of shame within the framework of the upbringing of the young was advocated by contemporary educators as an effective means of discipline and correction, and was preferable to the rod; '... checking and rebuking them when they do offend and do amisse, and in words reproving them discreetly', as the puritan author of a popular devotional work recommended.[17] To judge from letters dispatched to sons and daughters when they were sent away from home – to school or university, to an apprenticeship or other forms of service – the habits of moralizing and censure among the upper and middle classes were ingrained, with varied forms of shaming becoming intrinsic to the parental approach to the young. For example, in the late sixteenth century Anne Lady Bacon sent her son Anthony letters to counsel him on matters relating to his health and diet, his handling of finances and his lifestyle. Her advice was littered with reproof, berating him for his varied neglects and insinuating or directly inflicting a sense of shame. In instances of letters dispatched in the wake of familial conflict or dispute, her language became explicitly censorious, combining an authoritative style with more personal chiding, derision and rebuke.[18]

Epistolary advice written by elite parents to their offspring was habitually imbued with notions and insinuations of shame and condemnation. Offering advice and instructions, parents conveyed their expectations, warning their children against actual or potential deviations from their commendations, implicitly or explicitly raising the spectre of shame should they act otherwise, prompting in them a sense of guilt; 'I am confident you will not sleight myne advice, which if you should, I know not whose you will follow', as Sir Richard Grosvenor cautioned in his letter of advice to his son.[19] In other instances, elite parents were more forthcoming and blunt in their admonition and infliction of shame. As research has shown, elite parental reactions to wayward sons, and especially disobedient girls who failed to take their advice regarding marriage, could be intense, with parents admonishing and shaming them not only for their dishonesty and disregard of parental advice, but also for severely damaging their family's honour and reputation. In some of these instances, degradation and shame became imminent as parents threatened to withdraw financial support or disinherit their sons.[20]

Parental shaming also pervaded family correspondence among social classes below the elite. An insight into the intricate and expansive manner in which it was applied among these groups can be gained from the correspondence of Joseph Symson, a Lancashire mercer who traded in cotton and linsey manufactures from the 1670s onwards. By the time his surviving letter book opens, Symson had already been widowed with four sons and two daughters between the ages of 10 and 26.[21] The letters he dispatched to them in the decade of 1710–19 show how, among his numerous transactions and commercial affairs, he took great care in placing his children in careers in trade, arranging the sons' apprenticeships and setting up their shops, while also helping his daughters in their travels and sojourns away from home. The letters – the bulk sent to his sons – were sprinkled with instructions and advice that often turned into shaming and reprimand, which erupted in instances when Symson's expectations were not met. This was particularly marked in the case of his eldest (surviving) son, Robert, who succeeded his deceased brother in his shop in Liverpool, and whose relations with Symson over the years grew tense and sour. The letters show the father repeatedly rebuking the grown-up Robert, already in his 20s, on issues as diverse as his lifestyle and public appearances, his wavering between careers (the university, the military and overseas trade), and above all his mishandling of his business, especially his decision, in 1715, to begin investing in ships bound overseas, for Ireland, Africa and the West Indies.

Symson's critique and beratement often took a 'polite' mode of shame; moderate and indirect, it insinuated misdeeds through the use of soft words of suggestion and advice rather than bold accusations and shame. 'I doubt you'll find keeping a horse constantly more chargeable than you are aware of', Symson advised Robert when he began to keep a horse, which his father deemed not only above his means but also indicating idle ways and an extravagance.[22] On other occasions, Symson announced his own proper conduct, discreetly hinting at his son's shameful failure to act in a similar manner: 'Last night's post brought me yours of the 11th, which you see I neglect not [to] answer by next post'.[23] Elsewhere Symson disguised his critique and beratement by conveying surprise, apparently allowing it to be considered an error rather than a deliberate neglect: '… you strangely neglect sending the box of tobacco I so long since ordered for Mr Chambre'.[24] General instruction and moralizing conveying the father's perception of his son's idleness recurred; 'an honest calling was very consistent with religion and devotion and that it filled up the vacant time which we must all have much better than vain impertinent amusements could do'; 'No son, humility is the way to gain the favour and blessing of God and the respect of good men'.[25]

For all the polite moderation and apparent restraint, Symson's reproach could also become bold and direct, inflicting more punitive shame in which neglect and character flaws were exposed and disgraced. On some occasions, Symson directly conveyed his disapproval of Robert's conduct: 'I have long expected your full answer to mine … to which I now refer you and desire you'll read it carefully over and consider it well for therein I told you my deliberate thoughts'. On others he was scolding and bluntly confrontational: 'Neither do you as I desired in my last tell me how you succeed in your business, in which you are to blame'. And when Robert did not pay full attention to a moral tract he had referred him to, Symson accused him of disobedience and dishonesty, signing with an idiom of restraint that only barely concealed his condemnation, if not rage: 'I will say no more at present on this subject'.[26] When Robert decided to abandon the flax trade and turn to overseas trade, Symson erupted with a particularly harsh shaming, mixing his criticism with a torrent of scorn and ridicule; 'Your thinking to discontinue it is to me a plain demonstration that you have no mind to follow anything', he wrote in a long letter, in which he proceeded to ridicule Robert's reasoning, deriding his arguments as false and disingenuous and scorning him for his indecision. Highlighting his faults by referring to his brothers and sisters as the 'dutiful children', the mix of warning, derision and shame was unmistakable:

> Your fickle temper … must reflect upon you if it does not at last prove your ruin … To be one for the university, then for orders, then for trade and now to be for I know not what is such inconsistency as I dare say you yourself if you will but judge impartially must condemn … I cannot imagine what you would now be unless this soldiering and fine clothes has given your head another turn to live as a gentleman, … your unsteadiness … shall not break in upon mine or injure that of your brothers and sisters who I bless God are all very comfortable and good dutiful children.[27]

Other letters continued to expose and deride Robert's idle ways by closely scrutinizing and censuring his expenses and extravagances.[28]

Using a rhetoric that ranged between moderate warnings to harsh and punitive shame, Symson's approach to his son Robert was, above all, deeply personal. Rebuking Robert for his failure to follow godly command or fatherly advice, Symson simultaneously invoked his own emotional state and the ties that bound them as father and son. So, for example, he repeatedly announced that the letters he expected from his son were not only intended to convey information but also to contribute to his own 'comfort and satisfaction'.[29] His advice, too, went well above formal parental duty. Never directly forcing his opinion, he constantly mentioned his commitment, feelings and care for his son's wellbeing and future. 'I tell you my opinion and leave it to your consideration', 'This I think my duty to tell you and desire you consider it well, I write not this in passion, but out of affection as your father I deal plainly with you'.[30] References to his plain talk and openness – 'I deal plainly with you', 'to be plain with you' – abound, while ties and mutual acquaintances were also mobilized to embolden the ties of trust and care that bound them all together. 'Many of your and my good friends often enquire after your welfare'; 'Your brothers' and sisters' true love and my prayers', as he repeatedly signed his letters.[31] When Robert's overseas venture encountered difficulties, Symson castigated him for his failure to listen to his advice, prompting an obligation to respond to fatherly advice by stressing his fatherly duty to offer it. And while their clash of opinion and disagreement mounted, his letters still voiced emotional and personal bonds. The letter which denounced and derided Robert's decision to abandon the flax trade opened by insinuating that the decision resulted from Symson's emotional state; 'I can assure you there is something in your last letter very sensibly affected me, … [I] could not but be troubled [by it]', then proceeded to beseech 'Come let me beg of you to consider things'. Following his strong and lengthy rebuke, Symson still reiterated his commitment and determination not to give up on his son ('If I could but see you stick to anything I should have some hopes'), signing off by again commenting on the effect of the affair on his own state of mind: 'I am sure it gives me a very melancholy prospect'.[32]

These types of personalized pressures that raised the spectre of guilt by directly pointing to the consequences of his son's acts on his own emotional state, announcing the harm the son caused to a caring parent and hence to their mutual obligation to one another – were apparent in Symson's approach to his younger children as well. When young Benjamin announced his wish to discontinue his apprenticeship with a Kendal trader, Symson instantly drew a series of letters containing a mix of strong chiding along with emotional pleas; 'I cannot continue any longer thus perplexed. I am sure your unsteadiness has given me many uneasy hours', he grumbled, adding that he was 'surprised' at Benjamin's 'strange' alteration of mind, which exposed, so he declared, his 'unsteady temper', causing 'more disturbance [to me] than ordinary'. Scolding Benjamin for being dishonest with his master, he further raised the spectre of shame by retorting 'you did wrong. Have a care of such mistakes', again emphasizing that finding another honest master would 'give a great more trouble which I am unfit for'. In a postscript, Symson ultimately mounted the emotional pressures by assuring him that he would do 'nothing utterly against your will', while at the same time making his stand – and expectation – unambiguous: 'You know my opinion'. Unlike his brother Robert, who remained unyielding to his father's castigations and was determined to follow his own ways, Benjamin was far more attentive to his father's advice – and shame – thereafter abandoning his plan to leave his master.[33]

As other letters dispatched from parents to their sons show, the use of personalized pressures to impart shame or guilt could take nuanced and intricate forms. Parents could make ambiguous statements that left things hinted rather than said, stating one thing ('do as you wish') but implying the contrary, offering general moralizing which still connoted specific complaints against a son, arousing the shame of the young for betraying the ties that bound parent and son to one another. In the case of Isaac Lawrence, a merchant in the Levant who opposed his son's choice of a marriage partner, he sent a long letter in which he outlined a series of arguments against the choice, pouring affection and regard mixed with expressions of tolerance for his son's choice: 'for in this case of a wife I pretend only to advise not to choose; and only to direct your reason not to divert your love'. Nevertheless, the threat of shame and regret was unmistakable. 'And affairs of this binding nature require the most searching prudence; for we must not be so wrought upon ... as to commit any error that may leave us to repentance and an after game'.[34]

When the moralizing was not intended to point at a child's culpability, it could still be interpreted as such, and hence be experienced as an insult and a shame. The merchant Thomas Pelham, whose son was apprenticed in Constantinople, wrote to his son at one point: 'I must take this first opportunity of writing to you to send my best advice and earnest desires that you would behave yourself with all sobriety and diligence'. Making a special emphasis of the fact that he did not 'say this as if I had any [f]ault of you', he added not only the commonly-used claim regarding 'the duty of a father' to offer his advice to his son, but also his affection and care 'especially to a son who is so dear to me', while also stating that although the young Pelham already had formally finished his apprenticeship, 'you are still apprentice and must behave your self as such'. From a subsequent letter it is apparent that the son took his father's statement not simply as a critique of his inexperience, but also as an insult and a shame. 'I think you took my last letter a little wrong for I did not mean to show any suspicion of your doing anything amiss much less any anger towards you', his father wrote in response, again reiterating his kindness and care for his son.[35] This tangle of interactions, in which parental censure was imbued with expressions of care, causing in a child a sense of insult, or else of guilt or shame for betraying the obligations and ties of trust between father and son, is evident in family letters well into the early eighteenth century and beyond. 'Blemishes affixed to any one always carry shame with them: and the discovery, or even bare imputation of any defect is not borne without some uneasiness', as the philosopher John Locke articulated the kind of unspoken emotional response which habitually adjoined parental moralizing and reprimands.[36]

## Honour, bonding, and interpersonal ties

The language of shame pervaded letters exchanged amid networks of kin and friends. Among the landed elite, issues of honour and fierce conflicts arising from perceived assaults on a person's honour could generate outright and aggressive forms of verbal shaming. Taking the form of threats and harsh insults, verbal shaming was sometimes utilised to replace more violent confrontations, notably duelling. As research has shown, over much of the seventeenth century the practice of duelling was only rarely and sporadically applied, with notions of civility, as well as honour itself, being invoked to prevent violence and the deadly consequences of the duel.[37] Under these circumstances, elite men would find 'spilling ink rather than blood' a preferable and appropriate option. They wrote letters in which they declared their own honour while also alluding to the shame and knavery of their adversaries, exchanging slurs and denigrating insults which, for all the venom and lack of civility, still stopped short of a violent duel. In some instances, warnings and threats of shame were voiced against eager contestants by family members keen to avert the duel. In those cases when a duel did take place, verbal insults and shaming could still precede it, with vitriolic correspondence passing between adversaries, conveying slanders that undermined an opponent's gentle status by alluding to his servility, inferiority, cowardice or incivility.[38]

Alongside these aggressive forms of shaming, correspondence among the elite points to the pervasive use of more moderate, polite and restrained shaming, which came especially in the form of rebuke. Elite letter-writers routinely criticized, scolded, and reprimanded those whose behaviour they deemed to be disruptive or inappropriate; 'the landed ranks lived amid a constant chiding chorus of admonitions', as historian Linda Pollock put it.[39] The shaming was vital to monitoring the conduct of kin, peers, friends, and servants. It was critical in negotiating relationships and handling tensions or disputes about honour and other issues, including property or household management. Letter-writers sometimes used the criticism to force their kin to admit their fault (or amend their behaviour), inducing them to offer apology or expressions of regret and 'ashamedness', placing pressure to resolve conflicts and come to a reconciliation. When the shaming did not achieve its purpose and the shamed person refused to admit culpability, but rather took the rebuke as an insult, the exchange still had implications. In a community of peers bound by ties of honour and obligations, verbal shaming and reproof acted as reminders of obligations, signalling norms and expectations of proper gentlemanly and civil conduct, 'keeping peace' and other neighbourly commitments.[40]

A language of shame was entrenched across the gentlemanly and professional classes below the landed elite, amid intricate webs of patronage that tied patrons, clients and friends in bonds of dependence and personal loyalties. The expression of shame here could be excessively polite and formulaic, couched in a rhetoric of deference and apology. Echoing the formula of model letters, shame could be used as a form of supplication, signalling dependence and the inferiority of those seeking favours or aid, the expression of shame being integral to the deference they owed to their patrons or superiors.[41] Pouring praise and flattery that bolstered the honour of their addressee, writers exaggerated their pronouncements of humility and modesty, with an embellished idiom of shame at the same time invoking commitments and mutual obligations for the future. In March 1669–70, for example, Samuel Pepys wrote a letter of gratitude to Captain Thomas Elliott, the bailiff in Aldeburgh, Suffolk, for his assistance during his unsuccessful attempt at winning the election there. In his letter, Pepys not only stated that he was 'extremely ashamed to find myself so much outdone by you in kindness', but went on to elaborate on Elliott's exemplary discretion ('by your not suffering me to know the expense which this business has occasioned you'), pledging that Elliott's efforts and 'pains' were 'an obligation greater than I can foresee opportunity of requiting', and vouching 'though I shall by no means omit to endeavor it'.[42]

As Samuel Pepys' correspondence shows, his pronouncements of shame in his exchanges with his extensive network of family, friends, and clients were more varied and elaborate, going well beyond the formal rules of deference or even promises of reciprocal obligations. Not unlike the censure which, as noted, pervaded elite correspondence, Pepys repeatedly resorted to reproof in confronting kin, friends, or clients whose conduct he deemed improper. The shame and chiding could take a distinctly personalized form, as in the case of his brother-in-Law, Balthasar St. Michel, whom Pepys helped promote. In 1666, Pepys secured for St. Michel the post of muster-master at sea and in 1667 the post of a deputy treasurer of the fleet. In the ensuing years, Pepys' letters to St. Michel offered varied forms of advice mixed with admonition, invariably reprimanding him for his repeated requests for money, pointing out his wayward ways and misconduct; '...pray for the time to come keep your owne Credit to depend upon yourselfe, and not the good or ill deportment of other people', he writes in a letter of August 1675.[43] When Pepys realized that St. Michel was misusing his influence to interfere in a law suit involving a debt, he berated him not only for the moral implications of such conduct, but for the damage it brought on Pepys' own reputation, which amounted to betraying St. Michel's obligations and loyalty to Pepys:

> I find it to be a business much less becoming you ... for you to imbarke yourselfe in the merits of the quarrel [between these persons] ... is a piece of presumption and can by no means excuse you ... you know how often I have advised you to avoid any thoughts of [acting in this manner], as being, besides the injustice of it, too conscious of frailties of my owne and the care due to myself under them.

Pepys continued to urge St. Mitchel to tighten his belt, blaming him for being extravagant and possibly dishonest or neglecting to properly manage his financial affairs. His shaming was at times insinuated rather than inflicted outright; 'one thing I must observe to you with a little wonder' was a phrase he used often when implying his brother-in-law's misconduct. Carefully embedded within repeated expressions of commitment and care ('your very affectionate Brother and Servant', he signed all his letters), this mix of advice and beratement, invoking a sense of guilt or shame in betraying personal obligations and commitments, continued to sustain and nourish the relations between Pepys and St. Michel, with Pepys providing frequent financial assistance, and St. Michel, for his part, offering indispensable help when his patron was imprisoned in 1679.[44]

Pepys' correspondence also shows that beyond the practice of shaming others, he and his associates used the experience of shame to enlist the support of each other. Amidst a competitive patronage system rife with conflicts and shifting loyalties, they confided in one another, offering detailed narratives of the shame that engulfed them when confronting varied circumstances of disappointment and humiliation. When, in 1679, Pepys was forced to resign from the post of Secretary of the Admiralty, which he had held since 1672, he wrote his patron, the Duke of York, a long letter in which he chronicled in intimate detail the humiliation and shame inflicted by his parliamentary Whig adversaries, revealing not only his resentment but also his deep sense of betrayal by some of his supporters, as well as the King himself:

> I have from many years lived in a constant state of war, they censuring, and I defending, the management of the navy ... I should not promise myself any satisfaction from them [his adversaries], especially upon terms so unequal, as my being brought down to be a servant to them, when the dignity of the trust I have so long had the honour of serving his Majesty in, might, I hope, be thought to have set me upon a level with them.

Submitting 'the sincerity of my wishes for the weal of his service', Pepys then requested that the Duke entreat the King in his favour, again making clear the insult – and the shame – he would suffer should such recompense fail. 'I should be in very ill condition to bear its not being made up to me by his Majesty ... or at least making some other provision for me as one superannuated in his service'.[45]

Pepys' own clients and subordinates also turned to him for his support, requesting his aid in promoting their careers, offering financial aid, or admitting them as employees in his own household. Their requests were habitually emboldened by detailed narratives of the shame they had experienced in circumstances of degradation or misfortune. Sir Edward Morley, whose fortunes were allegedly ruined because he was 'led as a fool' into marrying a coachman's daughter 'no worth a shilling', disclosed that he was 'absolutely ruined in my fortune and reputation', feeling 'a derision to all the world'. Appealing for Pepys to intervene on his behalf at the Court, he likened his shame and suffering to that of the criminal going to the gallows: 'I beg you to put in a kind word for me ... for a criminal bound and going to execution is not in greater agonies, than has been my poor active soul'. In another case, Josiah Burchett, a servant, confidant, and long-term companion to Pepys, who had abruptly been dismissed on grounds of corruption, approached his master asking to be reinstated. In a letter offering a mix of apology and begging, he conveyed his experience of 'being thrown so suddenly out of a family I have soe long earned my bread in, into a wide world', describing how he was now 'so great a stranger, that I know not how or where to bestow myself', alleging he was forced to 'ramble in those parts where I think I may least expose myself to the sight of my friends, which is now grown equally cruel to that of my enemys'. Asking forgiveness for his shameful deeds ('I most humbly crave pardon for what I have done amiss') he beseeched Pepys to take him back.[46]

In the case of Pepys' close and more equal ties, revealing one's own innermost experience of shame could also indicate a particularly intimate sense of bonding and regard. In a letter to Pepys in April 1682, John Evelyn requested his assistance: 'I should not doubt but he would promote this ambition of mine'. In the letter, he offered a long and detailed account of the humiliation he had suffered during his service (on the commission for the sick and wounded) in the Anglo-Dutch Wars. First there was his thwarted ambition, when peace was concluded and his new patron, who was 'unkind and unjust to me', forced him to resign. Then there was also his wounded scholarly pride, when the Dutch ambassador criticized the treatise he wrote on 'Commerce and Navigation' as a preface to his projected history of the Dutch Wars. His pronouncements regarding his experience were unambiguous:

> In sum, I had no thanks for what I had done, and have been accounted since, I suppose, an useless fop, and fit only to plant coleworts, and cannot bend to mean submissions; and this Sir is the history of the historian. I confess to you, I had once the vanity to hope, had my patron continued in his station, for some (at least) honorary title that might have animated my progress, as seeing some amongst them whose talents I did not envy: but it was not my fortune to succeed.[47]

Having exposed the insult to his honour and the shame inherent in his failure, Evelyn not only asked Pepys for his assistance in promoting him but also offered drafts of the history of the wars he had begun to write, for Pepys' own use in writing the history of the Navy. The gesture, coupled with his account of his experience of humiliation and shame, bolstered his request while at the same time enhancing the mutual commitment, trust, and friendship that existed between the two men.[48] Other cases of letters exchanged between elite men point to the practice of disclosing shame and other negative feelings regarding honour in letters designed to sooth tensions or conflicts, and to nurture trust and intimate ties between elite male friends.[49]

Lower down on the social scale, shame could sometimes permeate letters addressed to family and friends. An illuminating case is the letter book of Nehemiah Wallington, the mid-seventeenth-century Puritan-artisan whose diary was discussed in a previous chapter. The letters Wallington meticulously copied (in 1650) were written to family members, neighbours and friends and were designed, as he explained it, not only 'to advise and console', but also 'to reprove and admonish'.[50] A host of transgressions prompted Wallington's reproach, from the adultery of a widowed kin, through breaches of the lord's day or drunkenness among his neighbours, to failures in the performance of ministerial obligations in his parish. The shame he inflicted on his addressees was inspired less by models of polite shame and more by his immersion in the Bible and the sermons he listened to in the church; 'according to the command of God in Leviticus 19:17 Thou shalt ... plainely rebuke thy neighbor and suffer him not to sinn', as he wrote in the opening of one of his letters.[51] Using a torrent of biblical quotations and pejorative idioms, his shaming could become extremely harsh and punitive. In this manner he condemned his neighbour, Mr Waddington, not only for 'the breach of the lords day in selling of your ware' but also for his deceit, fraud, lying and 'sleeping in church', overall being 'gilty of many abominations'. In a letter to his cousin John, Wallington vehemently admonished him for his drunkenness, describing his conduct as 'filthy, odious, loathesome, swinish, beastly', claiming it would lead him to 'speake lewed things', to 'strife and quarreling' and ultimately to 'eternal damnation'. In the case of his kin widow, Dorothy Rampaigne, who took an Irish Catholic lover, his denunciation and shame were at their utmost, describing her as 'woefull and miserable', her refusal to repent proving to be her 'everlasting disgrace and ruine ... For as the childe is so like the Father so is every wicked man and woman like the divel'.[52] Even ministers in his parish church were not spared of his judgemental tone and harsh and vituperative shame. Accusing Abraham Colfe, the absentee rector of his parish, for failing to prevent his parishioners from going astray – 'surely there would not have bine so many ignorant, drunken, swearers, mockers and profainers of the Lords day ... as now there be' – he claimed his church was 'as rude and profaine a place as ever they [the parishioners] did know which doth much abound in your old days to your discredit'. Wallington's shaming of independent ministers (Matthew Barker and George Griffiths) was no less scathing, pouring scorn and derision as well as denouncing them for their pride and cowardice in failing to reprove their audience for their innumerable sins and abominations.[53]

In this type of sermonizing and denunciation, Wallington repeatedly emphasized his own personal acquaintance and engagement with his addressee, amplifying the sense of shame and guilt in his friends. '... I have had a desire to speak with you but not finding a fit opportunity I now ... make bold to write something of my mind unto you', he wrote to his neighbour, Mr Waddington.[54] In many of his letters Wallington was keen to refer to rumours or information he received from mutual acquaintances, or point to acts he himself witnessed at church or the alehouse.[55] Constantly warning his acquaintances of the threat of damnation, he underscored the impact their misconduct had on his own sense of foreboding, passionately warning of the breach and abandonment such conduct could bring on their ties of friendship and support. To Dorothy Rampaigne he wrote that her adultery 'make us ashamed and tremble at your sinfull ways', warning not only that 'if you slite and reject this his (God's) forewarning of you, Then you are left without excuse', but also that his own letter of reproach to her 'will rise up in Judgement against you at the great day'. In the case of Abraham Colfe, his parish minister, he threatened that if Cole failed to 'admonish the wicked of his wicked ways', not only would the sinner 'dye in his iniquitye' but 'his blood will I require at thine hand'. In other instances, he went as far as to warn that his written reproach would not only bear witness to the sins of his friend, but add to his or her torments on the Day of Judgement.[56]

For all the vituperative language and threats, this type of personalized appeal also implied a more mitigated form of shame in which an enhancement of ties, rather than their utter disintegration, was conveyed. Wallington's letters of reproach were suffused with expressions of familiarity and regard, imparting a sense of affinity and affection which not only served to moderate his strong language of reproach, but also reinforced and strengthened his bonding and ties. In his letter to Dorothy Rampaigne, he took care to note that he wrote to her not only out of 'the obedience of God's command' but also because of 'the love I beare to your soule'. To Abraham Calfe he likewise wrote that 'it is out of my love I bare to you … I do it out of my love to you poore soule and the discharge of my conscience'.[57] While expressing great disappointment at the wayward ways of another friend – 'I now cannot but stand amazed to here of your wicked life' – he still referred to the depth of their connection and his overall admiration for 'those excellent parts which you are endued withal … and I having better thoughts of you then of myself'. Deep empathy also comes through in some of his letters: 'Sir my heart bleeds for you to thinke of your sad and miserable condition', he writes to one of his neighbours; 'goe on in a course of your sins still then my soule shall weepe in secret', to another.[58] Expressing his 'earnest desires' that his errant friends improve their ways, he offered prayers so that God 'would be pleased to bless and sanctifie this counsel which he by his holy spirit hath moved me to write unto you', placing himself as a guardian to his friends on their journey to a potential reconciliation with God, standing by them and remaining 'your sad and greved Freend such as he is Nehemiah Wallington', as he signed one of his letters to his neighbour, Mr Wade.[59]

One engaging example of Wallington's use of personalized shame to censure the conduct of a friend while at the same time reinforcing his ties and commitments was his exchange with his close and intimate friend James Cole, a tradesman with whom he shared his godly passion and way of life. When in 1634 Cole decided to leave London to escape his creditors, causing great anxiety among his friends in the godly community, Wallington wrote to him a long letter full of reproach, calling him to consider 'how many ways you doe dishonour your good God' and accusing him of yielding 'unto Satan your great enemie'. He not only entreated him to return home and resume his familial obligations but also scolded him; 'it is no shame to come home again. It was a shame to goe from home', further raising in him the potential for guilt by pointing to the harm his departure inflicted on his relatives and relations; it brought grief to his 'fellow members, the Saints of God', while in the case of his mother, who took his departure hard and is also 'very sick', he warned 'I feare it will be her death'. Yet for all the scolding and reproach, Wallington's shame was from the outset framed by the language of friendship. He addressed Cole as 'Loving and deere Freind Master Cole', highlighted their affinity and his sympathy for Cole's plight, along with the confidence, if not admiration, he had for Cole's generosity and moral character:

> you I say which hath been A Job in bearing of many sorrowes, And that hath been a foote to the lame and an eye to the blind, And a grate comfort to my sorrowfull soule: If such a captain as you fli, what shall become of such a weak soldier I am.

Travelling to Ipswich to deliver his letter to Cole in person, Wallington placed further pressure on Cole to change his mind and ultimately persuaded him to return to London.[60]

Wallington's correspondence with Cole and others also illuminates an altogether different aspect of his practice of shaming. Rather than solely concentrating on pouring reproach on others, Wallington confided in them, revealing his own deep sense of shame in his sins, betraying his innermost tribulations and suffering. From the preface to his letter book (addressed 'To all Readers'), it is clear that he was fully aware of the difference that existed between disclosing his inner tribulations in letters addressed to others and recording them down in his own diary, the former requiring greater restraint: 'Let your words be few, and digested. It is a shame for the tongue to cry the heart mercy much more to cast itself upon the uncertain pardon of others eares'.[61] Yet it is also evident that his diary style, with its focus on anguish and internal emotions, spilled into his letter-writing. In a long letter to his old friend Master Roborough, a curate of his parish, he complained deeply about his neglects and corruptions, likening his anguish to 'an Armie against mee ... cause my heart to drape (or break) asunder like drops of water and I am driven unto many sad and dismall thoughts', referring to himself as 'pevish, infidilious, unthankfull murmurere even a dead dogge ... so vile a sinner makes my heart to melt and my eyes to rune abundant of teers'. He also confided his sins and deep sense of shame to other friends in the community of the godly.[62]

This disclosure of the experience of shame in his letters offered Wallington an opportunity to console himself, with his friend and correspondent thereby becoming a witness and sharing in his efforts at soothing his agonizing pain. Thus, James Cole became an ear to his troubled mind, at the same time reaffirming his attempts at consoling himself; 'but I judg my selfe, therefore I shall not be judged', he wrote.[63] In other instances, Wallington received the solace and sympathy of others. His brother-in-law Zachariah Rampaigne responded to Wallington's letter, in which he chronicled his tribulations, offering a detailed set of considerations to soothe his pain and shame: 'do not aggravate nor make to much of those things which may move your sorrow. For a man to have his finger always in the gore is not the way to heale it'; 'lift up your eyes to the hills from whence commeth your salvation and see what causes of comfort the Lord reacheth out to you', are some of the comforts he conveyed.[64] These types of ongoing exchanges, pronouncing guilt and shame but also offering consolation to one another, reinforced the bonding and ties of affection and trust between Wallington and his friends. As James Cole expressed it outright:

> Being comforted in my troubles ... with the comforts of the same spirit of Christ that dwelleth in us, I am ashamed of my own inability, when I see thy excellency. But when such a freend as thou art importunate for there loves and I have half a loafe yet your importunity on one side and my love on the other side constraineth me to bring out what I have.[65]

In other instances, the letters show Wallington and his friends in the godly community confiding in one another, their revealed innermost sense of shame thereby becoming part of a continued and sustained dialogue that cemented their ties.[66]

## Women's letters and shame

A potent form of shaming and articulation of shame can be found in letters written by elite women. As indicated earlier in this chapter, female letter-writers in the sixteenth century habitually castigated or shamed their children. Yet, as their correspondence also shows, these elite women extended their shaming to a host of other relations, especially kin or friends, superiors and subordinates. Their shaming often took the form of polite language appropriate to their class and gender, offering deference and expressions of submission and apologies for approaching kin or patrons with their requests, or else submitting their misgivings and critique. Yet beyond deference and apologetic entreaty, letters written by elite women also point to their boldness in approaching their correspondents. Not unlike their male counterparts, they confronted them with their offences when the occasion required, reminding them of their obligations and chastising them for going amiss. The shaming could be direct, outspoken and threatening, even when directed at men of their own standing and above. In a letter to her brother-in-law, William Bouchier, Earl of Bath, Anne Dudley rebuked him for his ill-treatment of his wife, her sister: 'it seems you have altogether forgotten both your selfe and frendes'. She then moved to a severe and more punitive shame, criticizing him for his lack of respect for his wife and his 'posterity', declaring he was 'so voyd of judgment and descretion' and threatening to expose his conduct to 'the world'. Warning him to have no 'doubt that it shall be redressed', she vouched that unless he had 'more government' of himself, she would see to it 'that my sister may have her portion and go lyve from yow'.[67]

By threatening to expose male faults or misdeeds – their carelessness or neglect, the varied forms of 'unkindness' they showed – female writers could go well beyond polite shame, deliberately using the written letter to express 'outrage and incivility'. The use of shame and rebuke in their letters offered these women a means of response to men who injured, insulted or dishonoured them, belying expected norms of polite language and the submission appropriate to their gender, placing limits on male authority by challenging not only their conduct but also their honour. Addressing men of superior status, some women used a particularly bold and vituperative style, pouring scorn and deploying a strong language of sarcasm and spite. Elizabeth, countess of Shrewsbury, sent a message to Sir Thomas Stanhope, declaring she hoped he would be 'damned p[er]petuallie in hell fyre', announcing he was 'more wretched vyle and myserable than any creature lyveinge, and ... more uglie in shape than the vilest toade in the worlde, and one to whom none of reputacion would vouchsafe to send any messadge'. In the case of

Margaret, Countess of Bath, who defended her honour against the slights of a Master Savage, she asserted that she 'neuer offendid you in my lyffe wherfor the mor is your shame so to vse me', adding that 'this beastly blessinge of yours declare you to be more savage or brutish than discrete or reasonable', and resolving to publicly humiliate him by making others aware of his behaviour.[68]

The use of 'a little ink and paper' – as one writer put it – allowed women not only to delve into the shame of others, but also to elaborate on their own sense of gendered shame. A powerful case in this regard is that of Anne Dormer and her letters to her younger sister Elizabeth between the years 1685 and 1691, when the latter was living in France and Constantinople. Married in 1668 to a wealthy widower, Robert Dormer, Anne endured an abusive marriage, her husband proving jealous and rude, designing domestic rules to control and monitor every aspect of his wife's existence.[69] Her rich and detailed correspondence with her sister is first and foremost a record of her plight, of the torment, emotional distress and humiliation to which she was subject, leading to bouts of melancholy coupled with a strong sense of shame and guilt; 'the thoughts of my friends and the concern they take in my life and health makes me ashamed to suffer … and therefore I strive to cheer up myself but it is so unatruall to me', she reveals early on in the summer of 1685.[70] In her letters, she not only described her husband's hatred and verbal abuse in calling her worthless, undeserving, 'unworthy', 'the most abject pittifull creature in the world', but also exposed her vulnerability and doubts regarding whether she herself was to blame; 'I am so weary of being despised that if he will hate me I shall submit to it', as she writes. Striving to absolve herself from the guilt – 'I cannot accuse myself of having brought upon my self any of those cruelties that person shews me' – she consoled herself with the 'compassion and kindness' she found 'from every body'.[71] But as her letters make abundantly clear, the suffering and abuse to which she was subject had a profound effect on her, shattering her sense of self and engulfing her with an internal struggle to which shame and guilt regarding her moral worth were central.

For all the guilt and sense of shame in her melancholy and state of oppression, Anne managed, through her epistolary voice, to resist her husband and mitigate, if not altogether overcome, her shame. In letter after letter to her sister she exposed her husband in his own shame, formulating a clear and forthright judgement and condemnation of his abusive character. Exposing him as 'an obstinate hard hearted man', she proclaimed he was incapable of correction and improvement; 'to alter him impossible but he doth not mend', a man 'more and more governed by humour and less and less by reason'. She further demonstrated his rudeness and misogyny by referring to his repeated announcements that all women were 'whores', denouncing his shameful conduct and cruelty towards her kin: 'Nothing but a ray from heaven can soften that heart which is made of such a piece of stone'. Vainglorious in his 'resolution to believe well of himself in spite of all', he was above all mad: 'a man that seems to have his senses act in everything so like a madd man'.[72]

By thoroughly exposing her husband's comportment and character, Anne made her sister aware of her intimate domestic affairs, threatening to undermine his reputation among family and kin. No less important, despite his demand that she show him the letters she exchanged with her sister, she continued to write, her written denunciation of him gradually helping her to surpass her own sense of shame and guilt, proclaiming instead pity along with a growing sense of condescension and scorn. 'I assure you ... I am sorry for his sake'; it 'grieves me more then it angers me', she writes. And as she announced to her sister her decision to avoid appearing in public with him – 'for I can more easily beare a private affront then a publicke one', she explained, she also developed a set of arguments to challenge his aggression and claim her own moral superiority; 'he often says as one values themselves they shall be valued but I find that doth not hold true always for I know none values him as he values himself'.[73] Conceding that she would not deny her marital vows and would take care of her husband in sickness and old age, she then resolved to make herself 'less cheap' and suffer no longer 'to be scorned and vilified', withdrawing emotionally and distancing herself from him:

> I am weary now of playing the monkey any longer, and if I cannot deserve your [his] friendship I do not desire your fondness ... when I remember the passionate fondness I shewed him so many years and reflect what returnes he made me and how little good it did him and what hurt it did me I resolve no more to be allured into that nett againe.[74]

Anne's ability to overcome her shame did not remain a private process that affected solely her sense of self and internal travails. As she confided and divulged to her sister her experience in such passionate care, so her ties of trust and affection with her deepened. In some letters Anne conveyed gratitude and apology for burdening her sister with her troubles, placing herself in a humbled position of dependence on her sister's support: 'I must say as poore people do I can but love you and thank you'. In other instances, she also claimed to rely on God's assurances.[75] Yet overall, it is the affection that flows from Anne to her sister, and an ever-growing sense of solidarity and empathy between the two women, that governed her letters. 'I hope to live to have thee again in my arms and tell thee never sister loved more then thy faithfull friend'; 'I assure myself that as I do not pass any hour without thinking of you so your thoughts are as often and as kindly with me', as she expressed her sense of devotion and care with which the letters were suffused. In return, she found in her sister's letters consolation and encouragement, making her 'infinitely happy', and producing empathy and an intimate understanding of her plight:

> Tho I please myself often with a hope that you guess pretty well at all what is in my heart ... how perfectly I am every way satisfied of your affection for me how deeply I am sensible of all those testimonies you give me every way of your tender love and constant friendship.

And as the language of gratitude and humility that amplified her sister's emotional support persisted ('how grieved I am to be so little able to shew my gratitude to you'), the sense of bonding and trust between the two sisters became ever more profound.[76]

## Conclusion

Shame was a salient feature of the personal interactions of English women and men as they grew up and matured. In an early modern family regime governed by notions of the parental obligation to nurture, care and dispose children into the world, along with the children's obligation to obey parental authority and rule, feelings of shame were intrinsic to familial interactions and the upbringing of children from early on in their lives.[77] As writers of autobiographies that offer glimpses of early childhood experiences indicate, shame was the outcome of the breach – or perceived threat of a breach – of these obligations and the expectations they entailed. It could arise as an internalized sense of misconduct or inadequacy in failing to meet the parental expectations, a sense of sin or incompetence with which a writer concurred as an adult, if not already as a child. The shame could also be the consequence of the perceived parental failure to meet their obligations, with a child being engulfed by a sense of injustice, shamed in their punishment or alienation from an estranged and neglecting parent. In all these instances, the shame was not solely triggered by the infringement of a shared code of morality or even sin before God, but it was experienced as a deep sense of damaged relations and ruptured bonds between a parent and a child, variously leading to unease or embarrassment, a sense of betrayal, humiliation, guilt and shame.

This shame, which was the consequence of conflictual or damaged relations, permeated personal interactions amid networks of kin, patronage and friends across the elite and middle classes below. Among the elite, verbal shaming could go well beyond the perceived proper manner of politely shaming one's peers, with letter-writers sometimes inflicting harsh shame in reaction to assaults on their honour or other forms of disputes. They poured insult and scorn that escalated an already sour or damaged interaction, which, while averting more violent confrontations, utterly undermined the honour of an addressee and damaged their ties irrevocably. Elite women also mobilized the vocabulary and practice of harsh shame, threatening to expose male superiors in their abusive conduct, using aggressive forms of shame as a leverage in their relationships with husbands and other kin. Below the elite, harsh shaming could be embedded in notions of moral transgression and sin before God, bringing to the fore outright denunciation and vituperative scolding, as was the case of Nehemiah Wallington, who, inspired by sermons and biblical injunctions, took upon himself the position of the preacher, conveying threats of exclusion and the prospect of damnation and hell in his letters to kin and friends.

As the letters examined here also show, shaming and shame commonly came in softer forms of rebuke and reproach. Echoing to some extent the language and formula of reproach that pervaded epistolary manuals, writers invariably expanded the rebuke, using it in an attempt to amend the conduct of an addressee or admit them to a fault, or else to deter, place pressures, cause embarrassment or trigger guilt. The rebuke could take the form of a strong critique and censure of perceived misbehaviour, or else of a more restrained and polite expressions of apology, the latter sometimes concealing harsher reprimand and denunciation. The rebuke could also be insinuated, with a writer expressing more generalized moralizing which only implicitly referred to specific transgressions deemed a shame in an addressee. Issues of hierarchy and social distance permeated these exchanges, with model letters advocating a differentiated form of shame expression, recommending polite or insinuated shame in confronting peers, and a more robust form of rebuke in addressing and deterring inferiors. Such differentiation – and the relations of dependency underlying it – transpired in many letters; parents placed pressures to impart disgrace, shame or guilt on their dependent sons, patrons shamed their clients or servants, inferiors used the shame as a form of apology and a show of deference towards their patrons. No less important, the rhetoric of condemnation and admonishment could also be appropriated by inferiors themselves; women sent letters in which they scolded male kin, parishioners wrote letters of reproach to their local minister, adult children sometimes chastised and critiqued their own elderly parents.[78]

These habits and practices of castigation did not necessarily achieve the desired effect, nor were they always effective in averting conflicts and disputes or attenuating troubled ties. Elite contests of honour sometimes ended up in duels, or else involved cycles of insults and counter insults, with interpersonal disputes remaining pervasive among members of the elite over much of the era. Parental shaming, whether in the form of moderate reproach or robust denigration, could remain unhelpful in changing the mind of a stubborn or an independent offspring, as was the case of Joseph Symson's relations with his elder son. Nor did a letter-writer like Samuel Pepys always manage to amend the ways of those he repeatedly criticized and berated. Yet the habit and disposition to shame and reprimand others persisted. Invariably signalling status and varied forms of interdependencies, the shame acted as a reminder of obligations, nourishing and sustaining ties of exchange and expectations for cooperation, whether in families or amid networks that cut across the elite and middling groups below.

What ultimately gave the shaming its edge – and the distinct emotional pressure it could impart – was the personalized form in which it was applied. By berating kin and others, letter-writers exposed the misconduct of an addressee as uncivil or dishonourable, damaging norms of obedience and deference, or displaying immorality and sin before God. Yet over and above such transgressions, writers underscored the shame of breaching personal obligations and attachments. Their shaming was private and intimate, invoking betrayal of personal commitments, raising the spectre of embarrassment or guilt by pointing to the consequences of an addressee's actions to their own well-being, or to the threat these posed to mutual commitments and ties. Writers habitually imbued their critique and reproach with expressions of familiarity, personal attachment and vows of commitment, allowing space for tempering tensions, resolving conflicts and reconciliation. The shame could re-affirm and cement, rather than undermine, interdependencies and personal bonds.

In all these practices of negotiating and handling personal ties through shame, letter-writing came to acquire a pivotal role, greatly extending the use, communication and articulation of shame. Occupying a space mid-way between self-reflection and the relational self, letters conveyed varied forms of shame, both harsh or punitive and more moderate and inclusive, allowing individuals, men and women, to articulate the shame that would otherwise have remained unspoken or concealed. As the letters examined here also show, letter-writing was formative in the expression of an experience of shame, prompting writers not only to shame and reprimand others, but also to take account of their own experience of shame. Some writers examined here communicated an innermost sense of shame caused by an anxiety over what others think, by a foreboding sense of guilt over their own acts, or the fear for the loss of the respect of peers. Offering detailed accounts of the experience, writers placed their trust in those they addressed, affirming and enhancing their loyalty and ties. In the case of some female writers, recording and communicating a shame experience allowed them to overcome their deep sense of the humiliation caused by abusive men, claiming for themselves moral superiority and self-worth while at the same time enhancing their bonds of affection and trust with the women they addressed.

## Notes

1 For the expansion of letter-writing among the upper and middle classes, see James Daybell, *Women Letter-Writers in Tudor England* (Oxford, 2006), 17–26; Gary Schneider, *The Culture of Epistolarity: Vernacular Letters and Letter Writing in Early Modern England, 1500–1700* (Newark, 2005); Susan E. Whyman, *The Pen and the People: English Letter-Writers 1660–1800* (Oxford, 2009); Eve Tavor Bannet, *Empire of Letters: Letter Manuals and Transatlantic Correspondence, 1680–1820* (Cambridge, 2005).
2 Matthew Storey (ed.), *Two East Anglian Diaries 1641–1729: Isaac Archer and William Coe* (Suffolk Record Society, Vol. XXXVI, Suffolk, 1994), 46.
3 Richard Norwood, *The Journal of Richard Norwood, Surveyor of Bermuda* (New York, 1945), 8–9. For condescension towards children, especially younger children deemed impressionable, see Elizabeth Foyster, *Marital Violence: An English Family History, 1660–1857* (Cambridge, 2005), 138–9. For excessive erasure as marking unease and prevarication, in autobiographies, see Jane Humphries, *Childhood and Child Labour in the British Industrial Revolution* (Cambridge, 2010), 19.
4 Norwood, *The Journal*, 11–12.
5 Storey (ed.), *Two East Anglian Diaries*, 47–8, 49, 51. See also Ilana Krausman Ben-Amos, *The Culture of Giving: Informal Support and Gift Exchange in Early Modern England* (Cambridge, 2008), 278–80.
6 James Orchard Halliwell (ed.), *The Autobiography and Personal Diary of Simon Forman, The Celebrated Astrologer, from A.D. 1552 to A.D. 1602* (London, 1849), 5–6.

102  *Family, networks, and shame*

7 Ibid., 5; Norwood, *The Journal*, 10; Samuel Hartlib, *The true and readie way to learne the Latine tongue* (1654), Wing H1002, 13–4. See also Keith Thomas, *Rule and Misrule in the Schools of Early Modern England*, The Stenton Lectures, 1975 (University of Reading, 1976), 8–12. For whipping in public schools as a source of terror, guilt and shame, see also Anthony Fletcher, *Gender, Sex and Subordination in England 1500–1800* (New Haven and London, 1995), 302–3.
8 John Locke, *Some Thoughts Concerning Education* (1693), The Harvard Classics, www.bartleby.com, Vol. 37, Part 1, section 78.
9 For the rarity of disinheritance, see Ben-Amos, *The Culture of Giving*, 19–21, esp. note 10.
10 For varied experiences of stepchildren, including the difficulties they encountered, see Bernard Capp, *The Ties that Bind: Siblings, Family and Society in Early Modern England* (Oxford, 2018), 92–111. For physical abuse, see Elizabeth Foyster, *Marital Violence: An English Family History, 1660–1857* (Cambridge, 2005), 136–7, 141, notes 32–3; Patricia Crawford, *Parents of Poor Children in England, 1580–1800* (Oxford, 2010), 144–6. For vivid memories of physical punishment, in the eighteenth and nineteenth centuries, see Humphries, *Childhood and Child Labour*, 134–5.
11 For the effect of parental favouritism on children, see also Capp, *The Ties that Bind*, 20–31.
12 Angel Day, *The English secretorie* (1586), STC2 6401, 73–4; M. de La Serre, *The secretary in fashion: or, an elegant and compendious way of writing all manner of letters* (1640, 1668), Wing2 L461A. no pages; Daybell, *Women Letter-writers*, 17–24; Bannet, *Empire of Letters*, 55–63.
13 Day, *The English secretorie*, 75–6; S. (Samuel) Sheppard, *The secretaries studie containing new familiar epistles* (1652), Wing S3169, 182 and passim; John Hill, *The young secretary's guide* (1687), Wing2 H1991B, 44, 45, 73, 76, 92.
14 M.R., A president for yong pen-men: or, the letter writer (1638), STC2 20585, C, C2, D2; Sheppard, *The secretaries studie*, 106–24, 174–205, 182.
15 La Serre, *The secretary in fashion*, no pages.
16 Peter Mack, *Elizabethan Rhetoric: Theory and Practice* (Cambridge, 2002), 103–9, 113; Daybell, *Women Letter-Writers*, 169; Schneider, *The Culture of Epistolarity*; Bannet, *Empire of Letters*, 49–50, 63; Brant, *Eighteenth-Century Letters*, 28.
17 Edward Elton, *A plaine and easy exposition of sixe of the commandments of God* (1619), STC2 7620, 72.
18 Daybell, *Women Letter-Writers*, 179–81. See also Linda A. Pollock, 'Honor, Gender, and Reconciliation in Elite Culture, 1570–1700', *Journal of British Studies*, 46 (2007), 23–5.
19 Richard Cust (ed.), *The Papers of Sir Richard Grosvenor, 1st Bart. (1585–1645)* (Record Society of Lancashire and Cheshire, vol. 134, Oxford, 1996), 30.
20 Courtney Erin Thomas, *If I Lose Mine Honour, I Lose Myself: Honour among the Early Modern English Elite* (Toronto, 2017), 90, 175–80, 188–204.
21 S.D. Smith (ed.), *'An Exact and Industrious Tradesman': The Letter Book of Joseph Symson of Kendal, 1710–1720* (The British Academy, Records of Social and Economic History, new series 34, Oxford, 2002), xxxv, xIi, xcvii–cxxvii.
22 Ibid., letter 1141, dated 18 August 1715; letter 1161, dated 15 September 1715.
23 Ibid., letter 1724, dated 14 October 1717.
24 Ibid., letter 1217, dated 22 December 1715.
25 Ibid., letter 1533, dated 7 March 1716; 1724, dated 14 October 1717.
26 Ibid., letter 1245, dated 25 February 1715/6; 1217, dated 22 December 1715; 1533, dated 7 March, 1716.
27 Ibid., letter 1225, dated 5 January 1715/6.
28 Ibid., letter 1742, dated 14 October 1717.
29 Ibid., letter 1144, dated 29 August 1715.
30 Ibid., letter 1221, dated 31 December 1715; 1724, dated 14 October 1717.

31 Ibid., letter 1134, dated 6 August 1715; 1144, dated 29 August 1715; 1161, dated 15 September 1715.
32 Ibid., letter 1225, dated 5 January 1715/16.
33 Ibid., letter 1846, dated 21 April 1718.
34 British Library (hereafter BL), Mss EUR E 387/B, Letter book of Isaac Lawrence, 1672–79, fol. 16.
35 BL, Add 33085, Correspondence of Thomas Pelham, of Stanmer, Sussex, merchant at Constantinople, 1718–37, fos. 1, 4.
36 Ben-Amos, *The Culture of Giving*, 146–53; Locke, *Some Thoughts Concerning Education*, Vol. 37, Part 1. section 143.
37 Pollock, 'Honor, Gender, and Reconciliation', 7–8; Thomas, *If I Lose Mine Honour*, 29–75.
38 Ibid., 50–51, 52–3, 60–63.
39 Pollock, 'Honor, Gender, and Reconciliation', 28.
40 Ibid., esp. 24–8; Thomas, *If I Lose Mine Honour*, Chaps. 3–4, esp. 127–8, 141–3, 143–8, 157–8, 162–3.
41 For expressions of shame as part of the language of deference, see Ben-Amos, *The Culture of Giving*, 196–205, esp. 202.
42 Richard Lord Braybrooke (ed.), *Memoirs of Samuel Pepys, esq. F.R.S., Secretary to the Admiralty in the reign of Charles II and James II*, Vol. 5 (London, 1828), 29.
43 Helen Truesdell Heath (ed.), *The Letters of Samuel Pepys and His Family Circle* (Oxford, 1955), xxiv–xxviii, 34.
44 Ibid., 35–6, 111, 102. When Pepys was in prison, St. Michel unearthed information regarding the person who accused him; following the death of his wife, Pepys distanced himself from St. Michel, but for several more years the latter still turned to Pepys for help in providing for him in his old age. Ibid., xxiv–xxviii. For Pepys' habits of rebuking his siblings and other family members, see Capp, *The Ties that Bind*, 155–6.
45 Braybrooke (ed.), *Memoirs of Samuel Pepys*, 61–3.
46 Ibid., 114, 125.
47 Braybrooke (ed.), *Memoirs of Samuel Pepys*, 84.
48 The exchange persisted throughout the 1680s, with Pepys sending books and expressing care for the wellbeing of Evelyn and his wife, and Evelyn offering encouragement and care when Pepys was imprisoned in 1688. Heath (ed.), *The Letters of Samuel Pepys* 83–5, 103, 108, 140–1, 142, 148, 160–1.
49 Katharine W. Swett, '"The Account Between Us": Honor, Reciprocity and Companionship in Male Friendship in the Later Seventeenth Century', *Albion* 31 (1999), 1–30 esp. 12, 11–5, 25–6.
50 BL, MS Sloane 922, fol. 2.
51 David Booy (ed.), *The Notebooks of Nehemiah Wallington, 1618–1654: A Selection* (Aldershot, 2007), 258.
52 BL, MS Sloane 922, fos. 134, 160; Booy (ed.), *The Notebooks*, 258–9. See also Paul S. Seaver, *Wallington's World: A Puritan Artisan in Seventeenth-Century London* (Stanford, 1985), 68–9.
53 BL, MS Sloane 922, fol. 132; Seaver, *Wallington's World*, 106–7. For the practice of shaming and 'telling faults' in letters communicated among eighteenth-century Methodists, see Clare Brant, *Eighteenth-Century Letters and British Culture* (Basingstoke, 2006), 321–2.
54 BL, MS Sloane 922, fol. 134.
55 Ibid., fol. 132; Booy (ed.), *The Notebooks*, 258–9.
56 Ibid., 259; BL, MS Sloane 922, fos. 132, 138 ('This letter with two books and all the sermons that you have heard shall rise up in judgment and be a witnesse against you at the great day of judgment and shall adde to your torments in hell leaving you without excuse'.) See also Letters to Goodman Cox and Mr. Wade, fos. 143, 151.

57 Booy (ed.), *The Notebooks*, 258; BL, MS Sloane 922, fol. 132.
58 Ibid., fos. 148, 138.
59 Ibid., fos. 134, 150, 151.
60 Ibid., fol. 97; Booy (ed.), *The Notebooks*, 235; Seaver, *Wallington's World*, 95–9.
61 BL, MS Sloane 922, fol. 2.
62 Booy (ed.), *The Notebooks*, 241. See also letters to Master Edward Brown and James Cole, BL, MS Sloane 922, fos. 144–5, 174.
63 Ibid., fos. 174–5.
64 Ibid., fos. 80, 83.
65 Ibid., fol. 107.
66 For a letter written by Goodman Wilshmore, a trader in Nottingham, revealing his sense of shame and despair in his wayward son, see Ibid, fol. 120. For the role of letters in offering comfort and soothing despair among varied denominations in the eighteenth century, see Brant, *Eighteenth-Century Letters*, 318–23.
67 Daybell, *Women Letter-Writers*, 183, 184–7, quotation on 186. For women approaching their husbands with expressions of apology, being 'sory and ashamed' when actually criticizing them, see Thomas, *If I Lose Mine Honour*, 101–2.
68 Daybell, *Women Letter-Writers*, 185–6; Thomas, *If I lose Mine Honour*, 119. For elite women's honour, which they defended aggressively, using shame and the denigration of those offending them, see Pollock, 'Honor, Gender, and Reconciliation', 21–6; Thomas, *If I Lose Mine Honour*, Chap. 2, 76–124.
69 BL, Add. 72516, Trumbull Papers, Ann Dormer letters 1685–8; Mary E. O'Connor, 'Dormer, Anne (1648?–1695)', Oxford Dictionary of National Biography, online edition, https://www.oxforddnb.com. See also Sara Mendelson, 'Neighbourhood as Female Community in the Life of Anne Dormer', in Susan Broomhall and Stephanie Tarbin (eds.), *Women, identities and communities in early modern Europe* (Ashgate, 2008), 153–5.
70 BL, Add. 72516, fol. 163.
71 Ibid., fos. 169, 194.
72 Ibid., fol. 194.
73 Ibid., fos. 169, 165.
74 Ibid., fol. 169.
75 Ibid., fos. 163, 169.
76 Ibid., fos. 156, 190.
77 Foyster, *Marital Violence*, 141; Ben-Amos, *Culture of Giving*, 17–44.
78 For a letter of reproach from a son to his mother, see Linda A. Pollock, 'Anger and the Negotiation of Relationships in Early Modern England', *Historical Journal*, 47 (2004), 580; ('Are you three score and xvii yeares of agge and have noe better consyence, for shame goodmother for sake all worldly covetousenes and seek to serve god in trewth and to gett the good will of your neyghbours and to speake of yor chylderen wele that th[ey] may feare you and love you and hard[en] not their hartes agaynst you ... is this motherly dealinge, is not this unnaturall dealinge, let the world judge').

# 4 Commercial enterprise and exchange

The early modern era witnessed an immense expansion of commercial enterprise and trade, with an ever-increasing volume of goods travelling greater distances on hugely expanding trading routes, throughout England, Europe, and overseas. These fast-growing trade routes posed special challenges for traders. In a precarious economy lacking formal means of insurance or adequate technologies of transport and communication, long-distance trade presented numerous risks and required trustworthy agents and customers on whom a merchant could rely. An ability to keep promises and to gain the trust of others was indispensable for the conduct of trade.[1]

As a large body of research has shown, by the late sixteenth century a variety of formal and informal institutions created the conditions for establishing trust and enforcing commercial contracts and obligations. A broad spectrum of networks – based on family or religious and ethnic groups – generated 'reputational mechanisms', which offered rewards for trustworthiness while imposing sanctions on those who violated the trust of fellow members. The correspondence exchanged within such networks was uniquely important not only for providing a written record of transactions, but also for communicating precious information on market conditions or the aptitude and trustworthiness of agents and distant merchants. In addition, from the early middle ages there existed a host of more formal institutions that helped enforce commercial obligations and agreements. These included diverse contractual instruments, written records and accounts, as well as a system of courts – state, municipal, and local – that were, by the late sixteenth century, increasingly used to settle commercial disputes and debt litigation. Legal conventions and traditions were also effective in setting down rules of conduct, conveying expectations and enhancing broadly shared norms of behaviour.[2]

For all their importance in inducing trust and compliance with rules, the range of available institutions and networks did not wholly eliminate the uncertainty of economic transactions and ventures. As evidence from merchant correspondences indicates, the honesty and trustworthiness of associates remained deep concerns for traders well into the eighteenth century. 'But if you let any money, prey take care who you let it to, that he be a secure man, for now a days a great many comes out that are not worth a groat' – was a widespread sentiment that surfaced in merchant letters.[3]

DOI: 10.4324/9781003226871-5

Commercial networks in England and overseas did not always generate well-defined, closely regulated or exclusive units of exchange of the kind ordinarily associated with tight-knit kin or ethnic and religious groups. Instead, they formed loose, semi-open aggregations that reached at times distant locations, encompassing strangers.[4] Risks and hazards of trade through losses due to weather conditions, or as a result of careless handling of cargoes, fraud, and other human failings persisted, and dealings were frequently marked by suspicion and wariness over the betrayal of trust, even among kin and friends. Newly evolved forms of maritime insurance remained limited to overseas trade and particularly precious goods, and they could not wholly alleviate the threat of fraud; nor did the increased use of overseas and inland bills of exchange entirely address the hazards resulting from refusals to accept bills, protests, and limitations on information regarding the actions of sometimes remotely located agents. As for the legal system and the courts, for all their ability to impose sanctions and provide a framework that shaped traders' conduct and choice of action even outside the court, their role, too, was limited. As research has shown, litigation presented its own risks and tended to be used only as a last resort, if at all.[5] All of these considerations suggest that despite the safeguards offered by an elaborate set of institutions, trust was by no means a given or easily achieved and sustained.

It is against this background of the precariousness of trust that we will assess the pervasive use of shaming and shame, as it is revealed in letters merchants dispatched to one another. Based on the correspondences of several merchants operating in England and overseas over the course of the seventeenth and early eighteenth century, this chapter explores the circumstances and disputes that gave rise to shame, the manner and rhetoric through which shame was applied, the forms it took, and the responses it triggered in traders. As we shall see, shaming touched on essential mercantile values and assets, which, combined with a distinctive type of personalized shame, proved potent not only in inflicting penalties but also in enforcing obligations, cultivating loyalties and enhancing trust.

## Damaged reputations

The ability of merchants to gain the trust of their associates and establish their reliability depended first and foremost on their reputation, which remained 'the life and soul of … trade', as Daniel Defoe put it, well into the eighteenth century.[6] Reputation for 'good carriage' was built on the perception and observation of others – on conduct tested and monitored through information disseminated by word of mouth and in correspondences, one of the most important roles of which was to keep track of associates' conduct and affairs. Appraisals and character judgements passed between traders routinely, and these were crucial for ascertaining the probity of a trader and sustaining his reputation. 'But I trust Mr Askwith to bee soe honest a man, that if hee mett not with the party hee returned [the merchandize] unto you', as the young merchant Thomas Rogers wrote to William Hurt in a letter from Surat in early 1632. In the same letter, Rogers also related the case of John Kingstone, purser of the ship *Bart*, whom he accused of breaking his promise to put the debt owed to Hurt on record– '[he] hath done noething therein' – upon which Rogers resolutely concluded: 'therefore you may not depend on him herein'.[7]

The information and appraisals that were critical for ascertaining reliability were also crucial for exposing misconduct and inflicting shame. Merchant letters offer many instances of advice given to associates to withdraw their trust from those whose reputation had gone bad, often bolstered by unequivocal judgments and strong gestures of shaming. 'As for Pennicott, you know what a poor wretch it is. Wherefore we much wonder you'l trust such people, and had not better make your remittances in England directly in gold' – was how the attorneys and kin of John Scattergood worded their advice.[8] Letters invariably contained damaging reports of incompetence and misconduct, spreading rumours initially aired in public or at the London exchange, castigating alleged wrongdoers and relaying public denunciations that inflicted humiliation and exposed a trader's disgrace. Following the resolution of a dispute with his associate, Captain Greenhaugh, regarding their respective commissions, the merchant John Scattergood announced in a letter to his associate Charles Boone: 'I gained my point to goe head and he [Greenhaugh] was laughed at by most people'. Scattergood then concluded with his personal judgement: 'I find that I shall have but a troublesome companion of him, but I am resolved not to bate him an inch'.[9]

Traders who spread information on the misconduct and shame of others were simultaneously extremely apprehensive about their own reputation, worrying that they may become the object of shaming accusations or rumours based on some form of failure or misdeed. Such accusations provoked their instant reaction, displaying a need to dispel any rumour that might defame their character and dent their reputation. 'As baser a notorious lye as ever was invented … their story is [as] improbable as false', as John Moore's agent in Hull reacted to Moore's claims that he misled their associates regarding Moore's intentions towards them.[10] Traders' letters indicate that they took great care in replying to any claim that might wreak shame and sully their reputation, invariably expressing protest or insult, extending emphatic apologies, or begging to counter the claims, offering detailed refutations and counter-allegations that put the shame of misconduct on others while confirming their own fairness and exemplary character. Upon arriving in Balasore during his trading venture to India, Isaac Lawrence received information – 'word of mouth' – that his associate Edward Read had accused him of overcharging the goods he, Lawrence, had purchased for him in Surat, Lawrence immediately dispatched a letter to Read in which he gave a detailed account designed to vindicate himself – 'as if I had wronged you in an overcharge of what [the goods] cost'. Offering submissive gestures and pleas, Lawrence proclaimed his reputation for fairness: 'I stand upon my reputation as much as any man whatever'. On the same day, Lawrence also dispatched a letter to a prominent merchant and governor in the Bay of Bengal ('Mr Mathias President'), in which he laid out the affair in detail and justified his dealings, first denouncing Read for failing to confront him personally, then claiming his disinclination to cheat – 'I was ever guilty of any such dirty actions' – pleading honesty 'which tis well known I ever profest'.[11]

Unease about shame and reputational damage was particularly pronounced in the case of failure to pay debts or bills, widely perceived as not only a breach of promise but also as forfeiting the 'good opinion' of others. Under such circumstances, requests for postponement of debts could cast a long shadow over traders' reputations and result in poignant, if not humiliating, pleas designed to avoid the shame of being known to have made the appeal. Merchants sometimes urged that their financial difficulties be kept secret and out of the public eye; 'I only begg that you in return would not let me suffer in my reputation', the trader Alexander Orme put it in a letter to John Scattergood, in which he appealed to him to postpone a large debt he owed.[12] Overdue payments would affect the standing and reputation of the creditors themselves, as was the case of Philip Williams, the young Livorno factor of Henry Garway, who fell behind the repayment of his debts. Williams, still obligated to the senior merchant for his patronage and assistance, wrote an apologetic letter in which he asked 'brother Garway' to pay his dues by allowing him, Williams, to draw a bill on him in London. Williams then promised to make a convenient arrangement and 'extinguish your debt of interest by degrees', and invoked Garway's obligation towards him – 'I know you expect not your factor should suffer' – applying further pressure by pointing to the repercussions Garway's refusal might have on his own inability to pay other merchants their dues. 'And (I think I need not tell you) tis my credit only lies at stake, and you know it is but … [a] bud, if it bee apparent it will not thrive, decay it may'.[13]

The vulnerability of reputational standing and the shame of being known to have failed or been led astray could also be deployed as a form of deterrence to enforce compliance, a figure of 'forward-looking' shame treatment that presented correspondents with the potential consequences of their deeds. Merchant letters habitually contained warnings, threats, and reminders of the risks to reputation caused by misconduct. '[It] … will be registered to your shame shall you p[e]rish in this your politick' – was how Isaac Lawrence confronted William Hyde, an associate in Naples whom he accused of conspiring with another trader by concealing information regarding the whereabouts of his goods.[14] In his account to his agent in Newcastle, merchant Michael Mitford claimed that an associate of theirs, Robert Bailey, overcharged the costs of a voyage handled by Mr Knipe. Mitford, who contended that he had met Knipe and was persuaded by the soundness of the latter's allegations, informed his Newcastle associate, William Proctor, that he thought the costs were 'unjust', and moreover, that 'Baily is either knave or fool if not both', adding that he should pay the costs or agree to a compromise. He then further threatened, clearly assuming the information would be passed on to Bailey, that the latter would 'be condemned by everyone if he does not comply [and] will certainly suffer severly for it with due respect'.[15]

Once a trader was rumoured or suspected to have been engaged in misconduct or his noncompliance became exposed, he was liable to face distrust and bound to lose clients and associates. It must be emphasized that a damaged reputation and public exposure did not instantly reduce shamed traders' fortunes or end their careers. Information about misconduct could travel slowly and wrongdoings were at times kept in relative isolation, or circulated no further than among family members and a group of associates. While merchants tended to build their ties around a core network of agents, customers, and suppliers, their commercial relations could become widespread, involving dozens and hundreds of correspondents in England and abroad. As some of these correspondents had little or no contact with one another, transgressions could still occasionally remain only partially known.[16] Some merchants, moreover, willingly submitted to rumours that undermined their reputation, especially when faced with conflicting interests and if they determined that it was worth their while to breach the trust of one client in order to transfer their allegiance elsewhere. Others displayed *shamelessness*, openly disregarding norms of proper conduct and upholding obligations, taking advantage of their social standing and privileged status to act with impunity and ignore the appeals of creditors, using intimidation and displaying the type of attitude that earned them a reputation for being 'tough' and not open to negotiation. In a letter to John Lancelott, Philip Williams described an incident in Constantinople involving a 'grand difference' between 'my Lord Amber Mr Middleton' and several merchants who refused to pay a bill he presented, an action Williams condoned, as he thought these merchants 'have a greate deale of reason' for denying the conditions under which it was signed. Mr Middleton's reaction appears to have been ferocious. 'His Lordship uses a very sever way with them ... I tell thee I have beene made to tremble ... such hath been the malignity of the phrase as well as the over passionate expression'.[17]

Though Middleton's strategy of intimidation and verbal abuse appears to have succeeded in coercing others to comply and pay the bill, the information about the incident spread and its effects may well have eventually been counterproductive. Williams clearly presumed his correspondent, John Lancelott, was bound to know about Middleton's shameless conduct – 'I question not but you have already heard of this business if not you will doe shortly at large'. Williams thought that given Middleton's social position ('but his power is not to bee questioned amongst such as are newtrals') he would do well to avoid doing business with him and he resolved to stay away, conjecturing that others were likely to do the same:

[His] rigorous proceedings make many men more weary of the place ... I for my part ... wish myself in a more quiet climate, where such buzzing of contentions may not affright mine eares, which never were acquainted till I came hither with other than peaceable speeches free from violent and unsavory passion.

The incident indicates the difficulties Williams encountered among merchants in Constantinople, from where he moved to Livorno sometime later.[18]

Though the effectiveness of shame and reputational damage in curbing misconduct had its limits, and some merchants were never subject to it, overall the circulation of information regarding transgressions and breach of rules could have grave consequences for traders' fortunes and careers, as was the case of William Jearsey, a merchant in India (Masulipatam) who made his fortune in the diamond trade during the 1700s. When his deception was discovered and rumours spread among London's trading community, Jearsey's trade was greatly reduced and his commercial fleet substantially diminished; he ceased to be a leading merchant there.[19] More severe were the repercussions in the case of the Livorno associate of Isaac Lawrence, Mr Lee, whom Lawrence accused of embezzling the goods he had left with him. As Lawrence described in detail in letters dispatched in September 1672 to several associates in Livorno and Naples, instead of selling the goods and transferring the money to Lawrence's account as he had promised, Lee, with the conniving assistance of another associate, William Hyde, and several Jewish merchants ('I may chance to quit scores with those rogues the Jews' – he declared) fraudulently arranged for the goods to be confiscated and claimed Lawrence had to clear them first, before putting them up for sale. Lawrence's attempts at discovering the circumstances of the confiscation and recovering the goods by turning to associates in Livorno were to no avail, and he eventually turned to the London court, whereby Lee was forced to return to England to stand trial. Upon his arrival and before the judicial proceedings began, his household goods in Livorno had already been offered for sale, their value diminished as a consequence of the rumours of the affair. 'He setts a high value on it … a relique of his Pride', as Lawrence put it, further relating Lee's dire situation among associates and friends by the time he arrived in London:

> He hath bitterly lost himself here as to the title of a trusty and honest man, whatever he sayth here in relation to his affairs, it carryes noe better character with it then fabulous and falce, the great complaint of his nearest and dearest relations and friends which I am heartily sorry for, and the more since it hath been the prime occasion of all his present troubles out of which I pray God Almighty to deliver him … I doe not believe since his being in England he hath wrote a line to any of his friends abroad, though I have … prest him to it, and had as many promises from him, he hath noe care to preserve any mans friendship. I am sure without it his case will be but desperate.

While Lawrence himself was able to recover some of his goods in Livorno, his associate Lee not only faced legal charges but was also subject to public shaming in its harshest punitive form. Excluded from trade and subject to social isolation, Lee suffered a deep sense of shame, evident, as Lawrence saw it, in his loss of will and courage to face his friends.[20]

Lawrence's own career did not fare well either, and while he never faced legal charges of the kind encountered by Lee, his enterprise and reputation suffered badly in the ensuing years. By early 1677 he embarked on a voyage to India where, with the assistance of his London connections at the East India Company, he established ties in Bengal. As his extensive correspondence indicates, his enterprise was riddled with hardship and frustrations due to physical afflictions, unfavourable market conditions and, crucially, the difficulty he experienced establishing reliable contacts and building the kind of trust that would earn him a steady reputation among the English trading community on the Coromandel Coast and Surat. Upon his arrival, he had already acquired substantial connections in London and Livorno and managed to establish agency relations with merchants in east India and Persia. Yet overall his connections were loose and shifty, and his letters commonly reflect his attempts to revive early trading ties – 'Pray redeeme this neglect by a more exact correspondence in future', as he wrote to a London associate, or sending recurrent appeals in search of 'correspondence and friendship'.[21] Some of his dealings escalated into hostile disputes, and his letters indicate ample grievances and worries about shame and blame: 'their letters were full of expressions of disgust and anger with me ... as if I had done [them] an unparalleled injury'. Time and again he wrote to defend his good name and reputation against 'inconsiderate discourses' and the shaming he suffered from traders who sent 'complaints against me to [their] correspondents here, as if I had been a criminall of a rebellion and treason'. By early 1678 he was still in search of a new correspondent, reporting bitterly to his agent in Bombay about his dissatisfaction with another agent in Isfahan, where 'my goods remayne ... unsold and not one small price in returnes, the greatest disappointment I ever mett in all my life'. Turning to the East India Company for assistance in a final bid to promote his business by moving to Gombroon, Lawrence arranged for the transfer of his affairs, but shortly after his arrival there in March 1679, he despaired and decided to abandon the enterprise and return to Europe.[22]

In one of his last letters from Gombroon, Lawrence wrote emotively to his associate in Madras, James Bridger, recounting the hardship and difficulties he endured, pointing again to the blame and the complaints against him coming from traders in Surat, which he now attributed to their 'jealosies' over the favourable treatment he had received from the East India Company when it promoted his move to Gombroon. The letter conveyed his overwhelming sense of insult, frustration, and shame in failing the trust of these Surat traders. Informing Bridger about his decision to abandon the Company's employ 'which I am not longer ambitious to have that honour of', he asserted that such a move was the only possible route to reclaim his reputation, whereby 'the mouths of all these ill-natured people will be stopped'.[23]

## Honour, morality, proficiency

The shame of the recalcitrant merchant was not only tied to his public exposure and the injurious opinion of others. What people said also mattered because it hurt the traders' sense of themselves, harming their self-image, self-worth, or the sense of who they were. External and internal triggers of shame were inseparable; shaming needed to be answered and rectified not only because it carried potential punitive sanctions that might lead to exclusion from trade or financial ruin, but also because it touched and reflected on the merchant's social and moral world and the values and beliefs with which it was imbued.

Beliefs and values associated with mercantile conduct had long been articulated in a tradition of writing on trade and commerce, through which specialized knowledge, infused with assumptions regarding mercantile conduct and manners, was disseminated. *The Marchants Avizo* (1589), an early manual for young apprentices and factors embarking on a career overseas, set the standard for later guides by providing instruction of the principles of buying and selling, along with basic knowledge of weights, measures, currency or bills of exchange, all set within a broad moral frame that placed acts of buying and selling in the context of Christian duty, piety, and civility – virtue, good manners, gentleness and humility: 'Show yourself lowly and courteous ... if any rude and common sort of people will be chance offer you anie abuse or wrong, appease them againe rather by sufferance and gentlenesse, than by revenge'.[24] In the ensuing decades, a growing body of commercial literature offered specialized knowledge on the various components of trade, with publications on topics ranging from education and choice of calling to economic thinking, blending information with morality, and extolling the value of virtuous, fair dealing or an ethic of 'sympathy, concordance, and agreement'.[25] By the late seventeenth century, an enormously increased commercial literature presented readers with an elaborate, yet essentially similar mix of information and specialized knowledge, such as bookkeeping and commercial terminology, all firmly embedded in religious morality and civil mores. Richard Steele's *The Tradesman's Calling*, a popular handbook published in 1684, informed its readers on commerce while at the same time propagating politeness – prudence, discretion – alongside religious piety and the values of diligence, justice, veracity, 'shunning all unjust commendations', or 'abhorring untruth'. Other manuals were more practically oriented, but they, too, promoted a range of characteristics that combined trade knowledge and skill with piety and politeness – prudence, punctuality, justice, fair dealing, and so on.[26]

These idealized notions and the blend of commercial know-how, religious instruction, and civil mores they propagated did not directly impinge on the traders' daily interactions and conduct. As traders' correspondences indicate, in their everyday practice and exchanges they were, for the most part, preoccupied with practical concerns, managing transactions and vigorously pursuing their commercial interests. Their letters reveal apprehension about market conditions, tension between associates and suspicion about breaches of rules and dishonesty, pointing to disagreements that did not quite reflect 'sympathy, concordance, and agreement' or other qualities advocated by authors in the prescriptive literature. Nevertheless, and for all that actual practice offered no simple mirror image of prescribed norms, merchants' letters do show that in handling their affairs and managing their relationships, traders made use of a core notion of proper and improper behaviour, drawing on the set of prescribed values by selecting and modifying it according to needs and circumstances. Behaviour that adhered to certain values was referred to as 'honourable', that is, it not only earned a merchant the good opinion of others, but also added to his internal sense of standing, professionalism, and moral worth. Improper behavior signalled a breach of mores and called for dishonour and disrespect, a shaming treatment that could undermine honour, self-esteem, or pride. The shaming did not necessarily publicly expose traders and could remain within the purview of a small group of two or three associates, but it did involve reproach and strong moralizing that triggered negative feelings of hurt, insult, anger, or embarrassment, and shame. Moralizing appealed to a sense of unsuitable behaviour, presenting conduct as unbecoming, shameful, or a disgrace; it was 'ungentlemanly' or 'unchristian', and, referring to merchant values specifically, it was 'unmerchantlike'. 'My demands are noe other then such as are faire and just and merchant like', as John Oldbury, a London merchant, put it to his Livorno associate Ephraim Skinner.[27]

The role of honour, shame, and morality in managing personal interactions between traders can be illustrated with the case of John Scattergood, a merchant who spent most of his life and career in India. Born in Madras in 1685 when the city had already emerged as a large entrepôt of regional and international trade, Scattergood was educated in London and returned to India, where he began to act as supercargo on privately-owned ships and traded in commodities such as silks, quicksilver, pearls, tea, or chinaware on his own. By 1710, he was part or full owner of several ships, and his connections and correspondents encompassed merchants in Madras and Bengal, Surat, Bombay, Malabar, and Canton. His copious letters show not only the vigour and ruthlessness with which he pursued his career and amassed substantial fortunes, but also his social standing and intricate set of connections among the close-knit network of the gentleman-merchants acting between London and Madras. The letters also point to his sense of obligation to family, kin, and associates, as well as his self-esteem and honour which he earned, so he believed, through his experience and career as a merchant overseas. In his papers he also professed a notion of civic duty, of the kind current among the gentlemanly class at the time.[28]

Above all, Scattergood's honour related to the manner in which he handled his affairs and managed the trust of his associates. This came fully to the fore in an incident in 1717/18, when his three partners and owners of the *Bonita*, a China-bound ship on which he acted as supercargo, accused him of deceit, claiming that he deliberately misled them into believing he was invested in the voyage so that he might collect a share of the profit. Moreover, so they asserted, he did not provide an accurate picture of the profits made on the voyage and kept a large portion of it (allegedly his commission came to £3000) for himself and his associate, Thomas Harris. The letter that detailed their allegations was full of shaming and rebuke.

Chiding him on his apparent ignorance of the difference between profits in voyages conducted for the East India company, where benefits came solely in the form of a wage, and private ones like theirs whereby profits were divided according to shares, they proclaimed that concealing the profits and not paying their due share amounted to fraud and a breach of their honour and trust. 'As your owners have dealt so honourably by you, trusting entirely to you, they don't suppose but that you will bring such freight to their account', reiterating that

> The gentlemen thought this was not dealing with 'em with the same openness as they had dealt with you, nor according to the generous trust and confidence repos'd in you, for if you thought there was nothing amiss in not being concern'd in the ship, surely you might have trust'd such owners with so indifferent an affair, when they have trusted all to your honour and honesty'.[29]

As soon as the allegations reached him, Scattergood sent a letter to one of his partners, Francis Chamberlain, appealing to him as 'you being one that I have particular obligations to[o] makes me trouble you with this' and attempting to straighten out things and 'sett matters in a true light'. Chamberlain responded with a measure of restraint and refrained from full affront, instructing Scattergood to continue his voyage. He subsequently appears to have settled with Scattergood on some form of a financial arrangement and compensation.[30] As for the two other partners, the conflict with them became more fraught. While boasting that his connections extended to Madras and elsewhere – 'I have friends in abundance in Madrass Bengal and Surat, in either of those places I should not want for an employ' – Scattergood was clearly alarmed by their shaming treatment, which not only threatened his connections but severely damaged his sense of personal honour and pride. In his letter to them he reiterated his claims and vehemently denounced their reliance on 'barbarous usage' and rumours, furiously responding to their allegations that his conduct was dishonourable and 'unmerchantlike':

> You complain that we had not acted as merchants and had used you but indifferently ... I dare affirm that you would have mett but with very few men that could have managed your affairs better than us. As for using you ill, it never inter'd in our thoughts ... I do not understand what you mean about the word honour, except you thought we had none and so you design'd to instill it into us. You tell us you have dealt honourable by us, and I think (with very good reason) that we have delt as honourable by you for you are as much beholden to us for venturing our lives and working for you as we are for our imployments, for a labourour is always worthy of his hire.

Also evident was the deep insult and shame resulting from his partners' moralizing and overly didactic tone, which Scattergood perceived as aimed at both his integrity and skill. Instructing him on the difference between the East India Company voyages and their private venture, as if he did not know the difference between the two, was condescending and belittling, 'as if we were boys or not honest men'.[31]

Having declared his fury and insult over the violation of his honour, which obliged him to respond in kind – 'Truly gentlemen you have been very smart upon us, which made me answer as smartly', as he put it bluntly – Scattergood then took a more placatory approach in an attempt at reconciliation, reminiscent of his earlier mentioned letter to Chamberlain. Downplaying, if not wholly trivializing his initial proclamations, he now progressed to a more personal and less aggressive tone, expressing disappointment with 'especially … you two who I take to be my true friends and would prevent all suspicions or doubts that may lay upon you to our Prejudice'. He then expressed his willingness to comply, resorting to a temperate and subdued form of shame: 'Now I have discharged my fire, I am as coole as a militia musket … Therefore shall not [say] any more of the matter, but always to act so that you never may have any complaint against us'.[32] This more deferential mode, however, did not succeed in appeasing his partners, who, while not taking up legal proceedings, still resigned as his attorneys and do not appear to have maintained further contact with him.

This type of shaming, which took the form of strong moralizing aimed at an associate's integrity and credibility, could take different forms and, in terms of managing interactions between associates, have varied outcomes. Shaming an associate could target honour that was rooted in values of honesty or decency, or it could appeal to the honour earned in civil manners, charitable conduct, commercial skill, and acumen. Issues of proficiency and commercial judgement appear to have been particularly prominent in interactions between traders who were relative strangers or were not initially well known to each other, whereby the shaming that was aimed at the traders' sense of pride and honour in their skill functioned less as a form of punishment and more to assuage mutual suspicions, enforce greater cooperation and engender long-term relations of trust.

A case in point is the correspondence between William Turner, a London merchant-tailor who, in the 1660s, acted as alderman, sheriff and Lord Mayor, and his chief foreign clients and associates, the Paris firm of Boquelin and Sons. The correspondence between these merchants points to the strain and suspicion often inherent in the lucrative but volatile market for silks, with which they were engaged. In letter after letter Boquelin charged Turner with incompetency, stating that he was 'ill satisfied in the sale of the goods', bearing 'a great deal of discontent', and criticizing Turner for being 'insensible'. He also accused Turner of dishonesty, as when Turner allegedly dispatched goods (cloth) lying in his shop instead of buying them at Blackwell Hall as he was obliged to do. In his responses, Turner offered a mix of apologetics, self-defence, and flattery; 'I shall henceforth wave my and conforme unto yours'; 'I have great esteeme of you then to misdoubt anything that you saye', offering pronounced expressions of insult and hurt pride; 'I am very sure that noe body sells at better advantage then I doe', he writes repeatedly.[33]

Above all, Turner responded to Boquelin's charges of incompetence with counteraccusations and a great deal of moralizing and rebuke of his own – a sort of reciprocal shame treatment to counter Boquelin's shame and blame. Disparaging Boquelin for his unmerchantlike conduct, Turner denounced the charges as petty and not 'fit for discourse', amounting to lack of civility and want of 'charity'. He repeatedly referred to Boquelin's own lack of professionalism, accusing him of failing to send the proper silks or understand the market and its conditions in London. The silks dispatched by Boquelin were 'a mere drugg', displaying the wrong pattern (flowered tabys) and clashing with current London fashion. Refusing to apologize for his scornful words – '[I] beg pardon when I am soe just as to pay every man in his own coyne' – he proceeded by wavering between didactic instructions on how to handle profits, self-righteous rebuke ('there is nothing more against my inclinations then to bee always dislikeing and complyning'), to praise, rewards, warnings, commands, and threats. 'If you be exact in following my order ... our business [will] goe on cheerfully'; 'I am very glad you assure me by your letter to bee more scrupulous in bying then hitherto you have bin it is what gives courage and will make some amends for the deadnesse of the trade'. He also appealed directly to Boquelin's sense of shame and guilt for his apparent role in exposing Turner himself to the shaming of others. As he put it in a letter from June 1663, 'severall merchants ... tells mee they are old fashion laces and that the prices are soe deare as that they dare not meddle with them'; or in another similar instance, 'I am ashamed ... to shew the merchant such [goods]'.[34]

The entire exchange involving to-and-fro mutual shaming and moralizing persisted over the course of several years, with Boquelin sending silks and (according to Turner) disregarding specific orders and requests, and Turner selling some of the silks or else retaining them in his shop, but either way at a loss, as he claimed. The shaming and moralizing in the discourse of the two associates thus fuelled an ongoing exchange and collaboration in the face of difficulties and volatile profits, offering them a means for working out and overcoming suspicions and disputes, allowing them to preserve their sense of pride, honour, and proficiency, and over time to sustain their ties and mutual allegiances. By the summer of 1663, Turner was still declaring his losses through diminishing profits and reclaiming once again his honour, announcing that 'without vanity I can [say] it no man in England makes better clothes [than] I sell'. Yet when faced with the harshest blame and shame for returning unsold silks to Paris, his moralizing abated and he resorted to neither self-defence and flattery nor moralizing and shame, choosing instead a rather more personal appeal:

> I will say no more to make appear that neither an intent to reconquer my orders nor because I am difficult to please did give the occasions ... I do not think two pieces of damask worth so many words between us friends and therefore since you are so much concerned for it be pleased to returne me the factorie of them.[35]

Always facing the tests of daily conduct and its pressures, the relationship between the two traders became more personal and cooperative.

Moralizing and shame treatment that called for dishonour by threatening a trader's sense of morality and proficiency recurred under a range of circumstances and conflicts, including those involving agency relations, commissions, payment of bills, credit, and debts. When Philip Williams refused to accept a bill of exchange from his correspondent, he proceeded to instruct him on how to handle bills, charging him with dishonesty, and reflecting on his sense of insult and shame: 'you know how wisely such an instrument should be dealt withal ... nor could I think [it] a mistake either, for ... both jointly and particularly I had to show ... I was mistrusted'.[36] Threats to one's sense of honour were not exclusive to interactions involving lucrative and large-scale trading ventures, nor did they come solely in the form of sanctions, as in refusals to accept bills. They were vital to the management of interactions between people in various trades, men and occasionally women, acting as a deterrent and inducing greater cooperation and trust. 'That bill should be paid and I leave it to you, not doubting but you will do what becomes you in that matter', wrote merchant Symson to Mrs Irton, who long delayed an old debt but subsequently settled her account.[37]

Well into the mid- and late eighteenth century, honour and shame pervaded merchant letters and were integral to the regulation of their interactions and affairs, as was evident in the case of Joshua Johnson, who in the 1770s consigned goods from London to his partners in Maryland. When, during the prolonged recession following the financial crash of 1772, he was confronted with the demand by the London warehousemen (Mauduit, Wright & CO.) that he pay security for the shipment of his goods to America, he wrote to his partners:

> You see what a stroke credit has received and what a struggle I have had to supply you ... If any man breathing had told me once that I could have put up with such treatment I should have told him he knew me not.

Ashamed and humiliated at having lost the trust of a firm with which he had long been associated – 'I hope gratitude and honour will prompt you to use more than common exertion to enable me to extricate myself with honour', he told his partners – he was forced to comply with Maudit's demand. However, when the goods arrived at their destination he opted for retaliation, ceasing all contacts with Maudit. 'I scorn the act, but revenge calls aloud for it' he announced. He then proceeded with an all-out assault and an aggressive shame treatment of his own, confronting Maudit in person and branding him 'a mean puppy, a significant rascal and a deceitful fellow'.[38]

As for his partners, having forced them to pay and then cease all ties with Maudit, he was careful to offer them apologies so as to ensure their continued trust, and, in an attempt to reclaim his honour, also boasted, rebuked, and shamed them. Accusing them of their own failure to provide him with trusted bills that would keep his standing and reputation in London ('for indeed all your bills are good for nothing'), he justified his actions in agreeing to pay security by alluding to Maudit's intent 'in knocking us up', then announced his having gained the upper hand in the affair, which 'has made a good deal of noise', forcing Maudit to shamefully complain to other merchants about Johnson's 'ill treatment to him'. At last, Johnson signalled to his partners his own credibility and trustworthiness by announcing that another merchant, Peter Martin,

> still continues to act the most friendly part to me; he told me the other day that he had heard of Maudit's behaviour to me and that if I had but made him acquainted with it that he would have been our security.[39]

## Friendship and the personalization of shame

In describing an associate as acting 'the most friendly part' to him, Johnson articulated the single most desirable asset of the merchant, namely, his associates' binding commitments and obligations. Notions of friendship had long played an important role in sustaining relations of trust among traders, and uses of the idiom of friendship go back to medieval communities of merchants interacting in long-distance trade, and to fourteenth-century Italian traders who skilfully and elaborately used the language of 'amicizia'. In England, the concept of friendship was widely used to convey bonds of obligation in a range of social interactions, including family and kin, neighbourly ties or political patronage. Merchant letters, too, routinely made use of notions of friendship. 'Your true friend and servant', 'I am for self and son, your very much obliged friend and humble servant', 'I am for self and partner, sir, your friend and servant', 'your obliged friend and humble servant' – are some of the most common phrases with which Joseph Symson routinely signed his letters.[40]

As these correspondences amply demonstrate, friendship implied an obligation to offer a range of favours and services that tied traders in bonds of cooperation and mutual commitment. These favours invariably included information, advice, assistance in obtaining commission and assignments, recommendations, convenient credit terms, or mediation in disputes. Beliefs and expectations that friends be loyal, honest and keep their promises were particularly widespread. When Joseph Symson suspected his London correspondent might fail to pay a bill, he approached him on behalf of another merchant, Mr Gildard, stating that 'he [Gildard] is my good friend and I would not for more than I'll mention have him failed'. Powerful notions of confidentiality, too, bound merchant friends to one another; 'What you write to me you may depend shall be kept secret. Freedom prudently managed is the kindest service one friend can do for another', as Symson put it to Jeremiah Dixon, a Leeds merchant.[41]

While in some circumstances these pledges of friendship could reflect unequal relations and be associated with rank, service, and the kind of gratitude that bolstered social disparities, they were more consistently characterized by reference to notions of parity, with friends and friendship conveying a sense of equality and even enhanced affinity and empathy. As Henry Stanley wrote to correspondents who sold spices for him, in a letter requesting they reconsider their accounts:

> I desire you would do for us as for yourselves and give us what encouragement possible you can ... wee finding trade very dull and lowe and for the future you shall find us comply for your advantages as well as our owne,

Such formulations could go beyond promises of exchange and the idea of reciprocal favours, connoting a sense of closeness and empathy, putting oneself in the position of being one's 'friend', and acting accordingly. Stanley's partner, John Oldbury, applied this rhetoric while dealing with their regular correspondents, as in the case of the Plymouth merchant Daniel Barker, expressing disappointment with his performance of currant sales. Communicating latitude and approval nonetheless – 'if you cannot goe so much wee must be contended with lesse' – he then emphasized his expectations for affinity and kinship: 'pray doe for us as for your selfe, and Mr Stanley and myself shall acquiess therein and acknowledge ourselves engaged unto you'.[42]

These formulations and engagements bring to the fore the personal dimension of the trust that enduring bonds of obligation and friendship ties entailed. 'I have no friend in London that is so capable and hath always been willing to advise and assist me', as Joseph Symson put it. Long years of engagement in collaborative trading ventures could develop into special bonds of trust between merchants and a few select friends, be they their partners, major correspondents, or attorneys who handled their business affairs. 'My trusty friend John Scattergood', as George Woolaston, a merchant in Madras, referred to his newly appointed attorney, John Scattergood, in London. The two merchants had long belonged to the trading community in Fort St George and were part of a network of traders with particularly tight connections, whose personal affairs, family ties, and businesses were intimately interwoven. In a letter of instruction to Scattergood, Woolaston referred to Scattergood's wife Arabella and to the young daughter they had left behind in Fort St George when moving to London in 1714, and who was being raised and cared for by a Mrs Ramsden and other friends in the local trading community: 'Pray give my most humble Service to your lady and tell [her] your little girl was very well when I saw her last which was about ten days ago'.[43]

Underlying some of these formulations and appeals to friendship there still lurked a measure of uncertainty, and letters sometimes disclosed traders' wariness and apprehension over the durability and security, even of close and intimate ties. 'I assure I desire to doe for you as myself', John

Oldbury wrote to his partner, Henry Stanley, in his response to the latter's report from Malaga. Inserted almost imperceptibly in a long list of instructions regarding sales and transactions – an interposition that abruptly diverted from the flow of more practical contents of the letter – this gesture also betrayed Oldbury's hidden insecurity regarding a friendship that could never be fully taken for granted or assumed, needing constant assurances and reminders in the face of obstacles and the hazards of trading ventures, even among close associates and friends. The letter opened with a response to his partner's account of his dealings in Malaga, where Stanley apparently encountered considerable difficulties, alleging misconduct and despairingly referring to the 'unkindnesses' he had met with among traders there. Oldbury responded with sympathy, consoling Stanley by reminding him that there were still some worthy merchants – 'though some are believed not to be soe bad as you represented' – and then promptly counselling him to learn a lesson from the entire affair. 'I hope this will be warning to you for the future whom to trust', he wrote. These types of assertions of friendship, inadvertently revealing insecurity about trust, can be found in various merchant correspondences. In a letter dispatched from Virginia in August 1675, William Byrd wrote to his correspondent, Mr Lamport: 'I hope it [i.e., the settling of our accounts] will have the usual effect of making us long friends', adding an assertion that betrayed uncertainty, 'it shall not be my fault if it do not, for I shall be ready to do you any service I am able'.[44]

It is against this backdrop of prevailing notions of bonding and friendship, which at the same time never wholly diminished the uncertainties of trade and options for abuse, that we should note the use of a specific mode of shaming that involved neither public shame nor sanctions, nor humiliating insult to honour, but rather a type of shame that was linked to personal allegiances. This shaming came in the form of an appeal to personal engagements and obligations, highlighting broken promises and breaches of personal bonds. As in other instances presented in this chapter, this shaming entailed moralizing and reproach over perceived misconduct, yet it explicitly targeted personal allegiances and relationships between traders, stressing familiarity and the type of bonding that combined commercial ties with family, kin, or neighbourly ties and allegiances. So, for example, when George Sitwell, an ironmaster and trader in Derbyshire, confronted Godfrey Froggatt for meddling with his business by attempting to dissuade his associate, John Fresheville, from selling the ironstone (iron ore) he had purchased from him, Sitwell was uncompromising in his shaming, accusing Frogatt of failing to respect neighbourly and personal ties. In letters addressed to Froggatt in July 1662, he mixed threats to 'appeal to the whole country' along with derision – 'its probable you take most, except your self, to be tame fooles' – and then proceeded to add moralizing and reproach; 'Doe you think this is just? Have I not paid my rent? ... It seems you have will inough ... to be basely unjust and not blush at all', leaving absolutely no doubt about the breach of bonding that was at stake. John Freshville was the landlord of the Staveley ironworks, where Sitwell habitually purchased iron, while Froggart was Freshville's long-time servant, who was attempting to interfere with the transactions of these neighbouring traders and obliging friends. Frogatt's shameless conduct and his daring not to 'blush at all' was not only perceived as a matter of failed morality but one impairing neighbourly ties, causing dispute and raising 'a difference between [Mr Freshville] and his neighbours'.[45]

In other cases, this personalization of shame focused more squarely on friendship among traders and their personal acquaintances, conveying a sense of betrayal due to failure to act 'like a friend, as like a merchant', as Philip Williams wrote to John Lancelott in Livorno. By making a distinction between a 'friend' and a 'merchant', Williams affirmed the priority and more personal qualities of the former. In a similar vein, when Joseph Symson found out that John Howard, the London apothecary and one of his clients, returned his bill of £20 (to be paid to a Liverpool merchant) on the grounds that it was due only 'at 28 days', he accused Howard of being groundlessly 'scrupled' in demanding additional charges for an alleged loss in advance pay. He then claimed to be surprised at the breach of norm – 'it is news to me to have bills returned [with such demands]' – and proceeded to reproach Howard for betraying the leniency customary among friends. 'Had you drawn on me for double the same to serve any friend at sight your bill should have been honoured and the like freedom some friends in London takes with me and I with them'.[46]

This type of personalized shame was affected first and foremost by recurrent references to the personal acquaintance and familiarity between traders and their associates. 'I know your character so well', Symson announced to the abovementioned Howard when reproaching him for forsaking their friendship, contrasting it with his own habit of offering concessions to 'friends'. To a debtor (Richard Cranage) he wrote: 'I always thought you an honest man and doubt not but you'll continue my good opinion of you by freely complying with what I now do reasonably desire'. Symson also habitually singled out the uniqueness of his relations with his correspondents, emphasizing his preferential treatment of them, and shaming clients for not appreciating his commitment. 'I do truly esteem and use you as one of my best and most favourite customers', he wrote to a Shrewsbury merchant who complained of the high prices he charged for his commodities. No less important, Symson would stress his feelings and dismay at the harm or wrong done to him personally. 'You could not have contrived a greater disappointment to me', 'Such complaints do and will make me very uneasy … when bills are due pay punctually or else [I] shall grow weary' – he repeatedly wrote to debtors and clients who were behind in their payments. At other times he mobilized his material plight and circumstances, making use of his parental obligations towards his son who will 'soon be loose from his apprenticeship' and for whom it will require 'a considerable sum to raise to set up', as he explained to Mr Stanley, whose debt had been long overdue. When Richard Cranage informed him that he would be unable to pay his debt on the due date, Symson emphatically announced this 'was very hard upon us all circumstances considered', pointedly chastising him, 'you might see what confidence I had in you, which it is pity I should suffer for'.[47]

Symson's reproach was not only highly personal, alluding to personal attributes, emotional reactions, and uniqueness of ties, but it was also cautious. An apt illustration is his letters to Robert Shard, a client and major correspondent in London, who at one point in March 1716/17 returned a bill of £47, which Symson was then obliged to repay, along with postage charge. Furious at the rejection of his bill, Symson responded with a letter that conveyed strong, yet nevertheless guarded, shaming and reprimand. His reproach was voiced almost imperceptibly amidst regular instructions, mixing business with the personal request (to deliver a small parcel of shoes to his daughter), while also professing that Shard himself was not the main person at fault. 'I attribute it to the baseness of the fellow who came to you with the bill and not to you'. Symson then announced his continued feelings of obligation – 'I shall still be ready to serve you punctually and doubt not to meet with suitable returns from you', but still insisting that Shard write back to justify his deeds, 'how it happened this bill occasioned this charge and inconvenience'. On the same day, Symson also sent a letter to John Barwick, another London correspondent and supplier of merchandise, in which he gave an account of Shard's misconduct, a sort of 'informal' record of his complaint against him. Yet Symson was also careful to request Barwick's confidentiality – 'but this to yourself' – apparently still with the intent of protecting Shard from more public damage.[48]

Such a procedure, which conveyed a private, guarded and only partially confrontational shaming, was designed to avoid public insult and humiliation, and does not appear to have been intended as an instant threat. Instead, this mode of shaming was intended to place emotional pressures that would kindle and arouse lighter feelings – embarrassment, unease, guilt – urging Shard to greater compliance and cooperation. We do not know what Shard's immediate reaction to this form of shaming and pressures was. What we know is that over the years 1710–1720, when Shard was a major client of Symson, the two associates continued their dealings and engagement in the cotton trade, exchanging multiple favours while at the same time continuing their intermittent disagreements and complaints over prices (Shard) or transactions and delayed payments of bills (Symson). Overwhelmingly, Symson approached his client with muted shaming and reproach that invoked their familiarity and intimate contact, offering apologies and aiming not only to prevent a severe rupture in their transactions, but also to cement their ties. 'You desire me to be plain with you ... of late you have not paid my bills so well ... in true friendship I have honestly and truly told you my thoughts ... hope you will not think worse of me for it', wrote Symson, urging Shard to pay his debts and bills, as he apparently did.[49]

Symson was by no means unique in his excessive resort to a personal mode of shaming that placed far less emphasis on honour and punitive sanctions than on emotional pressures designed to trigger shame and guilt for betraying his friendship. All other merchants examined in this chapter had, at one point or another, resorted to this mode of shaming, aimed at evoking embarrassment and shame, at times quite explicitly triggering guilt; 'I believe your conscience will one day tell you how greatly you have abused yourselfe and friend, when t'may be to[o] late for you to quit yourself of so much self accusing guilt', as Isaac Lawrence wrote in his outburst against William Hyde, whom he accused of conspiring in a fraud against him.[50] As in the case of Symson, a set of tactics was repeatedly used to personalize shame and enhance guilt by highlighting familiarity and personal experience, distinctive qualities of the ties between correspondents, along with the emotional reactions of the shaming person or his material plight and constraints. More distinctive phrasing and idioms of expression were also used to emphasize personalized shame by singling out individual attributes or states of mind – unease or rage, affection or love. 'I hope you will not cause the Old proverb to be verified vizt Patienta Lesa fit furor [patience provoked turns to fury]'; 'if you fail actum est de amore [it is all done with love]' – George Sitwell, the ironmonger, wrote to Lionel Copley in a letter of 26 March 1663, in which he informed him about his intention to send a friend to collect the money due to him. Distinctive pronouncements of exaggeration, bold expressions, and phrasing surfaced in his letters as well. 'How unwilling I am to have any difference between us'; 'I would rather sell my coate than break my credit'; 'I doubt whether you would do as much for me if I stood in need'; 'you may see how you deale with me, my hope of better dealing hath made an ass of me'; 'you grumble and shuffle and have tried me soe much'; 'the cheape rates I sell iron for, is a great manifestation of my reall friendship to you', 'if you should fail me then you will do me a greater injury then I think you would willingly do to an enemy'. Such language resulted in powerful appeals that elicited misgivings, scruples, and shame; 'Having dunned him until he was ashamed and desired I would draw my bill on him to some other person, which he promised he would pay', Symson's friend described their associate's reaction when confronted with a demand to pay a bill.[51]

The force of personalized shame, with its reference to friendship and personal loyalties, was also evident in the recurrent use merchants made of this type of shaming treatment, even when they appealed to or threatened their associates' sense of honour and pride. It is clear that in shaming recalcitrant associates, traders appealed to their honour along with their loyalty and friendship, and that the two modes of shaming – one undermining honour and the other touching on personal allegiances – were quite often used jointly and indiscriminately. Still, beyond the pressure applied via honour and reputation, it was through personal allegiances, friendship, and loyalties that shaming was brought to bear. When Isaac Lawrence confronted James Bridger in Surat for his long-overdue debt, he made a direct appeal to his honour – 'let these for once prevayle with you to be a man of your honour and to give Mr Day [i.e., his agent] such satisfaction'. Yet this appeal to Bridge's honour was overwhelmingly couched in personal pledging and moralizing, which Lawrence presented in the opening part of his letter, setting the entire tone of the letter in terms that evoked personal trust and friendship, elevating it to a spiritual level:

> I am very sorry for the occasion you give me by your unkindness to tell you that your proceedings have not been with me like a friend ... I am really on all occasions to doe you all good and civil offices but when [I] meet with such ungratefull receptions pardon me if I tell you they are ill behaved ... to your great shame and discredit you have so often fail'd in breach of promises that ought to have some tye and obligation upon them as being made in the face of Heaven though couch't in paper and which will blast and lay a curse upon all your affairs.[52]

## Shame and formal litigation

The powerful role of personal shame in regulating interactions and maintaining trust was also evident in merchants' overall preference to inflict repeated shaming instead of pursuing formal litigation or turning to a court of law. As already noted, the increased role of litigation in resolving commercial disputes is well recorded, and suing people for debt through the common law courts, a practice well known already in medieval times, reached a zenith by the end of the sixteenth century. Throughout the seventeenth century and beyond, traders engaged in both domestic and overseas ventures intermittently approached urban courts such as London Mayor's Court at Guildhall, and increasingly also local courts of requests, seeking to enforce agreements and claim unpaid debts.[53]

The legal system thus offered a clear route for securing contracts and enforcing commercial obligations. It affected relations and interactions between merchants even outside the arena of the court, given that suits were only infrequently brought to a judgement and the great majority of litigation was resolved outside of court. The legal process could thus act as a form of intimidation that helped enforce payments or compromise without actually going to trial, inflicting punishment or committing defendants to jail.[54] As merchants' letters also indicate, traders were well aware of the viability of litigation in deterring associates from reneging on their commitments. Information regarding prosecution at court and legal proceedings regarding debts and other disputes circulated routinely through merchant correspondence, and it was used not only to inform, but also to threaten, intimidate, or cajole associates to act in a desirable manner. As Isaac Lawrence wrote on one occasion to his associate in London:

> Mr Charleton continues to prosecute Mr Thomas Vethicks on account of what he pretends of him, and [if] [h]e doe not speedily comply with him his Protection will be broake and so layed open to the law which may bring many other great inconveniences upon him,

When a dispute broke out between Henry Stanley and John Seward, Stanley's partner wrote Seward that he 'shall endeavor to settle all things in a friendly way between you', but then warned him 'otherwise have order to proceed against you at law, which am unwilling to doe being much more desirous to make peace, by a friendly composure, and I am sure that will be most to your advantage'.[55]

For all the importance of the law in maintaining commercial relations and obligations, it is clear that most merchants shied away from it and preferred to avoid it altogether. Not only did legal proceedings incur certain costs, but they also took months and sometimes longer until suits were handled and brought to a judgement. Turning to court could also adversely affect one's own reputation and business, depicting a trader as a person tending to disputes and conflict rather than a cooperative and desirable potential partner. As John Oldbury wrote, warning John Seward he would proceed against him in court, 'I assure you I never was nor will be a foementor of differences but shall endevour as much as in me lieth to make peace'. He then revoked his threat, beseeching Seward to meet with his partner to settle their differences: 'and I hartily wish you had given him a meeting beyond sea and agreed things yourselves'. While the benefits of litigation were not always obvious and the outcome less than satisfactory, a litigator's network of friends, neighbours and potential associates might also suffer damage. So, for example, Joseph Symson instructed Adam Ashburnham to avoid pursuing a debt owed to his late son, 'for I would avoid all things that may justly reflect on him that is gone or my Robert [his second son] that is coming to settle amongst them'. Well into the early eighteenth century, merchants deliberately avoided legal proceedings so as to safeguard their reputation and connections, even at the expense of forgoing overdue debts.[56]

As merchant correspondences also indicate, semi-formal alternatives for settling disagreements, such as forms of arbitration or reliance on a personal oath, were also sometimes preferred.[57] But overall a predilection for shaming – and especially personal shaming – was evident, even as disputes turned sour and some form of arbitration was considered. When John Oldbury's offer to Ephraim Skinner to turn to a third party for reference and reconciliation was met with resistance, he applied strong and consistent shaming, never raising the possibility of going to the law. The shaming was replete with personal attributions and allusions, alongside moralizing and instructions on the proper manner of handling relations between a merchant and his agent:

> [A] principalle would be in a bad condition if factor[s] might employ whom they please for the[i]re concern ... and the principal [is] to abide by the miscarriages of those whom the factors imploy.

In his letters, dispatched between August and October 1673, Oldbury repeatedly referred to Skinner's shame in betraying his loyalty:

> I never dreamed of having to doe with any factore besides yourselves or to have been charged with doble commission ... in short I am sorry to find in you soe little inclination to doe me right ... I value my right and conclude upon your deale not fair by with me ... I desire and expect

faire dealeing from you and no more than I would doeing selfe if in your place. If you refuse this my soe faile overture [i.e., going to a reference] I shall conclude you unkind I had almost saide unjust.[58]

Other merchants used the shaming procedure regularly, without turning to a court of law or even considering the use of intermediaries and informal arbitration. Joseph Symson regularly preferred the manoeuvres and pressures of shaming. When his debtors, Isabel Hall and her daughter, left their abode for London without notifying him, he requested that one of his London correspondents, John Fisher, collect their debt 'by piecemeal', as well as reproach and put pressure on Mrs Hall to comply:

> She will own I was always ready to serve them and I did expect she would have let me know before she went ... I should not have stopped her nor her daughter. I hope they will be just to me and make me suitable returns.[59]

George Sitwell, too, preferred to apply a shame treatment rather than go to a court of law. As his letters make clear, Sitwell was hardly unaware of the option to 'vindicate his right in a legal prosecution' and he resorted to the law in several disputes he had with neighbouring landowners. Yet it is also clear that in pursuing debts owed by his associates in the iron trade, Sitwell never used the law. As is apparent from a letter dispatched to Mr Jenkinson, a London merchant, Sitwell's unequivocal view was that one was not to use the law against friends and associates, and litigation was an option only when there were 'noe great bound of friendship ... [and expectations of] favour from one to an other'. Even in his relations with his Yorkshire associate, Lionel Copley, the most unreliable trader among his associates in the iron business who was persistently behind in his (bi-annual) payments, he never turned to litigation. At one point, when he became thoroughly impatient with Copley's delays, he threatened to go to court, apologetically announcing, 'I feare you will constraine me to do that which I am loath'. Yet during the period covered by the correspondence, between 1660 and 1666, the threat was aired only once, in a letter dated April 1663. In the remaining dozens of letters Sitwell dispatched before and after that date, he repeatedly resorted to the tactics of personalized shame. Often agreeing to Copley's request to postpone payment or else offering that he borrow from another 'friend', he constantly applied pressures and personal rebuke, highlighting his emotions, sacrifices made, and financial constraints – a direct appeal to the recalcitrant Copley's sense of shame and guilt. 'Is this all the thankes I must have for straitening myself to borrow of others upon interest to pleasure yow? ... and truly I am madd enough'; 'it makes me grumble'; 'you must upon necessity pay me', as he wrote in a letter that emphasized the need to assist his son, who was about to embark overseas.[60]

Sitwell also enhanced his shame treatment by allusions to his face-to-face encounters with Copley, bluntly exposing Copley's lies and duplicity allegedly performed in person and with no apparent shame. 'When we were last together… you then seemed to be deviseing something in your thoughts', as he wrote in November 1665, referring to Copley's broken promise to send the payment instantly. Several months later, he again exposed the face-to-face deceit: 'you and I have been together since [the bill miscarried] and when we were at London it was impossible but you should know it was not paid, so that I marvaill you told me not of it'.[61] Despite a certain imperviousness to the shame inflicted by Sitwell, Copley eventually paid his dues and transactions between these regular associates continued until Sitwell's death in 1667.

## Merchant shame, Protestant shame

Underlying some of these formulations of shame there were tacit or more explicit references to religious injunctions and values. Merchants at times explicitly linked honesty, adherence to truth or keeping promises with a sacred imperative – 'being made in the face of Heaven', as Isaac Lawrence put it. The shamed trader's conduct was referred to not only as 'unmerchantlike', but also occasionally as 'ungentlemanly' or 'unchristian' – a direct reference to values of civility and religion widely propagated in epistolary and trade manuals. For some merchants, the values of honesty, prudence, diligence, and frugality could carry weight and have a particularly important spiritual meaning.[62] Their letters also attest to the overwhelming prevalence of beliefs in the powerful presence of the Almighty on earth, with many of them harbouring a sense of god's intervention in their business affairs. 'I cannot attribute to anything but God almightys providence that we got the ship of', as merchant Scattergood's brother wrote to him after nearly experiencing a shipwreck in his trading venture to Madras. Statements placing the mutual interests of associates in the hands of God, prayers for delivery from troubles by 'God almighty', or for beneficial trade were common; 'Wee commend our interests to your care, and commit you to protection of Allmighty God', Henry Stanley wrote his Naples agent, Ephraim Skinner. '[I] hope God will enable you to make [the payment]', 'I duly pray for a blessing upon your concerns both at sea and land in which I hope you'll find both pleasure and profit' – were habitual expressions. Commonly held views regarding diligence, worldly affairs, and godly intervention could be mobilized for reproach and for triggering shame, as in the case of Michael Mitford, who, in response to a request from his former factor to assist him in covering the costs of his brother's funeral, rebuked him, 'be diligent in your business and then you may expect God will permit you to earn the bread to your mouth'.[63]

For all that religion offered a broad framework within which morality was conceived and daily affairs were explicated, it is apparent that in handling their interactions and enforcing obligations, and particularly in their shaming of correspondents and associates, traders scarcely alluded to or mobilized the power of the Almighty. Scant references were made either to the encompassing and active power of God and to the shame of sin as witnessed by God, the constant observer, or to his punishing powers. Nor was the exposure of a correspondent's deceit and dishonesty deployed to instil a sense of awe and trembling before God, or to invoke the Protestant habits of diligent self-scrutiny leading to shame for one's sins – a form of shaming in which what mattered was not what others perceived, but rather what God observed. When guilt was triggered more explicitly, it was not the guilt related to innate sin, but rather one consequent on transgressions, which, while sometimes revealing deep flaws in an associate's character, were first and foremost invoked as temporary lapses that contrasted with one's habitual loyalties and proper conduct. 'I know your character so well', Symson tells one of his trusted clients (as noted above), while inflicting his personal rebuke and shame. Shaming in this light was anchored in attachments and loyalties, with a personalized form of shaming unambiguously taking precedence over more pronounced forms of Protestant shame. Moreover, when traders did voice religious sentiments in their shaming, they were accompanied, and far exceeded, by a personal form of shame.

A telling illustration in this regard is merchant James Claypoole and his shame treatment of the Rogers brothers, long-time associates and fellow Quakers in Ireland, for whom he acted as their London factor. By the time he immigrated to Philadelphia in 1683, Claypoole continued to write to the Rogers and offer his services to them. But sometime later a dispute broke out regarding the accounts Claypoole had sent the Rogers on the eve of his departure overseas. In his letter of 23 November 1684, Claypoole responded to what must have been a strongly worded letter disputing his charges and bills and accusing him of cheating, expressing great outrage, humiliation and shame at the 'scornful' judgement of the Rogers and their 'exposing [me] as a cheat and of sneaking low-spirited, shabby tricks'. His long and detailed reply was suffused with self-justification, at times with references to his religious belief, as when he announced that he had nothing to be shameful about before God: 'I can commit myself to the Lord, who knows the secrets of all hearts … I have done nothing by you but what is excusable in the sight of God and man'. Elsewhere in his letter, he alluded to the devotion of fellow friends and the possibility of his reputation being tarnished should rumours be spread among them, countering, 'you cannot expose me to root me out of the hearts of the faithful friends of truth'.[64]

Yet these sole references to his friends' faith and to shame before God were inserted amidst a long list of counter-allegations and a shaming treatment that was thoroughly and judiciously personalized. Admonishing the Rogers for failing to clarify matters with him before making their accusations, he not only justified his calculations, but repeatedly referred to their past experiences and personal interactions, pointing to the Rogers' own negligence, and making accusations regarding past failures on their part – denying him assistance, for example – failures which Claypoole now alleged he had forgiven. Like other traders when reacting to accusations and shaming, Claypoole, too, employed a myriad of shaming tactics – from threats and warnings regarding their future interactions ('and the time may come when you may [have] occasion for my friendship, as much as you despise and scorn me') – to pleas and emotional pressures that highlighted his plight: 'The trouble and perplexity of it was so great that it made me sick, and many a sorrowful, careful hour I had about it'. And again, like other merchants in similar circumstances, Claypoole did not omit to mention the personal services he had offered and sacrifices he had made in helping the Rogers, as in the case of his exhaustive attempts to settle difficulties the Rogers experienced at one point with a reluctant and aggressive debtor in London, Thomas Clutterbooke; 'for it was with the hazard of my life and estate that I got it for you' he claimed. Throughout his long letter he conveyed a strong shame treatment wholly grounded in the Rogers' betrayal of friendship:

> What, could you not remember some kindness that I have done you formerly, how I have been out of cash to serve you … And I never wronged in all the course of our dealing of 1d. So pray reflect upon yourselves that you have been too severe and unkind.

Claypoole's shaming was neither strictly religious nor was it reputational or aimed at his associates' business honour. Rather, it was deeply personal, arousing shame and guilt that were associated with forsaking bonds and mutual obligations between friends. And while in his mind obligations towards God and towards friends were almost inseparable, his deployment of shame in handling his interactions was overwhelmingly inclined to the latter.

## Signals of trust

The abundant use of personal shame in regulating mercantile affairs not only took the form of shaming others for mismanagement or fraud. Merchants often used expressions of shame and ashamedness as positive signs of their trustworthiness and commitments, indicating their proficiency and integrity, which acted as a binding force and encouraged the trust and commitment of their associates. Merchant letters sometimes profusely expressed the writer's sense of shame, a type of professed ashamedness that took a polite and apologetic form; 'I am ashamed to give you all this trouble', merchant Symson wrote when requesting an associate to offer information about one of his debtors. Such an unassuming stance and polite expression of shame could also offer an indication of one's values and adherence to norms, taking the form of a didactic attitude, as in the letter Symson wrote to his son regarding their delay in settling accounts with his associate John Ducker: 'I am ashamed that I have not answered his letter. It is what I have not been used to'. Expressions of shame as a form of regret in the wake of one's own failure could also indicate a determined wish to continue to cooperate despite lapses of trust. As Lionell Copley, repeatedly behind in paying his debts, proclaimed in his letter to Sitwell: 'I am ashamed that as yet I have not your money for yow'. Or in the case of Philip Williams, who was also lagging in his debts and forced to ask his brother to pay a part on his behalf, imploring him to remain 'private' about it, 'for it shames mee extreamely to think of such an extravagant expense'. Williams quite obviously feared the ramifications his failure to pay his debt would have for his reputation, but by vowing to have been ashamed of the situation, he indicated his moral standards and attempted to enlist his brother's empathy and support.[65]

Professed shame thus intricately acted as an assertion of affinity and loyalty, aimed at solidifying ties and reinforcing obligations. When merchant Ellingsworth informed Francis Forbes, his associate in Bombay, about the great hardship he had met in conducting business among rival merchants in Bengal, describing it as having caused a 'great deal of dissatisfaction ... with the Rogueishness of the [traders] ... and other matters worse', he claimed he was on the verge of abandoning the ship including Forbes' goods; 'I protest I would have left the ship in Bengall'. But, as he was careful to indicate, he decided against it 'for I would not have the world to say that I have done a Base action'. By announcing the reasons for his decision, Ellingsworth showed consideration for the opinion of the 'world', while also conveying his loyalty to Forbes, and, no less important, his expectations and convictions regarding mutual returns. To abandon Forbes' goods, so he insinuated, would have been inexcusable and shameful, even if not doing so put him under great pressure and at tremendous risk; sacrificing one's own interest to some degree for the sake of safeguarding ties was the epitome of trust between friends.[66]

Some merchants used instances of public shaming as gestures of sympathy and regard for the injustice suffered by an associate whom they perceived to be wrongly accused of professional misconduct. Under such circumstances, shaming could be deployed for conveying empathy and outright solidarity rather than for inflicting sanctions or harm. Following the arrest of merchant John Seward in the wake of a dispute with his Bristol associate, Mr Colston, his London associate John Oldbury wrote him a letter in which he conveyed his support, affirming that he and his partner Henry Stanley were 'both sensible of the incivilities you have received, both in being arrested for the mony before due and that it should be done in that malitioce [malicious] manner upon the exchange and are sorry for it'. In his letter to Stanley, in which Oldbury reported Seward's arrest and Colston's denial of the allegations that he was behind it, he firmly asserted his siding with, and sympathy for, Seward, proclaiming it was Colston who broke the rules and deserved to be shamed: 'I look upon it to be a base envious act in Mr Colston first to doe it so publickly and before half the time for payment of the bill was expired'.[67]

Shame was also used to express expectations of fair trading and bargains. By designating certain acts or transactions as immoral and shameful, traders imbued market activities with morality and a perception of a moral economy within which fair and reasonable play was expected. 'I blush to tell you they write from your out ports that they ... had a good price for tobacco' was how merchant John Hanbury, in his letter to William Byrd, reacted upon learning about the price at which a French merchant in Virginia, with his 'ready money', purchased tobacco from local merchants. 'As it was they [the sellers] disposed of their sweet scented [tobacco] for a near third more than the worthies of your great city'. In a subsequent letter to Byrd, he reiterated his opinion more forcefully, expressing outrage at the abuse entailed in those earlier 'wretched sales', calling the high price at which the tobacco was sold 'shameful', and the deal an 'abominable sale', even 'a scandalous prostitution', for, as he explained, it was done 'at a time when there is not enough of that commodity in towne to answer his occasions'. These expressions of abhorrence and scorn served as a counterpoint to his dealings with Byrd, from whom he procured his tobacco, highlighting his expectations for fair and reliable transactions. 'No complaint can be fairly made of your sales of my tobacco, they being much upon a level with those of other people', he wrote, commending Byrd for his proper handling of the accounts: 'there is some merit too in the quick return of your accounts, that I may know how my affairs stand'.[68]

A moralizing stance over inappropriate bargains also came to convey Hanbury's credibility, anchored in his proficiency and understanding of the market play. Hanbury not only expressed his expectations and adherence to norms, but also signalled a certain 'hard headedness' and know-how, a form of warning in which he himself was featured as a shrewd negotiator who should not be meddled with or cheated. While condemning and expressing outrage at the shamelessness of those Virginia traders who overcharged their tobacco, his opinion of the French buyer was hardly favourable and no less shaming; 'A little patience would have brought that mighty purchaser to more reasonable terms', as he put it.

## Conclusion

In their engagements and interactions with one another, early modern traders made use of varied forms of shaming and shame. Amid fierce disputes and accusations of dishonesty, traders could voice damning allegations that presented an associate's conduct as a disgrace, with insults, disparaging comments, scorn, and humiliations of varied sorts engulfing their letters. A trader's shame could be spread more broadly in letters dispatched to associates, causing damage to his reputation and diminishing his contacts, or, in extreme cases, leading to outright exclusion from trade. More routinely, the shame merchants inflicted was restrained and polite, conveying criticism or moralizing in which the misconduct was branded 'unsuitable' or 'unbecoming' or 'unmerchantlike' rather than a disgrace. Softer forms of exhortation, rebuke, and warnings, or insinuations of negligence, were common. Merchant letters and correspondences show numerous instances of shaming that stopped short of full affront, an approach that included more guarded expressions of, or allusions to, misconduct, the shame tacitly concealed behind a rhetoric of pleading and commendations.

The traders' responses to their shaming were no less varied and vigorous, indicating the threat that it might pose. They communicated strong expressions of hurt pride, threatened self-esteem, insult, anger, or rage. Not unlike responses to an assault on honour among the elite (discussed in a Chapter 4), their retorts could be retaliatory; time after time we find merchants supplying detailed and prolonged responses to the slightest accusation or moralizing aimed to inflict shame, employing emotional rebuttal and retaliation, alongside boasting, counter-exhortation and a shaming of their own. Yet, in many instances merchants could also muster more positive responses that were intended to conciliate and appease. They wrote in self-defense, voicing apology and submission and employing a rhetoric of begging or flattery, ashamedness and guilt. In some instances, both strategies – the retaliatory and the conciliatory – would be implemented.

Shame was hence potently applied through a range of measures spanning the entire gamut between punitive shame and more integrative forms, variously aimed to penalize and deter or else to conciliate and appease. The shame targeted traders' most precious values and resources – their reputation, personal honour, sense of civility, morality or professionalism. Shame could hurt a trader's reputation, but also erode his honour, undermine his inner morality or integrity, and diminish his self-esteem and pride as a competent trader. It could unsettle exchanges and access to merchant networks, on which much of a trader's enterprises and transactions relied. Whereas varied shame strategies were applied selectively to fit specific circumstances and disputes, they could also be exacted concomitantly so as to increase the pressure on associates who reneged on their obligations. In their letters, merchants often inflicted shame that included threats to their correspondent's reputation, along with criticism that undermined his honour and self-esteem, his morality, integrity, and professionalism.[69]

One strategy particularly stands out. Like shame and shaming amid networks of family, kin, and friends, merchant correspondences appealed to the binding commitments that existed between themselves and their associates. The shame was personalized; an idiom of 'friendship' was summoned not only as an ideal or an abstract norm, but as a specific personal obligation, with traders condoning and castigating associates for breaches of their pledges regarding honesty, loyalty, or empathy ('pray doe for us as for your selfe'). Their shame could convey disappointment based on personal acquaintance and long familiarity, pointing as well to the consequences of an associate's misconduct on their own dealings and welfare. It could trigger embarrassment or guilt; and it could also send signals of one's creditworthiness and loyalty. This type of personalized shame was present in all the correspondences examined here, in some instances wholly dominating them, or repeatedly evoked in letter after letter during prolonged disputes and disagreements. This personalized shame also emboldened alternative strategies that related to honour, morality, or professionalism. Merchants shifted from allusions to agents' or clients' dishonour, or immorality and incompetence, to a personalized mode that evinced bonding and commitment, with broken promises and forsaken loyalties manifestly evoked as the highest most damning behaviour with which an associate could be castigated and shamed.

In all these practices and modes of operation, shame and its related emotions galvanized interactions between traders, allowing them to monitor associates and impose sanctions, or else to assuage suspicions and sustain cooperation even in the face of fissures and recurring lapses of trust. These practices did not always prevail, nor did they fully guarantee compliance or the resolution of disputes over honesty, fraud or mismanagement. Well into the eighteenth century and beyond, the credit market remained precarious, with failure to pay debts and insolvency, in trade and other sectors of the economy, being imminent, and imprisonment for indebtedness increasingly applied among the populace at large.[70] Nevertheless, amid traders' commercial networks, shaming practices remained effective in averting misconduct, facilitating conciliation, and allowing the resolution of disputes. Such practices predisposed traders to act in desirable ways; they enhanced dispositions for cooperation and imbued market transactions with the beliefs and norms associated with honesty and trust. Applied in increasingly wider and more global networks that could encompass distant associates and clients, these shame strategies reinforced trustworthiness, bringing to the fore commitments cultivated and habits maintained 'between us friends', as merchant-tailor William Turner articulated in one of his letters to his chief client, the Parisian drapers Boquelin and Sons.

# Notes

1 Nuala Zahedieh, 'Credit, Risk, and Reputation in Late Seventeenth-Century Colonial Trade', in Olaf Uwe Janzen (ed.), *Merchant Organization and Maritime Trade in the North Atlantic, 1660–1815* (St. John's, Newfoundland, 1998), 53–74; Craig Muldrew, *The Economy of Obligation: The Culture of Credit and Social Relations in Early Modern England* (Basingstoke, 1998), 148–72; Peter Mathias, 'Risk, Credit and Kinship in Early Modern Enterprise', in John J. McCusker and Kenneth Morgan (eds.), *The Early Modern Atlantic Economy* (Cambridge, 2000), 15–35; John Smail, 'Credit, Risk, and Honor in Eighteenth-Century Commerce', *Journal of British Studies*, 44 (2005), 439–56; Francesca Trivellato, *The Familiarity of Strangers: The Sephardic Diaspora, Livorno, and Cross-Cultural Trade in the Early Modern Period* (New Haven, 2009), 1–20, 155–62; Xabier Lamikiz, *Trade and Trust in the Eighteenth-Century Atlantic World: Spanish Merchants and their Overseas Markets* (Woodbridge, 2010).
2 Muldrew, *Economy of Obligation*; Richard Grassby, *Kinship and Capitalism: Marriage, Family and Business in the English-Speaking World, 1580–1740* (Cambridge, 2001), esp. 413–17; Nuala Zahedieh, *The Capital and the Colonies: London and the Atlantic Economy, 1660–1700* (Cambridge, 2010), 55–136; Sheilagh Ogilvie, *Institutions and European Trade: Merchant Guilds, 1000–1800* (Cambridge, 2011), 285–343, 371–6; Trivellato, *Familiarity of Strangers*, 10–6, 153–93.
3 British Library (hereafter BL), Add. MS 43730–3, The Scattergood papers, Vol. 1, 355.
4 Grassby, *Kinship and Capitalism*, 296–7; Trivellato, *Familiarity of Strangers*, 10–16, 194–223; Tijl Vanneste, *Global Trade and Commercial Networks: Eighteenth-Century Diamond Merchants* (London, 2011), 67–94.

134  Commercial enterprise and exchange

5 Muldrew, *Economy of Obligation*, 173–96; Zahedieh, *Capital and the Colonies*, 83–6, 96–103; Søren Mentz, *The English Gentleman Merchant at Work: Madras and the City of London 1660–1740* (Copenhagen, 2005), 126–36; Lamikiz, *Trade and Trust*, 141–61; Anne L. Murphy, *The Origins of English Financial Markets: Investment and Speculation Before the South Sea Bubble* (Cambridge, 2009), 6–7. On maritime insurance, see Christopher Ebert, 'Early modern Atlantic Trade and the Development of Maritime Insurance to 1630', *Past and Present*, 213 (2011), 102–8. For the precariousness of credit in the eighteenth century, see Alexander Wakelam, *Credit and Debt in Eighteenth-Century England: An Economic History of Debtors' Prisons* (London and New York, 2021), 18–50.
6 Muldrew, *Economy of Obligation*, 149–52, quotation on 155.
7 London Metropolitan Archives (hereafter LMA), MS 29393, Letters to William Hurtt, 12 January 1632, no fos.
8 BL, Add MS 43732, The Scattergood Papers, 119.
9 BL, Add MS 43730, The Scattergood Papers, 181.
10 LMA, MS 00507A, Papers relating to Sir John Moore's merchant business, fo. 67. For a case involving two merchants in Livorno, in which accusations of slander spread by letters from Livorno to London ended in violence, as described by Philip Williams, see BL, Stowe MS 759, Letter Book of Philip Williams, 1639–47, fo. 85.
11 BL, Mss EUR E 387/A, Letter book of Isaac Lawrence, 1672–79, fos. 28–9.
12 BL, Add MS 43730, 443.
13 BL, Stowe MS 759, fo. 79.
14 BL, Mss EUR E 387/A, fo. 2.
15 LMA, MS 11892A, Out-letter book of Michael Mitford, Russian and Baltic merchant of St Dunston East, chiefly correspondents in Newcastle, Amsterdam, Moscow 1703–06, fo. 37.
16 See note 4 above.
17 BL, Stowe MS 759, fo. 110.
18 See also Alison Games, *The Web of Empire: English Cosmopolitans in an Age of Expansion, 1560–1660* (Oxford, 2008), 91–2.
19 Mentz, *English Gentleman*, 164–5.
20 BL, Mss EUR E.387/A, fos. 7, 9.
21 Ibid., fos. 40, 67.
22 Ibid., fos. 50, 53, 74.
23 Ibid., fo. 110.
24 J.B. [John Brown], *The Marchants avizo: Verie necessarie for their sonnes and servants, when they first send them beyond the seas* (London, 1589) STC2 3908.4, 3, 4–5, 6. See also Trivellato, *Familiarity of Strangers*, 184–6.
25 Gerard Malynes, *Consuetudo, vel lex Mercatoria, or The ancient law-Merchant Divided into three parts* (London, 1622) STC2 17222, 3, 6.
26 Richard Steele, *The trades-man's calling being a discourse concerning the nature, necessity, choice, &c. of a calling in general: and directions for the right managing of the tradesman's calling in particular* (London, 1684), Wing S5394. See also Andrea Finkelstein, *Harmony and the Balance: An Intellectual History of Seventeenth-Century English Economic Thought* (Ann Arbor, 2000), 28–9; Natasha Glaisyer, *The Culture of Commerce in England, 1660–1720* (Woodbridge, 2006), 100–42.
27 LMA, MS 18470, Out-letter books of John Oldbury and Henry Stanley, Vol. I, 22 October 1673 (no fos.). For merchant honour, see also Smail, 'Credit, Risk and Honor'; Paul D. McLean, *The Art of the Network: Strategic Interaction and Patronage in Renaissance Florence* (Durham and London, 2007), 72–6, 87–9.
28 BL, Add MS 43730–3; Add. MS 42122, Bernard P. Scattergood, 'The Life of John Scattergood', reprint from *The Contemporary Review* (1928), 2–8; Mentz, *The English Gentleman*, 206–8. Sometime in 1721, in the wake of the South Sea

*Commercial enterprise and exchange* 135

Bubble, Scattergood devised a scheme to improve the state's finances by imposing new taxation on bachelors, concluding it with the statement, 'It would have be[en] a burning shame in me not to offer something being so very well qualified for sc[he]ams'. Add. MS 43732, 423.
29 BL Add MS 43731, 194, 236–7.
30 Ibid., 377, 446.
31 Ibid., 380–1.
32 Ibid., 381.
33 LMA, MS 05106/1 (no fos.), Journal and letter book of William Turner, 1664–67, 15/25 May 1662, 13/23 August 1663, 3/13 November 1662, 8/18 December 1664, 10/20 December 1663, 23 March 1662/3, 2 April 1662/3, 13/23August 1663. For the silk trade, see C.G.A. Clay, *Economic Expansion and Social Change: England 1500– 1700* (Cambridge, 1984), Vol. II, 39, 125; Linda Levy Peck, *Consuming Splendor: Society and Culture in Seventeenth-Century England* (Cambridge, 2005), 85–6.
34 LMA, MS 05106/1, 15/25 May 1662, 12/22 March 1662, 25 May/1 June 1662/3, 6/16 April 1663, 1/11 June 1663.
35 Ibid., 1/11 June 1663, 10/20 December 1663, 8/18 December 1664.
36 BL, Stowe MS 759, fo. 73.
37 S.D. Smith, *'An Exact and Industrious Tradesman': The Letter Book of Joseph Symson of Kendall 1711–1720*, British Academy Records of Social and Economic History, new series 34 (Oxford, 2003), 59.
38 Jacob M. Price (ed.), *Joshua Johnson's Letterbook, 1771– 1774: Letters from a Merchant in London to his Partners in Maryland* (London Record Society, Vol. XV, London, 1979), xviii, 90–2, 111.
39 Ibid., 111.
40 Jessica L. Goldberg, *Trade and Institutions in the Medieval Mediterranean: The Geniza Merchants and their Business World* (Cambridge, 2012), 38–9, 139–43; Trivellato, *Familiarity of Strangers*, 181–5; McLean, *The Art of the Network*, 62; Lamikiz, *Trade and Trust*, 150–61; Naomi Tadmor, *Family and Friends in Eighteenth-Century England: Household, Kinship and Patronage* (Cambridge, 2004).
41 Smith (ed.), *'Exact and Industrious'*, 528, 188.
42 LMA, MS 18470, 18 November 1699, 8 August 1671.
43 Smith (ed.), *'Exact and Industrious'*, 525; BL, Add MS 43731, fos. 97, 172. For the role of friends as attorneys, see Murphy, *Origins of English financial markets*, 135.
44 LMA, MS 18470, 15 November 1675; Marion Tinling (ed.), *The Correspondence of the Three William Byrds of Westover, Virginia, 1684– 1776* (Charlottesville, 1997), Vol. II, 456.
45 Philip Riden (ed.), *George Sitwell's Letterbook 1662–66* (Derbyshire Record Society, Vol. X, Chesterfield, 1985), x, xliv, 1–3.
46 BL, MS Stowe 759, fo. 73; Smith (ed.), *'Exact and Industrious'*, 534–5.
47 Ibid., 535, 519, 515–6, 60, 109, 10, 203.
48 Ibid., 470–2.
49 Ibid., 498.
50 BL, Mss EUR E.387/A, fo. 2.
51 Riden (ed.), *George Sitwell's Letterbook*, 26, 54–5, 51, 100, 60, 62–3, 78, 100, 175; Smith (ed.), *'Exact and Industrious'*, 521.
52 BL, Mss EUR E.387/A, fo. 66.
53 Muldrew, *Economy of Obligation*, 236–55; Zahedieh, *Capital and the Colonies*, 102–3; Margot C. Finn, *The Character of Credit: Personal Debt in English Culture, 1740–1914* (Cambridge, 2007). For the increased popularity of debtors' prisons in the eighteenth century, see Wakelam, *Credit and Debt*.
54 Muldrew, *Economy of Obligation*, 255.

55 BL, Mss EUR E.387/A, fo. 1; LMA, MS 18470, 17 December 1676.
56 Ibid., 13 Jan 1676/7; Smith (ed.), 'Exact and Industrious', lxv; Muldrew, Economy of Obligation, 255; Zahedieh, Capital and the Colonies, 102–3; Ogilvie, Institutions and European Trade, 297.
57 On the preference of using references or oaths in settling disputes over accounts, see LMA, MS 18470, 16 June 1673; MS 11892A, fo. 21. For arbitration, see also Ogilvie, Institutions and European Trade, 296–300.
58 LMA, MS 18470, 22 August 1673, 22 October 1673.
59 Smith (ed.) 'Exact and Industrious', lxv–lxvi.
60 Riden (ed.), George Sitwell's Letterbook, xxviii, xxix, 95, 12, 57, 26, 31, 51–2, 54–5.
61 Ibid., 195, 222, 254–5.
62 Matthew Kadane, 'Success and Self-Loathing in the Life of an Eighteenth-Century Entrepreneur', in Margaret C. Jacob and Catherine Secretan (eds.), The Self-Perception of Early Modern Capitalists (New York, 2008), 261–3.
63 BL, add MS 43731, fos. 146–7; LMA, MS 18470, 28 August 1670; Smith (ed.) 'Exact and Industrious', 203, 621; LMA, MS 11892A, fo. 5.
64 Marion Balderston (ed.), James Claypoole's Letter book: London and Philadelphia 1681–1684 (San Marino, 1967), 220–1, 226–9.
65 Smith (ed.), 'Exact and Industrious', 525, 621; Riden (ed.), George Sitwell's Letterbook, 7; Games, The Web of Empire, 92.
66 BL, Add. MS 43730, 43–4.
67 LMA, MS 18470, 2 December 1675, 13 December 1675.
68 Tinling (ed.), Correspondence of the Three William Byrds, ii, 463, 495.
69 For the centrality of proficiency and competence in enforcing obligations among eleventh-century Maghribi traders, for whom such skills were more important than notions of 'honour', see Jessica L. Goldberg 'Choosing and enforcing Business Relationships in the Eleventh-Century Mediterranaean: Reassessing the "Maghribi Traders"', Past and Present, 216 (2012), 3–40, esp. 30–7.
70 Julian Hoppit, Risk and Failure in English Business 1700–1800 (Cambridge, 1987); Wakelam, Credit and Debt in Eighteenth-Century England; Tawny Paul, The Poverty of Disaster: Debt and Insecurity in Eighteenth-Century Britain (Cambridge, 2019).

# 5 Communities as sites of shame

It has long been presumed that pre-modern societies, in Europe and elsewhere, were prone to shaming and shame. In these societies, typically governed by small communities and face-to-face relations, individuals were habitually subject to public shame, with women and men being watched, scrutinized, and effectively sanctioned through shame or its threat. Lacking access to more formal means of law-enforcing agencies, these communities relied on shame as a powerful mechanism for regulating conduct and enforcing conformity to norms. As these societies expanded and their communities eroded, and as more formal forms of governance developed with the rise of a centralized modern state, informal regulation through shame diminished and declined.[1]

As research in recent decades has shown, English communities in the period between 1500 and 1700 had already ceased to resemble these small 'close-knit' communities, as Lawrence Stone had once referred to them. The period witnessed population growth and market expansion, an intensified movement into towns along with increased levels of poverty. While agriculture continued to dominate the economy, urban populations grew substantially and communities throughout the countryside were transformed in multiple ways. These communities became not only more open but also more socially divided. With the Reformation taking firmer roots in society, they experienced greater religious divisions, as well. Overall, and most important for our discussion here, these communities became more regulated than before, as the state and an expanding machinery of courts, at both the local and national levels, attempted to curb mobility and confront the threat posed by poverty and disorder through the sanctioning of an increased array of perceived transgressions and misbehaviours.[2]

For all these modernizing forces and transformations, the regulation of conduct through shame hardly receded or declined. Rather than eradicating public forms of shame, the church and a centralized system of courts applied these shame punishments vigorously. No less important, shame was used by ordinary members of the community who took an active part in controlling and sanctioning misconduct amidst their communities, both informally and by turning to the courts. The Reformation created novel forms of division that could cut through communities, with shame being inflicted

DOI: 10.4324/9781003226871-6

on non-reformed and nonconforming groups; with its zeal to reform and discipline, the Reformed church intensified the use of shame in ways that continued to shape the everyday life of individuals and groups throughout the sixteenth and well into the mid-seventeenth century and beyond.[3]

This chapter examines the shame that resonated in English communities under these pressures and changing circumstances. Rather than focus on specific practices or rituals of shame, we investigate a broad array of practices, from communally organized shaming and the shame wreaked by individuals on their neighbours, through the shame inflicted by expanding state institutions and the courts. Here we pay special attention not only to the shame inflicted by a penal system administered by ecclesiastical and civil courts, but also the shame administered – purposely or inadvertently – through an emerging system of the Poor Laws (1601), which was designed to respond to the needs of the very poor. As we shall see, public shaming became markedly varied; in the mix of informal and institutionalized forms it took, the diverse uses to which it was put, and the differing ramifications it could have for individuals and the community at large. For all these variations, communities throughout the era remained sites of shaming practices and a shame that was above all coercive, exclusionary and harsh.

## Communal shaming

Informal shame was a salient feature of everyday life in communities and neighbourhoods across the countryside throughout the sixteenth and seventeenth centuries. In the public spaces, the streets, markets, the alehouse, or the threshold of private homes, individuals incurred the wrath of the community under a wide array of circumstances, with neighbours witnessing the shame inflicted on others, or orchestrating and partaking in these events. The centrepiece of these communally organized shaming were behaviours deemed inappropriate and transgressive of the social, moral, and religious order, with several offences looming large. First and foremost were sexual offences – especially adultery and fornication, reflecting on deeply held and intensely harnessed beliefs rooted in medieval Christianity and reinforced by Protestant notions of sin. Closely aligned were breaches of the patriarchal order, with women's unchastely conduct and insubordination posing a particular threat and becoming the target of public shame. A second cluster of offences were those committed against community values, with scolds (contentious women who disturbed their neighbours), refusal to give charity, disturbance of the common peace or neglect of neighbourly obligations being targets of special condemnation and shame. Third were infringements of the established religious order, as the defiance of core Protestant beliefs and customs was deemed malignant, and varied offences – idolatry or breaches of religious taboos – were tied to sins of the flesh and perceived as deeply offensive to God.[4]

Some of the most gruesome forms of communal shaming involved rituals of physical abuse and humiliation. Historians have long singled out the skimmington, or charivari, as the most potent of these rituals. Originating in popular customs and festivities, the skimmington targeted cuckoldry and domineering wives, forcing victims to ride on a horse, sometimes backwards, with their bodies subjected to assaults of mud and filth. The procession also featured parades of armed men, gunfire, raucous music, noise, laughter, and displays of animal horns (the traditional sign of a man whose wife had been unfaithful), sometimes 'tipped like gold and adorned with ribbons and flowers'. Victims occasionally ended up being ducked in a pond or a river. As a 'highly stylized representation of anarchy', the skimmington was rife with symbolism of the tensions between dominance and subjection (a horse and a rider), and between order and disorder (riding backwards, raucous music and cacophony). It also invoked animal symbolism, the misconduct of the victims being judged as inhuman and beastly. Other shaming events were also inspired by the skimmington, with pictures and effigies being used as signs of reproach and 'tokens of shame', or cuckold's horns being affixed about a man's porch or door with the head and skin of the animal still attached. In the case of high-ranking individuals, cuckolds' horns were sometimes thrown through the windows into the house, or set upon their horse.[5]

Rituals inflicting humiliation and bodily disfigurement were at the heart of the shame punishments inflicted on women, including instances of shaving the head of notorious whores and bawds, brutalizing women's bodies or sexual organs and, in exceptional cases, burning parts of their bodies.[6] Immense physical abuse was involved in the shaming of scolds, who were invariably subjected to the 'scold's bridle' or the 'branks' – a skeletal iron helmet secured in the back of the head with an iron loop and a chain by which a woman could be pushed around. From the early seventeenth century, as we shall see below, the cucking- or ducking-stool, a chair to which the woman was secured and then dunked into the river, was applied by the varied courts. The ducking punishment was sometimes exacted by neighbours, who would duck fornicating women, reproaching, ridiculing, and insulting them throughout the event. The 'branks', arguably the most brutal of these devices, was used in England only briefly, but it had a longer history in Scotland. Originally a torture device to extract confessions from alleged witches, the branks tied the female tongue with a long mouthpiece, causing immense pain and mutilation, with victims enduring physical and psychological scars long after the event. From 1600s onwards, branking was applied not only to scolds but also to other forms of conduct associated with female waywardness; 'evil tongued' women, violence, and fornication. In all these forms of the shaming of the scold, a crowd of onlookers jeering, mocking and laughing, was central to the scene.[7]

These rituals of shaming and physical abuse were fuelled by beliefs in the social and moral order, coupled with a sense of legitimacy, with the crowd's actions being perceived as legitimate because they were sanctioned not only by the community but by God and by the authorities.[8] The community-organized skimmington was, in some ways, inspired by the legal system itself, resting as it did on the belief that the populace had the right to chastise and reproach its own members, assuming a quasi-legal and political authority by punishing an offender so that 'other women also by her shame might be admonished [not] to offend in like sort'. Scolds were often shamed by urban and rural magistrates in civil and ecclesiastical courts, while in Scotland, the involvement of the church in shaming rituals was particularly pronounced, the evidence pointing to 'the symbiotic relations between customary practice, the church and the law', with church ministers acting as a conduit between the parties involved.[9]

Shame punishments also took the form of verbal rather than physical abuse. Over the course of the period, individuals believed to have lapsed in upholding community norms and beliefs risked being shamed through carefully orchestrated libels, invariably taking the form of a written epigram or more elaborate verse designed to scoff, satirize, and ridicule the victim. Composed by people of lowly status, often in the setting of an alehouse, the libel was primarily directed at high-ranking individuals, targeting occasionally ordinary members of the community as well. Once written down, libels spread rapidly; they could be found pinned to houses' gates or church doors, placed on alehouses' walls and attached to fence-posts or haystacks, or put inside the prayer book at the church. Some of these libels also appeared in print as derisive ballads, further circulating the disgrace and humiliation wreaked on their victims.[10]

Public spaces were also the scene of less ritualized and more diffuse personal insults and disgraceful speech. Conveyed face-to-face or indirectly through rumour and gossip, verbal abuse was deliberately designed to hurt, smear, and shame individuals, with neighbours witnessing and sometimes spreading the accusation further. The vocabulary of insults and abusive speech was immensely varied, with an entire arsenal of vicious words and synonyms being utilized to debase people by reference to their sexual conduct, status, and reputation, or else their religious persuasions and demeanour. While overtly gendered – abusive words against females invoked lust and unchastely conduct, while males were smeared for their lack of manliness – sexual insults were also loosely applied to both genders. Females would be shamed and humiliated by being dubbed 'whore', 'drab', or 'adulterer', and men would be likewise disgraced with accusations of 'whoremaster', 'bastard bearer', 'harlot monger', 'cuckold' – and more. The social standing and honesty of victims were particularly vulnerable to smear, with words of disgrace, including 'churl', 'rascal', 'varlet', 'rogue' and 'knave', along with 'boy', 'ape', 'slave', 'dog', or 'cheat', 'thief', 'liar' and 'villain'.[11] Special diatribes were reserved for the humiliation and shame of religious and ethnic minorities, with derogatory epithets including words such as 'heretic', 'papist', 'puritan', or 'rogue' 'Welsh', 'witch' and 'Devil'. Such labelling and invectives could elicit agitated responses and 'wars of words', making minority members a laughing-stock and carrying great shame. All verbal assaults could lead to physical abuse, or be accompanied by sexually degrading gestures directed at the body of the shamed individual.[12]

A significant aspect of all these shaming practices was that the allegations and insults often bore little relation to the actual deeds of those on whom the shame was inflicted. Verbal assaults often concealed disputes and discord in conflict-ridden communities; or they were the product of local politics, religious divisions, and economic anxieties, which could all trigger assaults on individuals or groups, inflicting great humiliation and shame. In the case of religious nonconformity, accusations such as fornication, incest, sodomy, and bestiality, which were aimed at Anabaptists, Ranters, and Quakers, were often part of the stereotype of the nonconforming group itself. Other forms of sexual insult bore little relation to the actual circumstances which led to these accusations, with verbal abuse often being the product of tensions and disputes over issues other than sexual, religious, or moral conduct, involving quarrels over debt or alleged theft, local feuds, long harboured resentments, brawls, and spiteful revenge. Vicious words of insult were used as a weapon in these rivalries, explicitly intended to humiliate and shame by denting the credibility, honour, or esteem of adversaries and foes.[13]

Whether based on presumed or actual conduct, communally organized or more personal, the shaming of people in public could have far-reaching and devastating consequences. Victims of the carnivalesque skimmington, or those facing cuckold's horns fastened on their doors, became a laughing-stock among their neighbours, sometimes long after the incident had occurred. As testimonies at court indicate, libels, insults, and shaming rituals could cause grief, sorrow, and great shame.[14] Women who were subjected to false rumours chose costly litigation to clear their names, fearing neighbours would think ill of them 'as long as [they] live[d]'; others would find their shame hard to eradicate. Victims of defamation, too, feared loss of face and ridicule, and when the defamatory language combined with gossip, the neighbours' reactions could be shattering. Verbal allegations could trigger further formal and informal sanctions or court litigation, leading to public scandals, loss of positions of authority or opportunities for work, or else the denial of access to employment and parish relief. For respectable members of the community, authority and status, economic worthiness, business partnerships, and credit networks – all were at stake.[15] As much research has shown, litigation over defamatory language reached its zenith by the mid-seventeenth century, the period witnessing a steep rise in defamation cases brought to the court by victims fearing the consequences of shaming and insults on their reputation, social standing, and livelihoods.[16]

Public shame could also affect one's closest kin, extending to husbands, wives, and whole households, who risked being labelled and shunned. Women who failed to reverse the damage resulting from accusations of whoredom or seducing married men might be shut out of their social networks; people with reputations for zealotry could be refused trade or else denied burial in the parish. Vicious derogatory language, savage mocking rituals, exposure on horse rides in raucous processions – all these invariably marked people as outcasts, ultimately depriving them, and those closest to them, not only of their social ties and reputations, but also of their sense of dignity, humanity, and belonging.[17] And while the exact frequency of these rituals is difficult to gauge, the sheer potential for being shunned through shame – and the fear of having to endure the consequences – would remain an imminent aspect of everyday lives and relationships in communities throughout the entire era.

Yet for all its severity, communal shaming still varied in its application and consequences. In the case of the skimmington, the full-fledged and highly stylized ritual was not always implemented, and in some instances a 'stang' was used rather than a real horse, or effigies rather than the person themself. Bodily abuse and physical pain, in other words, were in some cases less severe than in others. And while typically associated with a set of features – parades of rough music, displays of horns – many events applied some but not all of these elements. Variations also occurred between events that were evidently hostile but still light-hearted, and those that were more brutal and savagely applied; between minor incidents organized by a few individuals and larger spectacles involving hundreds of people. By comparison to its Scottish counterpart, the English skimmington appears to have been overall more jovial and humorous, the emphasis being less on actual physical abuse or torture and more on rebuke, mocking and intimidation.[18]

The shaming of the female scold, too, varied in form and implications. While the use of the tortuous 'branks' was popular in Scotland, in England the 'scold's bridle' was replaced, from the early seventeenth century, by the ducking-stool. Publicly performed in front of mocking crowds and hardly lacking physical pain, ducking in the water was perceived as 'less effective' and moderate, with the offenders sometimes managing to make speeches from the stool, claiming their innocence or pointing to the absurdity of the punishment. That is, the ritual allowed the shamed female to make her voice heard, which the more brutal 'branks' prevented. Here, too, there was a distinction between single, short-term performances of the ducking, and repeat episodes that prolonged the ordeal, with the consequences enduring long after it had initially been staged.[19]

In all these incidents of mocking and shame, the reactions of the crowds could vary as well. Neighbours and friends could at times become divided; while some acts of ridicule outside people's houses were an occasion for great merriment, in other instances at least some among the populace disapproved of the conduct and found it abhorrent, expressing grief and shame in the actions of the crowd rather than in the presumed deed of the victim. The ducked scold who gave her tongue 'liberty between each dip' and publicly denounced the injustice of the act, could also elicit sympathy among the crowd. In the case of slanderous speech and rumour, neighbours sometimes sided with the victim, judging the shaming slander malicious and rebuking the slanderer for their gossip-mongering and loose talk.[20]

All these variations implied that while communal shaming could be harsh and its implications enduring and irreversible, the practice could also be applied more moderately and its repercussions less stigmatic or durable. These shame punishments were all integral to the daily lives of the participants, invariably being part of popular culture and carnivalesque entertainment, of the laughter and satyr of youthful activities and pastimes or male culture in the alehouse or work environment.[21] While rife with scorn, disparagement and mock, these events could also take the form of insinuation and innuendo, jests, sniggers, and jeers, or tacit disparagement through rumours and gossip, all of which did not altogether disrupt the victim's ties and interactions in the community. In this sense, the shaming was more moderate, intended to place pressure on individuals to uphold the norms, or amend their ways, rather than inflict stigma and exclusion that utterly destroyed the position, prospects or personality of the shamed.[22]

This type of reformatory, and ultimately more inclusive, shame was evident in practices of verbal abuse and slanderous rumours. Here, too, the shame incited through derogatory speech varied; from instances where defamatory assaults and accusations marked the offender as an outcast and destroyed their character or livelihood, to episodes in which misconduct was exposed through shaming that forced conformity and a measure of conciliation. The latter allowed the restoration of the 'common peace', that is, a return to the routine of daily interactions and neighbourly exchange. Female networks of gossiping could thus generate collective pressure that forced women to conform, while among men slanderous assaults could expose misconduct and force offenders to mend their ways. As much evidence on court litigation regarding defamations has shown, formal accusations of slander invariably failed to reach the court, with most cases being dropped long before the proceedings at court came to an end. Instead, the participants – the shamed and the slanderer – sought mediation through friends, neighbours, the parish clergy, or other local authorities, which usually led to an informal settlement based on financial compensation and apology. The havoc caused by verbal shaming and affront was curtailed, the shame leaning less towards total exclusion and enduring stigmatization and more towards forgiveness through expressions of regret, apology, or acknowledgement of guilt.[23]

## Inferiors shaming superiors

Public shame was sometimes wreaked on persons of high status and in positions of authority, from high-ranking officers serving at court or acting as Parliament members, down to local magistrates, judges, landlords, or high constables and other men of gentle status. The shame directed at these people often came from below; that is, it was inflicted by ordinary people, women and men of the middle and lower orders who appropriated familiar forms of public shaming, subjecting their superiors to varied forms of insult, censure, and ridicule. In towns, the mayor and aldermen, councillors, and notable citizens were sometimes the targets of shame, while throughout the country puritans and clergy considered overly zealous could be singled out for condemnation or subjected to rituals of shame and mockery.

Some of these rituals were the outcome of festive entertainment that escalated into violent charivari and assaults directed against local magistrates or puritanically inclined constables, as was the case of the constable in Wells who in 1607 tried to suppress the May games, raising strong opposition that turned into a series of ridings savagely performed before thousands of people.[24] More frequent than these rituals, which overall remained a predominantly plebian affair, were incidents of verbal abuse, with ordinary people lashing out at their superiors using derogatory words, insults, and a language of shame.[25] Deeply touching on, and destabilizing, perceptions of the social and religious order, such defamation was considered an offence to authority – the gentlemanly classes, the Church and the Crown – and was dealt with special severity at the court. Yet for all the risk this type of slander entailed, the venting of rude and shaming words against superiors, in the public space, was a recurring incident. When collecting taxes or imposing fines, presenting ordinary villagers for various misdemeanours, officials and local authorities would invariably be confronted with verbal abuse and degrading speech, sometimes combined with derisory gestures of the face, limbs, hands, or thumbs. Mockery of the clergy at the church, in front of large audiences of all social strata, could also occur, with ordinary parishioners offending their minister and clergy, invariably using words such as 'fool', 'liar', 'varlet', 'rogue', 'knave', or 'rascal'. In towns, too, merchants and ordinary traders insulted their company's wardens, citizens sometimes abused the mayor or sheriffs, and parishioners degraded their vicar, all using rich vocabulary and imagery; 'more mete to dryve pyggs to the feyld than to be Justics of the Peace', 'worthy to kepe a stable rather than being fit for the ministry', were some of the words uttered in instances that ended up at the court.[26]

More potent still, especially at the local level, was the increased proliferation of libellous verse against individuals of high social standing or position of authority. Composed by people of humble status and sometimes aided by professional versifiers, these libels had distinctive features that turned them into a particularly potent weapon in satirizing, criticizing, and shaming superiors. The libels, which were often scrawled on a piece of paper amidst a social gathering in an alehouse, circulated rapidly and widely. Being affixed on the victim's house or porch, they were distributed in the market and read allowed in alehouses further afield. To enhance their effect and reach, composers sometimes made use of visual aids, highlighting the victim's humiliation by posting the written libel alongside horns, or with a graphic representation and picture of the victim. Some libels were pinned to the common whipstock, a setting associated with beggars, vagabonds, and criminals, further adding to the humiliation and provoking scandal, 'insomuch that the whole towne was in uprore', as it was described in one such instance brought before the court.[27]

Many of these offending compositions were also turned into ballads, with composers singing stories of shameful deeds of people of renown in inns and alehouses, teaching children and youngsters to sing libellous songs on the streets, 'in scoffinge manner in disgrace [of the local bailiff and rent collector]'.[28] Some ballads were passed to minstrels who moved from place to place, advertising and spreading songs of misdeeds and shame. Songs were sometimes manipulated to amplify the slander, with ridiculing rhymes being set to well-known and popular tunes adapted from printed ballads. Regardless of their specific words, libels could thus instantly carry potent undertones of sexual transgression and shame.[29] Some derisive verse was also sent to be printed in London, so that the short rhyme composed by amateurs in a locality ended up as a fully developed broadside, printed and dispersed in many duplicates, with people 'in diverse and sundrie alehouses and innes' being drawn to hear libelous ballads 'and to reioyce and laugh thereat in scornfull, derideinge and infamous manner'.[30]

Most important was the sheer content and language of libellous verse and rhyme. Libels invariably made an effective and creative use of satire and parody, shaming, mocking, and reproaching powerful or high-ranking individuals. For example, a libellous letter sent to the lord manor of Over Compton (on the border of Dorset and Somerset), which was subsequently fastened to the church gate, was titled 'Here be Andrew Abington's Commandementes'. Making use of the Second-Table Commandments, the verse turned their prohibitive mode ('Thou shalt not kill') into positive statements ('Thou shalt catch what thou canst;' 'Thou shalt paie no man'), through which Abington's alleged oppressions were exposed and his Christian morality was undermined. In other cases, balladeers made use of mock sermons, or exposed the conceit of eminent individuals by parodying their bodily demeanour and gestures when approaching their inferiors: 'He turnes his hat up in the brim,/ And lookes as though his eyes wold burne,/ He snappes poore people by the nose, And scornfully from them doth turne'.[31]

In still other cases, the balladeers' use of language was outright bawdy and far more abusive. Reflecting oral transmission that was ungoverned by rules of written language, ballads conveyed not only humour, scoffing wit, or even parody and sarcasm, but also far more debased, offensive, and spiteful language, typically employing excess and sexual imagery to intensify the humiliation and shame. Thus a group of artisans in a town in Essex in 1622 invented a shaming ballad against a councillor of the town, accusing him of harshly beating his daughter. Titled 'Whip Her Arse Dick', the ballad repeated the line over throughout: 'Hye thee home Anne,/Hye thee home Anne,/Whippe Her Arse Dicke,/ ... Come unto Parke Street, /And learne the songe,/Of Whippe Her Arse Dicke'.[32] In 1605, a ballad composed expressly to denigrate George Hawkings, a well-off gentleman landowner and leading officer in Worcestershire, who had fathered a bastard child, used multiple insults, calling him 'whore', 'knave', 'drabbe', 'cowardy', describing the place he committed his crime as 'most filthy' and 'a shame'. Hawkins was further degraded by being described as 'This is the bastarde,/ With his father the dastard', and the greatest knave in the shire: 'in all this shire,/There is not a squire,/More like a knave I trowe'. The final lines of this type of destructive shaming ballad highlighted its enduring stigma: 'O cursed seede,/My harte dothe bleede,/To thinke howe thowe woist born./To the whore thy mother,/And the knave thy father,/An everlasting scorne'.[33]

Adding to the stigma was the balladeers' deliberate and abusive use of names. All ballads were attuned to the names of their victims, publicly disclosing their identity and undermining their status and honour. Some ballads used nicknames, others dropped their subjects' titles, or else they mentioned the title but debased it through blatant use of sexual imagery, as in the case of the 'ballad of squire Hawkins and his whore'. Some ballads degraded their subjects by making playful use of their name. In a libel found fastened under the pillory in the marketplace at Lyme Regis, which was directed against a customs official of the harbour, the text decried his oppressions through the playful use of his name: 'His name in breef I will you tell,/ With two syllables you may it spell./A rope and a halter./Spells Robin Salter'.[34]

Some of the themes emerging from libels against superiors were common to other practices of communal shaming, observed earlier in the chapter. As in shaming of neighbours and ordinary villagers, here, too, a mix of ritual and verbal abuse, to which mocking was central, is observable, as is the affinity of public shame with popular entertainment and customs, centred around the alehouse. As in the shaming of ordinary villagers, there was also the pivotal role of sexual imagery and accusations, with allegations of sexual misconduct aimed to disgrace – and ruin – lives and reputations. And as in the case of communal practices, libels against superiors conveyed a sense of legitimacy and purpose, with ordinary people taking upon themselves the role of 'custodians of morality', notably sexual morality, conveying ideals and values of communal harmony and peace, of 'good neighbourhood' and especially notions of order and paternalism, including the perceived obligations of the powerful towards their inferiors and the poor.[35]

Yet libels directed at superiors also had specific, class-related features that distinguished them from other forms of public shame. Behind the mocking language and sexual imagery, there was not only tacit but also an explicit critique of varied oppressions and the specific individuals of higher rank or the 'better sorts' who were engaged in them; the earl who oppressed his neighbouring tenants, the wealthy clothier who employed 'many poore and distressed people', the village constable who regularly handed wrongdoers or criminals over to the authorities, manor lords who attempted to enclose the commons, placing fences that barred the poor from approaching it. Libels also harshly attacked zealous puritans who interfered with the flow of everyday life, suppressing popular sports or entertainments, and condemning the sociability of the alehouse.[36] Beyond a moral economy and the reminder of paternalist obligations, shaming ballads expressed an explicit denunciation of a host of cruelties and injustice committed against the lower classes and the poor, exposing the pretensions of officials and rulers who claimed their elevated status not only to birth and pedigree but also to civility and service, their morality or superior character:

> Were God I weare a head constable,
> And had a Justice of my name,
> Then would I whipp and stock the poore,
> And think it neither sinne nor shame.[37]

Above all, there was the distinct subversive language of the libel, which utterly defied the conventions of deference and subservience owed by inferiors to their superiors. In its outright denigration of eminent individuals, its excessive scoffing, rudeness, and lack of regard to rules of speech and proper address, libellous verse and songs directly challenged the status and authority of a ruling elite. Testimonies in court cases indicate that the language of the libels was deliberately intended to shock; 'such a thinge as he had never heard of in his life that he thought that yt was a libell', referring as well to 'bawdy libels' and 'filthy songs' that were perceived as stingy, infamous, 'most wickedlie endeavoured', provoking crowds to 'laughe and reioyce at the verses and contents thereof'. The libel was considered seditious and a threat to the social and political order, breeding 'a most dangerous opinion in the harts of the comon people', inciting 'the hatred and dispight bred in many of the baser sort of people against the gentlemen of the country'.[38]

By the early decades of the seventeenth century, the offensive language of libellous verse penetrated more established forms of 'high' literary culture and the political discourse around the royal court. Considered a 'debased mode' that was cultivated by popular traditions rather than classical authority, the libel was nevertheless increasingly used by poets, writers, and commentators in their polemics against rivals and opponents at court. Bawdy and free from the rules of proper writing, excessive in their denigrating and scoffing wit, libels allowed writers to go beyond the bounds of contemporary political discourse, freeing the more acceptable forms of satire from restraint and ambiguity, articulating a harsh critique of individuals in addition to more generalized forms of vice at the Jacobean court. By exposing the shame of corruptions at court through the language of libellous rhymes long used in localities throughout the country, such discourse contributed to destabilizing court politics, laying the ground for the development of satirical writing and the eruption of divisive revolutionary discourse in the mid-seventeenth century and well beyond.[39]

## The shamed poor

Early modern communities were suffused with the shame that was evoked not only in incidents of mock rituals or verbal abuse, but also through changing attitudes and practices relating to poverty and the poor. As communities across the country grappled with increasing levels of poverty and the rising proportion of poor people unable to provide for their needs, a new discourse on poverty emerged. By the mid-sixteenth century, it was promoted by Humanist and Protestant teaching and was also enshrined in the policies of welfare provision of the Tudor state that culminated in the Elizabethan Poor Laws (1601). Instead of the traditional understanding of poverty as sacred and the poor as being in an elevated position – 'God's poor' – the new discourse placed the burden of poverty on human nature, while also advancing the distinction between acceptable poverty and the unworthy poor, that is, between people who were unable to work (the sick and infirm, the very young and the elderly), and those who were able-bodied and capable of work. While the former deserved charity and relief, the latter merited neither; they were to be employed, or else ignored, punished, and excluded. A certain tension between compassion and disapproval thus came to govern attitudes towards poverty and the poor, with novel programs and ideas encouraging charity and aid to the poor, while simultaneously being buttressed by an overall view of poverty as the product of human idleness and sin, with failure to work and reliance on begging being perceived as a threat to the social order and abhorrent to God. Over much of the period, and as long as few, if any, attempts were made at wrestling with the roots of poverty or with the economic causes of the growing numbers of unemployed poor, these notions remained entrenched, especially among the elite and the 'better sorts'. Compassion and pity were invariably overwhelmed by the tendency to link poverty with idleness and sin, and by the perception of the poor as a potential threat and a burden on the community.[40]

Under these circumstances, the poor were liable to confront and experience varied forms of suspicion, humiliation, and shame. This was evident even in the case of those poor deemed deserving of relief and liable to obtain parochial support. It is indeed true that the novel system of the Poor Laws increasingly catered to the needs of the very poor, in the countryside as well in towns, and on an unprecedented scale. The system may also have engendered a growing sense of entitlement to welfare (in practice, if not in theory), especially among the poor themselves. Nevertheless, and in terms of its administration on the ground, the system was far from benign, nor was relief allocated on a purely objective and consistent assessment of material deprivation or the physical infirmity of the potential recipients of relief. As historians noted, the statutory specifications of the Poor Laws were limited and difficult to apply, leaving much room for discretionary distribution of resources, with varied and shifting considerations coming to dominate the distribution of relief in parishes across the countryside and in towns. As historian Steve Hindle showed, while practical considerations regarding the availability of communal resources loomed large in decisions to distribute relief, suspicion, and fear of poverty, in addition to the individual assessments of churchwardens and overseers, were widespread. Paupers who had long resided in their parish could find it difficult to secure access to parochial relief, and even those most clearly identified as 'objects of charity', like widows, could sometimes encounter the officials' contempt and disapproval. In many instances relief was withheld, suspended, and even cancelled on the basis of perceptions of the character and conduct of the recipients, who were required to show 'social respectability' and conformity. As Hindle also showed, the criteria most readily applied for assessing such respectability were church attendance, industriousness, sobriety, deference, and quality of parenthood.[41]

Parochial relief was thus conditional, and it had to be negotiated and begged for. When desiring relief, the poor would need to approach overseers or churchwardens, with applications probably being made in a face-to-face, doorstep encounter not unlike the kind made by the beggar seeking private relief. Paupers also made their pleas in writing, especially in cases when relief was denied or suspended, making their case against parochial decisions, with petitioners finding themselves repetitively begging officers to change their minds. Or else they would appeal to magistrates and the local JPs, at times waging long struggles vis-à-vis parish officers, involving overseers or magistrates who exercised their power of arbitration. In the decades following the passage of the Settlement Laws in 1662, paupers who resided in a place other than their parish of settlement regularly wrote (or had others write on their behalf) to their parish of settlement to apply for relief.[42]

These forms of appeal for relief could be deeply entangled with shame. Historians studying seventeenth-century petitions and pauper letters in the ensuing century argued that these petitions did, in fact, allow the petitioners some form of agency vis-à-vis the authorities, negotiating with parochial officers, sometimes threatening them, showing boldness or presenting their case by implicitly invoking their entitlement and right to relief. Petitions, in other words, were a tool in the survival strategies of the poor, and in their attempt to advance their case and enhance their chances for obtaining relief.[43] Nevertheless, it is important to emphasize that as parishioners struggled to negotiate their way and obtain the ears of parochial officers, their experience was invariably entwined with shame. Contesting parochial decision and turning to a higher authority, or appealing to a parish where they had no settlement, were permeated with humiliation and shame. The very formula of the written appeal manifestly and overly stressed a show of humility and deference to the authorities. That is, petitions were inherently and deliberately deferential, with shame built into the formula, whereby the poor who appealed presented their case not only by highlighting a desperate need for aid or their good character, but also by signalling their inferiority and the gulf that separated them from those on whom they depended for their relief. 'Your honours, who never faile to Contrive and provide for such miserable poor creatures as he'; your 'poor and without helpe miserable' petitioner, as some petitions expressed it.[44]

While overly conventional and formulaic, such rhetoric nevertheless was a powerful signal that reinforced and perpetuated the perceived lowly and dependent status of recipients of relief. Rather than a straightforward request or claim for relief, the written procedure postulated a position of personal begging and entreating, of gratitude and an apologetic stance vis-à-vis the authorities. Petitioners presented varied formulations of apology, expressing a desire not to be 'too troublesome' and a burden, or explaining that their turning to the parish was the absolute last resort after all else failed. Some expressed infinite gratefulness, belittling themselves so as to highlight their dependence on the goodwill of parish officers or vestry, asking not only to avoid being a burden on the parish but also not to cause personal offence nor trigger anger and scorn in officers: 'In regard your worshipfull have much business to trouble your heades withal'; 'that the worshipful would take noe affence att the preffering of this petition'; 'gentleman I desir that you Will not be angrey att me for sending to you' a request.[45] The formula fit well with other practices of written appeals to superiors, evidenced in pleas to private donors and charities in which aid was sought among the better off, as in the case of tenants seeking alms from landlords or aged urban citizens desiring relief from their guild. In all these petitions and appeals, the formula was a status signal that enhanced and reinforced the lowly status of the poor, framing it in terms of a shamed position of dependence and helplessness when facing the power and goodwill of an addressee.[46]

Beyond the formulaic shame, pauper letters also offer a glimpse of the actual experience of the shame entailed in poverty and destitution, or in the frustrations involved in confronting the authorities. A widowed petitioner in late sixteenth-century Exeter claimed to have 'sold and pawned all in her great want because she would not make her condition known', while a migrant labourer in 1662 allegedly 'obscured himself in a cottage about the space of three months unknown to the inhabitants, until exigency and necessity compelled him to crave their charity and relief'. The assize judges decided his plea should be conveyed to the parish of his abode.[47] Typically produced in erratic handwriting and phonetic spelling, pauper letters invariably used oral phrasing and everyday speech that went beyond the deference formula, conveying not only their material hardship and good character, but also a sense of dejection, hurt pride, or wounded self. In the 1690s, petitioners in Cumberland and Lancashire described how the charities they had relied on among neighbours had grown cold, while others exposed condescending and humiliating attitudes of overseers who were being 'uncharitable and inhumane', using 'wicked language' while turning them away. Still others reveal apprehension, fear, and shame at being treated with suspicion and mistrust by the officials. A petitioner at St Savior in London beseeched the overseers to resume paying her pension, for she was still unable to provide for her child, despite the fact that her husband was 'wearing an old black suit given him by a gentleman'. By the late eighteenth and early nineteenth century, pauper letters abounded with expressions that attest to a sense of vulnerability, apprehension, and fear of the shame entailed in wounded reputations.[48]

Recipients of relief were shamed in a myriad of other ways, being singled out, segregated, and stigmatized within their community, or, in the case of the pauper migrants, shamefully excluded. Hindle showed the varied parochial techniques with which poor migrants were excluded; from drawing up a census of all householders in which poor migrants were identified as potential burdens, through the requirement to provide 'indemnity bonds', guaranteeing they would never require relief in their new parish. Especially in times of economic difficulty, poor migrants were likely to be sent away, or shuttled back and forth across parish boundaries as vestries or parish authorities debated their fate. Local parishioners themselves sometimes voiced suspicion, fear and condemnation of the outsider poor person.[49]

As for residents of the parish who obtained relief, they, too, were subject to varied forms of 'small' humiliations that marked the gulf separating them from others in the community, signalling their position of dependency and want. Pensioners on regular relief were required to attend earlier services at church, and they often received inferior communion wine. From the late sixteenth century onwards, seating arrangements at church required that the poor be congregated in galleries that separated them from the rest of the community, with the recipients of alms and bread congregating at one end of the church and the bread presented to them for all to see. In the case of funds or bread allocated by the parish from private charities, the beneficiaries were required to 'show their respect'. Other forms of giving to the parochial poor resonated with public humiliation and symbols of shame that underlined their inferiority and dependence even as they received alms, whether at the house of a local landlord, elite funerals, or during feasts and celebrations in the countryside and in towns.[50]

Most conspicuous was the practice of badging the poor. Instated in the early sixteenth century, the badge initially presented a mark of approval and a testimonial of the paupers' status, which afforded them weekly alms or begging.[51] Even at this early stage, as Hindle observed, the line between the badge as a sign of approval and a stigma of poverty was blurred. Following the legislation that required a license for begging (1563, 1598), parish officers and vestries habitually badged the poor before and after offering the begging license, with the badge increasingly being viewed as a form of deterrence that would prevent the poor from begging, forcing them to stay at home 'and not go abroad'. A statute of 1697 reinforced the practice, stipulating that all poor persons receiving parish relief, together with their wives and children, would wear a badge with a 'P' and the initial letter of their parish, the badge of blue or red cloth to be placed on their shoulder 'in an open and visible manner'. Fines were also imposed on those who refused to wear the badge. While the statue was enforced somewhat haphazardly and applied only selectively on those who refused to conform, overall the badge remained a symbol of the stigma of poverty, with many among the poor resisting or refusing to wear it even if it meant forfeiting their entitlement to relief. By the late eighteenth century, critics of the relief system would point to the badge as a cruel 'mark of infamy' enforced on those relying for their livelihoods on parochial relief.[52]

Special programs initiated by parish authorities were also entangled with the humiliation and shame of the very poor. This was the case of programs to set the poor to work, intended for the most part for those among the poor who were capable of working – victims of injury or accidents and especially those overburdened with children.[53] Providing the poor with stock and material to spin, knit, or weave, at their homes or in special workshops and municipal workhouses, such programs were from the outset suffused with attitudes of suspicion towards the poor. Some workhouses stipulated careful supervision to avoid 'all prophaneness and vice', while in certain parishes the vicar and churchwardens distributed quarterly doles (from private charities) with the proviso that it would only be offered 'unto such as doe most worke and best' (in a workhouse).[54] These employment schemes remained erratic, but became more prevalent towards the later decades of the seventeenth century, when attempts to set the poor to work in workhouses were renewed, with at least 600 workhouses established, employing an estimated 30,000 people in them by the mid-eighteenth century. Statutory recognition in 1723 also empowered local vestries to withhold relief from those who were unwilling to enter a workhouse, often with the intention of discouraging the poor from turning to the parish for relief. Like the mandatory paupers' badges, parochial workhouses came to be used as a form of deterrence; as one member of Parliament declared in 1695, the intention was 'not only to employ the impotent in some measure', but also 'to terrify those of ability'.[55]

Among paupers themselves, the workhouse was widely perceived as a symbol of neglect, despair, and shame, a place where 'strong compulsion plucks the scrap from pride', as a poem in the late eighteenth century put it.[56] Historical research in recent decades has qualified this traditional dark image of the eighteenth-century workhouse, presenting a more benign picture of the role these institutions played in the lives of the very poor and their children, pointing to their benefits for young children and their families.[57] As Ottayway, in her study of the elderly, also showed, conditions in workhouses appear to have been tolerable, with instances of cruelty towards the elderly rare, and the workhouse serving as a hospice for the elderly among the 'poorest of the poor'. Nevertheless, as these studies also show, these institutions raised widespread apprehensions among the poor. Children were at times left in workhouses for long periods of time, while for the elderly, 'indoor' relief implied a decline in the quality of care provided by the community. With their strict rules regulating freedom of movement, along with the punitive measures against inmates who misbehaved, workhouses invoked widespread aversion, the poor preferring to avoid them, even at great cost. Above all, there was the stigma associated with entering a workhouse, symbolizing as it did not only loss of freedom but a failure to provide for oneself or obtain the support of family and friends.[58] In the case of paupers admitted to the workhouse when their children were still under their roof, there was the shame of failing to provide for their offspring, or exercising their authority over them, deeply harming the self-perception of the poor as parents and male heads of families. 'His wife and children look up to him no longer … [he] is sunk in the eyes of others and is altogether degraded in his own', as benefactor and reformer Catherine Cappe described the shame and humiliation of pauper fathers forced to enter the workhouse.[59]

The inability to provide for children was indeed among the deepest sources of poverty's shame. It was also evident in attitudes towards the compulsory binding of pauper children to apprenticeship and their removal from the parental home. Going back to parochial programs designed to alleviate the plight of parish orphans and those abandoned by their parents, plans for the binding out of older children as servants and apprentices were increasingly forced on the poor, with private charities invariably allocated to cover the costs of placing them with local masters. While the Elizabethan Poor Laws never made such practice compulsory, the seventeenth century, especially from the 1630s, witnessed intensive efforts to force apprenticeships on the children of the poor who obtained parochial relief, with the view of not only providing them with work and skills, but also reducing the burden on the rates.[60]

The evidence regarding parental reactions to these practices is sparse, but what there is suggests that, as in the case of the compulsory entry into workhouses, removing children from the homes of the poor caused resentment and shame. While in many cases these arrangements implied employment and care for the children by masters who benefited from their labour, the evidence also shows many masters who were hostile to these forced arrangements, consequently becoming fraudulent or abusive of these unwanted children who came to reside under their roof. Pauper parents themselves objected and were often reluctant to cooperate with these compulsory removals, even at the risk of being denied their own parochial assistance. While parents were apprehensive about the prospects of being deprived of their child's potential contribution to the family economy, it was their self-perception as parents that mattered the most, with removals threatening to expose them in their inability to perform their obligation towards their children. Some cases suggest that the poor would perceive any cooperation with the parish system of boarding out as tantamount to selling their children to others; 'What, would you sell my children?' was the response of a woman in Wickham (Durham) in reaction to a decision to offer her relief only if she entered a workhouse and agreed to have her children being bound apprentices.[61]

Most conspicuously was the shame of pauper mothers who gave birth to an illegitimate child. Well into the late seventeenth and early eighteenth century, the parenting, and especially the mothering, of 'a bastard child', entailed immense shame. The large body of research on illegitimacy has highlighted the great variations in the experiences of these women, but it has also confirmed that attitudes towards unmarried mothers remained negative throughout the era, and women pregnant with an illegitimate child were liable to go through a deep shaming ordeal.[62] The external expression of such shame is apparent in cases of women who aborted themselves or committed suicide, or of pregnant servants who lost their employment or became the subject of humiliation by masters, mistresses, or neighbours. Pregnant servants were forced to depart their parish and live in constant fear of being discovered, eventually giving birth in hiding, even amid the relative anonymity of the city of London. The delivery itself was a scene burdened with humiliation and shame, with women being pressured by midwives and others to reveal the name of the father. When the newborn was taken away and cared for, a servant might resume her life, but she still remained vulnerable to accusations and the stigma of whoredom, unless she permanently moved away from the parish.[63] For those who were determined to deliver and keep their infant, the shame and dishonour might become more public still, especially if the child was liable to fall on parochial relief. Mothers of illegitimate infants faced hostile questioning regarding fatherhood and were forced to confess their offence at church, or else be subject to inter-parish disputes, tossed around between parishes. Some would avoid presenting their illegitimate offspring for baptism. Many would find it difficult to obtain work as a live-in servant.[64]

Some of these mothers were forced to abandon their child, placing it on the church porch, the doorstep of wealthy families, or the street.[65] By the mid-eighteenth century, mothers of illegitimate children turned to London's newly established Foundling Hospital, where poor mothers – many of them unmarried women who had migrated from the countryside – placed their children in the care of the institution.[66] The notes some of them left with their infants, between 1741 and 1760, offer glimpses of their circumstances and the emotions surrounding child abandonment. Addressing the hospital governors with pleas of entreating and gratitude typically found in pauper petitions, these notes not only gave details of the child but also pointed to a sense of shame in being unable to provide for the newborn, with some bleakly stating their child was 'of honest but unfortunate parents', 'of an unhappy but truly virtuous woman', or claiming that when leaving the child to the hospital's care they did it 'from a Bleeding hart and Great destress'. Some avowed that they intended to leave the child only 'till such times as she can take it back', with many of the women leaving tokens of clothing or personal belonging (a silver box in a green silk purse, in one case) that would enable them to reclaim and reunite with their child. Some mothers indicated a deep sense of guilt, pleading that the governors of the hospital forgive them for 'this fault of ours' in deserting an infant to the care of others.[67]

Petitions presented to the Foundling Hospital from the 1760s onwards were more detailed and explicit about the poverty and destitution that enforced mothers to abandon their child, and the pain of shame it entailed. Some expressed insult and rage at being left to care for their child by men who after 'repeated promises of marriage humiliatingly forsook' them, obliging them to raise a child 'at her own expense without having received a single penny from the father of the child'. Others invoked a sense of alienation and estrangement in their communities, 'being left with no support nor relations family or friends to rely on'; 'being reduced to the lowest and most deplorable circumstances having no friend or relation to assist' them, at times referring to 'friends [who] in consequence of her imprudent Conduct Turned Their Backs on her and her infant'. Some mothers expressed outright humiliation and shame, stating that 'shame prevented me from applying to my friends … and might be a means of breaking my poor Mothers Heart if she knew my Unhappy situation'. Still others conveyed fear of 'not only being exposed to Shame amongst her friends but must be left in utmost want and Poverty' unless the child was admitted to the hospital.[68]

Children who were left to the care of the hospital were also likely to be subject to stigma and shame as they grew up and matured. Having benefitted from the hospital's provision of livelihood and education, and overall living in better conditions compared to those children living in workhouses, the future prospects of the children were still restricted, with most entering domestic service, lower trades, or sea service.[69] Beyond the lowly status to which they were destined, there was also the enduring stigma of their origins and upbringing at the hospital, as indicated in the instructions offered to them in a ceremony that marked their placing as apprentices and their departure from the hospital. Advising them to behave honestly, diligently, and avoid 'many temptations to be wickedly', the governors warned the children that if they failed in their conduct, they would bring upon themselves 'Misery, shame and Want'. Alongside moral advice, such instructions were also a strong reminder of the children's origins and the debt they owed the hospital; 'you were taken to it very young, quite helpless, forsaken and deserted by Parents and Friends. Out of Charity have you been fed, cloathed, and instructed'. Urging the children to make 'grateful acknowledgement to the Hospital for the benefits you have received', the governors encouraged them to overcome the stigma likely to be attached to life in the hospital: 'Be not ashamed that you were bred in this Hospital. Own it; and say, that it was through the good Providence of almighty God that you were taken Care of'.[70]

We may never know the full extent to which the type of shame alluded to by the governors was internalized by the youngsters who embarked on life on their own. Nor can we fully gauge the overall effect of poverty on a pauper's sense of shame, or how far the experience of shame pervaded and came to dominate their lives. As already noted, and as we shall also see in the next chapter, poor people invariably resisted or defied the shame wreaked on them by others. Yet it should also be pointed out that glimpses in the records still suggest varied forms of hidden, or unspoken, shame, as in the case of those left to fend for themselves, being 'harried across parish boundaries, begging for bread and ale, snatching a few hours' sleep in barns and church porches, and pleading with the parish for the right to belong'.[71] Testimonies at court in the seventeenth century sometimes reveal the shame endured by the elderly poor who lived on their own, sick and without the help of kin or a nurse, their failing body being degraded and exposed, to the dismay if not disgust of neighbours or passers-by; the fear of 'dying like a beggar' could be imminent.[72] By the early nineteenth century Francis Place would poignantly describe how 'adverse circumstances force on them [i.e., poor fathers] those indescribable feelings of their own degradation which sinks them gradually to the extreme of wretchedness'. As Snell also argued, the source of poverty's shame was not only poverty itself, or even an inability to provide for one's children, but the alienation and deprivation of those bereft of connectedness and the ties of family and friends.[73]

## The penal system and shame

The single most powerful agent of shame across communities was the penal system exercised through an array of ecclesiastical and secular courts. By

1500, a dense set of courts – archdeaconries and consistories, manorial courts and leets, municipal and guild courts, petty and quarter sessions, county assizes – prosecuted a host of transgressions, from sexual misconduct (adultery, fornication, bastardy) through offences against the community (scolding or eavesdropping), and those associated with poverty (taking subtenants, vagrancy). As the sixteenth century wore on, the range of transgressions increasingly embraced not only heresy, idolatry or sexual immorality, but also non-conformity, blasphemy or Sabbath-breaking, as well as a more intricate range of offences associated with poverty and the social order – vagrancy and begging, petty theft, dishonest dealings, fraud, slander and more. Offences long considered a capital crime – heresy and treason, homicide, rape and infanticide – were expanded to include additional types of misconduct, especially certain crimes against property, such as grand larceny.[74]

The punishments meted out on transgressors varied greatly, embracing a set of traditional along with more innovative penalties. In many cases, the penalty entailed the payment of fines, or, increasingly, confinement, with offenders being sent to houses of corrections ('Bridewells'), gaols, and prisons. Other punishments involved more traditional forms such as carting, riding backwards, or ducking offenders, with the courts in these instances reinforcing the kind of penal practices variably exacted by communities on their errant members. Other penalties were exclusive to the courts, and could include enforced public penance, the pillory or the stocks, hair cutting, eviction, branding, hard labour, and whipping. Offenders were carted, paraded, ducked, and put in stocks throughout the seventeenth century and well into the eighteenth, while whipping became, already in the late sixteenth century, the standard sentence for misdemeanours, especially in cases of petty larceny. Most conspicuously and looming above all these punishments were capital crimes punishable by death. Under the Tudors, executions appear to have become common for a wide range of crimes, with the government stiffening penalties for particularly heinous crimes by excluding them from the category of pardonable crimes (the 'benefit of clergy'). While by the mid- and late seventeenth century the rate of executions fell, significant numbers among those being acquitted were discharged with a branded thumb, subjected to whipping, and, increasingly, transported to the colonies in North America.[75]

As research has shown, the judicial authority played a pivotal role in asserting the sovereignty of the English state and its power to maintain control over individuals and the social order at large. The prime aim of the penal system was to deter, with offenders being punished so that they 'be made an example to all others, whether it be by cart, tumbrel, cookstool, the stocks, pillory, or otherwise by imprisonment', as an ordinance in Hull put it in 1563.[76] Judges and juries had wide discretionary powers, applying their sentences selectively; while most offenders were acquitted, reprieved, and pardoned, or, in the case of misdemeanours, punished with fines, a minority of those found guilty were punished publicly, their punishment being performed for others to behold and fear. In Tudor London, penalties

Communities as sites of shame 157

were performed at the church, the marketplace or both, with some offenders being compelled to traverse several marketplaces and amidst most crowded fares.[77] Stocks and the pillory, whipping, ducking, and hanging were all open events designed to attract large crowds of neighbours as well as strangers. The daily display of these punishing tools – a cucking-stool or a pair of stocks on show, whipping posts – served, so it was believed, as a reminder of the risks and costs entailed in misconduct. Historian Paul Griffiths estimated that there would have been 'something to view in most major marketplaces every weekend or mid-week market ... usually timed for the peak hour of buying and selling'.[78] Whipping parades and especially executions continued to draw large crowds throughout the seventeenth century and well into the mid-eighteenth and beyond.[79]

Yet over and above its power to deter, the penal system was blatantly designed to inflict humiliation and shame. Punishments were not only contrived to set an example, but to 'rebuke and shame'.[80] Penalties were turned into public events that featured varied and elaborate forms of ritual steeped with acts and symbols of disgrace. In the early sixteenth century, heretics performing penance in the church would not only stand or kneel on a platform to ensure complete visibility when admitting their sins, but were also compelled to walk barefoot, bareheaded, and garbed in a skimpy white shift, carrying faggots (symbol of the fire the heretic deserved). While some of these elements were omitted under the Reformed Church, public penance retained its features as a religious ritual, with culprits being forced to come to the church in penitential garb, attend a sermon and then confess their sins to the congregation.[81] Many punishments involved processions, headed by civil officers or minstrels, featuring musical instruments and raucous crowds, the offenders being forced to carry 'papers' announcing their offence, or ride backwards on a horse and hold the tail in a gesture that bolstered their disgrace. Actual objects associated with the offence – for example, goods allegedly stolen or traded dishonestly – were sometimes staged and carried along the parade.[82] Most conspicuous were public executions, which by the seventeenth century became an ostentatious ceremony blending spectacle and procession with religious rites. In London, the hour-long procession between Newgate and Tyburn displayed the malefactors on a cart, their hands or legs tied with a rope or chains, the great bell of St Sepulchre tolling throughout. The ritual came to its peak at the place of execution, where the crowds became dense, the Ordinary gave his exhortations, with the malefactors offering a last dying speech before the cart or ladder was drawn.[83]

At the heart of all these shaming rituals was the body of the condemned. Bodies were marked with shame – physically abused, disfigured, or mutilated, or helplessly and degradingly exposed. By the mid- and late sixteenth century, sexual offenders punished with penance were still forced to wear certain degrading clothes or go barefoot and carry a sign on their back and breast indicating their 'Fylthye lyveinge & shameless bragging' in large letters.[84] At the stocks and the pillory, where offenders were forced to sit or stand with legs, hands or head locked in a wooden board, their bodies were subject to physical torment and vulnerable to the abuse of passers-by, the culprits undergoing an ordeal laden with a sense of helplessness and indignity.[85] Ducking or cutting their hair would subject women to the torment of near suffocation and humiliation, with hair being publicly shorn 'for a deformitie' (as one contemporary put it) and as a mark of infamy. While cheek branding was not commonly implemented (the act allowing it was repealed in 1593), burning the hands of convicted criminals who were pardoned became common; in these cases, the stigma of the offence remained imprinted on the body long after the victim had endured the pain. In the case of flogging, offenders would be tied to a cart, stripped to the waist and at times almost naked, the rod or whip applied to their shoulders, back, or buttocks 'till his bodye blede', as court orders invariably specified.[86]

Nowhere was bodily shame more blatant than in the case of the death penalty. At the place of execution, the malefactors' body was exposed 'trembling and shaking to a great Degree, very naked, and in a most miserable condition', death by strangulation subsequently taking long painful minutes and the sufferer's body showing 'struggles and convulsions' – a 'very undecent Spectacle', as was reported in the early eighteenth century.[87] Bodies of particularly heinous offenders could also be subject to the still more ignominious hanging in chains ('gibbeting'). Above all, there was the degradation manifested in the treatment of the corpse following the execution. In the case of serious crime (treason, murder) male corpses were drawn, quartered, disembowelled, and decapitated; women committing similar crimes were burned at the stake. While the burning was intended to avoid 'the exposing and publicly mangling their bodies', the burning body of the female signalled, as in the case of heretics executed by fire, utter obliteration and the shame of being denied a decent burial and grave.[88] In lesser crimes, the corpse was supposed to remain hung for an hour, whence it was cut down and delivered to the deceased's family, with unclaimed corpses being buried in anonymous graves. By the early eighteenth century, the bodies of malefactors executed at Tyburn were also taken to be dissected and anatomized by surgeons of the College of Physicians, the practice raising the spectre of bodily shame further still; the prospect of having a body disfigured after death caused immense popular disdain. In a case in 1725 the malefactor pleaded to gibbet his body after the execution in order to 'escape the Mangling of Surgeons knives, which to him seemed ten Thousand times worse than Death itself'.[89]

It might be argued that the harsh and humiliating shame meted out on offenders could, under certain circumstances, be mitigated, its consequences allayed through notions of shame's capacity to correct culprits and re-integrate them into the community. Most of the public penalties were performed within communal spaces, with offenders going through an ordeal of humiliation and pain that was ultimately designed to lead to a return to the community, generating, in the process, unity and solidarity between all. The model for this mode of shaming was the public penance, in which admission of shame and sin before the congregation indicated a willingness

## Communities as sites of shame 159

to reform, the ritual culminating in community forgiveness and the restoration of harmony.[90] The physical torment that was linked to penance and other penalties could also be conceived as potentially re-integrative, the pain acting to purify the soul of the condemned along with the community as a whole.[91] This notion of re-integration was consistent with the judicial process itself, whereby magistrates handling petty crime encouraged victims and their offenders to reach conciliation rather than go to court. Shame punishments were only applied as a last resort and were designed to allow culprits to be brought back into the fold of the community. In the case of felonies, malefactors condemned to death could plead and obtain pardon, in which case they would also attend a public ceremony of shame and conciliation, being called by their names at court, pleading on their knees for pardon, the judges then announcing the goodness of the Majesties' act of grace.[92] The ritual of the execution itself exhibited a measure of re-integrative shame, the malefactors offering last dying speeches that could embrace repentance and assumption of shame and guilt, with crowds often responding with pity and compassion towards the condemned.[93]

For all this evident display of reformative and re-integrative shame, the penal system overall applied and inflicted punitive and exclusionary shame; the line between the two strands of shaming remaining blurred, with the punitive mode ultimately overpowering the more inclusive elements of the shame. This was evident in the ritual of execution, which subjected individuals to an extreme form of exclusionary and retributive shame. The site of the execution itself – in scattered locations on parish boundaries and increasingly in permanent sites at the peripheries of communities, mirrored the marginalization and ostracism of the condemned.[94] More important still was the treatment of the victim's body before, during, and following the hanging, and especially the denial of customary burial – all of which marked convicts as outcasts in life and even in death, depriving them of the last shreds of humanity and dignity; an utter exclusion not only from the community but from human kind.

Exclusionary shame pervaded all other shame penalties, even when these were designed as a form of re-integration. In public penance, which focused on contrition and conciliation, the stigma of having had to publicly confess one's faults could endure long after the ritual ended; and when penitents had to stand bareheaded or barefooted in church or the marketplace, wearing signs that advertised their offence, the shame experience was similar to spending long hours in the pillory.[95] The pillory and the stocks, riding backwards on a horse, ducking, whipping – all these penalties marked the culprit as an outcast, exposing their helplessly tormented and uncontrolled body, at times relegating them to the world of the inhuman and the beast. The shame was stigmatic; it indicated not simply faults and misdeeds, but a degraded identity stripped of status, honour, and dignity as a human being. This type of destructive shame could lead, as some contemporaries avowed, to illness and death. And as evidence in diaries also indicates, the prospect of the pillory could drive some individuals to commit suicide.[96]

## Conclusion

The shame inflicted amid early modern communities was a powerful tool in the regulation of conduct and enforcement of conformity. Deeply embedded in traditional attitudes and ideas regarding sexual morality and the patriarchal order, shame practices were reinforced by novel Protestant notions of sin and moral discipline, and by emerging new ideas regarding poverty and the poor. Growing class divisions and the tensions that could engulf communities also triggered – directly or more latently – incidents of shaming and shame, with ordinary people intermittently subjecting their superiors to ridicule and shame for their injustices and oppressions. Especially evident was the reinforcement of shame practices under the auspices and increased power of state institutions at the local level, the period overall witnessing the growth of a parochial system of poor relief, which, while extending aid and fostering charity to some among the poor, remained deeply anxious and suspicious, or even fearful, of its poor. More important was the role of the courts, ecclesiastical and increasingly civil, the latter coming to use an expanded range of shame penalties to counter a growing array of social and moral transgressions.

Public shame varied in its uses and ramifications. Some forms of community shame were applied moderately, or else they generated a process of conciliation, with the reactions of spectators acting to mitigate the effects of the initial disgrace. The shame could be implicit, taking the form of a rebuke, gesture, or tacit derision through rumours and gossip. More explicit forms of shaming – public insult and defamation – could still end with a process of reconciliation that entailed the payment of fines or the assumption of guilt and expressions of forgiveness. Some instances of shame could be short and cursory – a brief episode of communal riding, a short spell in the pillory – allowing individuals to sustain their ties and return to the daily routine of neighbourly relations and interactions. The shame of the poor – when forced to stand separately at church or plead for parochial relief – was mitigated by public gestures of compassion and communal offering, which tacitly acknowledged the needs of the very poor. Evident too was the shame aimed at reformation and rehabilitation through rituals of repentance and forgiveness, with the infliction of physical pain being conceived as a means of purifying the wrongdoer and the community. More important still, instances of mitigated shame were evident in the reactions of crowds to scenes of public humiliation and shame – posted libels, ducking, carting, whipping – when some among the crowd expressed shame over the abuse of victims, siding with the offenders against those orchestrating the event or the magistrates inflicting the shame. Acts of pardon along with repentance and forgiveness were invariably manifest in capital punishments and the ritual of the execution itself, with the crowds often showing pity and compassion that would attenuate the harsh shame inflicted on the condemned.

For all these instances of mitigated, or more explicitly re-integrative, shame, exacting shame amid public spaces was primarily punitive and exclusionary,

## Communities as sites of shame    161

the shame focusing on – and at times intentionally inflicting – humiliation, degradation, or retribution. Verbal assaults and slanderous accusations could have enduring implications for their victims, damaging their reputation, at times destroying the lives of their families. Some forms of popular and judicial shaming (riding, ducking) were deliberately vengeful, especially when the incidents turned into large-scale events or when the penalty was enforced repeatedly, leaving an indelible memory among neighbours and the community at large. When inflicted on religious or ethnic minorities, mock and derogatory epithets stereotyped and isolated these groups, marking them as outcasts, with contempt, rancour, and verbal or physical assaults engendering cycles of shaming and shame.

Especially significant was the role of state institutions in enhancing the coercive and exclusionary dimensions of public shame. Relief programs designed to aid the poor could still add shame to the humiliation entailed in a state of poverty and the inability to provide for oneself and one's offspring. Those deemed unworthy of relief – young people and vagrants seeking relief or employ and lacking a steady habitation, pregnant women with illegitimate offspring – were prone to experience the shame of ostracism and outright removal from the bounds of the parish. Coercive shame ultimately dominated the penal system, with scenes of ritualized shame imprinting the stigma of the culprits' offence on their bodies, exposing them to abuse and leaving them helpless in the face of sometimes hostile or vengeful crowds. Even public penance, which was designed to re-integrate the confessing culprit into the community, involved deep humiliation, with the shame stigmatizing the repentant as outright faulty. Most other shame penalties inflicted by the judicial system marked offenders as persons with a degraded personhood, denigrating their humanity and hurting their sense of dignity as human beings.

In all these practices of punitive shame, both formal and informal, ordinary people did not remain passive victims or observers of the shame perpetrated in their midst. As noted above, communities did not always take indiscriminate and unthinking part in public shaming, their reactions indicating divisions or else showing compassion towards the victims of shame. People of middle and lower classes sometimes appropriated the shame and subjected those above them to critique and verbal abuse that utterly defied the conventions of deference and the subservience they owed to their superiors. Nor did the poor fully cooperate or consent to their dependence as recipients of relief, with many among them negotiating and manipulating a parochial system that exacerbated their shame, showing boldness and invoking a perception of their entitlement and right to relief. Poverty-stricken people at times declined to cooperate with a relief program they deemed degrading, refusing to wear the badge or enter into a workhouse; mothers of illegitimate offspring defied their shame, showing resilience and raising their children in adverse circumstances and hardship. Sexual offenders forced to make penance at church remained obdurate or indifferent, defying their humiliation and public shame.[97] As we shall also see in the

## 162  Communities as sites of shame

following chapter, resilience, defiance, and expressions of self-respect in the face of brutal shaming and humiliating punishments were articulated and given greater voice as the period progressed from the early decades of the seventeenth century through the early eighteenth century, and beyond.

## Notes

1. Lawrence Stone, *The Family, Sex and Marriage in England 1500–1800* (New York, 1977), 142–50; Richard M. Smith, '"Modernization" and the Corporate Medieval Village Community in England: Some Skeptical Reflections', in A.H.R. Baker and Derek Gregory (eds.), *Explorations in Historical Geography* (Cambridge, 1984), esp. 148–9; John Braithwaite, 'Shame and Modernity', *British Journal of Criminology*, 33 (1993), 2; Peter N. Stearns, *Shame: A Brief History* (Chicago, 2017), 14–16.
2. The literature on these themes is vast. For an overall view of the findings, see Keith Wrightson (ed.), *A Social History of England, 1500–1700* (Cambridge, 2017). And see also Craig Muldrew, *The Economy of Obligation: The Culture of Credit and Social Relations in Early Modern England* (Basingstoke, 1998), esp. 15–94; Marjorie Keniston McIntosh, *Controlling Misbehavior in England, 1370–1600* (Cambridge, 1998).
3. Major recent studies include Simon Devereaux and Paul Griffiths (eds.), *Penal Practice and Culture, 1500–1900* (Basingstoke, 2004); David Nash and Anne-Marie Kilday, *Cultures of Shame: Exploring Crime and Morality in Britain, 1600–1900* (Basingstoke, 2010); Alexandra Walsham, *Charitable Hatred: Tolerance and Intolerance in England, 1500–1700* (Manchester, 2006); Bernard Capp, *England's Culture Wars: Puritan Reformation and Its Enemies in the Interregnum, 1649–1660* (Oxford, 2012); Martin Ingram, *Carnal Knowledge: Regulating Sex in England, 1470–1600* (Cambridge, 2017).
4. For an overview of the types of offences subject to popular shaming, see Nash and Kilday, *Cultures of Shame*, 26–9, 197, notes 8–12. And see also Walsham, *Charitable Hatred*, 120–49.
5. Martin Ingram, 'Ridings, Rough Music and Mocking Rhymes in Early Modern England', in Barry Reay (ed.), *Popular Culture in Seventeenth-Century England* (London, 1985), 166–97; Adam Fox, 'Ballads, Libels and Popular Ridicule in Jacobean England', *Past and Present*, 145 (1994), 62; Nash and Kilday (eds.), *Cultures of Shame*, 37–46. For skimmington rituals during bursts of anti-Quaker violence, especially against female Quakers, see Walsham, *Charitable Hatred*, 120, 145.
6. Bernard Capp, *When Gossips Meet: Women, Family and Neighbourhood in Early Modern England* (Oxford, 2003), 233–4.
7. Nash and Kilday, *Cultures of Shame*, 31–7, 197, notes 13–14.
8. Walsham, *Charitable Hatred*, 138. And see also Natalie Zemon Davis, 'The Rites of Violence', in *Society and Culture in Early Modern France* (Stanford, 1975), 152–88, esp. 164–9.
9. Martin Ingram, 'Ridings, Rough Music and the "Reform of Popular Culture" in Early Modern England', *Past and Present*, 105 (1984), 62–3; David Underdown, 'The taming of the Scold: The Enforcement of Patriarchal Authority in Early Modern England', in Anthony Fletcher and John Stevenson (eds.), *Order and Disorder in Early Modern England* (Cambridge, 1985), 116–36, esp. 123–4; Nash and Kilday, *Cultures of Shame*, 31–7, quotation on 43.
10. Ingram, 'Ridings, Rough Music and Mocking Rhymes', 178–97; Fox, 'Ballads, Libels and Popular Ridicule'; Adam Fox, *Oral and Literate Culture in England 1500–1700* (Oxford, 2000), Chap. 6.
11. Capp, *When Gossips Meet*, 189–203, 226–34; Alexandra Shepard, *Meanings of Manhood in Early Modern England* (Oxford, 2003), 152–85.

12 Walsham, *Charitable Hatred*, 124–9. Violence and debasing gestures could include the V-sign (cuckold's horns), touching the body of the shamed person, boxing the ears or face of an opponent, making him 'go down on their knees', spitting in their face, exposing body parts, pulling beards or gowns and kicking. Capp, *When Gossips Meet*, 232; Shepard, *Meanings of Manhood*, 144.
13 Capp, *When Gossips Meet*, 185–9; Shepard, *Meanings of Manhood*, 157–9; Walsham, *Charitable Hatred*, 129–49. For the use of libels and mock sermons in local gentry rivalries, see Fox, 'Ballads, Libels and Popular Ridicule', 69.
14 Ibid., 74–75.
15 Capp, *When Gossips Meet*, 203–17, quote on 208, 279–81. For considerable financial damages caused by slander, see also Shepard, *Meanings of Manhood*, 160.
16 For the extensive literature on defamation cases at the courts, see Shepard, *Meanings of Manhood*, 152–3, notes 2–4; David Cressy, *Dangerous Talk: Scandalous, Seditious, and Treasonable Speech in Pre-Modern England* (Oxford, 2010), 280, note 28.
17 Capp, *When Gossips Meet*, 193, 212; Walsham, *Charitable Hatred*, 128, 147. For the donkey ride as a 'blatant attempt to have the culprits removed or exorcized from the community on a permanent basis', see Nash and Kilday, *Cultures of Shame*, 37.
18 Ingram, 'Ridings, Rough Music and Mocking Rhymes', 168–9; Nash and Kilday, *Cultures of Shame*, 37–44.
19 Ibid., 35, 42–5; Martin Ingram, '"Scolding Women Cucked or Washed": a Crisis in Gender Relations in Early Modern England?' in Jennifer Kermode and Garthine Walker (eds.), *Women, Crime and the Courts in Early Modern England* (London, 1994), 48–80, esp. 60–4.
20 Fox, 'Ballads, Libels and Popular Ridicule', 76–7; Nash and Kilday, *Cultures of Shame*, 35; Capp, *When Gossips Meet*, 60. For divisions and community uproar caused by accusations of whoredom, see Steve Hindle 'The shaming of Margaret Knowsley: gossip, gender and the experience of authority in early modern England', *Continuity and Change*, 9 (1994), 391–419, esp. 407.
21 For mocking and derision as part of male alehouse culture and 'good fellowship', whereby fellows were shamed and disgraced in case they failed to control their body (bladder) and succumbed to a state of drunken stupor, see Mark Hailwood, *Alehouses and Good Fellowship in Early Modern England* (Woodbridge, 2014), 170–1. For shaming as an element of 'rite de passage' among mariners, where newly arrived apprentices suffering sea sickness were subject to ridicule and shame ('for mariners are apt to mock at such and scarcely esteem them sufficient seamen'), see Richard Norwood, *The Journal of Richard Norwood, Surveyor of Bermuda* (New York, 1945), 39.
22 Capp, *When Gossips Meet*, 199, 210.
23 Ibid., 59–60, 213–14, 224.
24 Ingram, 'Ridings, Rough Music and Mocking Rhymes', 171.
25 For the plebian character of the charivari, and the involvement of more substantial members as witnesses or instigators (rather than victims) of the ridings, see Ingram, 'The "Reform of Popular Culture"', esp. 104–5.
26 Cressy, *Dangerous Talk*, 27–33; Shepard, *Meanings of Manhood*, 173–85, quotation on 180.
27 Fox, 'Ballads, Libels and Popular Ridicule', esp. 61–3.
28 Ibid., 67–8.
29 Ibid., 65–6. And see also Christopher Marsh, *Music and Society in Early Modern England* (Cambridge, 2010), 325–7.
30 Fox, 'Ballads, Libels and Popular Ridicule', 61–3, 67–71.
31 Ibid., 78, 81–2.
32 Ibid., 73–4.
33 Ibid., 49–50.

34 Ibid., 65, 81. For libellers' attention to names as a form of stigmatization, see Andrew McRay, *Literature, Satire and the Early Stuart State* (Cambridge, 2004), 55–6.
35 Fox, 'Ballads, Libels and Popular Ridicule', 77–8.
36 Ibid., 76; Ingram, 'The "Reform of Popular Culture"', 95; Walsham, *Charitable Hatred*, 127, 145.
37 Fox, 'Ballads, Libels and Popular Ridicule', 80. Libel composed against Thomas Shillito, the high constable of Barkston, Yorkshire.
38 Ibid., 70–3, 76, 81–2.
39 McRay, *Literature, Satire and the Early Stuart State*, 51–84, 208–24. See also Alastair Bellany, '"Raylinge Rymes and Vaunting Verse": Libellous Politics in Early Stuart England, 1603–1628', in Kevin Sharpe and Peter Lake (eds.), *Culture and Politics in Early Stuart England* (Basingstoke, 1994), 285–310; Cressy, *Dangerous Talk*, Chaps. 7–8, 139–202. For satyr and shame from the mid-seventeenth-century through the mid-eighteenth, see Chap. 7.
40 Paul Slack, *Poverty and Policy in Tudor and Stuart England* (London and New York, 1988); McIntosh, *Controlling Misbehavior in England*, 193–203; Marjorie Keniston McIntosh, *Poor Relief in England 1350–1600* (Cambridge, 2012), 15–25; Steve Hindle, *On the Parish? The Micro-Politics of Poor Relief in Rural England c. 1550–1750* (Oxford, 2004), 99–104; Paul A. Fideler, *Social Welfare in Pre-Industrial England* (Basingstoke, 2006), 47–54. For an exceptional view of the causes of poverty as rooted in economic conditions, which deviated from the dominant ideology, see Patrick Collinson, 'Puritanism and the Poor', in Rosemary Horrox and Sarah Rees Jones (eds.), *Pragmatic Utopias: Ideals and Communities, 1200–1630* (Cambridge, 2001), 242–58.
41 Hindle, *On the Parish?*, 362, 379–98. For the historiographical debate on the notion of entitlement for relief among the poor, see ibid., 398–405.
42 Jeremy Bolton, 'Going on the Parish: The Parish Pension and its Meaning in the London Suburbs, 1640–1724', in Tim Hitchcock, Pamela Sharpe and Peter King (eds.), *Chronicling Poverty: The Voices and Strategies of the English Poor, 1640–1840* (Basingstoke, 1997), 19–46, esp. 32; Hindle, *On the Parish?* 405, 413–23. For pauper letters following the Acts of Settlement (1662, 1691 and 1697), see Steven King, 'Pauper Letters as a Source', *Family and Community History*, 10 (2007), 167–70.
43 Hindle, *On the Parish?*, 361–449, esp. 445–9; Steven King, 'Introduction: Voices of the Poor in the Long Eighteenth Century', in Alysa Levin (ed.), *Narratives of the Poor in Eighteenth-Century Britain* (London 2006), Vol. 1, *Voices of the Poor: Poor Law Depositions and Letters*, edited by Steven King, Thomas Nutt and Alannah Tomkins, xxxiii–liv; Thomas Sokoll (ed.), *Essex Pauper Letters, 1731–1837* (Records of Social and Economic History, 30, Oxford, 2001), 1–70. For a greater emphasis on the agency and boldness of pauper appeals, see also P.D. Jones and S.A. King, 'From Petition to Pauper Letter: The Development of an Epistolary Form', in P.D. Jones and S.A. King, *Obligation, Entitlement and Dispute Under the English Poor Laws* (Cambridge Scholars Publishing, 2016).
44 Hindle, *On the Parish?*, 414.
45 LMA, P92/Sav/749–780, Petitions for relief, St Saviour, Southwark. By the early nineteenth century, an apologetic stance still pervaded pauper letters: 'I ham sorry to have ... the unpleasant necessity of making applycation'; 'I bag pardon for writing a gain'; 'I humably beg pardon', 'I ham vary sorry to be under the necessity of trobeling you again'. Levene (ed.), *Narratives of the Poor*, Vol. 1, 9, 11, 14 and passim.
46 Ilana Krausman Ben-Amos, *The Culture of Giving: Informal Support and Gift Exchange in Early Modern England* (Cambridge, 2008), 196–203.
47 Slack, *Poverty and Policy*, 192; Hindle, *On the Parish?*, 337, 410–11.
48 Hindle, *On the Parish?*, 385–6, 407, 414–15; LMA, P92/Sav/765; King, 'Introduction', liv. See also K.D.M. Snell, 'Belonging and community: understandings of home and friends among the English Poor, 1750–1850', *Economic*

*History Review*, 65 (2012), 1–25. For letters' rhetoric that went beyond the formula of deference, see Thomas Sokoll, 'Writing for Relief: Rhetoric in English Pauper Letters, 1800–1834', in Andreas Gestrich, Steven King and Raphael Lutz (eds.), *Being Poor in Modern Europe: Historical Perspectives 1800–1940* (Oxford, 2006), 91–112.

49 For an extended treatment of these issues of the micro-politics of varied forms of exclusion, see Hindle, *On the Parish?*, 311–60.
50 Ibid., 383; Ben-Amos, *Culture of Giving*, 215.
51 The following paragraph is based on Hindle, *On the Parish?*, 433–45.
52 Patricia Crawford, *Parents of Poor Children in England, 1580–1800* (Oxford, 2010), 162. For the practice of badging pensioners in almshouses, see also McIntosh, *Poor Relief in England*, 204; Ben Amos, *The Culture of Giving*, 237.
53 Slack, *Poverty and Policy*, 148–56; Hindle, *On the Parish?*, 174–86, 379.
54 Slack, *Poverty and Policy*, 152; Hindle, *On the Parish?*, 183.
55 Ibid., 186–91 quotation on 187.
56 Susannah R. Ottaway, *The Decline of Life: Old Age in Eighteenth-Century England* (Cambridge, 2004), 248–9.
57 Alysa Levene, *The Childhood of the Poor: Welfare in Eighteenth-Century London* (Basingstoke, 2012), 107–29.
58 Ottaway, *The Decline of Life*, 247–76, esp. 258–9.
59 Crawford, *Parents of Poor Children*, 162–3, 149.
60 McIntosh, *Poor Relief in England*, 245–52; Hindle, *On the Parish?*, 191–223.
61 Crawford, *Parents of Poor Children*, 157–8; Hindle, *On the Parish?*, 222–3.
62 For the literature on illegitimacy, see Crawford, *Parents of Poor Children*, Chaps. 1–2, 30–111; Tanya Evans, *'Unfortunate Objects': Lone Mothers in Eighteenth-Century London* (Basingstoke, 2005).
63 Crawford, *Parents of Poor Children*, 41–6; Eleanor Hubbard, *City of Women: Money, Sex, and the Social Order in Early Modern London* (Oxford, 2012), 79–110, esp. 80–5.
64 By the early nineteenth century, about 40 per cent of illegitimate children were not recorded as baptized; Crawford, *Parents of Poor Children*, 32.
65 Crawford, *Parents of Poor Children*, 46–8; Hubbard, *City of Women*, 103–4.
66 For the history of the hospital, see Donna T. Andrew, *Philanthropy and Police: London Charity in the Eighteenth Century* (Princeton, 1989), 57–64; Levene (ed.), *Narratives of the Poor*, Vol. 3, *Institutional Responses: The London Foundling Hospital*, introduction by Elysa Levine, vii–xviii; Tim Hitchcock and Robert Shoemaker, *London Lives: Poverty, Crime and the Making of a Modern City, 1690–1800* (Cambridge, 2015), 162–5.
67 Levene (ed.), *Narratives of the Poor*, Vol. 3, 128, 142, 132, 166–7, 138.
68 Ibid., 181, 191, 199–200, 178, 228–9, 214, 215.
69 Levene (ed.), *Narratives of the Poor*, Vol. 3, introduction, xiii. For the negative aspects of the hospital (high rates of mortality, the policy of open admissions (especially after 1756) and forced removal of infants to the hospital), 'leaving a trail of heartbreak' among families torn apart by the policy, see also Hitchcock and Shoemaker, *London Lives*, 253–4.
70 Levene (ed.), *Narratives of the Poor*, Vol. 3, 123–4. For negative attitudes to illegitimate children, considered of 'base blood' and made to feel inferior, see Crawford, *Parents of Poor Children*, 111.
71 Hindle, *On the Parish?*, 432.
72 Hubbard, *City of Women*, 270–1.
73 Crawford, *Parents of Poor Children*, 149; Snell, 'Belonging and community'.
74 Major works on these themes include McIntosh, *Controlling Misbehavior*, 24–45, 54–107; Devereaux and Griffiths (eds.), *Penal Practice and Culture*, Introduction 1–35; Martin Ingram, *Carnal Knowledge: Regulating Sex in England, 1470–1600* (Cambridge, 2017); Bernard Capp, *England's Culture*

166  Communities as sites of shame

Wars: Puritan Reformation and its Enemies in the Interregnum 1649–1660 (Oxford, 2012); Robert B. Shoemaker, Prosecution and Punishment: Petty Crime and the Law in London and Rural Middlesex, c. 1660–1725 (Cambridge, 1991); J.M. Beattie, Crime and the Courts in England 1660–1800 (Oxford 1986), Chaps. 3–4, 74–198.

75 Devereaux and Griffiths (eds.), Penal Practice and Culture, Introduction 1–35; Martin Ingram, 'Shame and Pain: Themes and Variations in Tudor Punishments', in Devereaux and Griffiths (eds.), Penal Practice and Culture, 36–62; Beattie, Crime and the Courts; Ingram, Carnal Knowledge; J.M. Beattie, Policing and Punishment in London 1660–1750 (Oxford, 2001), 277–312.
76 McIntosh, Controlling Misbehavior, 205.
77 Beattie, Policing and Punishment, 277–312; Ingram, 'Shame and Pain', 42; Dave Postles, 'Penance and the Market Place: A Reformation Dialogue with the Medieval Church' (c. 1250–c. 1600)', Journal of Ecclesiastical History, 54 (2003), 441–68, esp. 457.
78 Griffiths, 'Introduction', Devereaux and Griffiths (eds.), Penal Practice and Culture, 14, 19–26; Paul Griffiths, 'Bodies and Souls in Norwich: Punishing Petty Crime, 1540–1700', in ibid., 91–3. For guild and university courts inflicting shame punishments (e.g., sitting in the stocks in the company hall in the presence of the whole company), on apprentices and students, see Shepard, Meanings of Manhood, 135.
79 Beattie, Policing and Punishment, 300; Griffiths, Introduction to Devereaux and Griffiths (eds.), Penal Practice and Culture, 14.
80 Ingram, 'Shame and Pain', 48.
81 Postles, 'Penance and the Market Place', 442; Ingram, 'Shame and Pain', 37; Ingram, Carnal Knowledge, 108–9; Walsham, Charitable Hatred, 69–70.
82 Ingram, 'Shame and Pain', 40–3, 55.
83 Griffiths, 'Introduction', Devereaux and Griffiths (eds.), Penal Practice and Culture, 1–13; Steve Poole, 'For the Benefit of Example: Crime-Scene Executions in England 1720–1830', in Richard Ward (ed.), A Global History of Execution and the Criminal Corpse (Basingstock, 2015), 71–101; Andrea McKenzie, Tyburn's Martyrs: Execution in England, 1675–1775 (London, 2007), 7–21.
84 Postles, 'Penance and the Market Place', 453, 460.
85 Ingram, 'Shame and Pain', 40–4.
86 Ibid., 45–6, 52–8, quotation on 55; Beattie, Policing and Punishment, 306–7.
87 McKenzie, Tyburn's Martyrs, 16–9.
88 Ibid., 18; Walsham, Charitable Hatred, 75.
89 Ward (ed.), A Global History of Execution, 8–9; McKenzie, Tyburn's Martyrs, 18–19.
90 Ingram, 'Shame and Pain', 37; Walsham, Charitable Hatred, 68–9; Postles, 'Penance and the Market Place'; J.R. Dickinson and J.A. Sharpe, 'Public Punishment and the Manx Ecclesiastical Courts during the Seventeenth and Eighteenth Centuries', in Devereaux and Griffiths (eds.), Penal Practice and Culture, 138–56.
91 Walsham, Charitable Hatred, 80–2; Griffiths, Introduction, 23–4.
92 Ibid., 16; Shoemaker, Prosecution and Punishment; Beattie, Policing and Punishment, 289.
93 McKenzie, Tyburn's Martyrs, Chaps. 6–7, 157–223. And see also Chap. 6.
94 Poole, 'For the Benefit of Example, 73.
95 Postles, 'Penance and the Market Place', 453, 460–1; Ingram, 'Shame and Pain', 38–9.
96 Ingram, 'Shame and Pain', 49 (quoting a sixteenth century report on the three men who were ridden backwards and who 'died all w[i]t[h]in VII days aft[er] for sham').
97 Postles, 'Penance and the Market Place', 462–6.

# 6 Crime narratives and shame

The shame penalties described in the previous chapter were vastly enhanced through an expanding market for printed news reporting on crime. These reports, which go back to late medieval descriptions of the public execution of traitors and criminals, were by the early modern period disseminated through an array of ballads and pamphlets, news-books, and, increasingly, serialized newspapers. Catering to a growing reading public and the demand for popular literature and news, these publications moved away from the early descriptions of how the condemned acted at the scaffold, to a longer and more detailed account of the lives of criminals and the history of their imprisonment, trial, and punishment. The writers of the reports were, for the most part, clergymen or 'Ordinaries', who from the 1630s onwards were appointed as official visitors to prisons, and whose role was to counsel and bring the condemned to repent, as well as to ensure an official and didactic version of their prosecution and punishment.[1]

The sources of information used by these clergymen-reporters were primarily official legal records of examinations, arraignments, and trial proceedings, to which writers added the information they extracted from the condemned themselves.[2] As many reports indicate, while not all prisoners responded to the Ordinary's inquests and exhortations, most of them cooperated with his pleas to confess, offering details of their lives and the circumstances that led to their crime. This cooperation, which generated a dialogue between the clergyman and the prisoner, resulted in a distinctive form of reports; while presenting the authoritative point of view of writers (and the prosecution), these accounts also incorporated the voices of the prisoners themselves. Writers recorded their conversations with the condemned, at times presenting fragments of their talk through semi-quotations or indirect speech ('the prisoner said that', he 'believes', 'insists', 'professes', 'laments' or 'alleges'), which they then supplemented with their own commentary and reflections on the prisoners' claims.[3] Dominated, as they were, by the authorial voice of the Ordinary, the reports afford a unique insight into the convicts' articulation of their crime, punishment, and shame.

In what follows we look into the shame reflected through these alternating voices of the writer and the condemned that were entwined in narratives of crime. Focusing on selected ballads and crime pamphlets from

DOI: 10.4324/9781003226871-7

1600 onwards, alongside the *Accounts* produced by the Ordinary of Newgate prison from the mid-1670s onwards, we explore the communication of shame and the means through which it was articulated and conveyed. As will become apparent, crime narratives resonated with divergent and contrasting notions of shame; while the line between these views was not always clear-cut, different versions emerge, with the convicts not only accommodating the Ordinary's pleas to repent and convey shame and regret, but also resisting, appropriating and reinventing their shame.

## The amplification of punitive shame

Written and disseminated under the shadow of the gallows, crime reports were structured by the politics of the penal system, with the reports being broadly intended to legitimize the judicial process and the punishment inflicted on the condemned. Closely aligned to this political agenda was the didactic and moral message, which writers and prison chaplains, many of whom puritanically inclined authors committed to godliness and evangelizing the populace, were keen to promote. Central to the message was the notion of the criminal as sinner, and of his punishment as the outcome of divine intervention and the retribution of an omnipotent deity, which was wreaked on notorious sinners. The discourse surrounding the gallows was hence imbibed with a potent form of punitive shame, which presented the malefactors as utterly deserving godly rage and retribution, their exclusion and death ultimately designed to 'sweepe them from off the face of the earth', as was expressed by Henry Goodcole, the Newgate Ordinary, in his report on the murder committed by Thomas Shearwood and Elizabeth Evans in 1635.[4]

This type of extreme punitive shame was voiced with special intensity in ballads that narrated stories of murder and crime. Taking the form of didactic exempla, crime ballads blatantly announced and magnified the deeds and evil character of the condemned. *'The cryes of the Dead'*, which related the story of a weaver who beat his apprentice to death, depicted the weaver, Richard Price, as immersed in total and unsurpassed evil: 'But a more graceless man/All I thinke was never made/All his life wicked was,/ And his minde bent to blood,/Nothing but cruelty/Did his heart any good'. Offering details of Price's cruelty and the physical torments he conferred upon his apprentices, the ballad highlighted his barbarity by contrasting it with the innocence of his apprentice (a 'gentle harmeless child'), concluding with the moral of a justly deserved punitive retribution: '(Oh Price,) dear is the price/ For this blood thou must pay,/Life for Life, bloud for bloud'. The ballad *The arraignment of John Flodder* described beggars who had committed arson, portraying them as being instigated by the devil, their act being repeatedly referred to as a devilish monstrosity, a cursed and 'blacke misdeed/that makes a thousand hearts with sorrow bleed', their own hearts being 'bespotted with blacke shame'. The ballad concluded with the vivid description of Flodder's shamed body on the scaffold, 'like a damned monster ... His hated body still on Earth remaines, (A shame unto his kin) hangd up in Chaines:/And must at all no other Buriall have,/But Crowes & Ravens mawes to make his grave'.[5]

Total denigration of character featured in many crime pamphlets and news reports, in which the history of the life, deeds, and punishment of the condemned were described in greater detail. Deeply immersed in the rhetoric of sin familiar from sermons and devotional guides, the authors of these reports attributed to the condemned numerous sins, blending together both general sins and the specific crime for which they were condemned, describing their deeds through the use of negative attributes and figures of speech that accentuated their sin and amplified the shame. The extreme and unsurpassed nature of the crime could often be gleaned from the title, as in the narrative of the conviction of Henry Robson, *The examination, confession, and condemnation of Henry Robson fisherman of Rye, who poysoned his wife in the strangest maner that euer hitherto hath bin heard of.*[6] Some pamphlets opened with a moralizing preamble that set the tone of the narrative from the outset, announcing and magnifying the shame and sinfulness of the malefactors. In the account of Thomas Sherwood and Elizabeth Evans, convicted of murder, the preamble denounced their 'abhominable' sins and crimes, offering a set of observations, from 'what a viperous brood of sinnes ... were ingendered, conceived, and brought forth by these monsters male and female', through an outline of their numerous sins – forsaking motherly obligations, sloth, 'forbidden' theft, 'beastly' lust, murder, then concluding by announcing to the reader utmost shame and disgrace: 'behold what a brand is set on them by Heaven, high scorne and derision; perishing before they perished, forgotten before they were dead'.[7] The report on *The Life and Death of Griffin Flood Informer* also presented a list of numerous sins and crimes, highlighting the anti-social implications of his crimes and his cruelty 'towards the weak and old ... the cruelty of this Flood expressed to his shame and disgrace'. The author not only described Flood's many abominations – he was 'full of quarrels', 'stubborne' and 'unruly', 'harsh in speech, and churlish in condition' – but amplified these by using superlatives and claims of unsurpassed conduct: 'a most debauched condition ... Never was there (I thinke) the like audacious and shameless fellow living in this citie'.[8]

Crime pamphlets also demonized the character of the offenders by using graphic and horrifying details of their crimes, and by associating their deeds with the devil, monsters, and beasts. In the report on Margaret Vincent, convicted for infanticide (the murder of her two eldest children), the account began with a description of the woman, who was married to a gentleman and 'with whom she lived in good estimation, well beloved, and much esteemed of all that knew her'. Diverging from other accounts that commonly attributed infanticide to the defective female nature, this depiction of the 'good' wife and gentlewoman still set the stage for the ensuing account of the 'bloody accident', which was described through the use of vituperative language intended to reveal her monstrous behaviour.[9]

Describing the murder in gruesome detail, the account demonized her as the anti-mother, crueller than 'the Viper, the inuenomed serpent, the snake, or any beast whatsoever, against all kind, takes a way those lives to whom she first gave life'. The narrative overall presented her as an 'abstinate papist', referring to her 'iron naturd heart', 'a pagan woman that knows not God ... nor have any feeling of his deity', and likening her to the 'Caniball, savage, Beast or fowle', finally associating her acts with the devil: 'this unhappy Gentlewoman was bewitched with, a witchcraft begot by hell and nursed by the Romish Sect, from which inchantment God of heaven defend us'. This demonization of the character of the condemned featured in other reports on crimes committed by women.[10]

Punitive shame and the verbal strategies used to amplify it persisted with no less intensity in the *Accounts* that came out of Newgate prison from the mid-1670s onwards.[11] More structured than the earlier pamphlets, the *Accounts* used a core format that included a summary of the trial proceedings, followed by an outline of the sermons and private exhortations the Ordinaries offered to the condemned, short biographies of the prisoners and the Ordinary's observations of their behaviour in their cells and up to their execution.[12] Such a format allowed authors ample space for delving into the character of the condemned, by offering comments, reflections, and exhortations regarding the prisoners' numerous flaws and defects. Going well beyond a focus on their specific crimes, the *Accounts* could utterly destroy the character of the condemned. Pejorative terms were intercepted throughout: 'idle', 'vile', 'impudent', 'vicious', 'wicked', 'profligate', 'perverse' – were some of the terms invariably used to refer to the prisoners. For example, the report on the life of Joseph Fretwell, convicted for robbery in 1733, described him from the outset as 'a most disobedient, untractable, foolish and unadviseable boy', proceeding to relate how he 'reduced himself ... into a state of insensible stupidity', and how he 'could never keep himself to close Work'; associating with the 'vilest and basest Companions', Fretwell became 'so perverse', delighting 'in the Company of none but the meanest Black-guards and Kennel rakers'.[13]

As in many earlier reports, the use of superlatives was profuse; 'the most horrid and crying sin', the 'greatest sin one can be guilty of', 'he was one of the most notorious street-robers'. Thomas Past was the 'most profligate and abandoned wretches in the world', Benjamin Loveday was 'one of the most mischievous, wicked, and profligate poor Black-guard creature ever... born'.[14] Of Samuel Burrard, a sailor indicted for robbery, the author stated that 'he scarce knew how to speak a true word'. Judith Defour, convicted in 1734 for infanticide, was described as hard-hearted, silent, and unconcerned with the Ordinary's exhortations. 'I have not seen one more stupid nor less thoughtful', was the sum of his observations of her behaviour.[15]

The demonization of the character of the malefactors was also enhanced by insinuating the total grip crime took over their routine lives. 'Among his other vices he did not absent himself from drinking', as Charles Patrick's conduct was described. Thomas Past, brickmaker and waterman convicted for murder, was described as 'having spent all the day in drinking, whoring and gaming', while Benjamin Loveday, a young plasterer, 'did nothing but thieving, stealing, and picking of pockets … a constant drinker'. Of William Fleeming, convicted for highway robbery, the Ordinary reported that 'when at home or abroad, he always robbed, stole and thiev'd'. John Mckgrady, so the Ordinary claimed, 'lived by stealing from everybody… he met with, [in] every place he came to'.[16] While the tendency to associate the criminals with the devil and references to demonic assistance had almost disappeared from the *Accounts*,[17] their authors persisted in evoking the inhumanity of the malefactors by associating them with beasts. The prisoners were 'intent upon the destruction of mankind, always going about like roaring lions, seeking whom they may devour', as the Ordinary claimed in his exhortations to the malefactors executed in 1731.[18] Lions, tigers, and wolves were mentioned so as to demonstrate the menace and total damage the felons posed to society. The malefactors were 'the Overturner[s] of Society'; they were 'like a Beast of Prey among an Herd of Cattle'. Those committing murder, theft or robbery were intent on destroying not only their victims, but the whole of 'mankind', arousing terror and hate 'by all', spoiling and ravaging 'all [which they] meet'.[19]

Claims regarding the tendency of the condemned to cheat and lie further served to undermine their reputation and demolish their character. The condemned were not only thieves and robbers, but were 'breaking sacred vows and obligations'.[20] Time after time in the *Accounts* the Ordinary laid doubt to their credibility, expressing disbelief in their claims regarding their motives and state of mind, remaining sceptical when they insisted not to have committed the crime for which they were indicted, or to have had no intent to murder, or no direct involvement in it. When prisoners expressed full penitence, the Ordinary tended to impute doubts in the minds of his readers regarding the sincerity of their words. For example, while describing the behaviour of a group of malefactors executed on 6 March 1732, he recorded that 'only Andrews cried and wept very much', and then even Andrews' truthfulness remained uncertain: 'Whether out of sincerity, or sheer reaction to the terror of death, we leave it to the readers to judge upon'.[21] In the case of Robert Hallam, the Ordinary observed that 'he at several times shed tears, but whether thro fear of death, or in evidence of a sincere repentance, we cannot possibly determine, for at other times he did not appear so much affected'.[22] In an account of the behaviour of several prisoners executed in 1732, the author, while telling the reader they 'wept a little at first', then reported that

> I was told that in the Cells they took Pleasure, in the Dead Hours of the Night, when all was quiet, to speak of their Street Robberies, and their manner of attacking and abusing People, and other wicked and idle Stories.

He then concluded, 'This was no good Sign of a due Sense of Sin or true Repentence'.[23]

No less damaging was the stigmatization of character that authors affected through their unfolding narratives of the lives of the condemned. In some *Accounts* the crimes of the malefactors were portrayed as being imprinted from early on in their lives; 'From childhood he was taken up in nothing but thieving, stealing, picking', as Benjamin Loveday was described, with other reports referring to crimes committed 'from the craddle', or 'from his infancy'.[24] This description, which conveyed a traditional notion of the criminal born into sin resulting from Original Sin, simultaneously insinuated the singular depravity of the condemned, marking them as incorrigible and with no hope for reform. In many narratives, the prisoners were portrayed as having been raised by honest and caring parents, who sent them to school and prepared them for the world as much as they could. Yet such accounts typically magnified the distinctive and irrevocable wilfulness of the condemned. Thus, Edward Curd was reportedly born to honest parents who gave him a good education, sending him to school to learn 'reading, writing, cyphering, and such things as were needful to accomplish him for business' and instructing him 'in our holy religion'. They then took care to bind him as an apprentice to a goldsmith who 'was a good master', yet Curd himself proved 'no less an insufficient servant'.[25] Many *Accounts* stated that the felons were placed with skilful and well-intentioned masters, as in the case of Rowland Turner, who was an apprentice at sea, and whose master and captain of the ship encouraged him to go to school, to learn navigation and 'other things that would fit him for the seafaring occupation'. 'But this excellent opportunity he neglected', the Ordinary asserted.[26] Other *Accounts* also described the condemned as having been sent to school and then placed as apprentices, but to no avail; they 'would learn nothing', as the Ordinary put it.[27]

This stigmatization of the condemned convict's character was also conveyed through life stories that portrayed the crimes for which they were punished as the outcome of the accumulation of vice over the course of their life. Here the condemned were typically described as descending down the 'slippery slope' – with small sins and crimes committed in childhood and youth inevitably leading to major crimes as they grew older.[28] The burden of responsibility for crimes was hence placed on the criminals' own voluntary will and choice, realized by their taking the first step in their criminal lives or deliberately picking a course that led them astray. 'This was the Origine of all his Misfortunes … for having contracted a Habit of Idleness, and an Intimacy with the most abandon'd Wretches … seldom did any thing to gain a Penny for his own Subsistence', as Rowland Turner, indicted for assault, was described. Edmund Neal, whose father, a blacksmith, 'was so much esteem'd by the best Men in the Town' that his son 'then [had] an Opportunity of keeping good Company', nevertheless still 'chose the worst'.[29] In other stories that traced the roots of criminal activities to bad company, the voluntary choice of the malefactors was emphasized. Thomas Edwards allegedly had in his childhood a particular inclination to go to Newgate and associate with the criminals there. 'He lov'd to visit the prisoners in

Newgate, where he got acquainted with [one criminal]'. In the case of William Chamberlain, he 'took himself to the most abandon'd life imaginable and chose for his companions the wickedest thieves, robbers, whores'.[30]

The effect of it all was utmost exclusionary and punitive shame. The malefactors were a 'dishonour' – to Christ, to the church of God, 'to our own souls'; 'Tis a Guilt in such, that they were once baptized'; 'tis a shame for them to own they have ever frequented the Church of God', as the Ordinary stated in his sermon to the malefactors executed on 29 January 1720. As the (19) prisoners who went to their death on 9 October 1732 were plainly told, 'because of their abominable, wicked and scandalous lives, now God's judgments had most Justly over taken them'.[31]

## Repentance and redemptive shame

Alongside punitive shame and at times closely associated with it, crime narratives were saturated with redemptive shame. Based on the Protestant understanding of a divine will working within a person to recognize sin and of shame as an act of awakening, potentially leading to redemption, crime reports presented accounts of criminals being delivered from their reprobate state of transgression to repentance, conversion, and spiritual rebirth. Here, too, the point of view of the author-clergyman, who was intent on bringing prisoners to confess and on proselytizing his readers, was evident. Felons were expected to repent not only the crime they had committed but also a whole lifetime of sins, with the clergy guiding them in the process of conversion. The result was an amplified account that highlighted an experience of guilt and shame through which the condemned were transformed from passive and deprived reprobates to spiritually reborn believers who willingly embraced their death. Ultimately, the felons' act of penitence manifested the power of mercy, indicating how the soul of even the most heinous criminal could emerge redeemed.[32]

Elements of this process of conversion and redeeming shame came into focus in ballads on crime and execution. Thoroughly infused with strong retributive shame aimed at the reprobate, these ballads still ended by invoking the prospects of mercy and redemption. 'On thy domes dying day/Pray thou for mercy there,/To save thy sinful soule,/For me thinks I doe hear,/ Thy pasing Bell doth toule' – was how *The cryes of the Dead*, which narrated the story of the punishment inflicted on the weaver who killed his apprentice, ended. In the ballad that related the story of the three beggars who committed arson (referred to above), the punitive and brutal shame inflicted on the body of John Flodder was juxtaposed against the redemptive shame of the two women who were indicted with him. While Flodder was executed and his body left to rot, his wife was fully penitent, admitting guilt not only for her crime of arson, but an entire life of sin:

> With weeping tears [she] bewailed her offence /... And how most leawdly she had lived long / A shamefull life, in doing deeds wrong/

And trode the steps of whoredome day by day,/ Accounting sinne and shame, the better way,

Finally, she embraced her death: 'For all her sinnes ... she did repent/ And said ... Christ was her content'.[33]

Some of these ballads were particularly suffused with repentance and expressions of shame, guilt, and sorrow, coupled with forgiveness and hopes for salvation. *Anne Wallens Lamentation* narrated the story of a woman who killed her husband, announcing from the outset, 'Ah me the shame unto all women kinde', presenting herself as being 'amongst my neighbours ... beloved well', and her husband forgiving her before he died: 'Yet he forgave me and for me did pray'. The ballad concluded with Wallen's appeal to audiences, pleading for her family's pardon, wishing to set an example to all wives, and vowing to accept her guilt and just death; 'in burning flames of fire I should fry, Receive my soule sweet Jesus now I die'.[34] In the ballad *Luke Huttons Lamentation, which he wrote the day before his Death*, Hutton, condemned for several robberies, gave an account of his 'bad life', entreating 'lord Jesus forgive me/ I have deserved death long since ... a viler sinner lived not than I', and appeal to the audience with hopes for conciliation and redemption: 'Adieu my loving friends ... think on me Lords when I am gone/be warned/then on the ladder you do me view/think I am nearer heaven then yoa'. Gamaliel Ratsey, whose repentance was written 'with his owne hand when hee was in New-gate', also took the form of a ballad that appeared at the end of the history of his many crimes, offering an enthusiastic proclamation of shame, guilt and hopes for redemption: 'Though sinne be great, thy mercies thrice as much/Oh thou that art in power and mercy great!'[35]

More elaborate accounts of shame and repentance became a regular feature of crime pamphlets, especially from the 1630s onwards, with many of these modelled on conversion narratives of the kind found in puritan sermons and devotional guides or spiritual autobiographies. *The Life, Confession, and Heartie Repentance of Francis Cartwright, Gentleman for his bloudie sinne in killing of one Master Storr* was an autobiographical account in which Cartwright described his sinful life, followed by his agonizing shame over the killing and his emergence as a true repentant. The account, so Cartwright asserted, was offered as a 'warning ... to all', so that readers could see his 'worst deformities' and 'hating them, may now pity my person, and comfort my soule', at the same time allowing them to 'see the power and goodnesse of the almighty, that hath not forsaken me when I fled from him and my self'.[36] Other murder pamphlets presented similar histories of a fall and redeeming shame. *A True Discourse of the practices of Elizabeth Caldwell*, which told the story of Caldwell poisoning her husband, presented an edifying narrative in which Caldwell was depicted as an exemplary penitent whose crime was the result of a momentary lapse, and who deserved a royal pardon. The account exalted in her conduct during the months of her imprisonment, when she transformed herself to a zealous penitent, urging many prisoners around her to convert. The pamphlet also included 'a most excellent exhortorie Letter' written to her husband, along with her 'words at the time of her death'. Both of these texts used godly rhetoric and exhortations profusely, urging her husband as well as others to seek conversion, admonishing all to follow their daily practice and keep the Sabbath so that the 'the glory of God might appear' in their conversion. Like other gallows speeches delivered from the execution cart or scaffold, and printed from the mid-seventeenth century on, Caldwell's speech may well have been rehearsed in advance with the help of Gilbert Dugdale, the prison clergyman and author of her narrative.[37]

Over and above the dominance of the author's voice in presenting a model of penitence, crime narratives also indicate what must have been a genuine experience of shame and hopes for salvation. The sheer detail of the description of Caldwell's conduct connoted a measure of sincere piety and penitence:

> ... from her first entrance into prison, till the time of her death, she acted ... with great zeale and industrie, continually meditating on the bible, excluding her selfe from all companie, saving such as might yeelde her spiritual comforts.

The account went on to describe the numerous visitors coming to her cell to watch her in her godly practice, her many conversations with ministers, her 'uttermost endeavores to obtain mercie', and her thorough acknowledgement of guilt during her trial. When Caldwell's request for royal pardon was denied, she

> Dutifully yielded thanks ... and said shee was very well content to receive the death ordained for her ... she very cheerfully answered I trust in my God and I am ready ... sung psalms and used other Godly meditations.

Her letter to her husband, too, displayed a mix of exhortations and personal prayers for their reunification – the 'joyfull meeting at the day of our Resurrection'. And there was also the gallows speech, which not only emphasized her personal agonizing in searching for God 'with broken and contrite hart', but also included references to her husband and children, sending prayers 'that her two children might have the fear of God', finally 'asking forgiveness of all', and 'making herslefe ready, saying her bodily death did not dismay her', concluding 'with these her last words Lord Jesus receive my spirit'.[38]

A mix of authorial rhetoric and the more genuine experience of repentance and redeeming shame emerge in the serial *Accounts* of the Ordinary of Newgate from the late seventeenth century onwards. The tone of these *Accounts* changed over time, with the godly zeal typical of the earlier pamphlets giving way to a more straightforward report of the Ordinary's sermons and his observations. Nevertheless, the author's intent in guiding the prisoners through shame and repentance towards a redeemed self was conspicuous and unmistaken throughout. 'I exposed to them the Freedom of God's Grace, and exhorted them not to despair of God's Mercy' – was a typical proclamation, as were his observations that the prisoners accepted their shame. 'He behaved modestly and christialy, and own'd that he suffer'd justly for the Sins of his Life'; 'He acknowledged himself the most wicked, flagitious, disobedient, undutiful young Wretch upon Earth, and that he suffer'd most justly, for the innumerable Villainies of his Life'.[39] References were sometimes made in the *Accounts* to weeping and tears as the deepest signs of contrition: 'He was very penitent, and wept bitterly, when I examin'd him'. Of Thomas Andrews, a glazier convicted of highway robbery, the Ordinary perceived that 'notwithstanding his pretended weariness of life, yet he often cried and wept like a child'.[40] Especially noted in the *Accounts* was the general willingness of the prisoners to 'die well' and 'in charity with the world'. Many among the condemned reportedly attended the Chappel, listened to sermons, prayed, and invariably showed a desire to qualify for the communion administered on the morning of the execution. Most of them also died 'in charity', forgiving others (as they hoped to be forgiven by God), including those who accused them, or else asking pardon of persons in the crowd they had wrongly accused of crimes, thus exonerating those suspected of crimes they had themselves committed.[41]

Some reports recorded in the Newgate *Accounts* show exceptionally deep and agonizing feelings of contrition and regret. Jane Griffin, who was indicted for the murder of her maidservant,

> could sometimes not be persuaded to sit on a chair, but would sit on the floor, saying that she ought to humble herself in dust and ashes; and that had she ten thousand hearts, she would willingly they *all* should bleed, to attone for her crime.[42]

Some malefactors apparently felt compelled to confess to those sins which lay on their conscience, including some unrelated to the crime of which they were accused. Other *Accounts* show agonizing feelings of remorse and suffering perceived as redemptive, with criminals reported as thanking God for the 'mercy in the foresight of Death', or dying in the belief that their misfortunes had saved them. Charles Weaver, hanged for murder in 1723, 'hop'd that his Misfortunes, like those of the prodigal Son, had reclaimed him, and that he should attain to the Portion of the Righteous, by dying the Death of the wicked'.[43] Some prisoners also left written gallows speeches that expressed the depth of their repentance and their hopes for mercy and salvation. Robert Hallam, convicted for murder, 'declar'd himself penitent for all the Offences of his Life; that he hop'd to be sav'd, by the Mercy of God'. On the morning of his execution he reportedly delivered a letter ('which he design'd to have spoke at the Tree') in which he beseeched the intercession of

You Good People ... to Almighty God, for my departing Soul, that the Greatness of his Mercy may supply the Imperfectness of my Repentance, the heavy Load of my Sufferings, efface the Guilt of my Crimes, and the Merits of my Saviour's Death ... bring me to everlasting Life.[44]

For all these varied descriptions of public contrition and expressions of shame, crime narratives only infrequently indicated full, unequivocal, and exemplary public confessions. Early seventeenth-century crime pamphlets describe many instances of prisoners who repented but showed no apparent signs of godly zeal, earnestness or sincerity, with Ordinaries perceiving their conversion 'faux', made only in order to obtain reprieves or royal pardon.[45] Repenting felons were invariably described as obstinate and hardhearted, grudgingly succumbing to the imperative to repent and express shame under great pressure, or only shortly before their death. When Henry Robson was urged during his trial to 'confess the truth and shame the devil [in him]', he persisted in denying he killed his wife, but finally succumbed; 'I perceive you glut after my blood, and if it will pleasure you you shall have it', he was quoted as saying. Margaret Vincent, condemned for infanticide in 1616, was described as tremendously obdurate throughout her trial and imprisonment – 'the blood of her owne body should have no more power to pearce remorse into her Iron naturd heart'. Only when 'certain Godly preachers' approached her, 'her heart by degrees became a little mollified, and in nature somewhat repentant for her most heinous offences'.[46] The Newgate *Accounts* typically show instances of a grudging acceptance of shame only after repeated sermons and exhortations. 'He was very hardhearted, and guilty of some little Miscarriages; but upon the Reproofs and Advices I gave him he turn'd better', was the report on Edward Perkins, sentenced to death on 9 October 1732. Ordinaries invariably reported on the strenuous efforts required to change the heart of the malefactors and lead them to confess, with some only becoming troubled when death was imminent. Martin Bellamy was reported as showing 'audacity', but when the death warrant was issued his conscience began to 'awake' and he finally 'acknowledge'd himself one of the greatest of Sinners, begg'd God and Man Pardon for the many offenses of his life'. In some extreme cases, the condemned confessed only after being subjected to the unbearable press. William Spiggot, a particularly obstinate and defiant prisoner who stood silent at his trial and was hence subjected to the press, finally submitted: 'he constantly attended the pryaers in the Chappel ... insisting he was truly penitent, and as sincerely so, as he who show'ed his Sorrow by his Tears'.[47]

No less important, penitent criminals invariably denied the specific crime for which they were going to die. Instead of offering a full confession and expressing repentance for all their sins, including the crime for which they were indicted, convicted felons admitted committing various 'general' sins. Typical in this regard was William Maw, indicted for burglary, who thanked the Ordinary for offering him 'great comfort and instruction', but admitted only vaguely that he was 'a great offender'.[48] Others admitted they were sinners and even confessed to varied sins for which they were willing to die, but they still utterly rejected committing the crime for which they were being punished and shamed. Edward Jackson, convicted of coining in 1684, reportedly swore during his gallows speech that he believed in God but was 'as innocent as the Child in the Mother's Womb'. Jackson then still declared that 'he had deserved this Death for his Sins, and he desired to take Public Shame to himself'. He forgave 'all the World', including 'those who swore falsely against him'. As the Ordinary described it, the speech and prayers Jackson delivered just before his death drew 'hundreds of spectators' to melt in tears.[49]

## Defiance of shame

Some prisoners not only confessed partially or grudgingly, but utterly denied their shame, refusing to go through penitence or confess to any sin or crime.[50] The mental anguish and desperation caused by the harshness of imprisonment and the terror of an approaching death could leave some convicts resigned and unresponsive to the Ordinary's pleas. The author of a pamphlet entitled *The Cruel Mother* (1670) reported that Mary Cook, accused of killing her daughter, was 'dejected in spirit and deeply afflicted with melancholy', persistently 'unheeding of ministers advice'. When she was offered to perform the speeches and prayers at the gallows, '[s]he told us she could only word it and not heart it'. The Newgate *Accounts* point to similar cases of passivity and desperation. Elizabeth Harwood, convicted for infanticide, reportedly told the chaplain she was sick whenever he approached her cell; she had, so the chaplain conceded, 'an aversion to be spoken to'. Other prisoners remained shamelessly indifferent; 'Confess or not confess, they would hang him on Wednesday', was how John Barnet was quoted as saying.[51]

Prisoners were also well aware of the repercussions a confession could have on their reputation. One crime pamphlet told of a prisoner who refused to confess because he 'had not a mind to be the Sport and Ridicule of vain idle Fellows in Coffee-Houses; who only laugh at unfortunate dying Men, who are frightened into a Confession of their private sins'. He also contended that 'he was satisfied in his conscience, ... [and] was oblig'd to confess to none but his Heavenly Father, who knew the Secrets of his Heart'. The Newgate *Accounts* show similar instances of apprehension. Mary Allen was quoted saying that she was resolved 'to give no account of herself ... because she would have no speeches made about her when she was dead'. John Edwards refused to talk to the Ordinary for fear of having his 'character blasted in London', and Peter Oldfield likewise 'chose not to have his name blasted in papers after he was dead'. These acts of defiance could also affect fellow prisoners. George Scroggs, indicted for assault, reportedly 'deny'd every thing he had confess'd before, having (it seems) got his Lesson from some of his graceless Companions, to make no Confessions'. Though the Ordinary preached Scroggs on 'the danger of going to Eternity with a Lie in his mouth', and warned him that 'he could not otherwise die in the peace of the Church', Scroggs remained silent: 'But all I could or did say availed not, for he still continued obstinate and obdurate, and would confess nothing'.[52]

In all these instances, felons declined to confess not only the crime for which they were convicted but also any other sin and wrongdoing; that is, they chose to forgo the entire process of penitence and redeeming shame, challenging the ritual of conversion as both a penalty and a means for obtaining divine grace. A majority of news pamphlets on crimes committed by women, as Randall Martin showed, gave no details on the prisoners' acts of conversion, possibly because no penitence and confession were performed. Other narratives offered only a partial confession or else completely rejected the Ordinary's appeal to repent and express shame. According to a pamphlet reporting on the behaviour of Newgate criminals executed on 6 May 1685, twelve out of the twenty-three prisoners rejected the Ordinary's exhortations to confess 'with greater Obstinacy, than ever any did for nine years past, as desperate and hardned in Wickedness, or being bold to venture into an Eternal State, without any desire to be Instructed or prepared for it'.[53]

This type of 'shameless' boldness in defiance of the conversion ritual featured increasingly – or was more openly reported – in news reports and the Newgate *Accounts* from the late seventeenth century onwards. A pamphlet from 1668 contrasted the negative and positive reactions of two prisoners, in order to spotlight Hannah Blay, convicted of murder, in her unwillingness to repent. While her fellow convict died 'shamefull-Happy death', Blay 'ended her wicked life by a shameful death, without the least sign of sorrow or Repentance for abominable whoredome and wickedness'. Phillipa Cary reportedly proclaimed her innocence while suffering excruciating fear at the gallows, with the clergyman refusing to comfort her unless she admitted her guilt; but 'She tells us. She cannot Confess that whereof she is not Guilty'. Mary Williamson, convicted for grand larceny in 1684, also refused to confess, begging mercy but denying the charges against her, declining to make 'any public speech to the People, as also to joyn in singing the Psalm to the last'. Occasionally, prisoners reportedly admitted the crime for which they were punished, but they still refused to follow the desirable course of repentance and shame. Margaret Osgood, who killed her husband and was convicted in 1680, admitted the deed but showed no shame nor remorse, even declaring that 'were it undone, she would yet do it'. When told she would be burnt, 'she replied, she burn'd already and that would prepare her for the Flames to come'. Descriptions of criminals who refused to confess and made 'the most solemn Protestations imaginable' to the charges brought against them invariably appeared in the Newgate *Accounts* well into the mid-eighteenth century.[54]

Some forms of shameless defiance were particularly bold, posing a challenge not only to the Ordinary and the conversion ritual which he strove to achieve, but also to the legal system and the assumptions underlying the judicial process itself. Instead of expressing shame and assuming guilt, some malefactors ridiculed juries, judges, and superiors. The Jacobite Thomas Coppach reportedly told a tearful fellow prisoner, 'What the Devil are you Afraid of? We shan't be Tried by a Cumberland Jury in the other world'. Stances of insolence were especially evident in cases of social crimes that were perceived as minor; smuggling, poaching, rioting, or returning from transportation before the expiration date, with the refusal to confess amounting to criticism and protest against the severity of the law or the social assumptions underlying it. A group of poachers executed in 1723 were described as 'hard to be persuaded that the Things they had committed were any Crimes in the Eyes of God', as 'Deer were wild Beasts and they did not see why the Poor had not as good a Right to them as the Rich'. While coming to chappel, listening to sermons or declaring they were 'forgiving the world', these prisoners persisted in refusing to acknowledge their guilt or undergo the ritual of public shame and confession of their sins.[55]

Subversive acts that challenged the legal system were most pronounced in the few cases of prisoners who refused to plead at the trial. According to a pamphlet reporting on *The Life and Death of Griffin Flood Informer*, executed in 1623, Flood 'by no perswasions would ... commit himself to the Law, but most obstinately stood to the severe justice of the Bench'. The author then proceeded to report that 'According to custom, the court censured him to the presse, where he received his deserts, by being bruised in terrible manner to a most fearful death'.[56] The Newgate *Accounts* also conveyed varied instances of prisoners who stood silent at their trial, risking death by being put under the press, their defiance presenting a form of resistance to the entire legal system and a trial in which they were denied an active voice. Their shamelessness not only undermined the deference owed to superiors and the appropriate forms of addressing judges – some malefactors reportedly cursed at the bar when they were convicted or left their hats on – but also allowed them to preserve their pride and sense of self-respect. Nathaniel Hawes, a street robber executed in 1721, refused to plead at his trial and only demanded that his 'handsome Suit of cloaths' be returned to him. He was put to the press and then relented, still claiming that 'as he had liv'd like a Man, he was resolv'ed to die so, and not be hang'ed in such a shabby coat as he then appear'd in'.[57]

Public shows of shameless subversion of the politics and culture of the executions were above all manifested in the conduct of prisoners who died 'hard' or 'game'; that is, they not only showed little signs of contrition, but advertised their indifference to their death, displaying courage and even cheerful demeanour while facing the gallows. At his 1728 execution, the robber Stephen Barnham 'laugh'd twice after he was ty'd up to the Gallows', and when the Ordinary had finished praying, he 'took his prayer-book and threw it up against the gallows with all the Passion and Folly imaginable'. Whereas such performance may have helped the condemned to cope with the pain and shame of death at the scaffold, ultimately, their conduct was thoroughly subversive. Conforming to the conventions of a good Protestant death – dying 'in peace' and forgiving the world – felons who died 'game' displayed indifference to the manner in 'which ... [they died] or when', coupled with high spirits and, occasionally, confidence in God's mercy. Scattered through the Newgate *Accounts* were stories of convicts who were unscarred to the last, making gestures to friends and acquaintances, smiling or laughing at them, throwing themselves off the ladder with great force, dying as self-styled heroes displaying calm composure and manly courage. James Hackett, a street robber hanged in 1707, was reported as saying it was 'a gallant and honourable thing' to 'shew a bold and undejected countenance'.[58]

## Bounded shame, inclusion, self-respect

Common to many crime narratives and news reports was a distinctive, subtle form of shame that involved neither punitive nor redeeming shame, nor an utter denial of shame. Instead, prisoners acknowledged responsibility for their shameful deeds – fully, partially, or only grudgingly complying with the imperative to show repentance and shame – but at the same time they introduced varied perspectives and arguments that attenuated their shame, undermining the total discredit and disgrace inflicted upon them by the published accounts of their crime and their brutal punishment and death.

This type of shame was closely aligned with popular perceptions and expectations of justice and equity, which by the sixteenth century were integrated into the legal system and were evident in pardons granted at the discretion of the Crown. Allowing greater leniency in the punishment of offenders and acting to mitigate the severity of the law, pardons were conditioned on the prisoner's show of penitence, and on a set of considerations that shaped the judgement of the court as well as the petitions presented by family and friends on behalf of the condemned. Already in the sixteenth century a wide range of circumstances could be considered grounds for granting a pardon; doubts expressed by judges about the malefactors' guilt, perceived gradations of responsibility for the crime or the intent and motivation behind the malefactors' acts. Individuals whose crime was deemed to have been committed in self-defence, along with the mentally ill, children under the age of seven, the weak and the poor – could all be exonerated and granted a reprieve. And while laws specified uniform punishments for particular actions, the pardon permitted room for issues of personal will and whether the crime was voluntary, overall encouraging discretionary individuation of punishments that could be tailored to the nature of the offence and the character of the offender.[59]

As crime narratives indicate, convicted criminals were aware of these perspectives and considerations that allowed mercy to be granted, and used them in order to attenuate their shame and guilt, admitting their sin or crime but at the same time presenting themselves more favourably to the Ordinary and the public at large. In his published account of his life and confession, Francis Cartwright admitted full responsibility for killing the minister of his parish and confessed a life full of sin: 'I stand forth here ... to condemne my selfe, ... Nay I dare not so much as ... cover my owne shame'. Yet while noting that he did not intend to 'use defences or mitigations', as he put it, he still claimed the existence of mitigating circumstances by asserting that his act was provoked by the minister himself:

> I might perhaps by way of extenuation say, that had he used greater words and milder reprehensions to me, he might by Gods blessing have plucked me out of the snare of Satan, and so had prevented this shortning of his owne dayes.

Cartwright also implied his lack of intention to kill: 'So must I neede acknowledge my selfe, because my heart, *though not before so intending*, yet as principall is guiltie of that which my hand did in the heate of fury'.[60]

Other pamphlets alluded to or directly qualified the criminals' guilt and shame. Luke Hutton, convicted for robberies and trespasses, wrote a confession that was suffused with shame and pleas for forgiveness; yet he, too, minimized the gravity of his crimes by claiming that while for three years he 'lived upon the spoil' of his robberies, 'yet did I never kill man nor wife'. Gamaliel Ratsey, who publicized his repentance for his many crimes and sins, wrote the story of his life and deeds in which he highlighted his conniving, deceitful, and devious manipulations of his victims. Yet he still reiterated his generous character when claiming to have robbed a poor man of his fortune but returning it and offering more, or lending another victim fifty pounds. When robbing a preacher he alleged to have told him that since he was preaching 'to others the Doctrine of good deeds and charity', he, Gamaliel Ratsey, did not doubt 'but your selfe will be respecting of such as are needy'. While confessing he was 'a great malefactor', Ratsey plainly articulated the rationale for his deeds, urging the preacher to 'consider the force and power of necessity which constraints them that are needy to rob, and take away the goods of their neighbors, and oftentimes to endanger their lives'.[61]

Pamphlets describing crimes committed by women were particularly prone to raise issues of mitigating circumstances, portraying female perpetrators in a more favourable light and undermining their total shame and stigmatization. The report on Elizabeth Caldwell, which (as noted above) presented her as performing exemplary penitence and going through a deep spiritual transformation, still indicated extenuating circumstances that led to the poisoning of her husband. It first described her good upbringing and character: 'she being framed and adorned withal the gifts that nature could challenge'. When she married and her young husband deserted her (he 'gave his minde to travel'), Elizabeth was left 'often time verie bare, without provision of such meanes as be fitting for her', forcing her into the arms of a neighbour who 'spared neither cost nor industrie ... to withdrawe her to his unlawfull desire', and enticing her to commit the crime. Ultimately, her act was presented as a momentary lapse rather than a vicious and corrupt character. Elizabeth Evans, convicted along with Thomas Sherwood for murder in 1635, was also presented by the author, Henry Goodcole, in harsh terms as a reprobate who utterly refused to repent. Yet Goodcole also introduced Evans' version of the events – 'as shee freely confessed' – which pointed to the influence of men, financial ruin, and social isolation as the sources of her crime. Born to good parents who sent her to London to become a servant, Evans met a young man 'who tempted her unto folly', leading her to abandon her friends and to utter destitution:

> Oh unnaturall blemish! Thus to forsake, cast off, and forget their owne deare flesh, all meanes of livelihood failing, her left thus destitute, and out of all, credit, friends, money apparell, and service.[62]

As Martin Randall showed, a wide range of circumstances was invoked as extenuating circumstances in cases of crimes committed by women, pointing to a shift from the moralizing and gender prejudice typical of early seventeenth-century crime narratives, to a more positive portrayal of female criminals in which self-defence and lack of intent to kill, marital relationship under duress, abusive husbands and female desperation – were all invoked as reasons for committing the crime for which a woman was accused. In cases involving infanticide, too, the responsibility of the women who committed such deeds was presented ambiguously, while in the case of poisoning – the least defensible of all crimes – the authors' presentation of the crime left room for a qualified shame and a certain resistance to reducing women's motives to sheer premeditation.[63]

More elaborate uses of notions of mercy, justice, and extenuating circumstances came to the fore in the Newgate *Accounts* published from the 1670s on. In their confessions to the Ordinary, prisoners invariably recounted – explicitly or implicitly – arguments affecting the mitigation of their crime, while also emphasizing aspects of their personality that diminished the totality of the misdeeds attributed to them by the chaplain, and the consequent stigmatization of their character. A common stance was to indicate or emphasize the boundaries of their crime, as in the case of Thomas Paxton, who admitted he deserved his punishment and even surmised that his approaching death would prevent the 'abominable Crimes' he might have continued to commit, but still stressed the fact that he was punished 'for his first Crime'. William Mead claimed that he was guilty of highway robberies 'but once or twice', while Rowland Turner proclaimed his act was 'the only robbery or Theft he ever committed in his Life'.[64] Other prisoners diminished the gravity of their crimes by suggesting gradations of crime and moral inhibitions; 'He owned also that he was guilty of a great number of petty thefts in picking of pockets, and stealing small things out of shops, but he never committed any notorious fact' – were typical assertions. Thomas Past confirmed that he deserved his punishment and shame, but still pointed to his moral restraint; he stole a wig, but 'no more, though several other things were in (the box)', adding, 'for my heart failed me'. Some alleged that the person they had killed was himself a great villain, asserting that their act eliminated great evil and menace to society. As the Ordinary reported in a case of two prisoners who committed a murder, 'as to the objection which they might possibly make, in alleviation of their Crime, I told them that altho' Waller whom they kill'd, was undoubtedly a wicked Person, yet they were by no means to prosecute private revenge against him'.[65]

The Newgate *Accounts* also point to instances of felons who emphasized their uncompromising compliance with the sixth commandment. 'He professed he had always taken Care, not to commit Murder: He said he had been Guilty of every Ill-Act except that' – was Richard Shefferd's statement. As in earlier pamphlets, there were also those who stated they had not intended to kill. In the case of Robert Hallam, referred to above, the chaplain told him 'it was of no avail to deny murder (of his wife)', yet Hallam 'persisted inflexible' in claiming it was unintentional; he struck and injured her, but she was alive and 'talked to him some hours after that', dying only two days later. Jane Griffin, who was fully penitent, imploring for pardon and mercy for the murder of her maidservant, still declared that the murder was 'wholly unintentional', a claim she 'requested me to deliver aloud to the people', as the Ordinary affirmed.[66]

Some felons attributed their misdeeds at least partly to the influence of others. Sara Malcolm, a servant who was hanged for burglary and the murder of her mistress, admitted being complicit in the plan to break into the house of her mistress, ('she was not averse to this proposal'), but still described her inhibitions and especially the part played by her collaborators in her decision to engage in crime: 'it was impossible for her to do it, without the assistance of some others'. Some narratives conveyed the impact of bad company in shaping the behaviour and life course of the condemned, or, among men, the effect of 'bad' spouses who failed in their roles as wives. Viner Whyte claimed 'that he was not long wicked, but only falling in with bad Company, he turned a Drunkard', and his account was also corroborated by other witnesses. Edward Jones blamed the killing of his wife on her habits of lavish expenditure ('his wife being no economist'), her drinking, lack of sexual mores and negligence in looking after him, which allowed him to succumb to idleness and drink. Other prisoners, too, insisted on the 'vanity', 'pride', and 'extravagance' of female companions as factors contributing to their immoral ways and crime.[67] The Ordinary himself sometimes confirmed the prisoners' statements regarding the effect of others; 'He appear'd to be a young Fellow of some good Dispositions, but was at once Ruin'd by bad Company' – as he observed in the case of Thomas Paxton.[68]

Especially pronounced in the Newgate *Accounts* was the invocation of drunkenness, poverty, and unemployment as the sources of the condemned person's criminality. William Mead claimed that 'he was very drunk when he did those facts … his falling into such crimes having only been the effect of his drinking and company-keeping'. Benjamin Loveday, a plaisterer whom the Ordinary described as 'the most wicked creature ever born', still insisted on having been diligent in his business 'till last Christmas', when an accident at work disabled him and forced him out of this employment and unto the streets. Other *Accounts* attributed their drift to criminality to being 'brought into great Straits by the hard Weather last Year', or else citing 'poverty', 'meer poverty', 'great necessities', or being 'reduced to a very low ebe of poverty', as the sources of their crime. Jane Williams, condemned for shoplifting in 1691, attributed her acts to poverty and the neglect of her husband, a sailor, to provide for her; male prisoners claimed that they turned to theft or robbery having been reduced to destitution and being unable to provide for their wives and children. Some felons invoked the influence of a menacing and brutal environment, as in the case of sailors who spent months and years on ships in long and arduous voyages overseas.[69]

In some *Accounts*, felons reportedly claimed that their early childhood experiences were the source of their aggression and criminality. Parental negligence and betrayal were sometimes invoked; 'O! that my parents had taught me something of the knowledge of God which I was never instructed in', was the lament of Judith Defour, indicted for infanticide. Edward Payne, indicted for highway assault, told the Ordinary that 'his Grandfather left him 250 l. but that his Father and Mother found a Way to get rid of it, while he was young', claiming that 'the want of which hindered him from doing Business to purpose'. Other prisoners spoke about broken homes, telling of friction between a father and his son following the death of the mother, mistreatment by stepmothers following the remarriage of fathers, or aggression and ingratitude of a son whose father died, and he directed his vengeance at his mother and grandmother. Parental death features prominently in many life stories that related the erosion of family obligations and care, consequently leading the child to engage in crime. 'Not having much to expect of the mother, [they] left her to shift for themselves', as the Ordinary described the case of John Maxworth, whose father died when he was about twelve years old.[70]

Over and above these notions of mitigating circumstances and the boundaries of criminal acts, the life stories presented in the *Accounts* illuminated aspects of the prisoners' character and personality that did not conform with their presentation as utterly shameful characters who deserved total exclusion and death. Some felons described their good behaviour and reputation early on in their lives; 'my father being exceeding fond of me', as William Shelton, an apothecary indicted for robbery, claimed. William Barkwith, indicted for embezzlement, professed that he was the son of reputable parents who educated him in Latin and Greek 'and other accomplishments fit for a gentleman'. Having served his master several years 'faithfully', he became a clerk and was 'looked upon by all who knew him to be a sober youth, and fit for business'.[71] Especially pronounced were the prisoners' repeated claims to have retained – despite their criminal activities – their reputation for honesty. In this manner, Viner White embraced his shame and admitted that 'he was lewed and drank to excess', but still asserted that 'otherwise' he was of an honest disposition. William Shelton confessed to numerous misdeeds and the mischief he caused already in his childhood, emphasizing his disobedience to his parents and several masters with whom he had served. Nonetheless, he also referred to instances that diverged from this steady progression of immoral ways, describing a master 'with whom I served six years very honestly, nor did I ever once wrong him'. He also related that when he embarked on his voyages overseas, he obtained letters of recommendation for his good character, which ensured that he was welcomed there 'with all possible marks of ... respect'. Others insisted that they were 'always honest, and never blam'd for any criminal action'; or they confessed to several robberies and an addiction to drinking, but at the same time asserted that 'in other part of his life, he was honest and wronged no body', or that 'in other respects he was not very vicious'. Robert Hallam, who admitted to being cruel to his wife, 'insistently professed' his good reputation among neighbours and friends.[72]

Most important were the subtle allusions the prisoners made to their conformity to social norms and the social or spiritual ties they had with family and friends. The condemned invariably conveyed their connectedness to human society rather than to that of outcast criminals, thus subverting their stigmatization and affecting a measure of rehabilitation of their character and reputation. Luke Nunny highlighted his childhood piety, when he felt 'strange inclinations to serve God ... [and] heartily wish'd that men would reform, and the world would grow virtuous and good'. He was also careful to stress his affinity with mainstream religion rather than with non-conforming groups, claiming that when 'he went to see how he liked the Quakers, he could not well relish their Way and Manner, but thought it was rather ridiculing Almighty God than Worshipping him'. Others referred to the norms of civility and polite manners which they shared with genteel classes. In describing at length the highway robberies he committed, William Shelton told the Ordinary, 'I met a Chariot with two well dress'd Ladies in it, whom I addressed with all the good Manners I was Master of, gently taking up their Aprons, and stroaking down their Gloves to search for Watches or Rings'. Some prisoners also alluded to patriotic feelings; 'he said he lov'd Old England the best', as George Brown, a sailor who talked about his return to England after long voyages oversees, declared.[73]

The life stories featured in the Newgate *Accounts* also included especially pronounced expressions of sentiments of caring, love, and loyalty to family and friends. James Johnson decided to become a highway robber when he was reduced in his fortunes and wanted to appease his mistress, 'with whom he liv'd, and whom he lov'd above all the World'. Robert Hallam, whose barbarity towards his wife culminated in her murder, still declared that 'he lov'd her to the last above all women'. Some accounts contained digressions in which love affairs, courting, and marital relations were described, with allusions to habits of sharing and mutual assistance. In his account of his robberies, William Shelton mentioned how at one point he disrupted his routine of going out for robberies, 'my wife being very ill, I did not think safe to leave her'. Shelton also referred to his grief over the demise of his wife, claiming that her 'dear memory at this unhappy juncutre gives me unexpressible pain'. Instead of the letters of repentance and godly instruction attached to some early crime pamphlets, the Newgate *Accounts* increasingly contained letters sent to wives or mistresses, replete with expressions of anguish and emotions 'beyond the power of language to express', as William Barkwith wrote in a letter he dispatched to a 'young lady'.[74]

Motherly love and filial obligation to parents were also expressed. The narrative of the life and crime of Judith Defour, whom the Ordinary contemptuously portrayed as ignorant, stupid, thoughtless, and averse to virtue, still recounted how, when she was forced to place her infant baby in a workhouse, 'she us'd sometimes to visit her and make much of her and to carry her out into the fields to give her the air'. After committing the murder, her guilt, anxiety, and longing for the child mounted; 'she never was at Peace since it happened', as the author related. The account of Elizabeth Harwood, also convicted for infanticide, indirectly conveyed her emotions by relating the care with which she treated the body of her infant following the murder:

> She took off his bloody shirt, put on his coat, breeches, and night cap, laid him down upon the bed, with some of the blankets to cover him; in which condition he was found at nine or ten o'clock next morning.

Filial obligations and loyalty to mothers were expressed by some prisoners, as in the case of Charles Patrick, who, in a letter attached to his confession, claimed that information reached him about 'several Persons' who talked about his mother and spread rumours that 'it was she that brought me to this untimely End'. Claiming, to the contrary, that if he had taken her advice he would 'never come to this untimely End', Patrick beseeched 'all People' to 'never reflect upon my dear Mother, nor any that belongs to me, for it was my own Doings that brought me to this shameful End'. Other prisoners showed care for the good name of their offspring, as was the case of Robert Hallam, who in his letter entreated 'all Christians, that they would not reflect on those poor Orphans, I leave behind me, ... As they cannot be thought in any Degree answerable for my Actions', adding as well his 'dying Desire' that 'the Dictates of every Man's Reason, will preserve them from any Reproach of this Sort'.[75]

In some reports, the chaplain reinforced the prisoners' declarations with his own observations of the intense feelings they were capable of expressing towards their kin, especially when describing the scenes of separation between the condemned and their families in the final days of their lives. In the case of Jane Griffin, indicted for the murder of her servant, the Ordinary described her husband and daughter's visit to her cell on the day of her execution, noting that 'it was not possible to view without tears the reluctance with which they left each other for ever'. The author went on to describe how Griffin then turned to her daughter, 'who hung upon her in tears', concluding by noting that 'after a very hard and difficult task in parting, her husband and daughter left her'. In the case of Thomas Past, convicted for robbery, his father and aunt who came to visit him cried out 'bitterly in a Flood of Tears', while his mother, who 'as they told me, ... indulg'd him above all her other Children, is now turned almost crazy, and cannot come Abroad, being inconsolable with Grief'. When the Ordinary asked Past 'how he could appear so hardened' in the face of these scenes, 'he said, he had unspeakable Grief and Vexation upon his Mind, though he could not express it outwardly'.[76]

Emotional attachments were also voiced by prisoners who reported the bonds of friendships and loyalty they formed over the course of their lives. Thomas Smith and Thomas Paxton, highway robbers, were described by the chaplain as having contracted 'an intimacy' and mutual obligations to one another, while David Delly and William Turner were 'born in the same neighbourhood, were acquainted from their infancy, and continued inseparable companions to the last'. Leonard Budley admitted that his mates were a bad influence on him, but he still insisted that 'he did not blame them as having any concern in his stealing or robbing'. Sara Malcolm and Mary Tracey, servants who were convicted of robbery and the murder of their mistress, were described as having 'contracted a great intimacy, and were often together', while the father, son, and brother-in-law who committed a robbery, were 'partners' all their lives, and 'companions' in their death. Other accounts report on criminals who refused to betray the names of their collaborators and friends; 'what good would it do me to hang three or four men, and ruin their families as well as mine?' one criminal was quoted in his response to the Ordinary.[77] Others expressed loyalty to friends whom they hoped would protect their own families. Richard Shepherd mentioned his loyalty to his two accomplices, whose names he refused to reveal, adding that these two friends sent him food during his confinement, and that he now hoped 'they would continue their Kindness after his Death to his dear Wife and his two poor young Children'. Appeals to friends or accomplices for the protection of wives and children are found in other accounts as well.[78]

In all these myriad forms of bounded shame, convicts aspired not only to obtain forgiveness and mercy, but also to restore their reputation among crowds and audiences, to reclaim moral character and earn for themselves a measure of self-respect. Scattered in the Newgate *Accounts* are instances of prisoners who wrote their confessions and placed them in a sealed envelope which they instructed to be opened and read to judges and benchers; others handed letters to the clergyman, wishing they be 'delivered to the people', or else they made 'declarations to numerous crowds of people' in prison and among acquaintances who came to visit them in their cell.[79] Calling upon varied dimensions of their personality and experience, the condemned constructed a more rounded presentation of their self, undermining the stigmatization of their character as shameful outcasts utterly deserving their death. Subtly and intricately, they pointed out that for all their crime and sin, they were nevertheless capable of sustaining human bonds and ties of obligation, loyalty and regard.

## Conclusion

Crime pamphlets and news reports published from the late sixteenth century onwards encompassed multiple voices and notions of shame. These voices were not always distinct, but rather intersected one with the other. Different notions of shame were invariably found in a single report, with the voice of clergymen-writers interrogating the prisoners converging with that of the condemned themselves. The prisoners sometimes complied with the author's expectations and exhortations, assuming full responsibility for their sins or crime, wholeheartedly embracing their shame, while offering penitence and expressing contrition and deep regret. Writers and Ordinaries, too, could at times embrace the perspective of the condemned, offering diverging, if not conflicting portrayals of felons, moving from denunciation and punitive shame to a more lenient and compassionate shame, showing sympathy and, at times, concurring or confirming the stories and pronouncements of the condemned.[80]

For all the lack of clear-cut boundaries, the divergence – and tension – between the voice of the author and that of the condemned, and between the different modes of shame presented by each, still stand out. An authorial voice that presented utmost punitive and exclusionary shame dominated crime narratives throughout, from the early seventeenth-century ballads and pamphlets, with their godly zeal and invocation of sin and shame, through the later Newgate *Accounts*, in which a vituperative rhetoric that stigmatized the condemned overwhelmed the clergymen's exhortations, permeating their biographical accounts and observations of the prisoners' behaviour in their cells. Alongside this thoroughly vindictive shaming, authors of crime reports also offered a more benign, redemptive shame, highlighting the power of God's grace in saving the criminal, presenting felons as penitent and transformed. For the prisoners, redeeming shame could offer a measure of alleviation for their suffering, raising the prospects of mercy and salvation, as well as of empathy and reconciliation with readers and the crowds who joined them in their final journey to their death.

Against this authorial and thoroughly Protestant voice and modes of shaming, the voices of the prisoners pervaded crime narratives throughout. Some prisoners complied with the Ordinary, fully acknowledging their sin and crime, expressing an agonizing shame and performing a 'good death' at the gallows. Most of the prisoners, however, displayed a far more partial and incomplete shame. Some repented grudgingly, expressing penitence half-heartedly or only at the very last moment of their lives. Many confessed they were sinners but still denied the shame and guilt for the specific crime for which they were being punished. Still others utterly denied their shame, refusing to cooperate and remaining obstinate and shameless in their fearlessness and resistance until the end. Above all, there were the many who, while admitting their shame and performing well at the gallows, still managed to diminish the shame by summoning varied arguments and considerations that presented their lives and deeds in a more humane, favourable light. They advanced an inclusive shame that did not rely solely on repentance and a plea for forgiveness and mercy, but rather on temporal arguments grounded in broadly shared notions of justice, mitigating circumstances, and pardonable crimes.

As the seventeenth century wore on, and as the early print media of ballads and godly pamphlets expanded into serialized newspapers, these arguments were advanced with greater intensity and force. They became 'public knowledge', reaching audiences and finding an open ear among readers of the reports and the crowds attending the execution.[81] As research has shown, and as some of the stories cited in this chapter also indicate, while spectators at the site of the execution sometimes exhibited hostility and vengeance towards the criminal, in many instances they displayed greater leniency and compassion, with crowds reportedly 'melting in tears' when witnessing the condemned or listening to their stories and claims. In the community or among readers of the reports, opinions were sometimes divided between those who viewed the convicts as monstrous and deserving death, and others who passionately defended them.[82] Within this range of diverse and conflicting attitudes, felons who resisted their shame or offered more circumscribed expressions of it, referring to their ties and emotional links to audiences and society, could hope to elicit understanding for their plight, raising the prospects of sympathy for themselves and the families they left behind.

These alternative stances on shame had implications not only for the reputation of the condemned but also for their perception and sense of an inner self. The minority of felons who defied their shame and resisted it until their death, shamelessly subverting the culture surrounding the gallows, presented a self which, on the eve of their brutal execution, assumed a measure of autonomy, honour, and pride. Those who invariably conveyed bounded shame, airing notions of pardonable crimes or mitigating circumstances, subtly alluded to their inner morality and capacity for sustaining human ties, despite their admitted sin and shame. The inclusive shame they expressed allowed them to construct a more complex, multifaceted self, linking themselves to human society, and to friends, neighbours, and crowds. Drawing a line between their deeds and their character, invariably hinting at or claiming moral character and a capacity for human attachments, felons increasingly and more vigorously attempted to affect their reputation and worth in the eyes of others, and, no less important, to earn for themselves a measure of self-respect.

As we shall also see in the final chapter, this articulation of bounded and more inclusive form of shame signalled, and in many ways anticipated, long-term changes in attitudes to public penalties and calls for reform of the justice system itself.

## Notes

1 Katherin Royer, *The English Execution Narrative 1200–1700* (London, 2013), esp. 9–14, 94; Randall Martin, *Women, Murder, and Equity in Early Modern England* (New York and London, 2008), 1–39; Andrea McKenzie, *Tyburn's Martyrs: Execution in England, 1675–1775* (London, 2007). For earlier studies, see especially Peter Linebaugh, 'The Ordinary of Newgate and His Accounts', in J.S. Cockburn (ed.), *Crime in England 1550–1800* (London, 1977), 246–69; J.A. Sharpe, '"Last Dying Speeches": Religion, Ideology and Public Execution in Seventeenth-Century England', *Past and Present*, 107 (1985), 144–67; Peter Lake, 'Deeds against Nature: Cheap Print, Protestantism and Murder in Early Seventeenth Century England', in Kevin Sharpe and Peter Lake (eds.), *Culture and Politics in Early Stuart England* (Basingstoke, 1994), 257–84.
2 Martin, *Women, Murder, and Equity*, 11–2.
3 For multiple and contesting voices in seventeenth-century reports on crimes committed by women, see ibid., passim.
4 Sharpe, 'Last Dying Speeches', esp. 166; Martin, *Women, Murder, and Equity*, 11–17, 80–97; Lake, 'Deeds against Nature', 268–73; Walsham, *Providence in Early Modern England*, 65–115; Henry Goodcole, *Heavens speedie hue and cry sent after lust and murther. Manifested upon the suddaine apprehending of Thomas Shearwood, and Elizabeth Evans, whose manner of lives, death, and free confessions, are heere expressed* (1635), STC2 12010, 2.
5 *The cryes of the Dead. Or the late Murther in South-warke, committed by one Richard Price Weaver*, in Hyder E. Rollins (ed.), *A Pepysian Garland, Black-Letter Broadside Ballads on the Years 1595–1639, Chiefly from the Collection of Samuel Pepys* (Cambridge, 1922), 223–8; *The Arraignment of John Flodder and his wife, at Norwidge, with the wife of one Bicks, for burning the Towne of Windham … of June last 1615*, in Rollins (ed.), *A Pepysian Garland*, 55–9.
6 *The examination, confession, and condemnation of Henry Robson fisherman of Rye, who poysoned his wife in the strangest maner that euer hitherto hath bin heard of* (1598), STC2 21131.
7 Goodcole, *Heavens speedie hue and cry*, 1–3.
8 Anon., *The life and death of Griffin Flood informer Whose cunning courses, churlish manners and troublesome Informations, molested a number of plaine dealing people in this city of London* (1623), STC2 11090, A3, B2, C2.
9 Anon., *A pittilesse mother That most vnnaturally at one time, murthered two of her owne children at Acton within sixe miles from London vppon holy thursday last 1616* (1616), STC2, 24757, A1.
10 Ibid., A4, B1–B2. For an analysis of the account of Margaret Vincent and its varied religious and politicized interpretations, and for the demonization of female criminals, see Martin, *Women, Murder, and Equity*, 164–7, 44–7.
11 *The Ordinary of Newgate His Account of the Behaviour, Confession and Dying Words of the Condemned Criminals … Executed at Tyburn.* Available on The Old Bailey Proceedings Online, 1674–1913 (www.oldbaileyonline.org), *Ordinary of Newgate's Accounts* (hereafter OBP/OA, date, and page no. from the original).
12 McKenzie, *Tyburn's Martyrs*, 261.
13 OBP/OA, 5 March 1733, 11–12. For the condemnation of criminals and the 'highly stylized practice of name calling' in the Restoration press reporting on crime, see also Phillippe Rosenberg, 'Sanctifying the Robe: Punitive Violence and the English Press, 1650–1700', in Deveraux and Griffiths (eds.), *Penal Practice and Culture*, 157–82, esp. 171–5.
14 OBP/OA, 14 February 1731, 5; 6 March 1732, 9; 9 October 1732, 13.
15 OBP/OA, 6 March 1732, 5; 8 March 1734, 5.
16 OBP/OA, 9 October 1732, 11, 13, 16.

192  Crime narratives and shame

17 McKenzie, *Tyburn's Martyrs*, 60–1.
18 OBP/OA, 14 February, 1731, 5.
19 OBP/OA, 29 January 1720, 2; 9 October 1732, 3.
20 OBP/OA, 9 October 1732, 4.
21 OBP/OA, 6 March 1732, 6.
22 OBP/OA, 14 February 1731, 14.
23 OBP/OA, 9 October 1732, 9. For suspicious attitudes regarding the sincerity of prisoners, see also McKenzie, *Tyburn's Martyrs*, 134, 194, 199, 209.
24 OBP/OA, 9 October 1732, 13, 11.
25 OBP/OA, 5 March 1733, 10–11.
26 OBP/OA, 6 March 1731, 6. See also McKenzie, *Tyburn's Martyrs*, 68–9.
27 OBP/OA, 6 March 1732, 11.
28 McKenzie, *Tyburn's Martyrs*, 59–67.
29 OBP/OA, 5 March 1733, 6; 31 December 1722, 1.
30 OBP/OA, 6 March 1732, 11; 5 March 1733, 10.
31 OBP/OA, 29 January 1720, 1; 9 October 1732, 2.
32 Martin, *Women, Murder and Equity*, 88–94; Sharpe, 'Last Dying Speeches'.
33 *The cryes of the Dead, Or the late Murther in South-warke, committed by one Richard Price Weaver*, in Rollins (ed.), *A Pepysian Garland*, 228; *The arraignment of John Flodder*, in Rollins (ed.), *A Pepysian Garland*, 57–8.
34 *Anne Wallens Lamentation. For the Murthering of her husband John Wallen a Turner in Cow-Lane neere Smithfield; done by his owne wife* (1616), in Rollins (ed.), *A Pepysian Garland*, 85–8. For emotional scenes of the suffering of the repentant criminal in ballads, see also Joy Wiltenburg, 'Ballads and the Emotional Life of Crime', in Patricia Fumerton and Annita Guerrini (eds.), *Ballads and Broadsides in Britain, 1500–1800* (Farnham, 2010), 173–88.
35 Luke Hutton, *Luke Huttons lamentation which he wrote the day before his death, being condemned to be hanged at Yorke this last assises for his robberies and trespasses committed* (1598), STC2 14032; Gamaliel Ratsey, *The life and death of Gamaliell Ratsey a famous theefe of England, executed at Bedford the 26. of March last past* (1605), STC2 20753, F3.
36 Francis Cartwright, *The life, confession, and heartie repentance of Francis Cartwright, Gentleman for his bloudie sinne in killing of one Master Storr, Master of Arts, and minister of Market Rason in Lincolnshire* (1621), STC2 4704, A2.
37 Gilbert Dugdale, *A true discourse of the practises of Elizabeth Caldwell, Ma: Ieffrey Bownd, Isabell Hall widdow, and George Fernely, on the parson of Ma: Thomas Caldwell* (1604), STC2 7293. See also Martin, *Women, Murder and Equity*, 47–50, 107. For printed gallows speeches from the late seventeenth century onwards, see McKenzie, *Tyburn's Martyrs*, 33–41.
38 Dugdale, *A true discourse*, B2, C3, D2.
39 OBP/ OA, 3 March 1733, 4; 9 October 1732, 15, 16. For the Ordinaries' exhortations regarding the necessity to confess, see also McKenzie, *Tyburn's Martyrs*, 140–4.
40 OBP/OA, 5 March 1733, 7; 6 March 1732, 13.
41 McKenzie, *Tyburn's Martyrs*, 147–8, 157–70.
42 OBP/OA, 29 January 1719–20, 4, 6.
43 McKenzie, *Tyburn's Martyrs*, 145–6, 238, 240.
44 OBP/OA, 14 February 1732, 14, 16–7.
45 Martin, *Women, Murder and Equity*, 107, 114–6.
46 Henry Robson, *The examination, confession, and condemnation of Henry Robson fisherman of Rye, who poysoned his wife in the strangest maner that euer hitherto hath bin heard of* (1598), STC2 21131; Anon., *A Pittilesse mother*, B2.
47 Martin, *Women, Murder and Equity*, 107; OA, 9 October 1732, 15; McKenzie, *Tyburn's Martyrs*, 137, 135, 193.
48 Ibid., 137.
49 Ibid., 146–50.

50 For different historical interpretations of the degree to which prisoners resisted their punishment, see Martin, *Women, Murder and Equity*, 110–4.
51 Ibid., 107–8; OA, 21 December 1739, 7; Linebaugh, 'The Ordinary of Newgate', 258.
52 Martin, *Women, Murder and Equity*, 28, 214, note 90; Linebaugh, 'The Ordinary of Newgate', 258; OBP/OA, 14 February 1732, 16.
53 Martin, *Women, Murder and Equity*, 97, 113.
54 Ibid., 106, 115, 67; OBP/OA, 9 October 1732, 17 (report on Serjeant Griffiths). See also McKenzie, *Tyburn's Martyrs*, 146–8, 162.
55 Ibid., 231, 231–2, 241–9.
56 Anon., *The life and death of Griffin Flood*, C4.
57 McKenzie, *Tyburn's Martyrs*, 243–7.
58 Ibid., 191–223, quotations on 194, 203–4, 209. For McKenzie's suggestion that accounts of felons dying 'game' but still expressing confidence in God's mercy indicate the influence of antinomian beliefs, see 204.
59 K.J. Kesselring, *Mercy and Authority in the Tudor State* (Cambridge, 2003), 91–135; J.M. Beattie, *Crime and the Courts in England, 1660–1800* (Oxford, 1986), 400–49; Martin, *Women, Murder and Equity*, 47–51, 114–6.
60 Cartwright, *The life, confession, and heartie repentance*, A4. Italics added by the author.
61 *Luke Huttons lamentation*; *The life and death of Gamaliell Ratsey*, C3, D3. For similar accounts of highwaymen aspiring to a chivalric code, in the Newgate Accounts, see McKenzie, *Tyburn's Martyrs*, 108–15.
62 Dugdale, *A True Discourse*; Goodcole, *Heavens Speedie Hue and Cry*, B2. See also Martin, *Women, Murder and Equity*, 47–50, 103–4.
63 Ibid., 51–68.
64 OBP/OA, 6 March 1732, 15; 9 October, 1732, 12; 5 March 1733, 7.
65 OBP/OA, 5 March 1733, 9; 6 March 1732 10; 9 October 1732, 4.
66 OBP/OA, 29 January 1720, 4; 14 February 1731, 11; 29 January 1720, 6. See also McKenzie, *Tyburn's Martyrs*, 111–2.
67 OBP/OA, 5 March 1733, 21; 9 October 1732, 12; 21 December 1739, 5, 12, 14.
68 OBP/OA, 6 March 1732, 15.
69 OBP/OA, 9 October 1732, 12, 13; McKenzie, *Tyburn's Martyrs*, 75–8, 81.
70 OBP/OA, 8 March 1734, 8; 20 December 1731, 6; 11 August 1736, 14. For negligent masters contributing to the criminal course of the condemned, see also McKenzie, *Tyburn's Martyrs*, 76–7.
71 OBP/OA, 9 November 1732, 33; 21 December 1739, 10.
72 OBP/OA, 9 October 1732, 12, 33, 35; 5 March 1733, 9; 21 December 1739, 8; 4 February 1731, 11.
73 OBP/OA, 25 May 1723, 4; 9 October 1732, 37; 6 March 1732, 7.
74 OBP/OA, 9 October 1732, 10; 14 February 1731, 14; 9 October 1732, 35, 37; 21 December 1739, 15–16.
75 OBP/OA, 8 March 1734, 5; 21 December 1739, 7; 9 October 1732, 11–12; 14 February 1732, 17.
76 OBP/OA, 29 January 1720, 6; 6 March 1732, 10. For these 'moving and affecting scenes', see also McKenzie, *Tyburn's Martyrs*, 214–17, where the author attributes these descriptions to the eighteenth-century culture of sensibility.
77 OBP/OA, 6 March 1732, 13; 5 March 1733, 7, 8, 20; 21 December 1739, 9; McKenzie, *Tyburn's Martyrs*, 200–1.
78 OBP/OA, 29 January 1720, 4.
79 OBP/OA, 14 February 1732, 14.
80 For converging voices, see also McKenzie, *Tyburns' Martyrs*, 59, 78–82.
81 Martin, *Women, Murder, and Equity*, 203.
82 Martin, *Women, Murder, and Equity*, 103–4, 116–22; McKenzie, *Tyburns' Martyrs*, 33–4, 149–50. For the complexity of crowds' emotional reactions, in the late eighteenth and nineteenth centuries, see also V.A.C. Gatrell, *The Hanging Tree: Execution and the English People 1770–1868* (Oxford, 1994).

# 7 Transformations of shame

By the late seventeenth century, the shame punishments discussed in the previous two chapters were waning. Ducking, carting, and locking in stocks, with convicts placed on display for crowds to behold, mock, and deride, diminished throughout the seventeenth century. Public whipping, long central to the punishment for petty crime and misdemeanours, also decreased. In Norwich, the process was evident before 1700, while in London a long-term decline was observable from the 1730s onwards. Both whipping and executions disappeared from the public purview, to be performed behind or outside prison walls. The notorious procession to Tyburn, with convicts led to their hanging via a long and humiliating route, was abolished in 1783. Executions from then onwards moved to Newgate prison, where the size of the audience able to watch the hanging was dramatically reduced.[1]

This fading of the shamed criminal from the public arena by no means implied an overall decline of shaming and shame. The eighteenth century witnessed major shifts in sentencing practices, evident first and foremost in the introduction, from 1660, of the penalty of transportation, which was increasingly used following the Transportation Act of 1718. Imprisonment became more prominent as the century progressed, as well.[2] Yet overall, the penal system remained severe and the punishments it administered continued to inflict ostracism, stigmatization, and shame. Transportation to the colonies, which was imposed as a condition for pardon (instead of the death penalty) or as a punishment for lesser offences, was perceived from its inception as internment in an outdoor prison. Although some mid-eighteenth-century observers judged the penalty as weak and ineffectual, transportation wreaked immense hardship and was thoroughly entangled with shame; prisoners awaited transportation for months, embarking on a long and hazardous voyage confined in the hold of the ship, their displacement to remote places utterly uprooting them from family and friends. The penalty could arouse contempt, indignation, and a sense of 'utmost degradation'; by the end of the century some prisoners refused to accept transportation and preferred the death penalty instead.[3] Imprisonment, which increased substantially by the 1770s, exacted its own isolation and shame, being inflicted in combination with a fine and branding. Despite calls and attempts at reform, prisons became greatly overcrowded, and were overall designed to enable

DOI: 10.4324/9781003226871-8

the survival of prisoners or prevent their escape, rather than offer them a route for reform or rehabilitation. Death by hanging, whipping, branding on the cheek – all remained standard forms of punishment well into the late eighteenth century, inflicting utmost punitive shame and disgrace even as they came to be performed indoors and away from the public eye.[4]

No less important, as indicated throughout this book, shame could take different forms, from harsh and punitive through more benign modes, the shame being inflicted not only via the penal system nor even through the observation of large crowds, but rather in varied social encounters, public and private. These diverse modes of shame were intricately linked to a set of beliefs and values, which over the course of the era were disseminated through print and other media and had a powerful hold on society at large. These values and ideas did not present a unified belief system, nor were they consistently applied by all social groups or even within a specific social class or setting. As repeatedly observed in this book, it was precisely the coexistence of strongly held ideals and beliefs on the one hand, and inconsistent practice, or outright disregard for these ideals, which could produce some of the most intense forms of shaming and shame. All this implies that if we are to assess whether shame was on the decline, we need to probe a range of contexts within which the emotion was triggered and applied, along with broader cultural shifts and transformations that could affect the practice and experience of shame.

The purpose of the following chapter is to assess the changing contours of shame by looking into some of these changing contexts and cultural transformations. Taking a long chronological view that encompasses the middle decades of the eighteenth century, we examine a set of cultural and intellectual transformations, focusing on the implications they had for the practice and experience of shame. We begin with the effect that the enhanced diffusion of civility and politeness had on the infliction of shame, in English society itself and in its encounters with foreign peoples across the seas. We then move to discuss the impact of novel enlightenment ideas regarding sin and sexuality, along with changing conceptions of the role of shame as a form of punishment in education and the penal system administered through the courts. We further explore the uses of shame in the vastly expanding world of print, where public shaming and shame took a new and vigorous role. Finally, we look into shifts in practices long associated with the early modern honour culture – elite duels, public insult – probing the implications these had for notions of male honour and shame. As will become apparent throughout, by the mid- and late eighteenth century, the possibilities for the use and expression of varied forms of shame – public and private – expanded; and while some shame practices diminished or faded altogether, others were transformed, reformulated and vastly enhanced.

## Shameful incivility, class, race

As civility was increasingly adopted by an English elite keen on maintaining its status, and as the pressure for refinement and polite manners came to dominate the lives of generations of elite women and men, so shame shaped their mental habits and comportment, navigating and controlling their social relationships and interactions. Books of manners, which continued to be published well into the eighteenth century and beyond, became ever more detailed, with every minute injunction for accomplished conduct enhancing the potential for embarrassment and shame.[5] As we saw in previous chapters, shame also reverberated in daily lives and interactions within families and networks of kin, friends, patrons and clients, or commercial ties. The shame applied in these contexts could be overly polite, coming in the form of reproach or couched in a strong rhetoric of deference and apology, acting as a reminder of obligations, smoothing disputes or allowing space for conflict resolution. The shame could also come in a far less polite form; an outright threat of disgrace, insult or humiliation, forms of punishment that could undermine reputations, social standing, and sense of honour, at times with devastating consequences for the shamed.

By the 1700s, polite idiom and comportment were adopted by social groups below the elite, politeness becoming instrumental in the creation of an ethos for merchants, the professions, and other urban trades. It came to be associated with proficiency and improvement, metropolitanism, and a set of 'genteel' comportments and accomplishments – from fashion and taste to conversation and sociability. Polite manners not only defined these elite groups, but also distinguished them from the rest of society, buttressing their distinctive status and exclusiveness.[6] Those with no access to these groups carried the mark of an increasingly intense and exclusive shame, their lack of manners being not only designated 'indecent', 'uncivil', or 'uncomely', but also associated with beastly instincts or an incapacity to feel human shame. The vocabulary for marking and shaming the 'vulgar' classes became more varied, encompassing an increasingly wide range of terms, from 'lewd', 'filthy' and 'rude' through 'savage', 'barbarous' and much more. The rhetoric penetrated everyday discourse and imbued the lives of polite classes, men and women, with a sense of superiority and distinctiveness well into the eighteenth century and beyond.[7]

Shameful incivility also came to delineate more intricate hierarchies and classifications among middling groups and the lower classes themselves. A mercantile ethos of proficiency, credit, and honesty was linked to civil manners, with certain trading occupations being designated 'genteel trades' to distinguish them from lower, 'common trades'. Some of these common trades would be dubbed rude and 'most uncivilized'; others, seamen, for example, were perceived as rough, plain-spoken and difficult to discipline; they were the 'most unconversable Part of Mankind'.[8] Divisions along lines of civility and vulgarity could cut through the middling classes, generating praise for the refinement, cleanliness, and good manners of artisans or those lacking gentle status, or else criticism, derogation, and shame for their ignorance, 'ill discourse' 'raillery' or 'noise'.[9] The language of civility could also penetrate the discourse on poverty, bolstering the classification of the poor into categories of deserving and undeserving. Those deserving of charity were selected on the basis not only of their age or inability to work, but also on the criteria of character and civil conduct, their civility being associated with industriousness, deference, and adherence to civil mores. Through decent conduct and conversation, the poor could earn respectability and hence be considered worthy of relief. The undeserving poor, on the other hand, were labelled idle and sinful, with beggars and vagabonds described, at times, as 'rats' and 'vermin', overall being shamed for their unruliness and 'most beastly manners'. Incivility was ultimately the mark of the criminal, who was castigated not only as sinful or devilish but also as the epitome of incivility – a cannibal, savage, the beast deserving outright shame and punishment by death.[10]

As Englishmen came into contact with non-English peoples and foreigners, in England and increasingly beyond, these distinctions and hierarchies marked with a shame idiom of incivility were greatly extended and reinforced. The Welsh, Irish, and Scots, all possessing the same legal rights as the English, were regularly dubbed wild, barbarous, and in dire need of being civilized. The Welsh were ridiculed and mocked in caricatures (in ballads and woodcuts) for their coarse habits, and their filth and ugliness were regularly commented upon; sons of Welsh gentry attending English universities were derided for their accent and broken speech. The Welsh themselves were quite aware of the English scorn, which they found distressing and hard to endure.[11] The Irish had long been approached with disdain and shame. In 'A view of the Present State of Ireland' (c. 1590), Edmund Spenser, Lord Deputy's secretary between 1580 and 1589, was at pains to dispel any notion that they conformed in any manner to English habits and accomplishments. Descending from the Scythians (the notorious barbarians of the ancient world), the Irish were nomads and their customs were perceived as hopelessly savage, posing a threat to civilized society. They not only needed to be civilized, but the entire edifice of their institutions and culture had to be dismantled and destroyed for such an enterprise to succeed. Spenser's views, carefully and elaborately argued, were not uncommon in the 1590s, and in the ensuing decades Englishmen continued to insist on the contrast between the savagery of Ireland and the civility of their homeland. Despite some dissenting opinions, the stigma of shameful incivility – the Irish being presented as brutish, filthy, and savage – persisted and continued to provide the justification for a civilizing mission, implemented, if need be, by force.[12]

Beyond the seas, English attitudes towards foreigners and the populations they encountered were initially more benign. Small clusters of English merchant communities were created in European cities and more remote places, from the Mediterranean and North Africa to India, the Far East and North America. As historian Alison Games showed, English merchants in these places pursued their lives and businesses discreetly, both a part of and apart from the dominant local population, relying on local people for their communication and adapting to local customs and ways, their attitude characterized by caution, accommodation, and flexibility. These overseas trading centres were also diverse, inhabited by migrants of a wide variety of ethnic groups and religions, including other Europeans or people of European origins – German, Dutch, French – and a growing slave population. Almost everywhere, the English were in a minority and hence forced into a measure of coexistence with, and dependence on, others.[13] Some of the English who embarked on journeys overseas, among them traders and sailors, travellers and explorers, came to espouse a favourable view of the peoples they encountered, becoming aware of their history and culture, commenting on their 'civilized' ways or praising their manners and habits. Some also adapted a critical stance towards the notion of an English civilizing mission beyond the seas; others mixed with and became immersed in the local population, adopting their customs and dress, acquiring language skills and knowledge of the indigenous ways.[14]

For all the pragmatism and accommodation, a deep strain of prejudice mixed with arrogance, condescension, and loathing was evident in English attitudes towards the foreign peoples they encountered. Native populations were typically viewed as deviating from English norms of civility, and were presented in derogatory terms that conjured up, and exposed them to, utmost humiliating and exclusionary shame. A large and growing literature of travel and exploration habitually associated African, Asian, and American people with 'bestial barbarity', the term 'barbarous' denoting an ever-growing range of deficiencies, from lack of moral self-restraint through want of education, religion, or laws and an orderly and civil society. English dictionaries related 'barbarous' people to rudeness in speech and behaviour, cruelty, violence, and 'a wilderness of life and manners'. Indigenous forms of dress (or lack thereof), alongside hairstyles, diet, bodily gestures and ornaments, were perceived as proof of uncivil and barbarous condition.[15] Like the lower classes in England, native populations were intuited as lacking the human capacity to feel shame, 'a nation ... without any sense of shame' as was still observed in the late eighteenth century, referring to the nakedness and sexual manners of Amerindians.[16] Criticism and ridicule of local attitudes towards women were common. In North America, Englishmen ridiculed Amerindian societies for what they considered to be perverse gender roles, with women performing agricultural labour while the men engaged in sporadic activities such as hunting.[17]

As the seventeenth century wore on and the English state expanded its hold over the colonies overseas, displacing and controlling foreign and local natives, such attitudes became increasingly rigid. With the accelerated reliance on Africans as slaves, incivility was invoked not only to signal the gap between the civil and uncivil, nor only to justify invasion, conquest, and colonization, but also to indicate innate and intrinsic racial differences between the English and non-white peoples or species.[18] In practice, by the early eighteenth century the separation between a 'civilized' English colonizer and local people of colour became entrenched. In the North American settlements, English inhabitants were seeking closer cultural ties with England, emulating English polite manners and sociability, adapting their fashion in architecture and the consumption of goods, in part to distinguish themselves from Amerindians and Africans or those of African descent. All people of colour, enslaved and free, became subject to slave codes, which consolidated and amplified their inferiority and exclusion, placing harsh restrictions on their movement, marriage, possession of property, and other freedoms. The shame and stigma of racial inferiority were extended to the offspring of these people, including those born of sexual liaisons between English men and non-English women. While some of these mixed-race children were integrated into the white population, by the eighteenth century they increasingly faced barriers to their full participation in colonial society. In Jamaica and Barbados, laws were passed barring 'mulattoes' (anyone with one African great-great-grandparent) from holding office and testifying against whites. Other restrictions, including a cap on inheritance, hindered economic activity. In some colonies, such as Antigua, free people of colour were required to obtain a white sponsor or otherwise become enslaved; in others, such as Jamaica, free people of colour had to wear a badge that marked them as inferior, excluded and disgraced.[19]

## Sin, sexuality, enlightened shame

While civility propagated and deepened varied forms and uses of shame, new ideas and attitudes could, at the same time, bring about its erosion and transformation. These ideas, broadly associated with the Enlightenment, placed doubt on a set of beliefs regarding the nature of God and his activity in the world, advancing notions of rational thinking and rational religion based on scientific ideas concerning the laws of the universe. The emergence and dissemination of these ideas entailed a long and protracted process, affecting only some sectors of society and the church, coming in piecemeal and infiltrating only certain religious denominations, while also encountering much resistance. Nor did the shift necessarily imply a complete rejection of Christian religiosity. Yet, as the eighteenth century progressed, these ideas were gradually taking roots, reshaping and transforming minds and attitudes not only among scientists or intellectuals and theologians, but also among pastors, their audiences and the population at large.[20] The result was the unsettling of some traditional notions of shame, along with the reconfiguration of ideas regarding its uses and application.

Critical for the waning of shame was the undermining of beliefs in the twin ideas of providentialism and original sin. By the late seventeenth century, the influential belief in godly intervention in the world receded, and with it the threat of a shameful humiliation wrought by godly wrath and retribution. Publications that had long inflicted and broadcasted utmost retributive shame – with graphic details of bodily shame and horrible degradation – were increasingly replaced by stories designed, for the most part, to entertain.[21] The rhetoric of punitive and degrading shame inflicted on sinners who violated godly commands gave way to a belief in more perfectible, elevated humans. The doctrine of original sin, long inscribing humans with the shame of ineradicable depravity and corruption, was challenged as well, potentially liberating some believers from the burden of an internal, agonizing shame generated by self-scrutiny and the sense of constant godly supervision, of the kind long recorded in spiritual diaries. As we saw in Chapter 2, by the mid- and late seventeenth century there were already those who distanced themselves from the puritan self-inflicted punitive shame, focusing instead on an experience of persecution and redeeming shame which offered them hope, if not assurance, of grace and salvation. As we also saw, there were radical sectarians who altogether defied the notion of original sin and shame, embracing instead an 'indwelling light' that connoted perfection and sinlessness. By 1730, some evangelical autobiographers displayed, in yet a different vein, a certain tendency to focus on contemplation and devotion to the bodily suffering of Christ, rather than on soul-searching and the monitoring of inner emotional states and shame.[22]

By then, moreover, there were some dissenters, especially among Presbyterians, who also took the more radical stance, touting a full-fledged denial of the doctrine of original sin and the burden of shame it entailed. For these heterodox Presbyterians, the rejection of original sin offered a way out of the agonizing dilemma between living 'in the flesh' and inevitably succumbing to sin, on the one hand, and the aspiration to godly life and ascetic conduct in the world on the other. As the case of the wine merchant Pentecost Barker, studied by historian Mathew Kadane, indicates, this merchant made the transition from a deep sense of guilt for his numerous lapses – his accumulation of wealth, his drinking habits – to outright denial of the doctrine of original sin, as it was preached by some heterodox Presbyterians and espoused by a correspondent of his, the proto-Unitarian pastor Samuel Merivale. Starting out as a traditional puritan, Barker kept a diary that strictly followed the model of Puritan spiritual autobiographies, typically displaying an acute awareness of sin, self-examination, and loathing for the idle ways of his youth and his habits of drinking thereafter. In his melancholy and despair, he was also tempted to put an end to his 'wretched life'. Yet sometime in the 1740s, Barker reconfigured himself as a rational dissenter, denouncing the doctrine of original sin, and attributing his drinking to his personal experience rather than sinful nature. Rejecting the notion that the species was depraved by nature, and ridiculing the idea that sin was transmitted from Adam to posterity, Barker concluded that the view of human nature that justified self-loathing and shame had to be abandoned. For him, the burden of a sense of corruption and shame had indeed been muted, if not altogether removed.[23]

Other novel ideas, especially regarding sexual morality and conduct, brought about an erosion of traditional notions of shaming and shame. By the late seventeenth century, an emerging discourse regarding religious tolerance and freedom of conscience in politics generated new ways of thinking about sexual freedom, with some thinkers extending the political discourse to sexual matters and morality. In 1660 the Adultery Act (which made adultery punishable by death) was abolished, and while there were some attempts at reinstituting the Act, prosecutions for sexual crimes like adultery and fornication decreased, and the shame penalties inflicted on victims of sexual transgression gradually came, by the mid-eighteenth century, to an end. Behind this change in the criminal law was a broader intellectual shift in opinion, in which personal instinct and conscience – rather than state magistrates or the church – were deemed the arbiters in matters of sexuality. This emphasis on sexuality as a private matter, reinforced by new scientific ideas and the separation of morality from religious rule, paved the way to a new understanding of sexual pleasure as natural, positive, and unhinged by sin and a sense of shame.[24] Already in the Restoration period, arguments in defence of sexual promiscuity and elite habits defying sexual decorum undermined long-cherished notions of male civility, decency and rationally controlled sexuality. By the eighteenth century, an explosion of erotica literature gave voice to this libertine tradition, signalling new habits and attitudes regarding sexuality, with the circulation of hundreds of eclectic books depicting erotic acts with explicit descriptions, scenes, and illustrations. The literature catered to a male and female literate audience, with erotic material also being read and listened to in male coffee-house gatherings. Although typically exhibiting a measure of polite restraint and refinement, erotica literature and the culture surrounding it indicated attitudes to sexual pleasure that were quite unhinged by, if not altogether liberated from, notions of sin, corruption, and indeed shame.[25]

Closely related to these attitudes was the enlightenment reconfiguration of masculinity and femininity, which reinforced the erosion of traditional notions of gendered shame. Increasingly infiltrating public commentary, literature, drama, and intellectual discourse, a new reversed distinction between the genders came to be pronounced. Instead of the traditional division between male-controlled and disciplined sexuality vs female lust and unrestrained appetites, men were now perceived as overwhelmingly sexual and passionate, while women were viewed as chaste by nature, asexual and virtuous. Both views could imply a more positive evaluation of sexuality and the diminution of the shame traditionally perceived as inherent to it. The new ethos of male sexuality, moreover, was perceived not only as positive but also as enhancing masculine honour. Masculine power and sexual urges were increasingly extolled, and a cult of seduction boldly cultivated men's sexual conquests, rapacity, and licentiousness, along with their power to control and humiliate women.[26] No less transformative was the new configuration of female sexuality, with women increasingly being perceived as innocent, chaste, and even morally superior to men. Commentators, judges, playwrights, and novelists depicted women as innocent victims of aggressive and seductive males, femininity being identified with suffering, male exploitation, and innocence. Prostitutes were increasingly presented as victims and 'fallen angels', and whoredom came to be approached with greater sympathy and understanding for the female plight. For many reformers and commentators, whores became an object of compassion, deserving support and rehabilitation rather than contempt, punishment and public shame.[27]

For all their novelty and radicalism in arresting some forms of traditional shame, new enlightened ideas and attitudes did not imply a wholesale erosion of shaming and shame. Older traditions regarding sin remained entrenched. Mid-eighteenth-century evangelical awakening, for example, inspired a generation of diarists who recorded their conversion experience, where sin and agonizing shame remained vital. Other prolific diarists, like Joseph Ryder, a clothier in Leeds, were well within the puritan tradition of writing under the shadow of a watchful God, expressing a deep, troubling, and ongoing sense of sin and shame.[28] Nor did the espousing of notions of freedom of conscience and religious toleration necessarily imply an endorsement of sexual liberty or a license to engage in adultery and fornication. The new agenda of gendered sexuality did not acquire a consensus, but rather triggered a great deal of reaction, contest, and debate, reflecting a greater plurality of moral views rather than an outright rejection of sexuality as the source of human corruption and sin. As we shall also emphasize below, liberated sexuality would trigger moral condemnation, with male rapacity and sexual urges being viewed as immoral and shameful. By the mid- and late eighteenth century, calls were aired for a law to be passed against seduction, and a certain 'backlash' against male licentiousness and promiscuity became evident.[29]

Nor did the traditional understanding of female sin and shame altogether abate. The celebration of gentlemanly sexual conquests could, in fact, reinforce the humiliation of the victimized females, and the shame they experienced would be harsh and unbearable. The identification of female characteristics with vanity, vileness, and unchastity persisted, although these were now typically explained as the product of education rather than of an innate nature or the female anatomy and humoral complexion.[30] Erotica literature, which promoted erudite libertinism and the pleasure of sexuality, was suffused with traditional perceptions of the gender divide between male sexual agency vs female passivity and modesty.[31] For many contemporaries, whoredom continued to signal utmost sin and shame, with women engaged in prostitution being regarded as depraved, immoral, loathsome, and dangerous.[32] Rape was likewise viewed ambiguously, with contemporary responses to sexual violence remaining inconsistent, and the stigma of unchastity being attached to the victim herself. As rape trials at the Old Bailey indicate, the ordeal was extremely damaging for women, whose cross-examination at court could be intimidating and a source of deep shame. In most of these cases, the victims remained reticent and unable to divulge the details of their ordeal in the face of a hostile and disapproving audience. The reporting on these trials was vicious and usually rendered the women's accusations false.[33]

No less important, shame became integral to enlightenment thinking itself, coming to the fore in a host of theories and calls for reforms – from education through law and the penal system. John Locke, whose views on religious toleration and freedom of conscience came to dominate the political discourse on these issues, accorded shame a central role in his treatise on the upbringing of children, *Some Thoughts Concerning Education* (1693). Written in the tradition of humanist advice literature, the treatise advocated the role of education in cultivating civil manners; decency and gracefulness, accommodation and respect to others, self-control, fortitude and courage.[34] Yet the treatise also incorporated a new understanding of human nature, based on Locke's theory of human knowledge (laid out in his '*An Essay Concerning Human Understanding*', 1689), according to which a child was born 'tabula rasa' and all knowledge came from sensual experience. Placing great emphasis on nurture rather than nature, and on the power of education in shaping character, Locke advocated the role of parental tending to the special needs of children and their individual character. While not fully rejecting the idea of original sin and remaining pessimistic in his view of the goodness or lack of corruption in humans, Locke discarded and ridiculed the idea of innate corruption caused by Adam and Eve.[35] Rather than delving into the ravages of original sin, he argued that humans can be ameliorated, and that a child's occasional display of cruelty, for instance, was the product of a bad parental example. Children, in his view, were not naturally wilful and selfish, but rather capable of reasoning and understanding. Particularly innovative was his plea against rote learning and the overt use of the rod – 'the usual lazy and short way' of chastisement, as he described it. Corporal punishment, so he reasoned, induced fear and a sense of impunity in a child, instead of the desired rational understanding and reflection on one's misdeeds and culpability.[36]

In this mix of traditional notions of civility and a novel attitude to child understanding, capabilities, and needs, shaming and shame acquired a central role. Given that children lacked judgement and were in need of restraint and discipline, parental indulgence was harmful: 'for liberty and indulgence can do no good to children'.[37] Instead, the proper method of education involved the two 'most powerful incentives to the mind', namely, a show of esteem and infliction of disgrace. While the former induced the pleasure of being cherished and esteemed 'especially by their parents', the latter triggered 'an apprehension of shame and disgrace'.[38] Here the persistence of the traditional notion of shame as a bridle on vice, and of the benefits of shame for cultivating not only good manners but also morality and virtue, were evident; 'Ingenious shame, and the apprehension of displeasure are the only true restraints on children conduct'; the 'Shame of doing amiss, and deserving chastisement, is the only true restraint belonging to virtue'.[39] Yet, more than his predecessors, Locke went into great detail in probing the psychological and emotional factors at play, pointing out the link between the two methods. Children who were sensitive to praise and commendation would also become particularly sensitive to any 'neglectful countenance' which they encountered when they misbehaved. And while the shaming should start early and upon the first 'irregularities' occurring in a child, it need not be frequent, for 'once they are shamed out of their faults, they will be in love with all the ways of virtue'. Frequent chiding, moreover, will 'lose all its influence' once it becomes 'learned lectures … daily inculcated into them'.[40]

Locke also elaborated on the desired method of applying shame, which constituted, so he avowed, 'the great secret of education'.[41] The shame should take the form of rebuke or chiding for faults, and be managed in a 'sober, grave and unpassionate' manner. Crucially, the shame ought to be performed 'alone and in private', for if exposed to others in their faults, children would give up their attempts to improve, suspecting 'that their reputation with them is already blemish'd'.[42] Overall, shame should involve 'gentle remedies of advice, direction, and reproof', including the use of insinuation, a gesture or a disapproving look:

> If any vicious inclination in him be, in the first appearance and instances of it, treated as it should be, first with your wonder, and then, if returning again, a second time discountenanc'd with the severe brow of a father ... and this continu'd till he be made sensible and asham'd of his fault ... And the best remedy to stop them, is, as I have said, to shew wonder and amazement at any such action as hath a vicious tendency, when it is first taken notice of in a child. For example, when he is first found in a lie, or any ill-natur'd trick, the first remedy should be, to talk to him of it as a strange monstrous matter, that it could not be imagin'd he would have done, and so shame him out of it.[43]

If Locke championed the practice of private shame in face-to-face relations and the education of children, others accorded a greater role for public shame in the treatment and punishment of criminals. Especially relevant here are the insights of Cesare Beccaria in his *On crimes and Punishments* (1764), in which he famously offered a thorough critique of the law and the justice system, proposing a new agenda for penal reform on the basis of a broader understanding of the nature of society and the need for social change.[44] Following Locke in attributing human knowledge, including morality, to the operation of impressions upon the senses, and insisting, again like Locke, that human reason could still channel and control these impressions, Beccaria called to replace the existing criminal justice system. Instead of a penal system that was arbitrary, he proposed a more rational scheme, in which laws were clear and precise, with judicial discretion reduced to a minimum so that citizens knew where they stood and could reason and calculate their acts accordingly. Laws were to be established by the legislative authority and applied by the state equally to all, while punishments ought to be speedy and certain, ensuring an indisputable proportion between the crime and the punishment. Beccaria called for eliminating the humiliation of criminals as much as possible, dispensing with torture and altogether abolishing the death penalty, all of which he deemed ineffective and unjust.[45]

Despite this call for a sweeping penal reform, Beccaria still embraced the practice of public shame, with 'infamy', or public disgrace, remaining integral to his proposed reforms. His reasoning was grounded in his understanding of honour, esteem, and pride as basic human sentiments. Honour, which had emerged when societies were formed, remained necessary for the sustenance of moral norms and standards of behaviour, especially when the law was unable to secure them. Undermining the principle of mutually respected honour in society ought therefore to be punished with disgrace:

'Personal injuries which damage honour, that is the proper esteem that a citizen can rightly expect from others, ought to be punished with public disgrace'. The aim was to deprive the culprit of the 'public goodwill ... the nation's confidence, and that sense almost of brotherhood which society inspires'. Beccaria did not go into specific detail on this matter, but made several provisos regarding the application of public disgrace. The penalty ought to be incorporated into the law so as to ensure a correspondence between morality – which public disgrace represented – and the law. It should not be applied 'too often nor on too many individuals', which would make it ineffectual; and it ought to avoid corporal pain, for the criminal who showed fortitude by enduring physical suffering enhanced 'glory and nourishment'. Public disgrace, on the other hand, acted to subdue such vain pride: 'ridicule and public disgrace are far more appropriate (than corporal punishment), being punishments which use the pride of the onlookers to put a brake on the pride of fanatics'.[46]

This reconfigured shame-based penalty was closely related to Beccaria's distinctive approach in his understanding of the purpose and application of the law, which combined two enlightenment theoretical strands: the utilitarian and the contractual. Beccaria argued that penalties ought to be evaluated by the benefit they brought to society, acting as a deterrent

> to prevent the offender from doing fresh harm to his fellows and to deter others ... Punishments and the means adopted should, consistent with proportionality, be so selected as to make the most efficacious and lasting impression ... with the least possible torment to the body of the condemned.[47]

Yet alongside this utilitarian understanding of the purpose of the law, Beccaria endorsed the contractual argument, according to which penalties should not only prevent crime in the future for the benefit of all, but also ensure that wrongdoers suffer in proportion to their wrongdoing. That is, society should punish those individuals who intentionally broke the social agreement between citizens, allowing considerations of guilt and morality that involved neither issues of utility nor even the rehabilitation of the criminal, but rather a measure of retribution; wrongdoers should suffer for what they had done, albeit in proportion to their wrongdoing and in accordance with the laws. In this context, public disgrace, which deprived individuals of their honour when they abused the honour of others, was considered a measured and appropriate penalty.[48] Other reformers elaborated the role of shame in punishment, with shame remaining integral to public debate and proposals for penal reform well into the late-eighteenth and nineteenth centuries.[49]

## Print, satire, and public shame

As observed in previous chapters, public shame in the early modern era was inflicted not only by state authorities and through the penal system, but also by ordinary people amidst their communities and the public at large. Here shame rituals – skimmington, ducking – were used against individuals deemed to have transgressed the accepted norm of conduct, subjecting them to mockery, physical abuse, and humiliation. Public abuse and shame also took the form of libels – in verse, ballads, or epigrams – invariably targeting persons of high status, including high-ranking officers, local magistrates, or landlords. Both of these forms of shame – ritual and verbal abuse – were rooted in popular tradition; while the former was rife with degrading symbols and connotations, the latter reflected a form of oral transmission that was ungoverned by rules of the written language, with the balladeers' offensive and spiteful language making creative use of satire and parody, typically employing excess and sexual imagery to intensify the humiliation and shame of the victim. As also noted in Chapter 5, the offensive language of popular libels penetrated more established forms of 'high' literary culture and the political discourse around the Jacobean royal court, freeing the traditional literary genre of satire from restraint and ambiguity, and allowing writers to articulate a harsh critique of individuals and of perceived vice at the Jacobean court.

Unlike the ritualized forms of public shame, which persisted throughout the seventeenth century but thereafter began to deteriorate, verbal shaming and abuse expanded immeasurably through the growing market for print. By the early seventeenth century, some libellous ballads were printed as broadsides and dispersed in many duplicates, disseminating the shame of the victims beyond the local alehouse to nearby villages and beyond. Illegal libellous verse, ballads, and mocking rhymes, which satirized and critiqued court aristocrats, continued to circulate by word of mouth or in manuscript form, among elite circles and a broader social milieu. By the 1640s, with the collapse of censorship and the breakout of civil war, the production of libels became the centrepiece of an intense and divisive political culture. Partisan writers broached previously taboo politics, ridiculing, maligning, using 'scandalous and disgraceful words' to denounce and mock rivals, with political leaders at the highest levels of government, including the King and the Queen, subjected to scurrilous and derogatory commentary and shame. The extraordinary textual production of the revolutionary decades also triggered fresh outbursts of satire in the populace at large. Combining early forms of high and popular satire, writers of middling and lower ranks boldly asserted themselves as political agents, using the printed satire to ridicule, satirize, and shame their opponents. Their pamphlets mixed popular debates on religion and politics with bitter, personal invectives, offering critique and condemnation, stigmatizing rival religious or political positions and exposing opponents for their shortcomings and lapses.[50] With the coming of the Restoration, the printing of political satire was halted, but as a literary genre the satire continued to flourish in manuscript form, with thousands of poems being composed and circulating among a restricted audience of the elite. Preserving the biting and shaming edge of the satire, the poems used polite language mixed with blatant and indecent idioms to convey moral condemnation, public insult and shame.[51]

In the ensuing decades, the thriving print market vastly increased the scope and use of satire and other forms of verbal condemnation and shame. An enormous increase in the number and variety of books and pamphlets, alongside the spectacular rise of the periodical press, allowed events and opinions to be publicized much more widely to a far larger readership among polite society and classes below it, in London and beyond. Journals, magazines, and newspapers included essays, commentaries, and correspondence, generating and broadcasting a range of polemic, critical, and didactic stances, presenting editorials and offering the public opportunities to pronounce their complaints or respond with opinionated letters to editors. Reading the papers was often not a solitary activity, but also occurred in a public arena of the coffee-house.[52] The explosion of printed satire, literary and graphic, was especially momentous. Going back to the revolutionary decades of the mid-seventeenth century, graphic satire was by the early eighteenth century produced by some of the most distinguished graphic artists working in London. The genre obtained pictorial and aesthetic distinction, developing a complex variety of techniques, skills, and styles. Like other forms of print, the dissemination of satire became far more sophisticated, with varied engravings imitating and complementing one another, maintaining a dialogue with each other and with other forms of print, offering verbal captions that highlighted the derision and shame embedded in the graphic image itself. Satirical prints and pictures were sold following or alongside journalistic commentary, poems, descriptions, and satirical accounts, all merging satire with moral condemnation that greatly increased the scope for ridicule and public shame.[53]

The themes targeted for shame through these satirical and literary works reflected an array of issues, debates, and contemporary preoccupations. As was already the case in previous decades, intimate links existed between satire and political debate, with satirical engravings fusing pictorial representation as a weapon of political attack and condemnation. So, for example, at the height of the Sacheverell controversy in 1709–10 (and the riotous assault on dissenting houses that ensued), hundreds of pamphlets were published, with some describing the clergyman Henry Sacheverell in the grossest language and 'street dialect', and engravings depicting him as a grotesque figure associated with the devil and the Pope.[54] The emergence of the new financial markets also became a topic of commentary and satire, heightened in the wake of the financial catastrophe of the South Sea Bubble in 1720, when newspapers attacked and denounced those involved as both stockbrokers and investors. Adding to the scene were satirical engravings – all on sale at shops – which represented the Exchange Alley through excessive detail and imagery, conveying a chaotic world of folly, crowd perversions, and craving for stocks, alongside hospitals and asylums that blatantly hinted at the ultimate – and shameful – destination of the bubble's victims. By the mid-eighteenth century, engravings with explicit political content came to dominate satirical art, with some of the images being used as instruments of party politics and propaganda, which was occasionally connected to an organized programme of political attack, or else published as independent graphic products.[55]

Moral issues loomed large in these overlapping worlds of painting, journalism, and literature, again reflecting public concerns and shifting preoccupations, with satire at times used as a guardian of public morality, exposing and castigating a host of vices and social ills. William Hogarth's famous morality tale, *The Rake's Progress* (1735), depicted the life of young Tom Rakewell, the son of a merchant whose idleness and profligacy brought him to financial and personal ruin, in eight scenes. The final pictures show the hero in his ultimate degradation and shame; in debt and imprisoned, then going mad and placed in the notorious Bedlam, where he is seen sitting on the floor, without a wig, half-naked and tearing his flesh, with elegant ladies watching him at a distance with disgust and scorn. Hogarth's series was part of a body of works produced by other satirists, artists, and commentators who subjected varied perceived social ills, especially pertaining to the metropolis, to critique, ridicule and condemnation.[56]

In its scathing criticism and denunciation, satire and moral commentary not only addressed topical issues generally, but also targeted specific groups, genders, social classes, and individuals for shaming. Stockbrokers or 'stock-jobbers', brothel keepers, rakes and pimps, seductive and lecherous males, female prostitutes, plebian women and lower classes in general – could all be the object of stigmatized representation, subjected to denigration and shame. Newspapers published stories and intimate accounts of male seduction, blaming and shaming men for their libidinous treachery; graphic satire presented the female as an object of sexual commodification, with grotesque scenes displaying flirtatious men with their hands creeping across women's breasts and crawling underneath their skirts.[57] The centrepiece of William Hogarth's widely distributed *A Harlot's Progress* (1731) was the seduction and ruin of an innocent young woman, her seducers, a notorious procuress and an infamous rake and rapist, enticing her into the world of prostitution. Yet the series also shames the victimized heroine Moll herself. In the final engravings, Moll dies of venereal disease, her coffin, from which only her face is seen, is surrounded by a flirtatious undertaker and a crowd of whores who playfully use the coffin as a tavern bar. The series reflected contemporary discourse and debates on prostitution, highlighting ambiguous attitudes by depicting the prostitute as the innocent victim while also targeting her for ridicule, denunciation and shame, her body ultimately becoming an emblem of metropolitan corruption.[58]

Women of the lower classes were condemned and shamed for other vices, especially their proclivity to drink. Censorious comment of alcoholism, which surged as an intense topic of concern by the mid-eighteenth century, produced varied shocking descriptions of the victims, with the drunk plebeian woman presenting the personification of drunkenness and a 'portrait true of shame'.[59] In Hogarth's *Gin Lane* (1751), the central dominating figure is a woman sprawled on her back across the stairwell of a St. Giles gin shop, her breasts bare, legs showing signs of disease and her eyelids heavy with alcohol as she abandons her child to the street – a symbol of moral breakdown and shame. Both *Gin Lane* and Hogarth's *Beer Street* (1751) resonated with a chaotic plebeian world full of vulgar, grotesque, and bestial figures; beggars and cripples with clothes ripped, women pouring gin for one another, men with huge stomachs drinking, laughing, flirting, or collapsing on the ground. According to the press announcement of the forthcoming publication of these prints, they reflected the 'reining vices peculiar to the lower Class of people', with the lower classes being construed not only as gin-prone but idle, feckless, and grotesque.[60] In verse satire and jestbooks, the lower orders were viciously ridiculed and mocked, with numerous jokes replete with bawdy and insulting humour being directed at the poor and other marginal groups – beggars, the crippled, deformed, or handicapped. Like the prints produced by Hogarth and other artists, which hung in taverns and shops for respectable viewers to behold, verse satire and jestbooks were produced for, and widely consumed by, the middle classes and the polite, women as well as men.[61]

Blunt and demeaning satire not only targeted the lower classes, but was also widely used as a weapon against polite society itself. If in the early seventeenth century satirical verse and ballads were directed at the local magistracy or court aristocrat, by the eighteenth century the critique and satirical presentation of the elite was vastly expanded to include a broader world of an urban, polite society – the *beau monde* – including both men and women. Some forms of perceived misconduct – adultery, gaming – were identified as the quintessential vice of the 'Great and Powerful' and others 'among Persons of the Greatest Fashion and Distinction'.[62] The hypocrisy of the polite, their fashionable excess, fraudulent conformity to religion or their attempt at hiding (in the case of women) signs of ageing, were common themes of written and graphic satire. Juxtaposing the Beau against the plebeian, such works dramatized class boundaries, exposing the tensions and disjunctions between the polite and the middling or lower classes, reinforcing the animosity of the latter by presenting the Beau in a grotesque light, stripped of honour and pride.[63] So, for example, in a 1716 description of a traffic accident involving a coach with its protected wealthy rider crashing into the mud, the narrator joined the onlooker's relish at the spectacle of embarrassment and shame: 'Crushed is thy Pride, down falls the shrieking Beau/ The slabby pavement crystal fragments strow,/ Black floods th' embroider'd Coat disgrace,/ And Mud enwraps the Honours of his face'.[64]

Disgrace of the polite was robustly presented in Louis Phillipe Boitard's engraving *Taste A La Mode* (1740), which depicted a parade of polite figures and flamboyantly dressed courtesans in St James Park, the central figure being a woman dressed in a huge and ludicrous hooped petticoat, a symbol of gross fashionable excess. In John June's *The Lady's Disaster* (1746), a fashionable lady is subjected to plebeian gaze and ridicule when she is forced to toss her Hoop too high to avoid a chimneysweep's boy suddenly falling under her feet. The boy is shown peeping underneath her skirt at her bare legs, while a crowd of soldiers and fashionable walkers alongside window-cleaners and carmen gather around and laugh. At the side is a beggar, his clothes ripped and hat battered, while his dog, in an ultimate gesture of insubordination and ridicule, is urinating on the hem of one of the women's embroidered dress. Prostitutes also look down on the 'disaster' from the first-floor windows of the brothel, where the scene takes place.[65]

Satirical and condemnatory presentations of polite society could become particularly destructive when directed against individuals, exposing them to public mockery and shame, invariably targeting their political or religious stances, their misconduct, corruption, or lapses. In 1710, Daniel Defoe, the writer and journalist already famous for his publications and attacks on the High Church, was himself subjected to ridicule and shame in George Bickham senior's engraving *the Whig's Medley* (1711), which showed him as a bewigged, stylishly dressed and self-satisfied figure being advised by the Pope and the devil. At the top was also a card that showed his head caught in the pillory (a reference to a punishment he had received for his views in 1702), with a caption denigrating his embarrassing facial features, 'with blobber Lips, & Lockram Jaws, Warts, Wrinkles, Wens and other Flaws'.[66] Other satirical attacks on politicians – often linked to a series of political articles or debates in the press – increasingly used the art of portraiture, with the decorous and idealized image of the portrait punctured and destabilized, recasting it as deformed faces or with face gestures indicating shame. Satirically detaching these portraits from their original dignified context and transplanting them in a crowded street or the brothel, graphic satire presented politicians in a grotesque and comic form, rich with allusions to their alleged shameful misdeeds. At the dawn of the premiership of Robert Walpole, George Bickham junior produced *The Stature of a Great Man, or the English Colossus* (1740), depicting him as a gigantic statue, situated in a landscape crowded with signs of overseas defeat and commercial collapse, his pocket full of cash from the Sinking Fund (a National Debt provision) he was accused of plundering, with a parodied verbal defence of his failed foreign policy introduced on a piece of paper into his hand. Bickham's *The Late P-m-r M-n-r* (1743), produced soon after Walpole was deposed, presented a shockingly ugly composite of grotesquely exposed facial features; a huge yawning mouth, teeth and gums laid bare, upturned nostrils and half-open eyes – a symbol of indignity and a grotesque leadership.[67]

As court politicians increasingly came under the gaze of the public, their private lives and exploits became special targets for criticism, denunciation, and shame. The flow of information on the sexual impropriety of leading courtiers became far more regular than in the previous century, provoking a huge amount of commentary and debate, with liaisons between leading courtiers and their mistresses subjected to criticism and increasingly to harsh and savage caricatures. The surge in the publications of paintings and biographies of leading aristocratic courtesans further expanded the scope for comment and condemnation, with some satirical prints of these immoral lovers and mistresses being produced in order to arouse shame and contempt. Well-known courtesans began to publish their own autobiographies in an attempt to vindicate their conduct, whereby they named and shamed their enemies, detractors and former lovers.[68]

It should be emphasized that the publicity generated through these satirical works and commentary did not always imply harsh punitive shame. In its appeal to polite audiences and viewers, some graphic satire tended to conform to more established 'high' forms of satirical conventions, offering an unthreatening critique or polite reproach, displaying elegance, refinement and restraint rather than bawdy and savage mockery. Satirical publications were also designed to entertain, offering audiences a humorous respite, and revelling in the public's appetite for sensational and salacious news and gossip.[69] No less important, the exaggeration and excess typical of satirical works could also empower their subjects, boosting and broadcasting their status and prestige, even conferring an inverse celebrity status on their victims. In the case of royal and aristocratic courtesans, their denigration could at times be overwhelmed by pictures that invoked admiration, with the prints enhancing the popularity and fame of these women. The courtesans who published narratives of their lives could also actively build their reputation, celebrating their exploits and sexual conduct, and partaking in what some historians refer to as the 'first age of celebrity'.[70]

For all these different functions of the satire, there is no doubting the power of satirical works and condemnatory comments as forms of public shaming and shame. Some graphic satire (as in the case of Hogarth's prints of the mid-century) presented chaotic scenes of immorality and decay, with the figures dominating them presented as not only comic or grotesque, but also deviant and utterly degraded, an epitome of a horrifying and menacing shame. Other images buttressed vitriolic attacks on politicians in the press, denigrating their misdeeds, causing humiliation, embarrassment, and shame. As noted above, the notoriety of well-known whores could ultimately lead to contempt, while sexual scandals, which were publicized and debated in print and regularly commented upon in editorials and letters to newspapers, could also elicit mockery and denunciation.[71] From the 1760s, when the identity of those involved in sexual scandals was regularly exposed – instead of remaining in anonymity or only being hinted at – such reports presented blatant criticism of leading court politicians linked to the Crown itself. Among commentators and readers – or rivals of these politicians – there were those who viewed the publicity as a means of reform that would shame corrupt and powerful individuals into changing their ways.[72] For the victims, the publicity could have harsh implications for their family lives and careers. In the case of aristocratic women, being 'scandalously talked about' caused anguish, with family members expressing a sense of being 'frightened to Death' when an affair only began to be rumoured and reported. The subsequent publication of adultery trials, replete with stories of the sordid actions and scandalously embarrassing letters written by those involved, vastly enhanced the humiliation and public shame. An active press coverage came to be considered a form of not only chastisement or ridicule, but an 'inquisitorial instrument', a 'pure impartial justice' and a justly deserved punishment.[73] By the late eighteenth century, politicians became vulnerable to blackmail, as courtesans and scandalous women threatened to publish their former lovers' names and letters. Reports of sexual histories and sexual scandal, publicizing the names of politicians and their courtesans, or with stories of disreputable conduct and immorality more broadly, came to be used as a political weapon, greatly discrediting and at times destroying the careers of opponents. Well-known public figures – artists, actors – also risked their careers when the details of their liaisons and the legal cases brought against them were publicly exposed and widely talked about.[74]

## Honour, pride, and shame

Some practices that had long been associated with early modern notions of honour and shame receded over the eighteenth century. Aristocratic duelling, whereby to avert the shame inflicted through an infringement of honour elite men resorted to the sword, became a subject of contention. The duel had long been condemned by some critics as immoral and a shame, and by the early eighteenth century it encountered vociferous opposition, with critics accusing the practice as unchristian, savage, or absurd, governed by the 'tyranny of passions' and based on false notions of civility.[75] While in the early decades of the eighteenth century the duel appears to have flourished, it also began to change; pistols replaced swords, seconds took on a new role as mediators and, as a consequence, injuries and fatalities decreased. Some duels retreated indoors, or else contestants took them to the press or the court, insisting on an apology rather than succumbing to the ritual's deadly hazards. By the 1780s the practice was restricted to politicians and military men, and while a resurgence occurred during the Napoleonic Wars, thereafter the duel was increasingly considered obsolete, unpatriotic and an object of ridicule.[76]

Public insult and litigation over verbal abuse among the middling and urban classes also dwindled. As we saw in Chapter 5, verbal abuse reverberated across communities throughout the country, inflicting shame and humiliation and invariably denting or destroying the honour and social standing of community members. Male honour – his 'worth' and 'good name' – was associated with qualities such as credit and trustworthiness, sexual propriety, an ability to provide for a family; women's honour resided in their chastity, honesty, and honest dealing. Verbal abuse that shattered any one of these qualities could lead to violent brawls and prosecution at court, and well into the mid-seventeenth century, victims of slander, women and men, were willing to go to court to clear their name and restore their reputation. Following a collapse in defamation prosecutions during the Interregnum and a partial recovery in the late seventeenth century, court litigation over insults declined. In London, the decline in the number of cases prosecuted at the consistory court and quarter sessions was observable by the 1730s, while in other places the process was protracted and persisted longer. In Edinburgh, levels of defamation litigation at the consistory court remained high through the 1770s, but thereafter declined.[77]

For all the manifest significance of these changes, they did not imply a decline in the honour culture, nor the varied forms of shame embedded in it, first and foremost among the elite. As noted in Chapter 3, duels were only the most extreme manifestation of reactions to infringement of honour, and the number fought throughout the seventeenth century appears to have been small. The practice was criticized by many and was often avoided, with honour itself being invoked to prevent violence and uphold restraint rather than proceed to a contest. Elite honour was based not only on a display of masculine courage, or even on birth and lineage, but also, as described in this book, on appropriate manners and courtesy, on accommodation and moderation – an ideal of civility in which outward appearances were often perceived as inextricably linked to inner morality, charitableness and virtue. In this world, interpersonal tensions and disputes, including affronts to honour, were managed or averted through self-control and restraint rather than outbursts of violence or outrage, with varied tactics employed to diffuse passions and circumvent dishonour and shame, including use of emotional pressures, rebuke, scolding, or the threat of shame. Nor were honour and shame confined to elite men. Honour and repute were crucial assets for elite women as well, gained through chaste and modest comportment, efficient domestic management, sociability and family reputation, which elite women defended aggressively; that is, they perceived any infringement on their claim to being 'women of honour' a shame. Among both men and women, these assets continued to nourish a strong sense of reputation and honour, the violation of which remained a source of deep shame well into the eighteenth century and beyond.[78]

Lower down on the social scale, among urban tradesmen and craftsmen, the decline in litigation over public insult did not indicate a diminishing significance of honour, nor the decline in the susceptibility to shame among these groups. Shaming and shame continued to pervade social interactions as not only sources of tensions and disputes, but also the means through which the ensuing confrontations could be resolved. Already in the seventeenth century, clashes over degrading speech and insult did not always lead to violent brawls, the use of violence being constrained by considerations of what were considered acceptable and unacceptable forms of male aggression, or else being tempered by notions of civility, self-constraint, and morality. Alternative responses to violence could take the form of denunciation and counter-allegations, social pressures and verbal shaming, with many disputes being settled informally without reaching the court. Appeals to the court often did not proceed to indictment and trial, ending up in mediation that aimed at conciliation through financial compensation along with apology or expressions of regret or guilt.[79]

As defamation prosecutions declined during the eighteenth century, the use of these non-violent and more constrained or 'civilized' forms, to which shame was crucial, remained entrenched and even intensified. Concomitantly, the use of arenas other than the court to resolve issues of honour also became more common.[80] In London, the records of prosecution for homicide at the Old Bailey show instances where attempts were made to pacify disputes and prevent fights from taking place, with passers-by or friends, all of them men, acting as mediators. While in these cases the attempts failed and the brawls ended with fatal injuries or death, in other instances such interventions would have been more successful in moderating a dispute and allowing space for apology or conciliation.[81] In Edinburgh, only a small number of incidents of public insult ended up at the court, and the level of violence they involved, while declining towards the end of the eighteen century, was still overall low.[82] No less important, as these court cases also reveal, responses to insult could include non-violent means in which shame was pivotal; not only 'mad rage and passion' but also cool and dispassionate responses, non-verbal displays of disparagement, signals of shame or threats of shaming and social exclusion (refusing to drink with someone), alongside persuasion in the context of more 'polite conversation'. As in the earlier decades, these cases suggest that face-to-face affronts to honour and shame continued to be resolved informally outside the court, in a public space in front of witnesses, or in face-to-face encounters and domestic settings, in the company of small groups and acquaintances. Disputes were also increasingly negotiated and mediated publicly through the press.[83] In all these cases, affronts and intense confrontations could culminate with a show of remorse, 'coming to senses', or an offered apology whereby shame was partially averted and honour restored.

Elsewhere in the public arena, issues of honour, pride, and shame also remained vibrant, with some aspects of masculine honour and shame being reconfigured and reinforced. In Bernard Mandeville's well-known works *The Fable of the Bees* (1714/24) and *An enquiry into the Origin of Honour* (1732), the philosopher placed these issues at the heart of his analysis of human nature and the emergence of social, civilized life. Starting from the Hobbesian assumption that humans were deeply selfish and social life was an unnatural imposition on them, Mandeville still asserted the presence of a germ of sociability in the human nature, without which no civil society could exist, nor be governed. This sociability resided in the universal passions of honour, pride, and shame. Honour was defined strictly in terms of the 'extraordinary concern' we all have 'in what others think of us', with pride and shame being core innate elements of human existence, both of them facets of honour.[84] While pride was associated with what Mandeville called self-liking and the need to gain the good opinion of others (or gratify the self-liking and honour of others), that is, it was oriented outwards, shame was associated with self-love and oriented internally, that is, to the sacrifices and restraints people impose on themselves in their attempt to gain esteem and avoid disapproval, contempt, and dishonour. The shame in Mandeville's analysis was intensely interior; 'a sorrowful Reflexion on our own Unworthiness', which was followed not only by a host of physical symptoms but also by 'the sinking of the spirits', a weariness of one's 'being' and the wish one 'could make himself invisible'. Acquiring a habit of shame was a difficult task which required strenuous education, training and the acquisition of polite manners, whereby individuals learnt to subdue their selfish impulses to gain the admiration of those around them, thus allowing society to thrive. 'It is incredible ... how necessary an Ingredient Shame is to make us sociable ... no society could be polish'd, if the Generality of Mankind were not subject to it'.[85]

Mandeville's views regarding the selfish nature of humans and his assault on morality, especially his assertion that human traits perceived weaknesses and a source of shame (like pride) were, in fact, powerful engines of society – were considered provocative and radical, or eccentric. His challenge of cherished ideas and his defiant denigration of Christian values (benevolence, for example) were also met with criticism and often also contempt.[86] Mandeville's insistence on the dissociation between civility and morality was not broadly shared; his assertion that civility and politeness were based solely on selfish instincts and the desire for honour, displayed strictly through outward appearances and divorced from virtue, honesty, and morality, did not conform to more conventional contemporary thinking on these matters.[87]

Yet some of Mandeville's insights regarding honour, pride and shame resonated with broader preoccupations regarding the centrality of the passions, including pride and shame, in the formation of the self and its relations with others, and these would continue to play a role in the discourse of some enlightenment thinkers in the following decades, and beyond.[88] Especially relevant for our discussion here is his notion of masculine honour gained through the display of bravery. As Mandeville reasoned, pride and the eagerness for praise predisposed men to seek revenge when honour was evaded, preferring the opinion of others over anything else, including self-love and even life itself; such passions encouraged men to fight and engage in duels and wars, overcoming the fear of death. 'A man of honour must fear nothing', courage being the 'grand Characteristic of a Man of Honour'. In contrast to early forms of honour which had been practised among the ancient Greeks and in medieval times, the honour of the modern male was based on the sole rule of 'suffering no affront', refined through guidelines for fighting and polite conduct. 'There is a spirit of Gentility introduced among military Men, both officers and soldiers, ... which now shines through all their Vices and Debaucheries'.[89] Intricately tied with, and essential to, politeness, male honour and courage were not only beneficial to society but comprised an invaluable asset for the creation of a good army and fighting wars, with men of honour always ready to defend their country.[90]

These arguments fitted all too well with the early eighteenth-century emerging discourse on militarism and the ideal military man, which evolved in the wake of the professionalization of the army and the waning of more traditional perceptions of elite military prowess.[91] As the British state grew and its military forces greatly expanded, waging wars on the Continent and increasingly in the colonies and across the globe, questions regarding the desirability of a standing army, the nature of military training and the ideal modern soldier were brought to the fore.[92] Like Mandeville, some commentators promoted the view that the modern soldier was steeped in polite culture, combining good manners and a calm mind with physical prowess and bravery, with professionalism, military skill and courage acquired and cultivated through proper civic education, sports, and physical exercise. Against these writers were those who postulated a notion of soldiery based strictly on male physical prowess and courage. Good soldiery, in this view, derived from masculine instinct rather than from nurture and training, as military skill and courage were thought to be rooted in male nature from time immemorial. 'Where there is sheer Courage in a nation, Men are Soldiers by instinct', as one author put it.[93] As the century wore on, additional views of the military man were articulated, from literary constructions (in gothic and sentimental literature) that looked upon the medieval chivalric hero as the prototype of the modern soldier, through images of the modern soldier as a man of feeling capable of expressing inner emotions and sentiments.[94]

For all their different emphases, these shifting conceptualizations of soldiery shared a renewed and invigorated vision of masculine honour and pride displayed through prowess and courage, with the failure to perform honourably perceived as cowardice and becoming a source of public humiliation and shame. These renewed notions of honour affected the standing of politicians and military men, reverberating across a public who became keenly interested in military matters and affairs. By mid-century, public enthusiasm for the military man who fought bravely without succumbing to the fear of danger or death, fighting to the end, impinged on several military trials, in which highly ranked navy officers were accused of failing to secure victory in combat (against the French fleet). These trials, which took place in the 1740s and 1750s, exposed debates and conflicting versions of appropriate conduct in war and in engaging the enemy, and their outcomes varied. Yet throughout the duration of the trials, public opinion was adamant in its condemnation of the officers for their failure to do their utmost, their shame and humiliation being widely publicized beyond the confines of the courtroom or the military itself.[95] By the late eighteenth century, the public embrace of military men as heroes intensified, with high-ranking officers becoming celebrities in their own right. Among military men, the pressure to display courage and avoid shame at all costs, that is, to abide by a code of honour, was particularly pronounced, as was evident in the surge of duels in which they were engaged.[96] As England faced wars in America and with the French, the cult of heroism and aggressive masculinity merged with patriotic fervour and an emboldened sense of British national identity. Manly desire to show prowess and an eagerness to fight, and the concomitant concern not to seem a coward and avoid the shame inflicted by friends and family, all fed on the mobilization of volunteers from among the lower classes and the young during the French and Napoleonic Wars.[97]

Among the elite, heroic endeavours, and aggressive maleness as signifiers of social status, feeding on a sense of honour, pride, and shame, were particularly pronounced. By the late eighteenth century most sons of upper-class families received their education at several exclusive public schools, where the ideas of empire, patriotism, and service to the nation were instilled alongside notions of manliness and male bonding, with fortitude and virility being acquired through tough discipline, manly sports and competitive displays of courage. In this schoolboys' society, failure to display resolution and courage incurred indignity, insult, and shame.[98] These formative experiences were crucial to the consolidation of a more uniform ruling elite founded on service to the nation; it was also constitutive of a renewed sense of elite honour and shame that would persist well into the nineteenth century and beyond. In his *The Life of Samuel Johnson*, James Boswell offered a succinct expression of these prevalent attitudes in Johnson's avowal that 'Every man thinks meanly of himself for not having been a soldier, or not having been at sea'. When Boswell objects – 'Lord Mansfield (the Lord Chief Justice) does not' – Johnson retorts, 'Sir, if Lord Mansfield were in a company of General Officers and Admirals who have been in service, he would shrink; he'd wish to creep under the table'.[99]

## Conclusion

Early modern notions and experiences of shame changed over the course of the period from the mid-seventeenth century onwards, but the shift was neither linear nor homogenous, and nor was it complete. Instead, several different trajectories can be observed, involving a decline, along with the reconfiguration and enhancement, of shame. Public shame punishments that had long dominated the penal system – carting, locking people in stocks – decreased, or else retreated from the public purview, as was the case of whipping and the death penalty. Communal rituals of shame (skimmington) were also waning, alongside forms of verbal abuse and public insult wreaked by individuals amidst communities. It is difficult to know whether English women and men became less inclined to thrust angry insults at one another. What is clear is that the use of violence as a means of responding to affront dwindled, that is, the urge to instantly and aggressively react to verbal abuse – and the shame entailed in it – appears to have become more inhibited or controlled. Use of the court as an arena for reclaiming honour and defying shame lessened as well. Among the elite, the aggressive and hazardous response to dishonour – the duel – persisted longer, but it also became more ritualized and less deadly; by the early and mid-nineteenth century it disappeared altogether.

More protracted and less complete was the decline in shame emotions related to notions of sin and sexuality. Here the undermining of beliefs in providentialism and original sin had a profound effect, paving the way towards the easing of the burden of sin, and in some instances – as in the case of radical dissenters – altogether freeing individuals from the sense of guilt and shame which had long been an essential component of the process of self-scrutiny and the sense of failure under the constant gaze of God. Attitudes to sexuality also shifted, with notions of sexual freedom – more lenient attitudes regarding adultery, a view of sexual pleasure as natural, positive and unhinged by sin and shame – taking root among sections of society, including the polite. Long-standing notions of masculinity and femininity altered as well, with men being increasingly perceived as sexually rapacious while women came to be viewed as by nature chaste and virtuous; prostitutes became an object of compassion rather than of shame and disgrace. These novel attitudes did not acquire a broad consensus, triggering a great deal of reaction and debate as the eighteenth century progressed, with notions of gendered shame, and especially the depravity of women, remaining entrenched. Nevertheless, these attitudes signalled the unsettling of deep-seated Protestant notions of shame, allowing greater space – in public and private lives – for new options of critique, defiance, and liberation from enduring religious practices and experiences of shame.

Alongside these shifts, which point to the erosion of the traditional notions of shame, the eighteenth century witnessed continued vitality and invigoration of shaming and shame, evident first and foremost in the enhanced and evolving role of notions of civility and politeness. As the period progressed and an ideal of civility was disseminated among the elite and the urban classes, the role of shame in social exchanges and relations was emboldened and reinforced. Conduct deemed uncivil and shameful came to mark the gulf that separated the polite from the impolite, with shame being applied to stigmatize individuals, social classes as well as ethnic groups and races, in English society and across the seas. Native populations and races were viewed as uncivil, being presented in disparaging terms that exposed them to harsh, humiliating, and exclusionary shame. As the English state expanded its hold over the colonies overseas, increasingly relying on Africans as slaves, shameful incivility was invoked not only to justify conquest and colonization, but also to indicate innate and intrinsic racial differences between the English and nonwhite peoples or species.

More benign and less exclusionary forms of shame were also being reconfigured and explored, with shame becoming integral to novel theories of human nature and the formation of society. The authors discussed in this chapter – John Locke, Cesare Beccaria, and Bernard Mandeville – all elaborated on shame and its role in varied settings, each pointing to different options and possibilities for thinking about shame and its dynamics in social life. For Locke, shame was central to educating children and inculcating civility and virtue in them. Acting as a powerful psychological incentive in a child, parental shaming, so he believed, needed to be moderate, reformative, non-violent, and private; allowing onlookers to witness a child being shamed by a parent was counterproductive and harmful. For Beccaria, shame was an appropriate manner of punishing criminals, the shame being public and retributive, that is, designed not only to prevent future crimes or even reform the criminal, but also to exact a moral price; wrongdoers should suffer for what they had done. Yet like Locke, Beccaria also insisted that public disgrace be non-violent and rational, that is, in proportion to the criminal's deeds. For Mandeville, shame was a basic component of an otherwise utterly selfish human nature. The emotion was essential to the sustenance of civil life, civility being defined strictly in terms of appearances and altogether divorced from morality or virtue.

Despite their different vantage points and conceptions, these thinkers shared a secular view of shame, one in which the emotion was rooted neither in sin nor immorality, but rather in social formation and human psychology. Shame was not only essential to civil life and governance, but constituted a component of the human psyche, inextricably linked to additional 'universal' emotions or 'passions', namely, esteem, honour, and pride. While they all elaborated on the external facet and dynamics of shame, with shame being triggered when honour or esteem was damaged, they were also cognizant of shame's internal orientation and impingement on a sense of personhood. Even Mandeville, who perceived honour and shame as aspects of a wholly external notion of civility, still made it clear that shame impinged on internal feelings, needs and an innermost sense of 'being' and the self.

Shifting arenas and the means through which shame was invoked also point to a renewed vitality and enhanced susceptibility to shame. Especially manifest was the explosion of the market for print, whereby shame was publicized and broadcast to a growing reading public below the elite. An expanding array of techniques – from traditional forms of moral commentary and reproach through more innovative forms of written and graphic satire – were used to address a host of political, moral and social issues, targeting various social groups, genders, classes, and individuals for criticism and shame. The shame inflicted through these means could be benign – refined in its idiom or style, didactic in intent, limited in its political edge. Catering to the polite classes, moral and satirical works adapted to their tastes and aspirations along with their appetite for gossip, scandal, and entertainment. Satire could even sometimes enhance rather than impair the personal repute and fame of the individuals concerned. Nevertheless, the shame inflicted through moral condemnation and satire could also become more savage and punitive. Combining the popular and bawdy with high and more refined idioms of speech or presentation, many satirical prints and caricatures presented their subjects not only as grotesque but also as deviant, destructive, and a menace. Newspaper commentaries and satirical works offered a means for public critique, defying the upper classes and the polite, exposing social tensions and animosities towards the elite and polite classes. Personalized invectives could damage and destroy the reputations, status or careers of the elite, men and women as well.

Honour-related shame was also reconfigured, and the arena where it came to be expressed was transformed. It is true that violent responses to dishonour – evident in elite duels or male reactions to public insult – decreased over the course of the eighteenth century. Yet other, and no less dominant, facets of the early modern honour culture were sustained, and the shame triggered by varied forms of infringement of honour remained ever imminent. Elite honour had long been attained – and reasserted – by means other than duels, male honour being nurtured by an ideal of civility and the display of self-control, restraint, virtue, and moral obligation, with non-violent means and tactics, including threats of shame and shaming, being used to diffuse assaults on honour, in the private and the public domain. By the mid- and late eighteenth century, these notions and practices were nourished, among elite women no less than men, by a renewed emphasis on polite manners and domestic virtue. Lower down on the social scale, non-violent forms of settling disputes regarding insult and shame had been practised throughout the seventeenth century, with varied forms of reconciliation allowing adversaries to reaffirm their reputation, whether through the civil and ecclesiastical courts, or else by more informal means of mediation, whereby an expression of guilt or regrets could prevail. By the mid-eighteenth century, as litigation over public insult receded, these informal means were sustained, increasingly moving outside the arena of the court into domestic settings or public spaces, where the intercession of small groups of friends or other acquaintances enabled the shame of insult to be attenuated and honour restored.

No less important, notions of honour-related shame that had long been embedded in perceptions of male courage and physical prowess were emboldened and came to pervade the public sphere. As the English state expanded its army and empire, and wars were fought with increased intensity overseas, the traditional conception of civic education, in which physical exercise and valour were aligned with politeness, was given new meanings. A new discourse regarding the ideal modern soldier emerged, and a vision of masculine honour displayed through prowess, courage, and military service was broadly disseminated; military men deemed to have failed in combat increasingly risked being humiliated and shamed, both at court and by the public at large. By the late eighteenth century, when England waged wars in America and with the French, this new cult of militarism and the elevation of male willingness to die merged with a growing patriotism and an emboldened sense of nationalism across varied classes and sectors in the population. Among the elite, a renewed sense of honour based on aggressive maleness and service to the nation was cultivated in the prestigious public schools; a sense of honour based on physical prowess and fortitude – and of the shame of cowardice and physical frailty – would continue to be instilled in generations of elite youths throughout the nineteenth century, and beyond.

## Notes

1 The process was protracted and uneven, with some shame penalties lingering into the nineteenth century. See Simon Devereaux and Paul Griffiths (eds.), *Penal Practice and Culture, 1500–1900* (Basingstoke, 2004), Introduction, esp. 13–26; Robert Shoemaker, 'Streets of Shame? The Crowd and Public Punishments in London, 1700–1820', in Devereaux and Griffiths (eds.), *Penal Practice and Culture*, 232–57; Tim Hitchcock and Robert Shoemaker, *London Lives: Poverty, Crime and the Making of a Modern City 1690–1800* (Cambridge, 2015), 244–6, 361–7. For the decline in popular rituals of shame (with sporadic episodes in the eighteenth and nineteenth centuries), see E.P. Thompson, *Customs in Common* (London, 1991), 469–77; David Nash and Anne-Marie Kilday, *Cultures of Shame: Exploring Crime and Morality in Britain 1600–1900* (Basingstoke, 2010), 46, 113–33.

2 J.M. Beattie, *Crime and the Courts in England 1660–1800* (Oxford 1986), Chaps. 9–10, 450–618; Cynthia Herrup, 'Punishing Pardon: Some Thoughts on the Origins of Penal Transportation', in Devereaux and Griffiths (eds.), *Penal Practice and Culture*, 121–37; Hitchcock and Shoemaker, *London Lives*, 244–52.
3 Herrup, 'Punishing Pardon', 129–33; Hitchcock and Shoemaker, *London Lives*, 251–2, 322–5, 389–92; Robert Jütte, *Poverty and Deviance in Early Modern Europe* (Cambridge, 1994), 167–8; Gwenda Morgan and Peter Rushton, *Banishment in the Early Atlantic World: Convicts, Rebels and Slaves* (London, 2013), 119–23.
4 For fluctuations in rates of imprisonment, whipping, and branding, from the 1760s, see Hitchcock and Shoemaker, *London Lives*, 323–30, 362–3. For harsh conditions, overcrowding, and limits of prison reforms, ibid., 325–9, 334–42. For branding as a mark of shame allegedly preventing convicts from obtaining employment and making them 'desperate', see J.M. Beattie, *Policing and Punishment in London 1660–1750* (Oxford, 2001), 331; Hitchcock and Shoemaker, *London Lives*, 64–5. For increased imprisonment for debt, see Alexander Wakelam, *Credit and Debt in Eighteenth-Century England: An Economic History of Debtors' Prisons* (London and New York, 2021); Tawny Paul, *The Poverty of Disaster: Debt and Insecurity in Eighteenth-Century Britain* (Cambridge, 2019).
5 Keith Thomas, *In Pursuit of Civility: Manners and Civilization in Early Modern England* (Waltham, Massachusetts, 2018), 23–48, esp. 39.
6 For notions of civility among merchants, see Chap. 4. And see also Thomas, *In Pursuit of Civility*, 49–62; Felicity Heal and Clive Holmes, *the Gentry in England and Wales, 1500–1700* (Stanford, 1994), 276–318; Henry French, "Gentleman': Remaking the English Ruling Class', in Keith Wrightson (ed.), *A Social History of England 1500–1750* (Cambridge, 2017), 278–9; Lawrence E. Klein, 'Politeness and the Interpretation of the British Eighteenth Century', *The Historical Journal*, 45 (2002), 869–98, esp. 875–85.
7 Chap. 1 above; Thomas, *In Pursuit of Civility* 55–62, 65–6; Amanda Vickery, *The Gentleman's Daughter: Women's Lives in Georgian England* (New Haven and London, 1998), 195–224, esp. 211, 213. For a more nuanced view of the dominance of politeness, which nevertheless recognizes its hold over society, see Rosalind Carr, 'A Polite and Enlightened London?', *The Historical Journal*, 59 (2016), 632–3.
8 Thomas, *In Pursuit of Civility*, 63, 65; Marcus Rediker, *Between the Devil and the Deep Blue Sea: Merchant Seamen, Pirates, and the Anglo-American Maritime World, 1700–1750* (Cambridge, 1987), 153–4.
9 Vickery, *The Gentleman's Daughter*, 210–11, 213.
10 Steve Hindle, *On the Parish? The Micro-Politics of Poor Relief in Rural England c. 1550–1750* (Oxford, 2004), 164, 410; Thomas, *In Pursuit of Civility*, 70; Patrick Collinson, 'Puritanism and the Poor', in Rosemary Horrox and Sarah Rees Jones (eds.), *Pragmatic Utopias: Ideals and Communities, 1200–1630* (Cambridge, 2001), 245. See also Chap. 6 above.
11 Alison Games, 'The English and 'Others' in England and beyond', in Wrightson (ed.), *A Social History of England*, 356–7; Jane H. Ohlmeyer, '"Civilizinge of those rude partes": Colonization within Britain and Ireland, 1580s–1640s', in Nicholas Canny (ed.), *The Oxford History of the British Empire* (Oxford, 1998), Vol. I, 127; Prys Morgan, 'Wild Wales: Civilizing the Welsh from the Sixteenth to the Nineteenth Centuries', in Peter Burke, Brian Harrison, and Paul Slack (eds.), *Civil Histories: Essays Presented to Sir Keith Thomas* (Oxford, 2000), 269–72.
12 Nicholas Canny, 'Reviewing A View of the Present State of Ireland', *Irish University Review*, 26 (1996), 252–67; Thomas, *In Pursuit of Civility*, 157–8. For the argument that Spenser's views were common in his time, see also Andrew Hadfield, 'Another Case of Censorship? the riddle of Edmund Spenser's 'A View of the Present State of Ireland (c.1596)', *History Ireland*, IV (1996), 26–30.

13 Alison Games, *The Web of Empire: English Cosmopolitans in an Age of Expansion 1560–1660* (Oxford, 2008), 81–115; Games, 'The English and 'Others', 360–3.
14 Thomas, *In Pursuit of Civility*, 183–218; Games, 'The English and 'Others', 368.
15 Thomas, *In Pursuit of Civility*, 87–93, 121–7.
16 Faramerz Dabhoiwala, *The Origins of Sex: A History of the First Sexual Revolution* (London, 2013), 104. See also Brian Cummings, 'Animal Passions and Human Sciences: Shame, Blushing and Nakedness in Early Modern Europe and the New World', in Erica Fudge, Ruth Gilbert, Susan Wiseman (eds.), *At the Borders of the Human: Beasts, Bodies and Natural Philosophy in the Early Modern Period* (Basingstoke, 2002), 26–50.
17 Games, 'The English and 'Others', 365; Thomas, *In Pursuit of Civility*, 162–3, 166–7.
18 Games, *The Web of Empire*, 289–99; Thomas, *In Pursuit of Civility*, 173–82.
19 Games, 'The English and "Others"', 366–8.
20 For an overview of these themes, and the related historical literature, see Mathew Kadane, *The Watchful Clothier: The Life of an Eighteenth-Century Protestant Capitalist* (New Haven and London, 2013), Chap. 7, 156–70.
21 Alexandra Walsham, *Providence in Early Modern England* (Oxford, 1999), 33–4.
22 Bruce Hindmarsh, *The Evangelical Conversion Narrative: Spiritual Autobiography in Early Modern England* (Oxford, 2005), 186–92.
23 Kadane, *The Watchful Clothier*, 158–63; Mathew Kadane, 'Original Sin and the Path to the Enlightenment', *Past and Present*, 235 (2017), 105–40, esp. 114–16, 121–8, 139–40. For the secularization of the autobiography in the eighteenth century, see also Michael Mascuch, *Origins of the Individualist Self: Autobiography and Self-Identity in England, 1591–1791* (Stanford, 1996), esp. 137–42.
24 Dabhoiwala, *The Origins of Sex*, 50–5, 85–110.
25 Anna Bryson, *From Courtesy to Civility: Changing Codes of Conduct in Early Modern England* (Oxford, 1998), 247–52; Dabhoiwala, *The Origins of Sex*, 144–53; Karen Harvey, *Reading Sex in the Eighteenth Century: Bodies and Gender in English Erotic Culture* (Cambridge 2004), esp. 54–68, 222.
26 Anthony Fletcher, *Gender, Sex and Subordination in England 1500–1800* (New Haven and London, 1995), 322–46, 376–400; Dabhoiwala, *The Origins of Sex*, 141–69.
27 Ibid., 153–69, 234–47.
28 Hindmarsh, *The Evangelical Conversion*; Kadane, *The Watchful Clothier*, 32, 43–83.
29 Dabhoiwala, *The Origins of Sex*, 138–40, 153–69, 212–15.
30 Ibid., 190–1.
31 Harvey, *Reading Sex in the Eighteenth Century*. For the persistence of traditional notions of manhood, with emphasis on self-control and domestic authority, see the comments and works cited in Carr, 'A Polite and Enlightened London?', 630–1.
32 Dabhoiwala, *The Origins of Sex*, 145, 158–60, 190–201. See also next section, below.
33 Ibid., 168; Esther Snell, 'Trials in Print: Narratives of Rape Trials in the Proceedings of the Old Bailey', in David Lemmings (ed.), *Crime, Courtrooms and the public Sphere in Britain, 1700–1850* (Farnham, 2012), 23–42. See also the comments and works cited in Carr, 'A Polite and Enlightened London?', 628, 631.
34 John Locke, *Some Thoughts Concerning Education* (1693), The Harvard Classics, www.bartleby.com, Vol. 37, Part 1. For Locke's stipulations regarding the cultivation of courage and fortitude in a child, see especially section 113.2 ('[children] should be harden'd against all sufferings, especially of the body, and have no tenderness but what rises from an ingenuous shame, and a quick sense of reputation').

35 John Locke, *The Reasonableness of Christianity* (1695), in *The Works of John Locke in Nine Volumes* (London, 1824), Vol. 6, Online Library of Liberty, https://oll.libertyfund.org/titles/1438, 5. See also W.M. Spellman, *John Locke and the Problem of Depravity* (Oxford, 1988).
36 Locke, *Some Thoughts Concerning Education*, Sections 40–47, 50 (quotation section 47). Locke still endorsed corporal punishment in some extreme cases of 'obstinate disobedience'; 'But in these cases, I would have it ordered so, if it can be, that the shame of the whipping, and not the pain, should be the greatest part of the punishment'. Yet overall he thought corporal punishment as a form of correction 'never produces any good' and 'is much to be avoided as may be' (Sections 78, 60, 80).
37 Ibid., Section 40.
38 Ibid., Sections 56–7.
39 Ibid., Sections 60, 78.
40 Ibid., Sections 57–60, 67, 84.
41 Ibid., Section 56.
42 Ibid., Section 62.
43 Ibid., Sections 84–5.
44 Richard Bellamy (ed.), *Beccaria: On Crimes and Punishments and Other Writings*, Trans. Richard Davies (Cambridge, 1995).
45 Regarding corporal punishment, Beccaria argued that it should be administered only in cases of violent crimes, i.e., 'crimes that are assaults on persons'. Ibid., 50.
46 Ibid., 26–7, 54–5.
47 Ibid., 31.
48 Ibid., Introduction, ix–xxx.
49 Nash and Kilday, *Cultures of Shame*, 88–112.
50 Andrew McRay, *Literature, Satire and the Early Stuart State* (Cambridge, 2004), 208–22; Nigel Smith, *Literature and Revolution in England 1640–1660* (New Haven and London, 1994), 295–355; Alastair Bellany, '"Raylinge Rymes and Vaunting Verse": Libellous Politics in Early Stuart England, 1603–1628', in Kevin Sharpe and Peter Lake (eds.), *Culture and Politics in Early Stuart England* (Basingstoke, 1994), 285–310; David Cressy, *Dangerous Talk: Scandalous, Seditious, and Treasonable Speech in Pre-Modern England* (Oxford, 2010), Chaps. 7–8, 139–202; David Como, *Radical Parliamentarians and the English Civil War* (Oxford, 2018). For a recent discussion and an overview of the literature on libelous print and sexual politics in these decades, see Samuel Fullerton, 'Fatal Adulteries: Sexual Politics in the English Revolution', *Journal of British Studies*, 41 (2021, published online 14 June 2021), 1–29, and notes 30–4.
51 Harold Love, *English Clandestine Satire, 1660–1702* (Oxford, 2004); Cressy, *Dangerous Talk*, Chap. 9, 236–58; Fullerton, 'Fatal Adulteries'.
52 Dabhoiwala, *The Origins of Sex*, 313–19; Donna T. Andrew, *Aristocratic Vice: The Attack on Duelling, Suicide, Adultery, and Gambling in Eighteenth-Century England* (New Haven and London, 2013), 9–10, 37–41.
53 Mark Hallett, *The Spectacle of Difference: Graphic Art in the Age of Hogarth* (New Have and London, 1999), 1–2, 27–8, and passim. And see also Andrew, *Aristocratic Vice*, 37; Dabhoiwala, *The Origins of Sex*, 286–93.
54 For a detailed analysis of the political and aesthetic context of the engraving, see Hallett, *The Spectacle of Difference*, 46–55.
55 Ibid., 58–59, 67–71, 131–51, 167.
56 Ibid., 172–3, Chaps. 5–6, 169–234. See also Peter Temin and Hans-Joachim Voth, *Prometheus Shackled: Goldsmiths Banks and England's Financial Revolution After 1700* (Oxford, 2013), 7–12.
57 For the contemporary view of the stock market as a system of fraud, and of stock jobbers as 'the lowest element of London society', see Anne L. Murphy, *The Origins of English Financial Markets: Investment and Speculation before*

224  Transformations of shame

the *South Sea Bubble* (Cambridge, 2009), 66–72. For the condemnation of male seduction and treachery, Dabhoiwala, *The Origins of Sex*, 157–69. For graphic satire's stereotypical representation of different classes, sexes and professions, Hallett, *The Spectacle of Difference*, 131, 177–8.

58 For an analysis of *A Harlot's Progress* in the context of the artistic and graphic culture of the 1730s, and of the social world and discourses informing it, see ibid., Chap. 3, 93–129.

59 Ibid., 197, quoted from W.H. Draper, *The Morning Walk; Or, City Encompass'd* (1751) ('Behold! What shocks the eye, intoxicate, / A tatter'd female drunk, with sulph'rous GIN,/ ... her legs wide-sprawling, portrait true of shame').

60 Ibid., 196, 204, 206, 216–18; quotation on 216. For Hallett's analysis of the darker features of *Gin Lane*, compared to *Beer Street*'s lighter and more polite and satirical approach, see 197–233.

61 Simon Dickie, *Cruelty and Laughter: Forgotten Comic Literature and the Unsentimental Eighteenth Century* (Chicago, 2011).

62 Andrew, *Aristocratic Vice*, Chaps. 4–5, 127–218, quotation on 128.

63 Hallett, *The Spectacle of Difference*, 170–7, 180–7.

64 Ibid., 184, quoted from John Gay, *Trivia; or, the Art of Walking the Streets of London* (1716).

65 Ibid., 174–6.

66 Ibid., 45–52.

67 Ibid., 2–5, 151–4, 131–2.

68 Dabhoiwala, *The Origins of Sex*, 306, 310–11, 338–9; Andrew, *Aristocratic Vice*, Chap. 4, 127–74.

69 Hallett, *The Spectacle of Difference*, 169–95.

70 Ibid., 10–11; Marilyn Morris, *Sex, Money & Personal Character in Eighteenth-Century British Politics* (New Haven and London, 2014), 103–4; Dabhoiwala, *The Origins of Sex*, 296–313, 334–42.

71 For the case of the notorious courtesan Kitty Fisher, whose accident (in the late 1750s) was used to ridicule and humiliate her through comments, songs, and prints showing her fall from a horse, to which she also reacted by publishing an announcement condemning the representation by some 'wretches, mean, ignorant and venal' people, see ibid., 322–3, 282.

72 Andrew, *Aristocratic Vice*, 10, 40–1, 136–40; Morris, *Sex, Money & Personal Character*, 1–23, 102.

73 Ibid., 144, 172, 246.

74 Dabhoiwala, *The Origins of Sex*, 338–9; Andrew, *Aristocratic Vice*, 147–8. For a detailed analysis of court intrigue and gossip spreading into a broader and more public political arena, becoming also a source of moral condemnation and caricature, see Morris, *Sex, Money & Personal Character*.

75 Markku Peltonen, *The Duel in Early Modern England: Civility, Politeness and Honour* (Cambridge, 2003), 108–31, 244–62; Andrew, *Aristocratic Vice*, 20–31, 43–4.

76 Robert B. Shoemaker, 'The Taming of the Duel: Masculinity, Honour and Ritual Violence in London, 1660–1800', *The Historical Journal*, 45 (2002), 525–45; Andrew, *Aristocratic Vice*, 43–81; Stephen Banks, *A Polite Exchange of Bullets: The Duel and the English Gentleman 1750–1850* (Woodbridge, 2010), 70–1, 77–82, 93–4, 214–15.

77 Robert B. Shoemaker, 'The Decline of Public Insult in London 1660–1800', *Past and Present*, 169 (2000), 97–131, esp. 99–108; K. Tawny Paul, 'Credit, reputation and masculinity in British urban commerce: Edinburgh c.1710–70', *Economic History Review*, 66 (2013), 226–48.

78 Chaps. 1, 3 above; Pollock, 'Honor, Gender, and Reconciliation', 9–16, 21–6, 27–9; Courtney Erine Thomas, *If I Lose Myself: Honour among the Early Modern English Elite* (Buffalo, 2017), 8–9, Chap. 2, 76–124; Vickery, *The Gentleman's Daughter*; Andrew, *Aristocratic Vice*, 15–41.

79 Chap. 5; Capp, *When Gossips Meet*, 218–9, 224–7, 242–3; Shepard, *Meanings of Manhood*, 130–2, 143–51.
80 Shoemaker, 'The Decline of Public Insult', esp. 130–1; Paul, 'Credit, Reputation and Masculinity', 244–5.
81 Robert Shoemaker, 'Male Honour and the Decline of Public Violence in Eighteenth-Century London', *Social History*, 26 (2001), 190–208, esp. 200–1. About a quarter of cases ending in homicide were preceded by attempts at mediation and pacification.
82 Paul, 'Credit, Reputation and Masculinity', 231–4, 245, Fig. 3 (between 1710–19, the percentage of cases involving violence was 15, declining thereafter to between 4 and 7 percent).
83 Ibid., 242–4, 246–7. On the replacement of litigation at court with advertised apologies in the press, see Donna T. Andrew, 'The Press and Public Apologies in Eighteenth-Century London', in Norma Landau (ed.), *Law, Crime and English Society 1660–1830* (Cambridge, 2002), 208–29.
84 Jerrold Seigel, *The Idea of the Self: Thought and Experience in Western Europe Since the Seventeenth Century* (Cambridge, 2005), 111–16, quotation on 114.
85 *An Enquiry into the Origin of Honour, and The usefulness of Christianity in war. By the Author of Fable of the Bees [B. de Mandeville]* (London, 1732), 11–12; Peltonen, *The Duel in Early Modern England*, 269–74, quotation on 273.
86 Seigel, *The Idea of the Self*, 111; Thomas Dixon, *From Passions to Emotions: The Creation of a Secular Psychological Category* (Cambridge 2003), 81; Peltonen, *The Duel in Early Modern England*, 270.
87 For the argument that Mandeville reasserted a specific strand in early modern theories of civility, in which emphasis had been placed strictly on external appearances, see ibid., 267.
88 Seigel, *The Idea of the Self*, 117–21. See also above, on shame in John Locke and Cesare Beccaria. For passions in eighteenth-century intellectual discourse, see Dixon, *From Passions to Emotions*, 62–97.
89 Peltonen, *The Duel in Early Modern England*, 289–94, quotations on 289, 291, 293.
90 Ibid., 290–96; Andrew, *Aristocratic Vice*, 19.
91 For the decline of the traditional ideal of elite military prowess and manly courage, from 1660 onwards, see Keith Thomas, *The Ends of Life: Roads to Fulfilment in Early Modern England* (Oxford, 2009), 62–76.
92 Julia Banister, *Masculinity, Militarism and Eighteenth-Century Culture, 1689–1815* (Cambridge, 2018), 1–18.
93 Ibid., 14–43, quotation on 18. Note also Banister's emphasis on the tension between the two models, and on the continuing power of an ideal of 'natural' militarism and masculinity throughout the eighteenth century. For the argument that there was a shift from an ideal of the courageous military-man to the 'polite' soldier, see Andrew, *Aristocratic Vice*, 17–36, esp. 34–5.
94 Banister, *Masculinity, Militarism and Eighteenth-Century Culture*, Chaps. 4–5, 97–150.
95 Ibid., Chaps. 2–3, 44–96.
96 Ibid., Chap. 6, 151–84; Shoemaker, 'The Taming of the Duel', 540; Andrew, *Aristocratic Vice*, 58–62; Banks, *A Polite Exchange of Bullets*, 70–1, 78–9.
97 Linda Colley, *Britons: Forging the Nation 1707–1837* (New Haven and London, 1992, ed. 1994), 300–19, esp. 302–3.
98 Ibid., 167–72; Anthony Fletcher, *Gender, Sex and Subordination in England 1500–1800* (New Haven and London, 1995), 297–309; Banks, *A Polite Exchange of Bullets*, 27–9.
99 Quoted in Banister, *Masculinity, Militarism and Eighteenth-Century Culture*, 1–2.

# Conclusion
Early modern and modern shame

Early modern English society was suffused with shame. Some of its most potent sources were embedded in the beliefs and convictions that marked the era from the sixteenth century onwards. Ideas regarding civility, politeness, and honour, Protestant notions of sin and immorality, perceptions of patriarchy, gender, and community relations – all these generated strong injunctions and norms, predisposing contemporaries to feel or inflict shame when these were, or perceived to be, violated. Other forces were also at play. Growing religious divisions, the frictions and disparities attendant on economic and social change, widening webs and networks of distant connections along with increased state control of the localities – these processes left ample room for a host of practices and experiences of shame. Especially pronounced was the expanding print market and the diffusion of reading and writing practices, through which shame and shaming were communicated, broadcast, elaborated, or intimately shared.

Our inquest brought to light many variations in practices, expressions, and experiences of shame, both overt and covert, public and private. Yet these experiences, it has been repeatedly shown, clustered around, or ranged between, two major patterns. Especially conspicuous was punitive shame, in which emphasis was placed on the totality of the emotion, the shame wholly defining the character of the shamed, invariably affecting utter disgrace, humiliation, and exclusion. Punitive shame was the hallmark of a host of public penalties exacted by courts, and occasionally the populace, on transgressors and perceived wrongdoers, the brutal shaming marking the body of the condemned, stigmatizing them as outcasts deserving pain, ostracism, or death. Punitive shame could also penetrate a state relief system designed to address the needs of the poor, the deserving poor being subjected, intentionally or otherwise, to stigma and marginalization. This type of harsh shame could also surface elsewhere. It penetrated the private and domestic domains, engulfing believers with a sense of sin as a profound, infinite experience of humiliation and worthlessness before God. It played a role in a host of interpersonal conflicts – in families or amid varied networks – where a dynamic of shaming and shame escalated, leading to verbal or physical abuse, and ultimately to disruption or dissolution of ties. Disinheritance, diminished standing, loss of careers and livelihoods, even death, could all be at stake.

DOI: 10.4324/9781003226871-9

Punitive shame, with its exclusionary connotations, had intimate ties with hierarchies of power and social divisions. It bolstered the status and authority of rulers over the ruled, acting as a form of deterrence, reinforcing obedience, conformity, and the subordination of those perceived inferior – lower classes, religious minorities, the female gender or non-English races. The shame could also be turned upside down, with members of the middle and lower classes appropriating moral authority and inflicting shame on their superiors, destabilizing elite authority and privilege through varied means of critique, verbal abuse, satire, and mockery, which by the eighteenth century saturated the market for print. Other forms of authority could be savagely subjected to verbal shame; the early Protestants targeted the traditional church for shame, while in subsequent decades nonconforming puritans invariably shamed the established church, their parish ministers or those they deemed profane and unregenerate among their neighbours and friends. Men's conduct could be exposed to shame, with elite women asserting moral authority and challenging men's rule through verbal abuse and threats to their honour and reputation. Nor were shamed victims among the poor wholly submissive in responding to their treatment. While many accepted or admitted their shame, expressing repentance and showing deference and submission, instances of resistance to coercive shame recurred. Poor people declined to cooperate with a relief program they deemed degrading, offenders forced to make penance at church remained obdurate, criminals condemned to death shamelessly subverted the justice system itself by refusing to admit their crime, showing no signs of contrition and facing the gallows with indifference or a cheerful demeanour.

A second major pattern of shame involved more lenient, conciliatory, and inclusive shame. Historians readily recognize the religious context of this type of shame, as in those cases when repentance for sin and expression of shame were publicly performed, leading the way to re-integration and bringing offenders back to the fold of the community. No less important was the Protestant understanding of sin, which triggered harsh and tormenting shame upon the recognition of sin, but also offered the believer a mitigated and soothing experience, the shame being oriented towards redemption and overcoming, at least partly, the effects of the initial punitive shame. Both punitive and redemptive shame pervaded spiritual autobiographies written throughout the seventeenth century and well into the mid-eighteenth.

Mitigated and more integrative forms of shame were generated not only by notions of repentance and redemption, but also by the beliefs and practices rooted in interactions and the reciprocities that flowed amid a wide range of family and other networks, including those handled across long distances and commercial exchange. The shame took varied forms, from polite and insinuated shame through more robust forms of rebuke, scolding, and criticism. It was personalized, invoking breach of personal loyalties and extending the emotional pressure by reminding individuals of the obligations tying them to one another. While the shame could bring in its wake anger, embarrassment, or guilt, it also offered a space for conflict resolution or apology, acting to sustain and enhance, rather than disrupt, personal bonds and relations based on trust.

Moderate and inclusive forms of shame, with no apparent links to religious perceptions and assumptions, transpired in the public domain as well. Some informal forms of community shaming – verbal insults, mockery, gossip – were short-term and more benign, intended as they were to monitor or amend the conduct of neighbours and friends and allowing a return to the routine of everyday life. The justice system administered by the civil courts also left a scope for moderate forms of shame that focused on conciliation rather than punishment, especially in cases of petty crime, in which compromise, accommodation through mediation along with some form of apology or admission of guilt and shame prevailed. No less important was the increased role of notions of pardonable crimes and mitigating circumstances. Rooted in early forms of popular perceptions and expectations of justice and equity, which by the sixteenth century were evident in pardons granted at the discretion of the Crown, such perceptions allowed greater consideration of the circumstances leading to crime, and of gradations in the responsibility to criminal acts. The result was the emergence of a distinctive, subtle understanding of bounded or partial shame, which was increasingly expressed by convicted offenders themselves. Here criminals admitted their transgression and shame, but still claimed moral character and a capacity for human attachments and ties. Drawing a line between their character and the deed for which they were convicted, they thus eroded or subverted the total discredit and the stigmatic, exclusionary shame inflicted on them through their punishment and brutal death. As the seventeenth century wore on and newspapers broadcasting these accounts multiplied, views of bounded shame were disseminated among readers and crowds, anticipating long-term changes in attitudes to public penalties that were embodied in humanitarian calls for a reform of the justice system.

In all these uses and intricate ramifications, shame deeply touched on contemporaries' notion of personhood and sense of the self. While much of what we have seen points to the preponderance of shame's external facets and to a self that was oriented towards others, ultimately, notions and experiences of shame impinged on both the external and internal dimensions of the self. That is, these experiences reflected a relational self and its socially constituted elements, while also indicating a sense of interiority and reflection on the self itself.[1] In their devotional practice, puritans were oriented outwardly towards God, but still focused on rigorous self-scrutiny, writing about their inner spiritual lives and presenting an introspective self that was governed, to one degree or another, by an overwhelming internal sense of shame. Notions of civility, politeness, and honour dictated rules of conduct that focused heavily on courtesy and outward appearances, but, in both theory and practice, they reflected and enhanced internal values relating to character, morality, or integrity. Personal honour was tied to public standing and reputation, but also to a strong sense of internal worth and self-esteem, shame being experienced not only as the outcome of the dishonour inflicted by others but of failure of internal standards, invariably perceived in terms of morality, excellence, capabilities, skill, or professionalism.

This dual dimension of shame – and the multifaceted selfhood it connoted – was revealed and amplified through the correspondence increasingly exchanged amid family, kin, and more distant networks. It is impossible to grasp the pervasive use of rebuke – and sometimes angry responses to it – without reference to this internal dimension of shame that induced self-awareness and assessment of interior standards. The rebuke not only threatened the status or social ties of an addressee, but also damaged their self-esteem and sense of worthiness, their very sense of 'being', as Bernard Mandeville referred to it.[2] No less important, in their letters writers condemned, rebuked, and shamed their addressees, but they also shared intimate experiences of shame, disclosing – and taking stock of – an experience of guilt, hurt pride, and an agonized internal self that was the outcome of experiencing dishonour, abuse, or humiliation inflicted by others, with external and internal shame being inextricably linked. In the case of the lower classes, the two facets of shame were poignantly elaborated and communicated in the life accounts of condemned felons awaiting their death, in which they constructed multiple dimensions of their self in an attempt to both reclaim their reputation and the good opinion of others, and assert for themselves moral character, a measure of dignity, sense of worthiness and self-respect.

Our enquiry into the forms and patterns of early modern shame also brought to the fore the complexity of shifts across time, underscoring a lack of unidirectional course – decline or gradual increase of shame – in the transition to modernity. In some areas, first and foremost in penal practice, the decline was evident and robust, as the notorious public shame penalties were eliminated, culminating in the late eighteenth-century abolition of public executions. Informal practices of slander or public insult, along with the use of the courts to regain one's reputation by reversing the shame, likewise declined. Yet other trajectories of change involving partial or ambivalent withdrawal from shame, along with the re-evaluation of the emotion, can also be observed. By the mid-eighteenth century, changing attitudes to sin and sexuality reduced the burden of guilt and the shame attached to sin in earlier generations, allowing a greater expression of sexual desire, and subduing the shame attached to female sensuality. This shift was protracted and by no means complete, and sexual misconduct, especially of women, continued to be perceived as sinful, deplorable, and full of shame. Other trajectories entailed not only the decline or persistence of shame, but also its reformulation. With the spread of new enlightenment ideas, philosophers and reformers denounced practices of punitive shame in both the public and domestic domain, while still offering a re-evaluation and articulation of shame's role in education or in novel schemes for penal reform.

The invigoration of shame from the late seventeenth century onwards can also be observed elsewhere. As the British Empire expanded its territories beyond the sea, the shameful incivility attributed to the lower classes was extended to reflect on indigenous populations, shaping racial relations and greatly stiffening racial divisions in the colonies overseas. In England, the public sphere witnessed an eruption of shaming and shame, which targeted the perceived misconduct of individuals, genders and classes, with polite urban classes themselves being subjected to renewed forms of satire, mockery, and moral criticism. Under the pressures of population growth and increased (if fluctuating) levels of poverty, institutional relief expanded, and the shame that was attendant on some forms of relief, as in the case of the workhouse, was augmented. Nor did the new penal regime ameliorate the shame and degradation of convicted felons. While punishments for crime were removed from the public view, imprisonment increased substantially, inflicting great physical hardship and humiliation. New prospects for shame were also entailed in the growth of commerce and financial enterprises, which generated not only wealth and prosperity but also an array of failures leading to imprisonment for debt. The insecurity of the credit market and the shame entailed in imprisonment pervaded the lives of the middle classes, destroying lives and haunting generations of traders and artisans well into the nineteenth century, when debtors' prisons were formally abolished by law (1869).[3]

Honour-related forms of shame, too, were reanimated. As research on early modern honour showed, and this study has emphasized, early modern honour was based on a plurality of claims and virtues – physical, moral, public, and domestic. The violation of any one of these claims brought dishonour and shame, first and foremost among the elite, and invariably among classes below it as well. By the mid decades of the eighteenth century, elite honour based on politeness and domestic virtue, among men and women, persisted. Among the populace, more constrained and non-violent forms of averting shame and restoring honour became more pronounced, with expressions of shame or shaming being central to resolving issues of insult outside the arena of the court, privately or even publicly through the press. Elsewhere in the public at large, traditional notions of virility and courage – and the shame of physical fragility or cowardice – were reformulated and reasserted. Under the impact of imperial expansion, warfare, and a new military culture, along with an emerging British nationalism, a whole new arena for inflicting and experiencing dishonour, humiliation, and shame emerged, greatly affecting not only the military elite but also the public at large.

These different trajectories, whereby some forms of shame diminished as others were reformulated or revitalized across social arenas and broader shifts in culture and society, appear to have persisted throughout the nineteenth century and beyond. It has been shown that beginning around the 1820s, references to the word 'shame', in Britain as in other Western societies, declined steadily. The change in terminology may indicate a certain re-evaluation or 'downgrading' of shame, the consequence of broader shifts associated with the emergence of notions of modern selfhood and the autonomous self. As the relationship between the self and the world was redefined and greater emphasis was placed on an individual free from the observation of God or the judgement and ascriptions of others, the susceptibility to shame – and the inclination to apply it – decreased.[4]

Yet the evidence also points to the persistence, reformulation, and renewed vigour of shame in the vastly changing configurations of modern life. From the perspective of the themes discussed in this book, the persistence of shame throughout the nineteenth century is particularly noticeable in family life and the upbringing of children. Despite innovative forms of education and novel views regarding the upbringing of children (of the kind promoted by John Locke and other enlightenment thinkers), the mix of parental care and affection along with a pervasive use of rebuke and punitive shame, typically applied in earlier decades, persevered. A nineteenth-century contemporary could thus describe an incident in his childhood when his father struck him 'a very sharp blow' with a stick; upon being shown the marks left on his arm, the father 'took me in his arms and kissed me', saying 'but I am afraid, you deserved it'. In extreme instances of an embattled relationship between a father and a teenage son, as was the case of the early nineteenth-century merchant William Jackson and his profligate son, the constant censure, reprimand and condemnation on the part of the headstrong and disappointed father turned far more retributive, with the son ending up in prison and transported to Australia, going through immense suffering and shame. Lower down on the social scale, working-class autobiographies indicate parental care along with a mix of punitive and moderate shame in the discipline of boisterous sons. While fathers used the rod, mothers invariably resorted to chastisement and reproach; 'his mother's 'softest look' was 'most penetrating in reprehension', as one autobiographer recalled.[5]

Victorian values and moral regime gave rise to novel forms and expressions of shame, especially among the middle classes and the bourgeoisie. A distinctive blend of traditional and novel attitudes – among them the enduring power of evangelical morality, the persistence of traditional notions of civility and attention to 'character' qualities, along with a new heightened perception of the human power to direct individual conduct – combined to produce a rigid and demanding morality that amply induced shaming and shame.[6] Nineteenth-century literature points to intensified notions of shame and the remarkable power it had on novelists. In the emerging literature for children, shame became a staple of the stories, and remained the core of children's literature over the course of the nineteenth and twentieth centuries.[7]

The shame that had long been associated with sexuality persisted, and the stigma of adultery, prostitution, and other perceived vices hardened. Over the course of the nineteenth century, instances of communal shaming surrounding alleged indecent or coarse behaviour emerged in some rural communities; in the metropolis and elsewhere newspapers and pamphlets continued to be filled with detailed accounts of adultery in high life and the sexual impropriety of the monarchy itself. Among families of the middle classes, homosexuals ('bachelor uncles') were accepted only as long as they did not reveal their relationship with other men, the furtiveness and secrecy indicating deep-seated shame. From the late nineteenth century onwards, under the impact of new scientific ideas regarding the heredity of character traits, the shame of homosexuality and a host of other character or physical defects became ever harsh and stigmatic. Well into the mid-twentieth century, middle-class families were prone to concealment and secrecy in matters concerning adultery, homosexuality, or the illegitimacy and disability of their children. Disabled children were increasingly sent away to institutional care, remaining a source of profound shame for the families and the children themselves.[8]

Intensification, reformulation, a renewed vigour of shame – these can all be discerned amid the shifts and upheavals of the early and mid-decades of the twentieth century. Imperial domination and notions of British superiority, along with heightened nationalism and a military spirit that denigrated conduct deemed cowardly, were fertile ground for widespread practices of shaming and shame during the Great War; World War II witnessed, in the European zones of wars, horrifying forms of humiliation being inflicted on ethnic groups, races, and individuals.[9] Well into the 1960s, institutions such as mental hospitals, military establishments and boarding schools ('total institutions', as they were labelled by Erving Goffman) were prone to produce or trigger shame, subjecting inmates to a host of humiliations through a regime designed to strip them from their identity and exact obedience and conformity.[10] While twentieth-century penology and the punishment system presented aspirations and practices of isolation quite removed from the public penalties and the conditions of imprisonment of earlier centuries, prisons were, and in many ways still remain, full of potential for punitive and exclusionary shame rife with individual and collective humiliation.[11] In the public arena, class and race relations were still marred by feelings and experiences of shame caused by prejudice and the stigma attached to low-status origins or lack of respectability, poverty, neglected appearance, or being part of an ethnic group, the stigma penetrating public institutions, including those under the protective arms of a welfare state. In the private domain, varied forms of abuse were, and still are, sources of agonizing shame. Child and female abuse, spousal violence, and rape remained sources of complex forms of shame triggered by the shock, insult, loss of dignity and body control, or else by the sense of being complicit with the abuse and blaming oneself for it, or witnessing abuse and failing to prevent it. For much of the twentieth century, the subject of the sexual abuse of children was barely acknowledged formally, and when such cases were disclosed (either by force or voluntarily), they were met with silence or disbelief, incurring deep, debilitating and life-long shame.[12]

Yet the modern era also witnessed the resurgence of shame as a moral and social critique, and the reformulation of shame's potential for solidarity, empathy, and inclusion. Novel thinking and approaches to shame and its place in the penal system emphasized the importance and potential of acknowledged shame for reconciliation, acknowledged shame being viewed as functional for constructing and maintaining social relationships more generally. The late twentieth century witnessed the increased recognition of the role of shame in restorative justice and innovative initiatives for mediation between victims of crime and their offenders.[13] More consequential was the shame that animated a host of movements and calls for reform. The nineteenth-century abolitionist campaign against slavery decried slavery a shame; it not only appealed to morality, justice, and humanity, but argued that slavery was shameful, its wrongness a source of a collective British shame, 'an indelible disgrace'.[14] Processes of democratization and liberalization that Western European societies underwent from the nineteenth century onwards engendered a host of criticisms of social arrangements and institutions, shame and guilt being invoked for rethinking about reform and change. The public sphere became, perhaps more than ever before, an arena for moral and social critique, with ideas, movements, and protests invoking shame to galvanize people to accept and recognize the rightful claims of others, arousing empathy and regard for the protection of other human beings against degradation and the corrosive effects of harsh practices of discrimination, humiliation and punitive shame.[15]

This study has uncovered shame as a culturally shaped emotion, inextricably linked to beliefs and convictions, social relations, politics and the institutions specific to early modern times. We have also observed mutations of shame running along several paths concomitantly, if at times in contradicting ways. Yet some robust features of shame appear to have sustained across time and amid the vast transformations of early modern and modern times; the enormous range of manifestations of shame in both the public and private domains, its alignment with a multifaceted, relational and internal, self, and, lastly, the destructive and constructive potential intrinsic to shame. Over time, shame was repeatedly and at times overwhelmingly applied, manipulated and enhanced to punish and exclude, control and extract conformity, draw boundaries and bolster disparities, causing resentment, rage, humiliation, and pain. But shame also surfaced in more moderate and mitigated forms, pointing to its subtle capacity to negotiate and facilitate relations, ameliorate or mend damaged ties, bringing in its wake inclusion or empathy and regard for the wellbeing and dignity of other human beings belonging to one's immediate circles of personal ties, and well beyond.

## Notes

1 For a history of evolving ideas of the self from the seventeenth-century onwards, in which emphasis is placed on both the external and the internal dimensions of the self, see Jerrold Seigel, *The Idea of the Self: Thought and Experience in Western Europe since the Seventeenth Century* (Cambridge, 2005).
2 *An Enquiry into the Origin of Honour, and The Usefulness of Christianity in War. By the Author of Fable of the Bees [B. de Mandeville]* (London, 1732), 12. For Mandeville's dual notion of the self, and other discourses articulating a multidimensional selfhood from the seventeenth century onwards, see Seigel, *The Idea of the Self*, 111–24.
3 Julian Hoppit, *Risk and failure in English business 1700–1800* (Cambridge, 1987); Tawny Paul, *Poverty of Disaster: Debt and Insecurity in Eighteenth-Century Britain* (Cambridge, 2019), esp. Chap. 6, 191–213; Alexander Wakelam, *Credit and Debt in Eighteenth-Century England: An Economic History of Debtors' Prisons* (London and New York, 2020).

234  Conclusion

4 Peter N. Stearns, *Shame: A Brief History* (Urbana and Chicago, 2017), 59–61, 68–9, 70–1, 91–2.
5 Joanne Bailey, *Parenting in England 1760–1830: Emotion, Identity, and Generation* (Oxford, 2012), 76–7, 87, 90–1, quotation on 90; Elizabeth Foyster, *Marital Violence: An English Family History, 1660–1857* (Cambridge, 2005), 135–8; Nicola Phillips, *the Profligate son: Or, A True Story of Family Conflict, Fashionable Vice, and Financial Ruin in Regency Britain* (New York, 2013); Jane Humphries, *Childhood and Child Labour in the British Industrial Revolution* (Cambridge, 2010), 143–4.
6 The literature on these themes is vast, but see especially Jerrold Seigel, *Modernity and Bourgeois Life: Society, Politics, and Culture in England, France and Germany since 1750* (Cambridge, 2012), 336–75; Faramerz Dabhoiwala, *The Origins of Sex: A History of the First Sexual Revolution* (London, 2013), 350–60.
7 Andrew H. Miller, *The Burdens of Perfection: On Ethics and Reading in Nineteenth-Century British Literature* (Ithaca, 2008), 162–90; Ute Frevert, 'Piggy's Shame', in Ute Frevert et al., *Learning How to Feel: Children's Literature and Emotional Socialization, 1870–1970* (Oxford, 2014), 134–54.
8 David Nash and Anne-Marie Kilday, *Cultures of Shame: Exploring Crime and Morality in Britain, 1600–1900* (Basingstoke, 2010), Chaps. 6, 8, 113–33, 153–72; Dabhoiwala, *The Origins of Sex*, 350–60; Deborah Cohen, *Family Secrets: Shame and Privacy in Modern Britain* (Oxford, 2013).
9 Anne-Marie Kilday and David Nash, *Shame and Modernity in Britain: 1890 to the Present* (Basingstoke, 2017), Chap. 2, 21–62; Ute Frevert, 'Shame and Humiliation', in *History of Emotions – Insights into Research*, October 2015, https://www.history-of-emotions.mpg.detexts/shame-and-humiliation#drei; Ute Frevert, *The Politics of Humiliation: A Modern History* (Oxford, 2020), 54–70; Stearns, *Shame*, 90.
10 Erving Goffman, *Asylums: Essays on the Social Situation of Mental Patients and other Inmates* (New York, 1961); Frevert, *The Politics of Humiliation*, 104–10.
11 Frevert, 'Shame and Humiliation'.
12 Lucy Delap, '"Disgusting Details Which Are Best Forgotten": Disclosures of Child Sexual Abuse in Twentieth-Century Britain', *Journal of British Studies*, 57 (2018), 79–107. The evidence presented by Delap also points to condescending attitudes of social workers towards the low origins and lack of respectability of victims of rape. For varied additional sources of shame, and for public shaming in the twentieth century (evident in sexual scandals, attitudes to abortion, the role of media in inflicting shame), see Nash and Kilday, *Shame and Modernity*. For a broader discussion of the complex impact of shame in modernity, arguing that shame declined but unevenly and inconsistently, indicating also the revival of shame in a host of social settings (youth culture, business failure), see Stearns, *Shame*, Chaps. 4–5, 57–130, esp. 86–91.
13 Eliza Ahmed, Nathan Harris, John Braithwaite and Valerie Braithwaite (eds.), *Shame Management through Reintegration* (Cambridge, 2001); Tony F. Marshall, 'The evolution of restorative justice in Britain', *European Journal on Criminal Policy and Research*, 4 (1996), 21–43; Danielle Sered, *Until We Reckon: Violence, Mass Incarceration, and a Road to Repair* (New York, 2019). For a broader formulation of the importance of shame in integration and social relations, building on Norbert Elias and other sociologists, see Thomas J. Scheff, 'Shame and the Social Bond: A Sociological Theory', *Sociological Theory*, 18 (2000), 84–99.
14 Kwame Anthony Appiah, *The Honor Code: How Moral Revolutions Happen* (New York, 2010), 93–8, 103–35, 172, quotation on 114.
15 Martha C. Nussbaum, *Hiding from Humanity: Disgust, Shame and the Law* (New Jersey, 2004), 211–16; Frevert, 'Shame and Humiliation'.

# Bibliography

## Archival sources

### British Library, London (BL)

Add MS 33085, Correspondence of Thomas Pelham, of Stanmer, Sussex, merchant at Constantinople, 1718–1737.
Add. MS 43730–43733, Scattergood Collections. Vols. XIV–XVII, Transcripts of papers of John Scattergood (1681–1723), merchant of Madras, 1698–1725.
Add. MS 42122, Bernard P. Scattergood, The Life of John Scattergood, reprint from *The Contemporary Review* (1928).
Add. MS 72516, Trumbull Papers, Ann Dormer Letters, 1685–1688, fols. 156–241.
Mss EUR E 387/A–B, Letter Book of Isaac Lawrence, 1672–1679.
Sloane MS 922, Profitable and Comfortable Letters, 1650–1658, by Nehemiah Wallington.
Stowe MS 759, Letter Book of Philip Williams, 1639–1647.

### London Metropolitan Archives, London (LMA)

CLC/B/227/MS 29393, Letters to William Hurtt (Hurt), merchant of Bishopsgate and official of East India Company, from Thomas Rogers, His Nephew and East India Company factor, 1632–1636.
CLC/509/MS 05106/00, Journal and Letter Book of William Turner, Citizen and Merchant Taylor, 1664–1667.
CLC/480/MS 00507A, Papers Relating to Sir John Moore's Merchant Business, Mostly Letters Addressed to Him by His Country and Foreign Agents, 1666–1687.
CLC/B/MS 18470, Out-Letter Books of John Oldbury and Henry Stanley, Merchants of London, 1669–1678.
CLC/521/MS 11892A, Out-Letter Book of Michael Mitford, Russian and Baltic Merchant of St Dunston East, Chiefly to Correspondents in Newcastle, Amsterdam, Moscow, 1703–1706.
P92/Sav/749–780, Petitions for Relief, Parish of Saint Saviour, Southwark.

## Printed primary sources

*Anne Wallens Lamentation. For the Murthering of her husband John Wallen a Turner in Cow-Lane neere Smithfield; done by his owne wife* (1616), in Rollins (ed.), *A Pepysian Garland*, 85–8.

## Bibliography

Anon., *A pittilesse mother That most vnnaturally at one time, murthered two of her owne children at Acton within sixe miles from London vppon holy thursday last 1616* (1616), STC2, 24757.

———, *The life and death of Griffin Flood informer Whose cunning courses, churlish manners and troublesome Informations, molested a number of plaine dealing people in this city of London* (1623), STC2 11090.

Aristotle, *On Rhetoric: A Theory of Civic Discourse*, trans. George A. Kennedy (Oxford, 1991).

Balderston, Marion (ed.), *James Claypoole's Letter book: London and Philadelphia 1681–1684* (San Marino, 1967).

Beard, Thomas, *The theatre of Gods judgements revised, and augmented: Wherein is represented the admirable justice of God* (1631), STC2 1661.5.

Bellamy, Richard (ed.), *Beccaria: On Crimes and Punishments and Other Writings*, trans. Richard Davies (Cambridge, 1995).

Booy, David (ed.), *The Notebooks of Nehemiah Wallington, 1618–1654: A Selection* (Aldershot, 2007).

Brathwaite, Richard, *The English gentleman: Containing sundry excellent rules or exquisite observations, tending to direction of every gentleman, of selecter ranke and qualitie; how to demeane or accommodate himselfe in the manage of publike or private affaires* (1630), STC2 3563.

———, *The English gentleman, and The English gentlewoman both in one volume couched, and in one modell portrayed: To the living glory of their sexe, the lasting story of their worth* (1641), Wing2 B4262.

Braybrooke, Richard Lord (ed.), *Memoirs of Samuel Pepys, esq. F.R.S., Secretary to the Admiralty in the reign of Charles II and James II*, Vol. 5 (London, 1828).

Brinsley, John, *The true watch, and rule of life Or, a direction for the examination of our spirituall estate, and for the guiding of our whole course of life* (1632), STC2 3784.

Brown, John [B., J.], *The Marchants avizo: Verie necessarie for their sonnes and servants, when they first send them beyond the seas* (London, 1589), STC2 3908.4.

Browne, Thomas, *Religio Medici* (1642), Wing2 B5166.

Bunyan, John, *Grace Abounding to the Chief of Sinners* (1666), Wing2 B5523.

Burton, Robert, *The Anatomy of Melancholy* (1621), STC2 4159.

Cartwright, Francis, *The life, confession, and heartie repentance of Francis Cartwright, Gentleman for his bloudie sinne in killing of one Master Storr, Master of Arts, and minister of Market Rason in Lincolnshire* (1621), STC2 4704.

Cleland, James, *Hero-paideia, or The Institution of a young noble Man* (1607), STC2 5393.

Coeffeteau, Nicolas, *A table of humane passions With their causes and effects* (1621), STC2 5473.

Courtin, Antoine de, *The rules of civility, or, Certain Ways of deportment observed in France amongst all persons of quality upon several occasions* (1671–1678), Wing2 C6604.

Crooke, Helkiah, *Mikrokosmographia a description of the body of man. Together with the Controversie thereto belonging* (1615).

Cust, Richard (ed.), *The Papers of Sir Richard Grosvenor, 1st Bart. (1585–1645)* (Record Society of Lancashire and Cheshire, Vol. 134, Oxford, 1996).

Day, Angel, *The English secretorie* (1586), STC2 6401.

Dent, Arthur, *A sermon of repentance a very godly and profitable sermon preached at Lee in Essex* (1630), STC2 6666.4.

Disney, Gervase, *Some remarkable passages in the holy life and death of Gervase Disney, Esq.* (1692), Wing2 D1671A.

Dugdale, Gilbert, *A true discourse of the practises of Elizabeth Caldwell, Ma: Ieffrey Bownd, Isabell Hall widdow, and George Fernely, on the parson of Ma: Thomas Caldwell* (1604), STC2 7293.
Elton, Edward, *A plaine and easy exposition of sixe of the commandments of God* (1619), STC2 7620.
Elyot, Thomas, *The boke, named The gouernour deuised by Sir Thomas Elyot Knight* (1532, 1580), STC2 7642.
──────, *The castel of health. Corrected and in some place augmented* (1561), STC2 7651.
Erasmus, Desiderius, *The ciuilitie of childehode with the discipline and institucion of children, distributed in small and compe[n]dious chapiters ... translated oute of French into Englysh, by Thomas Paynell* (1560), STC2 10470.3.
Ford, John, *Tis Pity She's a Whore* (1633).
Fox, George, *An Autobiography*, ed. Rufus M. Jones (Philadelphia, 1909), https://archive.org/details/georgefoxautobio00foxg.
Foxe, John, *Actes and monuments of these latter and perillous dayes touching matters of the Church* (1563), The Unabridged Acts and Monuments Online, or TAMO (1583 edition), HRI Online Publications, Sheffield, 2011, https://www.johnfoxe.org.
Goodcole, Henry, *Heavens speedie hue and cry sent after lust and murther. Manifested upon the suddaine apprehending of Thomas Shearwood, and Elizabeth Evans, whose manner of lives, death, and free confessions, are heere expressed* (1635), STC2 12010.
Halliwell, James Orchard (ed.), *The Autobiography and Personal Diary of Simon Forman, The Celebrated Astrologer, from A.D. 1552 to A.D. 1602* (London, 1849).
Hartlib, Samuel, *The true and readie way to learne the Latine tongue* (1654), Wing H1002.
Heath, Helen Truesdell (ed.), *The Letters of Samuel Pepys and His Family Circle* (Oxford, 1955).
Heywood, Thomas, *A Woman Killed with Kindness* (1603).
Hill, John, *The young secretary's guide* (1687), Wing2 H1991B.
Hutton, Luke, *Luke Huttons lamentation which he wrote the day before his death, being condemned to be hanged at Yorke this last assises for his robberies and trespasses committed* (1598), STC2 14032.
Keeble, N.H. (ed.), *The Autobiography of Richard Baxter* (London and Melbourne, abridged edition, 1985).
Knappen, Marshall Mason (ed.), *Two Elizabethan Diaries by Richard Rogers and Samuel Ward* (Chicago, 1933).
Lemnius, Levinus, *The touchstone of complexions expedient and profitable for all such as bee desirous and carefull of their bodily health* (1633), STC2 15458.
Levene, Alysa (ed.), *Narratives of the Poor in Eighteenth-Century Britain* (London, 2006), Vol. 1, *Voices of the Poor: Poor Law Depositions and Letters*, eds. Steven King, Thomas Nutt and Alannah Tomkins; Vol. 3, *Institutional Responses: The London Foundling Hospital*, ed. Alysa Levene.
Locke, John, *Some Thoughts Concerning Education* (1693), The Harvard Classics, www.bartleby.com.
──────, The Reasonableness of Christianity (1695), in *The Works of John Locke in Nine Volumes* (London, 1824), Vol. 6, Online Library of Liberty, https://oll.libertyfund.org/titles/1438.
Malynes, Gerard, *Consuetudo, vel lex Mercatoria, or The ancient law-Merchant Divided into Three Parts* (London, 1622), STC2 17222.

Mandeville, Bernard, *An Enquiry into the Origin of Honour, and The usefulness of Christianity in war. By the Author of Fable of the Bees* [B. de Mandeville] (London, 1732).

Mulcaster, Richard, *Positions Concerning the Training Up of Children* (1581), ed. William Barker (Toronto, 1994).

Norwood, Richard, *The Journal of Richard Norwood, Surveyor of Bermuda*, ed. W.F. Craven and W.B. Hayward (New York, 1945).

Price, Jacob M. (ed.), *Joshua Johnson's Letterbook, 1771- 1774: Letters from a Merchant in London to his Partners in Maryland* (London Record Society, Vol. XV, London, 1979).

Primaudaye, Pierre de la, *The French Academie Wherein is Discoursed the Institution of Manners ... by Precepts of Doctrine, and Examples of the Lives of Ancient Sages and Famous Men*, trans. T.B. (London, 1594), STC2 15235.

R., M., *A president for yong pen-men: Or, the letter writer* (1638), STC2 20585.

Ratsey, Gamaliel, *The life and death of Gamaliell Ratsey a famous theefe of England, executed at Bedford the 26. of March last past* (1605), STC2 20753.

Reynolds, Edward, *A treatise of the passions and faculties of the soule of man* (1640), STC2 20938.

Riden, Philip (ed.), *George Sitwell's Letterbook 1662–66* (Derbyshire Record Society, Vol. X, Chesterfield, 1985).

Robson, Henry, *The examination, confession, and condemnation of Henry Robson fisherman of Rye, who poysoned his wife in the strangest maner that euer hitherto hath bin heard of* (1598), STC2 21131.

Rollins, Hyder E., *A Pepysian Garland: Black-Letter Broadside Ballads of the Years 1595–1639 Chiefly from the Collection of Samuel Pepys* (Cambridge, 1922).

S[eager], F[rancis], *The schoole of vertue, and booke of good nurture teaching children and youth their duties* (1621), STC2 22137.7.

Sansom, Oliver, *An Account of Many Remarkable Passages of the Life of Oliver Sansom, etc.* [Written by himself] (London, 1710).

Serre, M. de La, *The secretary in fashion: Or, an elegant and compendious way of writing all manner of letters* (1640, 1668), Wing2 L461A.

Sheppard, S. (Samuel), *The secretaries studie containing new familiar epistles* (1652), Wing S3169.

Smith, S.D. (ed.), *'An Exact and Industrious Tradesman': The Letter Book of Joseph Symson of Kendal, 1710–1720* (The British Academy, Records of Social and Economic History, New Series 34, Oxford, 2002).

Sokoll, Thomas (ed.), *Essex Pauper Letters, 1731–1837* (Records of Social and Economic History, 30, Oxford, 2001).

Steele, Richard, *The Trades-Man's Calling Being a Discourse Concerning the Nature, Necessity, Choice, etc. of a Calling in General: And Directions for the Right Managing of the Tradesman's Calling in Particular* (London, 1684), Wing S5394.

Storey, Matthew (ed.), *Two East Anglian Diaries 1641–1729: Isaac Archer and William Coe* (Suffolk Record Society, Vol. XXXVI, Suffolk, 1994).

The arraignment of John Flodder and his wife, at Norwidge, with the wife of one Bicks, for burning the Towne of Windham ... of June last 1615, in Rollins (ed.), *A Pepysian Garland*, 55–9.

The Cryes of the Dead. Or the Late Murther in South-warke, Committed by One Richard Price Weaver, in Rollins (ed.), *A Pepysian Garland*, 223–8.

The Examination, Confession, and Condemnation of Henry Robson fisherman of Rye, Who Poysoned His Wife in the Strangest Maner that Euer Hitherto Hath Bin Heard of (1598), STC2 21131.

The Lamenting Lady, Who for the Wrongs Done by her to a Poore Woman, for Having Two Children at One Burthen, Was by the Hand of God Most Strangely Punished, in Rollins (ed.), *A Pepysian Garland*, 121–31.

The Ordinary of Newgate His Account of the Behaviour, Confession and Dying Words of the Condemned Criminals … Executed at Tyburn. Available on Tim Hitchcock, Robert Shoemaker, Clive Emsley, Sharon Howard and Jamie McLaughlin, et al., *The Old Bailey Proceedings Online, 1674–1913* (www.oldbaileyonline.org, version 7.0, 24 March 2012), Ordinary of Newgate's Accounts (OBP/OA).

Tinling, Marion (ed.), *The Correspondence of the Three William Byrds of Westover, Virginia, 1684–1776* (Charlottesville, 1997), Vol. II.

Trosse, George, *The Life of the Reverend Mr. George Trosse*, ed. A.W. Brink (Montreal and London, 1974).

Webster, John, *The Duchess of Malfi* (1623).

Wright, Thomas, *The Passions of the Minde in Generall in Six Books* (1601–1621), STC2 26042.

## Secondary sources

Ahmed, Eliza, Nathan Harris, John Braithwaite and Valerie Braithwaite (eds.), *Shame Management through Reintegration* (Cambridge, 2001).

Andrew, Donna T., *Philanthropy and Police: London Charity in the Eighteenth Century* (Princeton, 1989).

———, 'The Press and Public Apologies in Eighteenth-Century London', in Norma Landau (ed.), *Law, Crime and English Society 1660–1830* (Cambridge, 2002), 208–29.

———, *Aristocratic Vice: The Attack on Duelling, Suicide, Adultery, and Gambling in Eighteenth-Century England* (New Haven and London, 2013).

Appiah, Kwame Anthony, *The Honor Code: How Moral Revolutions Happen* (New York, 2010).

Bailey, Joanne, *Parenting in England 1760–1830: Emotion, Identity, and Generation* (Oxford, 2012).

Bailey, Merridee L., *Socializing the Child in Late Medieval England c. 1400–1600* (Woodbridge, 2012).

Banister, Julia, *Masculinity, Militarism and Eighteenth-Century Culture, 1689–1815* (Cambridge, 2018).

Banks, Stephen, *A Polite Exchange of Bullets: The Duel and the English Gentleman 1750–1850* (Woodbridge, 2010).

Bannet, Tavor, *Empire of Letters: Letter Manuals and Transatlantic Correspondence, 1680–1820* (Cambridge, 2005).

Beattie, J.M., *Crime and the Courts in England 1660–1800* (Oxford, 1986).

———, *Policing and Punishment in London 1660–1750* (Oxford, 2001).

Bellany, Alastair, '"Raylinge Rymes and Vaunting Verse": Libellous Politics in Early Stuart England, 1603–1628', in Kevin Sharpe and Peter Lake (eds.), *Culture and Politics in Early Stuart England* (Basingstoke, 1994), 285–310.

Ben-Amos, Ilana Krausman, *The Culture of Giving: Informal Support and Gift Exchange in Early Modern England* (Cambridge, 2008).

Benedict, Ruth, *The Chrysanthemum and the Sword: Patterns of Japanese Culture* (Boston, 1946).

Bolton, Jeremy, 'Going on the Parish: The Parish Pension and its Meaning in the London Suburbs, 1640–1724', in Tim Hitchcock, Pamela Sharpe and Peter King (eds.), *Chronicling Poverty: The Voices and Strategies of the English Poor, 1640–1840* (Basingstoke, 1997), 19–46.

Bourdieu, Pierre, *Outline of a Theory of Practice*, trans. Richard Nice (Cambridge, 1977).

Braithwaite, John, 'Shame and Modernity', *British Journal of Criminology*, 33 (1993): 1–18.

Brant, Clare, *Eighteenth-Century Letters and British Culture* (Basingstoke, 2006).

Bryson, Anna, *From Courtesy to Civility: Changing Codes of Conduct in Early Modern England* (Oxford, 1998).

Burke, Peter, Brian Harrison and Paul Slack (eds.), *Civil Histories: Essays Presented to Sir Keith Thomas* (Oxford, 2000).

Burrus, Virginia, *Saving Shame: Martyrs, Saints, and Other Abject Subjects* (Philadelphia, 2008).

Cadden, Joan, *Meanings of Sex Difference in the Middle Ages: Medicine, Science, and Culture* (Cambridge, 1993).

Cairns, Douglas L., *Aidos: The Psychology and Ethics of Honour and Shame in Ancient Greek Literature* (Oxford, 1993).

———, 'Honour and Shame: Modern Controversies and Ancient Values', *Critical Quarterly*, 53 (2011): 23–41.

Canny, Nicholas, 'Reviewing A View of the Present State of Ireland', *Irish University Review*, 26 (1996): 252–67.

Capp, Bernard, *When Gossips Meet: Women, Family and Neighbourhood in Early Modern England* (Oxford, 2003).

———, *England's Culture Wars: Puritan Reformation and Its Enemies in the Interregnum, 1649–1660* (Oxford, 2012).

———, *The Ties that Bind: Siblings, Family and Society in Early Modern England* (Oxford, 2018).

Carr, Rosalind, 'A Polite and Enlightened London?', *The Historical Journal*, 59 (2016): 623–34.

Clay, C.G.A., *Economic Expansion and Social Change: England 1500– 1700* (Cambridge, 1984), Vol. II.

Cohen, Deborah, *Family Secrets: Shame and Privacy in Modern Britain* (Oxford, 2013).

Colley, Linda, *Britons: Forging the Nation 1707–1837* (New Haven and London, 1992).

Collinson, Patrick, 'Puritanism and the Poor', in Rosemary Horrox and Sarah Rees Jones (eds.), *Pragmatic Utopias: Ideals and Communities, 1200–1630* (Cambridge, 2001), 242–58.

Como, David, *Radical Parliamentarians and the English Civil War* (Oxford, 2018).

Conrad, Lawrence I., Michael Neve, Vivian Nutton, Roy Porter and Andrew Wear (eds.), *The Western Medical Tradition 800 BC to AD 1800* (Cambridge, 1994).

Crawford, Patricia, *Parents of Poor Children in England, 1580–1800* (Oxford, 2010).

Cressy, David, *Dangerous Talk: Scandalous, Seditious, and Treasonable Speech in Pre-Modern England* (Oxford, 2010).

Cummings, Brian, 'Animal Passions and Human Sciences: Shame, Blushing and Nakedness in Early Modern Europe and the New World', in Erica Fudge, Ruth Gilbert and Susan Wiseman (eds.), *At the Borders of the Human: Beasts, Bodies and Natural Philosophy in the Early Modern Period* (Basingstoke, 2002), 26–50.

Dabhoiwala, Faramerz, *The Origins of Sex: A History of the First Sexual Revolution* (London, 2013).

Davis, Natalie Zemon, 'The Rites of Violence', in *Society and Culture in Early Modern France* (Stanford, 1975), 152–88.

Daybell, James, *Women Letter-Writers in Tudor England* (Oxford, 2006).

Delap, Lucy, '"Disgusting Details Which Are Best Forgotten": Disclosures of Child Sexual Abuse in Twentieth-Century Britain', *Journal of British Studies*, 57 (2018), 79–107.

Demos, John, 'Shame and Guilt in Early New England', in C.Z. Stearns and P.N. Stearns (eds.), *Emotions and Social Change: Toward a New Psychohistory* (New York, 1988), 69–86.

Devereaux, Simon and Paul Griffiths (eds.), *Penal Practice and Culture, 1500–1900: Punishing the English* (Basingstoke, 2004).

Dickie, Simon, *Cruelty and Laughter: Forgotten Comic Literature and the Unsentimental Eighteenth Century* (Chicago, 2011).

Dickinson, J.R. and J.A. Sharpe, 'Public Punishment and the Manx Ecclesiastical Courts during the Seventeenth and Eighteenth Centuries', in Devereaux and Griffiths (eds.), *Penal Practice and Culture*, 138–56.

Dixon, Thomas, *From Passions to Emotions: The Creation of a Secular Psychological Category* (Cambridge, 2003).

Ebert, Christopher, 'Early Modern Atlantic Trade and the Development of Maritime Insurance to 1630', *Past and Present*, 213 (2011): 87–114.

Elias, Norbert, *The Civilizing Process: The History of Manners and State Formation and Civilization* (1939), trans. Edmund Jephcott (Oxford, 1969, new edition, 1994).

Evans, Richard E., *Rituals of Retribution: Capital Punishment in Germany, 1660–1987* (Oxford, 1996).

Evans, Tanya, *'Unfortunate Objects': Lone Mothers in Eighteenth-Century London* (Basingstoke, 2005).

Febvre, Lucien, 'Sensibility and History: How to Reconstitute the Emotional Life of the Past', in Peter Burke (ed.), *A New Kind of History and Other Essays*, trans. K. Folca (New York, 1973), 12–26.

Fernie, Ewan, *Shame in Shakespeare* (London, 2002).

Fideler, Paul A., *Social Welfare in Pre-Industrial England* (Basingstoke, 2006).

Finkelstein, Andrea, *Harmony and the Balance: An Intellectual History of Seventeenth-Century English Economic Thought* (Ann Arbor, 2000).

Finn, Margot C., *The Character of Credit: Personal Debt in English Culture, 1740–1914* (Cambridge, 2007).

Fletcher, Anthony, *Gender, Sex and Subordination in England, 1500–1700* (New Haven and London, 1995).

Fox, Adam, 'Ballads, Libels and Popular Ridicule in Jacobean England', *Past and Present*, 145 (1994): 47–83.

———, *Oral and Literate Culture in England 1500–1700* (Oxford, 2000).

Foyster, Elizabeth A., *Manhood in Early Modern England: Honour, Sex and Marriage* (London and New York, 1999).

Foyster, Elizabeth, *Marital Violence: An English Family History, 1660–1857* (Cambridge, 2005).

Fredricksen, Paula, 'The *Confessions* as Autobiography', in Mark Vessey (ed.), *A Companion to Augustine* (Oxford, 2012), 87–98.

French, Henry, '"Gentleman": Remaking the English Ruling Class', in Wrightson (ed.), *A Social History of England*, 269–89.

Frevert, Ute, *Emotions in History – Lost and Found* (Budapest, 2011).
Frevert, Ute et al., *Emotional Lexicons: Continuity and Change in the Vocabulary of Feeling 1700–2000* (Oxford, 2014).
Frevert, Ute, 'Piggy's Shame', in Ute Frevert et al. (eds.), *Learning How to Feel: Children's Literature and Emotional Socialization, 1870–1970* (Oxford, 2014), 134–54.
———, 'Shame and Humiliation', in *History of Emotions – Insights into Research*, October 2015, https://www.history-of-emotions.mpg.detexts/shame-and-humiliation#drei.
———, *The Politics of Humiliation: A Modern History* (Oxford, 2020).
Fullerton, Samuel, 'Fatal Adulteries: Sexual Politics in the English Revolution', *Journal of British Studies*, 41 (2021): 1–29.
Games, Alison, *The Web of Empire: English Cosmopolitans in an Age of Expansion, 1560–1660* (Oxford, 2008).
———, 'The English and "Others" in England and beyond', in Wrightson (ed.), *A Social History of England*, 352–72.
Gatrell, V.A.C., *The Hanging Tree: Execution and the English People 1770–1868* (Oxford, 1994).
Glaisyer, Natasha, *The Culture of Commerce in England, 1660–1720* (Woodbridge, 2006).
Glannery, Mary C., *Practising Shame: Female Honour in Later Medieval England* (Manchester, 2020).
Goffman, Erving, *Asylums: Essays on the Social Situation of Mental Patients and other Inmates* (New York, 1961).
———, *Stigma: Notes on the Management of Spoiled Identity* (New York, 1963).
Goldberg, Jessica L., 'Choosing and enforcing Business Relationships in the Eleventh-Century Mediterranean: Reassessing the "Maghribi Traders"', *Past and Present*, 216 (2012): 3–40.
——— *Trade and Institutions in the Medieval Mediterranean: The Geniza Merchants and their Business World* (Cambridge, 2012).
Grassby, Richard, *Kinship and Capitalism: Marriage, Family and Business in the English-Speaking world, 1580–1740* (Cambridge, 2001).
Greenblatt, Stephen, *Shakespeare's Freedom* (Chicago, 2011).
Griffiths, Paul, 'Bodies and Souls in Norwich: Punishing Petty Crime, 1540–1700', in Devereaux and Griffiths (eds.), *Penal Practice and Culture*, 85–120.
Grimes, Mary Cochran, 'Saving Grace Among Puritans and Quakers: A study of 17th and 18th Century Conversion Experiences', *Quaker History*, 72 (1983): 3–26.
Gundersheimer, Werner L., 'Concepts of Shame and Pocaterra's Dialoghi Della Vergogna', *Renaissance Quarterly*, 47 (1994): 34–55.
Hadfield, Andrew, 'Another Case of Censorship? The Riddle of Edmund Spenser's "A View of the Present State of Ireland (c. 1596)"', *History Ireland*, IV (1996): 26–30.
Hailwood, Mark, *Alehouses and Good Fellowship in Early Modern England* (Woodbridge, 2014).
Hallett, Mark, *The Spectacle of Difference: Graphic Art in the Age of Hogarth* (New Haven and London, 1999).
Harvey, Karen, *Reading Sex in the Eighteenth Century: Bodies and Gender in English Erotic Culture* (Cambridge, 2004).
Heal, Felicity and Clive Holmes, *The Gentry in England and Wales, 1500–1700* (Stanford, 1994).

Herrup, Cynthia, 'Punishing Pardon: Some Thoughts on the Origins of Penal Transportation', in Devereaux and Griffiths (eds.), *Penal Practice and Culture*, 121–37.

Hill, Christopher, 'Bunyan's Contemporary Reputation', in Anne Laurence, W.R. Owens and Stuart Sim (eds.), *John Bunyan and his England 1628–88* (London and Ronceverte, 1990).

Hindle, Steve, 'The Shaming of Margaret Knowsley: Gossip, Gender and the Experience of Authority in Early Modern England', *Continuity and Change*, 9 (1994): 391–419.

———, *On the Parish? The Micro-Politics of Poor Relief in Rural England c. 1550–1750* (Oxford, 2004).

Hindmarsh, Bruce, *The Evangelical Conversion Narrative: Spiritual Autobiography in Early Modern England* (Oxford, 2005).

Hitchcock, Tim and Robert Shoemaker, *London Lives: Poverty, Crime and the Making of a Modern City, 1690–1800* (Cambridge, 2015).

Hodgkin, Katharine, *Madness in Seventeenth-Century Autobiography* (Basingstoke, 2007).

Hodgkin, Katharine (ed.), *Women, Madness and Sin in Early Modern England: The Autobiographical Writings of Dionys Fitzherbert* (Farnham, 2010).

Hollander, Martha, 'Losses of Face: Rembrandt, Masaccio, and the Drama of Shame', *Social Research*, 70 (2003): 1327–50.

Hoppit, Julian, *Risk and Failure in English Business 1700–1800* (Cambridge: Cambridge University Press, 1987).

Houlbrook, Ralph, *Death, Religion and the Family in England, 1480–1750* (Oxford, 1998).

Hubbard, Eleanor, *City of Women: Money, Sex, and the Social Order in Early Modern London* (Oxford, 2012).

Humphries, Jane, *Childhood and Child Labour in the British Industrial Revolution* (Cambridge, 2010).

Hunt, Arnold, *The Art of Hearing: English Preachers and their Audiences, 1590–1640* (Cambridge, 2010).

Ingram, Martin, 'Ridings, Rough Music and the "Reform of Popular Culture" in Early Modern England', *Past and Present*, 105 (1984): 79–113.

———, 'Ridings, Rough Music and Mocking Rhymes in Early Modern England', in Barry Reay (ed.), *Popular Culture in Seventeenth-Century England* (London, 1985), 166–97.

———, '"Scolding Women Cucked or Washed": A Crisis in Gender Relations in Early Modern England?', in Jennifer Kermode and Garthine Walker (eds.), *Women, Crime And The Courts In Early Modern England* (London, 1994), 48–80.

———, 'Shame and Pain: Themes and Variations in Tudor Punishments', in Devereaux and Griffiths (eds.), *Penal Practice and Culture*, 36–62.

———, *Carnal Knowledge: Regulating Sex in England, 1470–1600* (Cambridge, 2017).

James, Mervyn, *Society, Politics and Culture: Studies in Early Modern England* (Cambridge, 1986).

Jones, Peter and Steven King, 'From Petition to Pauper Letter: The Development of an Epistolary Form', in P.D. Jones and S.A. King (eds.), *Obligation, Entitlement and Dispute Under the English Poor Laws* (Cambridge Scholars Publishing, 2016), 53–77.

Jütte, Robert, *Poverty and Deviance in Early Modern Europe* (Cambridge, 1994).

## 244  Bibliography

Kadane, Matthew, 'Success and Self-Loathing in the Life of an Eighteenth-Century Entrepreneur', in Margaret C. Jacob and Catherine Secretan (eds.), *The Self-Perception of Early Modern Capitalists* (New York, 2008), 253–71.

Kadane, Mathew, *The Watchful Clothier: The Life of an Eighteenth-Century Protestant Capitalist* (New Haven and London, 2013).

———, 'Original Sin and the Path to the Enlightenment', *Past and Present*, 235 (2017): 105–40.

Kane, Brendan, *The Politics and Culture of Honour in Britain and Ireland, 1541–1641* (Cambridge, 2010).

Karant-Nunn, Susan C., *The Reformation of Feeling: Shaping the Religious Emotions in Early Modern Germany* (Oxford, 2010).

Keeble, N.H., 'Baxter, Richard', *Oxford Dictionary of National Biography*, online edition, https://www.oxforddnb.com.

Kesselring, K.J., *Mercy and Authority in the Tudor State* (Cambridge, 2003).

Kilday, Anne-Marie and David Nash, *Shame and Modernity in Britain: 1890 to the Present* (Basingstoke, 2017).

King, John N., *Foxe's Book of Martyrs and Early Modern Print Culture* (Cambridge, 2006).

King, Steven, 'Pauper Letters as a Source', *Family and Community History*, 10 (2007): 167–70.

Klein, Lawrence E., 'Politeness and the Interpretation of the British Eighteenth Century', *The Historical Journal*, 45 (2002): 869–98.

Krieken, Robert van, 'Norbert Elias and Emotions in History', in Lemmings and Brooks (eds.), *Emotions and Social Change*, 19–42.

Lake, Peter, 'Deeds against Nature: Cheap Print, Protestantism and Murder in Early Seventeenth Century England', in Kevin Sharpe and Peter Lake (eds.), *Culture and Politics in Early Stuart England* (Basingstoke, 1994), 257–84.

———, 'Reading Clarke's Lives in Political and Polemical Context', in Kevin Sharpe and Steven N. Zwicker (eds.), *Writing Lives: Biography and Textuality, Identity and Representation in Early Modern England* (Oxford, 2008), 293–318.

Lake, Peter and Isaac Stephens, *Scandal and Religious Identity in Early Stuart England: A Northamptonshire Maid's Tragedy* (Woodbridge, 2015).

Lamikiz, Xabier, *Trade and Trust in the Eighteenth-Century Atlantic World: Spanish Merchants and their Overseas Markets* (Woodbridge, 2010).

Lemmings, David and Ann Brooks (eds.), *Emotions and Social Change: Historical and Sociological Perspectives* (New York and Abingdon, 2014).

Levene, Alysa, *The Childhood of the Poor: Welfare in Eighteenth-Century London* (Basingstoke, 2012).

Lewis, Michael, 'Self-Conscious Emotions: Embarrassment, Pride, Shame and Guilt', in Michael Lewis, Jeannette M. Haviland-Jones and Lisa Feldman Barrett (eds.), *Handbook of Emotions*, 742–56.

Lewis, Michael, Jeannette M. Haviland-Jones and Lisa Feldman Barrett (eds.), *Handbook of Emotions* (London, 2008).

Lindemann, Mary, *Medicine and Society in Early Modern Europe* (Cambridge, 1999).

Linebaugh, Peter, 'The Ordinary of Newgate and His Accounts', in J.S. Cockburn (ed.), *Crime in England 1550–1800* (London, 1977), 246–69.

Love, Harold, *English Clandestine Satire, 1660–1702* (Oxford, 2004).

Lynch, Kathleen, *Protestant Autobiography in the Seventeenth-Century Anglophone World* (Oxford, 2012).

Mack, Peter, *Elizabethan Rhetoric: Theory and Practice* (Cambridge, 2002).
Margalit, Avishai, *The Decent Society* (Cambridge, 1998).
Marsh, Christopher, *Music and Society in Early Modern England* (Cambridge, 2010).
Marshall, Tony F., 'The Evolution of Restorative Justice in Britain', *European Journal on Criminal Policy and Research*, 4 (1996): 21–43.
Martin, John, 'Inventing Sincerity, Refashioning Prudence: The Discovery of the Individual in Renaissance Europe', *The American Historical Review*, 102 (1997): 1309–42.
Martin, Randall, *Women, Murder, and Equity in Early Modern England* (New York and London, 2008).
Mascuch, Michael, *Origins of the Individualist Self: Autobiography and Self-Identity in England, 1591–1791* (Stanford, 1996).
Mathias, Peter, 'Risk, Credit and Kinship in Early Modern Enterprise', in John J. McCusker and Kenneth Morgan (eds.), *The Early Modern Atlantic Economy* (Cambridge, 2000), 15–35.
McIntosh, Marjorie Keniston, *Controlling Misbehavior in England, 1370–1600* (Cambridge, 1998).
———, *Poor Relief in England 1350–1600* (Cambridge, 2012).
McKenzie, Andrea, *Tyburn's Martyrs: Execution in England, 1675–1775* (London, 2007).
McLean, Paul D., *The Art of the Network: Strategic Interaction and Patronage in Renaissance Florence* (Durham and London, 2007).
McRay, Andrew, *Literature, Satire and the Early Stuart State* (Cambridge, 2004).
Mendelson, Sara, 'The Civility of Women in Seventeenth-Century England', in Burke, Harrison and Slack (eds.), *Civil Histories*, (2000), 111–26.
———, 'Neighbourhood as Female Community in the Life of Anne Dormer', in Susan Broomhall and Stephanie Tarbin (eds.), *Women, Identities and Communities in Early Modern Europe* (Ashgate, 2008), 153–64.
Mentz, Søren, *The English Gentleman Merchant at Work: Madras and the City of London 1660–1740* (Copenhagen, 2005).
Miller, Andrew H., *The Burdens of Perfection: On Ethics and Reading in Nineteenth-Century British Literature* (Ithaca, 2008).
Miller, Ian William, *Humiliation: And Other Essays on Honor, Social Discomfort, and Violence* (Ithaca, 1993).
Moore, Rosemary, *The Light in their Consciences: Early Quakers in Britain 1646–1666* (University Park, Pennsylvania, 2000).
Morgan, Gwenda and Peter Rushton, *Banishment in the Early Atlantic World: Convicts, Rebels and Slaves* (London, 2013).
Morgan, Prys, 'Wild Wales: Civilizing the Welsh from the Sixteenth to the Nineteenth Centuries', in Peter Burke, Brian Harrison and Paul Slack (eds.), *Civil Histories: Essays Presented to Sir Keith Thomas* (Oxford, 2000), 265–84.
Morris, Marilyn, *Sex, Money and Personal Character in Eighteenth-Century British Politics* (New Haven and London, 2014).
Muldrew, Craig, *The Economy of Obligation: The Culture of Credit and Social Relations in Early Modern England* (Basingstoke, 1998).
Murphy, Anne L., *The Origins of English Financial Markets: Investment and Speculation before the South Sea Bubble* (Cambridge, 2009).
Nash, David and Anne-Marie Kilday, *Cultures of Shame: Exploring Crime and Morality in Britain, 1600–1900* (Basingstoke, 2010).
Neill, Michael, *Issues of Death: Mortality and Identity in English Renaissance Tragedy* (Oxford, 1997).

## 246  Bibliography

Newton, Hannah, *The Sick Child in Early Modern England* (Oxford, 2012).
Nussbaum, Martha C., *Hiding from Humanity: Disgust, Shame and the Law* (Princeton, 2004).
O'Connor, Mary E., *'Dormer, Anne (1648?–1965)'*, *Oxford Dictionary of National Biography*, online edition, https://www.oxforddnb.com.
Ogilvie, Sheilagh, *Institutions and European Trade: Merchant Guilds, 1000–1800* (Cambridge, 2011).
Ohlmeyer, Jane H., '"Civilizinge of those rude partes": Colonization within Britain and Ireland, 1580s–1640s', in Nicholas Canny (ed.), *The Oxford History of the British Empire* (Oxford, 1998), Vol. I, 124–47.
Ottaway, Susannah R., *The Decline of Life: Old Age in Eighteenth-Century England* (Cambridge, 2004).
Paster, Gail Kern, *The Body Embarrassed: Drama and the Discipline of Shame in Early Modern England* (Ithaca, NY, 1993).
———, 'The Unbearable Coldness of Female Being: Women's Imperfection and the Humoral Economy', *English Literary Renaissance*, 28 (1998): 416–40.
Pattison, Stephen, *Shame: Theory, Therapy, Theology* (Cambridge, 2000).
Paul, K. Tawny, 'Credit, Reputation and Masculinity in British Urban Commerce: Edinburgh c. 1710–70', *Economic History Review*, 66 (2013): 226–48.
Paul, Tawny, *The Poverty of Disaster: Debt and Insecurity in Eighteenth-Century Britain* (Cambridge, 2019).
Peck, Linda Levy, *Consuming Splendor: Society and Culture in Seventeenth-Century England* (Cambridge, 2005).
Peltonen, Markku, *The Duel in Early Modern England: Civility, Politeness and Honour* (Cambridge, 2003).
Peristiany, J.G. (ed.), *Honour and Shame: The Values of Mediterranean Society* (London, 1965).
Phillips, Nicola, *The Profligate son: Or, A True Story of Family Conflict, Fashionable Vice, and Financial Ruin in Regency Britain* (New York, 2013).
Plamper, Jan, *The History of Emotions: An Introduction* (Oxford, 2015).
Pollock, Linda A., 'Anger and the Negotiation of Relationships in Early Modern England', *Historical Journal*, 47 (2004): 567–90.
———, 'Honor, Gender, and Reconciliation in Elite Culture, 1570–1700', *Journal of British Studies*, 46 (2007): 3–29.
———, 'The Practice of Kindness in Early Modern Elite Society', *Past and Present*, 211 (2011): 121–58.
Poole, Steve, 'For the Benefit of Example: Crime-Scene Executions in England 1720–1830', in Richard Ward (ed.), *A Global History of Execution and the Criminal Corpse* (Basingstoke, 2015), 71–101.
Postles, Dave, 'Penance and the Market Place: A Reformation Dialogue with the Medieval Church' (c. 1250–c. 1600)', *Journal of Ecclesiastical History*, 54 (2003): 441–68.
Preston, Claire, *Thomas Browne and the Writing of Early Modern Science* (Cambridge, 2009).
Rediker, Marcus, *Between the Devil and the Deep Blue Sea: Merchant Seamen, Pirates, and the Anglo-American Maritime World, 1700–1750* (Cambridge, 1987).
Rosenberg, Phillippe, 'Sanctifying the Robe: Punitive Violence and the English Press, 1650–1700', in Devereaux and Griffiths (eds.), *Penal Practice and Culture*, 157–82.
Rosenwein, Barbara H., 'Worrying about Emotions in History', *American Historical Review*, 107 (2002): 821–45.

Rosenwein, Barbara, *Generations of Feeling: A History of Emotions, 600–1700* (Cambridge, 2016).
Royer, Katherine, 'Dead Men Talking: Truth, Texts and the Scaffold in Early Modern England', in Devereaux and Griffiths (eds.), *Penal Practice and Culture*, 63–84.
———, *The English Execution Narrative 1200–1700* (London, 2013).
Ryrie, Alec, *Being Protestant in Reformation Britain* (Oxford, 2013).
Scheff, Thomas, 'Pride and Shame: The Master Emotions', in *Bloody Revenge: Emotions, Nationalism and War* (Boulder, 1994), 39–55.
Scheff, Thomas J., 'Shame and the Social Bond: A Sociological Theory', *Sociological Theory*, 18 (2000): 84–99.
———, 'Elias, Freud and Goffman: Shame as the Master Emotion', in Steven Loyal and Stephen Quilley (eds.), *The Sociology of Norbert Elias* (Cambridge, 2004), 229–42.
———, 'The Ubiquity of Hidden Shame in Modernity', *Cultural Sociology*, 8 (2014): 129–41.
Schneider, Gary, *The Culture of Epistolarity: Vernacular Letters and Letter Writing in Early Modern England, 1500–1700* (Newark, 2005).
Scribner, Robert, 'Incombustible Luther: The Image of the Reformer in Early Modern Germany', *Past and Present*, 110 (1986): 38–68.
Seaver, Paul S., *Wallington's World: A Puritan Artisan in Seventeenth-Century London* (Stanford, 1985).
Seigel, Jerrold, *The Idea of the Self: Thought and Experience in Western Europe since the Seventeenth Century* (Cambridge, 2005).
———, *Modernity and Bourgeois Life: Society, Politics, and Culture in England, France and Germany since 1750* (Cambridge, 2012).
Semenza, Gregory M. Colón, *Sport, Politics and Literature in the English Renaissance* (Newark, 2003).
Sered, Danielle, *Until We Reckon: Violence, Mass Incarceration, and a Road to Repair* (New York, 2019).
Sharpe, J.A., '"Last Dying Speeches": Religion, Ideology and Public Execution in Seventeenth-Century England', *Past and Present*, 107 (1985): 144–67.
Shepard, Alexandra, *Meanings of Manhood in Early Modern England* (Oxford, 2003).
Shoemaker, Robert B., *Prosecution and Punishment: Petty Crime and the Law in London and Rural Middlesex, c. 1660–1725* (Cambridge, 1991).
Shoemaker, Robert, 'The Decline of Public Insult in London 1660–1800', *Past and Present*, 169 (2000): 97–131.
———, 'Male Honour and the Decline of Public Violence in Eighteenth-Century London', *Social History*, 26 (2001): 190–208.
Shoemaker, Robert B., 'The Taming of the Duel: Masculinity, Honour and Ritual Violence in London, 1660–1800', *The Historical Journal*, 45 (2002): 525–45.
Shoemaker, Robert, 'Streets of Shame? The Crowd and Public Punishments in London, 1700–1820', in Devereaux and Griffiths (eds.), *Penal Practice and Culture*, 232–57.
Slack, Paul, *Poverty and Policy in Tudor and Stuart England* (London and New York, 1988).
Smail, John, 'Credit, Risk, and Honor in Eighteenth-Century Commerce', *Journal of British Studies*, 44 (2005): 439–56.
Smith, Emma, *The Cambridge Shakespeare Guide* (Cambridge, 2012).
Smith, Nigel, *Literature and Revolution in England 1640–1660* (New Haven and London, 1994).

## 248  Bibliography

Smith, Richard M., '"Modernization" and the Corporate Medieval Village Community in England: Some Skeptical Reflections', in A.H.R. Baker and Derek Gregory (eds.), *Explorations in Historical Geography* (Cambridge, 1984), 140–245.

Snell, Esther, 'Trials in Print: Narratives of Rape Trials in the Proceedings of the Old Bailey', in David Lemmings (ed.), *Crime, Courtrooms and the Public Sphere in Britain, 1700–1850* (Farnham, 2012a), 23–42.

Snell, K.D.M., 'Belonging and Community: Understandings of Home and Friends among the English Poor, 1750–1850', *Economic History Review*, 65 (2012b): 1–25.

Sokoll, Thomas, 'Writing for Relief: Rhetoric in English Pauper Letters, 1800–1834', in Andreas Gestrich, Steven King and Raphael Lutz (eds.), *Being Poor in Modern Europe: Historical Perspectives 1800–1940* (Oxford, 2006), 91–112.

Spellman, W.M., *John Locke and the Problem of Depravity* (Oxford, 1988).

Stearns, Peter N., 'History of Emotions: Issues of Change and Impact', in Lewis et al. (eds.), *Handbook of Emotions*, 17–32.

———, *Shame: A Brief History* (Urbana and Chicago, 2017).

Sternberg, Giora, *Status Interaction during the Reign of Louis XIV* (Oxford, 2014).

Stewart, Frank Henderson, *Honor* (Chicago, 1994).

Stone, Lawrence, *The Crisis of the Aristocracy, 1558–1641* (Oxford, 1965).

———, *The Family, Sex and Marriage in England 1500–1800* (New York, 1977).

Swett, Katharine W., '"The Account between Us": Honor, Reciprocity and Companionship in Male Friendship in the Later Seventeenth Century', *Albion*, 31 (1999): 1–30.

Tadmor, Naomi, *Family and Friends in Eighteenth-Century England: Household, Kinship and Patronage* (Cambridge, 2004).

Temin, Peter and Hans-Joachim Voth, *Prometheus Shackled: Goldsmiths Banks and England's Financial Revolution After 1700* (Oxford, 2013).

Thomas, Courtney Erin, *If I Lose Mine Honour, I Lose Myself: Honour among the Early Modern English Elite* (Toronto, 2017).

Thomas, Keith, *Rule and Misrule in the Schools of Early Modern England*, The Stenton Lectures, 1975 (University of Reading, 1976).

———, *The Ends of Life: Roads to Fulfilment in Early Modern England* (Oxford, 2009).

———, *In Pursuit of Civility: Manners and Civilization in Early Modern England* (Massachusetts, 2018).

Thompson, E.P., *Customs in Common* (London, 1991).

Todd, Margo, 'Puritan Self-Fashioning: The Diary of Samuel Ward', *Journal of British Studies*, 31 (1992): 236-64.

Trivellato, Francesca, *The Familiarity of Strangers: The Sephardic Diaspora, Livorno, and Cross-Cultural Trade in the Early Modern Period* (New Haven, 2009).

Underdown, David, 'The Taming of the Scold: The Enforcement of Patriarchal Authority in Early Modern England', in Anthony Fletcher and John Stevenson (eds.), *Order and Disorder in Early Modern England* (Cambridge, 1985), 116–36.

Vanneste, Tijl, *Global Trade and Commercial Networks: Eighteenth-Century Diamond Merchants* (London, 2011).

Vickery, Amanda, *The Gentleman's Daughter: Women's Lives in Georgian England* (New Haven and London, 1998).

Wakelam, Alexander, *Credit and Debt in Eighteenth-Century England: An Economic History of Debtors' Prisons* (London and New York, 2021).

Walsham, Alexandra, *Providence in Early Modern England* (Oxford, 1999).
———, *Charitable Hatred: Tolerance and Intolerance in England, 1500–1700* (Manchester, 2006).
———, 'The Reformation of the Generations: Youth, Age and Religious Change in England, c. 1500–1700', *Transactions of the Royal Historical Society*, 21 (2011): 93–121.
Watkins, Owen C., *The Puritan Experience: Studies in Spiritual Autobiography* (1972).
Webster, Tom, 'Writing to Redundancy: Approaches to Spiritual Journals and Early Modern Spirituality', *Historical Journal*, 39 (1996): 33–56.
Whyman, Susan E., *The Pen and the People: English Letter-Writers 1660–1800* (Oxford, 2009).
Wierzbicka, Anna, *Emotions Across Languages and Cultures: Diversity and Universals* (Cambridge, 1999).
Willis, Jonathan, *The Reformation of the Decalogue: Religious Identity and the Ten Commandments in England, c. 1485–1625* (Cambridge, 2017).
Wiltenburg, Joy, 'Ballads and the Emotional Life of Crime', in Patricia Fumerton and Annita Guerrini (eds.), *Ballads and Broadsides in Britain, 1500–1800* (Farnham, 2010), 173–88.
Wrightson, Keith (ed.), *A Social History of England, 1500–1700* (Cambridge, 2017).
Zahedieh, Nuala, 'Credit, Risk, and Reputation in Late Seventeenth-Century Colonial Trade', in Olaf Uwe Janzen (ed.), *Merchant Organization and Maritime Trade in the North Atlantic, 1660–1815* (St. John's, Newfoundland, 1998), 53–74.
———, *The Capital and the Colonies: London and the Atlantic Economy, 1660–1700* (Cambridge, 2010).
Zhao, Han, '"Holy shame shall warm my heart": Shame and Protestant Emotions in Early Modern Britain', *Cultural and Social History*, 18 (2021): 1–21.

# Index

abuse 109, 42, 83, 109, 112, 120, 131, 140–7, 158, 160–1, 206, 212–3, 217, 226, 229, 233; *see also* insult; rape; shame (and sexuality); shame punishments; whipping
adultery 33, 35, 38, 92–3, 138, 156, 200, 202, 209, 211, 217–18, 231–2; *see also* sexuality
advice manuals: commercial 112; epistolary 81–4; conduct 16–24; devotional 37–8
affection 65, 69, 83, 86, 88, 93–4, 95–6, 98–9, 101, 123, 231; *see also* bonding
anger 7, 21, 53, 79–80, 88, 111, 113, 132, 149, 227–8
apology 6, 82, 83, 89, 91, 96, 98, 100, 107, 117, 122, 132, 143, 149, 196, 212–14, 227–8
apprenticeship and apprentices 54, 55, 58, 60, 63, 68, 79, 84, 85, 87, 84, 85, 87, 88, 112, 121; pauper 152–5; in crime narratives 168, 172, 173
Archer, Isaac 54, 55, 58, 59–60, 62, 72, 78, 79

badging 151
ballads 11, 38, 140, 144–7, 167–9, 173, 189, 190
bastard 140, 145, 153, 156; *see also* illegitimate children
Baxter, Richard 58, 66–8, 72
Beard, Thomas 38
Beccaria, Cesare 204–5, 218
begging: and the poor 148, 151, 155, 156; rhetoric of 91, 107, 132, 149, 179
Bickham, George 210

blush and blushing 1, 15, 22, 23, 25, 28, 34, 41, 43, 120–1, 130
Boitard, Louis Phillipe 211
bonding 6, 11, 36, 82–3, 87, 88–96, 91–2, 93–6, 99, 120, 132–3, 188, 217, 228
Brathwaite, Richard 24, 27
Browne, Thomas 31–2
Bunyan, John 55–6, 64–6
Burton, Robert: *The Anatomy of Melancholy*, 13, 23
Byrd, William 120, 131

Caldwell, Elizabeth 174, 182
charity 116, 138, 148, 150, 151, 153, 155, 160, 176, 182, 196–7
childhood 53, 54, 57–9, 64, 67, 68, 70, 71, 78–81, 82, 99, 172, 185–6, 231
children 20, 29, 62, 68, 70, 80–1, 85, 84–8, 99, 100, 162, 175, 181, 188, 199, 202–4, 218, 231–3; abandonment of 151–55; disabled 232; whipping 80–1, 203, 205; *see also* bastard; illegitimate children
Civil War and Revolution 51, 66, 206
civility and incivility 3, 4, 12, 15, 16–23, 24–7, 28, 31, 78, 81, 83, 89, 112, 115–6, 132, 147, 186, 195–9, 201–3, 212–3, 215, 218–9, 220, 228, 232; *see also* politeness
Claypoole, James 128–9
Cleland, James 25, 26, 27
colonies and colonization 194, 198–9, 215, 218, 229–30
condemnation 38, 40, 58, 77, 81, 84, 86, 97, 100, 138, 143, 151, 169, 202, 206, 207, 208, 210, 217, 220, 231
courage 24–7, 110, 180–1, 202–3, 215–17, 220, 230; *see also* cowardice

Courtin, Antoine de 17, 18, 19, 22, 24, 27
cowardice 24, 25–7, 29, 33, 89, 93, 145, 216–7, 220, 230, 232
credit 108, 117, 123, 141, 183, 196, 212; *see also* reputation and reputations; trust
credit markets 133, 230; *see also* debt and debts
Crooke, Helkiah 30, 31

Day, Angel 81
debt and debts 90, 117, 118, 105, 107, 107, 108, 117, 122–30, 141, 230
defamation (prosecutions) 23, 141, 143, 160, 212–3
defiance 10, 11, 39, 138, 161–2, 178–81, 201, 218, 219; *see also* insubordination; shamelessness
Defoe, Daniel 107, 210
Defour, Judith 170, 187
Dent, Arthur 37
devil 38, 64, 140, 168, 169, 170, 171, 177, 196, 207, 210
dishonesty 20, 21, 22, 84, 86, 112, 115, 117, 128, 131
Disney, Gervase 53, 54, 63, 66, 72
Dormer, Anne 97–9
ducking 139, 142, 156, 157–61, 195, 206
duels and dueling 20, 21, 88–9, 100, 196, 212, 213, 215; decline of 217, 219; surge of 216

Elias, Norbert 3–4, 6, 8, 9, 23
Elton, Edward 37
Elyot, Thomas 25–6, 31
education and educational 3, 10, 12, 16, 22, 24, 25–7, 28, 42, 55, 59, 80, 84, 112, 172, 195, 202–4, 214–15, 216–17, 220, 229, 231; *see also* schools
embarrassment 7, 9, 22–3, 29, 43, 99, 100, 113, 123, 132, 196, 209, 211, 227–8
emotions 1, 3, 56, 81, 95, 126, 133, 154, 187, 216–17, 219; theoretical approaches to 5–10; *see also* affection; anger; embarrassment; empathy; fear; guilt; honour; humiliation; passions; pride; shame
empathy 6, 11, 43, 94, 98, 119, 130, 132, 189, 232–3; *see also* sympathy
Enlightenment, the 12, 195, 199, 201, 202, 205, 215, 229, 231

Erasmus, Desiderius 20, 25, 43
evangelical awakening 64, 200, 202, 232
Evans, Arise 80, 81
executions 156–60, 168, 175, 177, 180, 187, 190, 194–5, 229; *see also* shame punishments
exhortation 34, 131, 132, 157, 167, 170, 175, 178, 179, 189; *see also* condemnation; rebuke

fear 6, 8, 9, 19, 24, 44, 53, 54, 56, 62, 64, 70, 80, 81, 141–2, 148, 153, 154, 155, 171, 178, 179, 203, 215, 216
Febvre, Lucien 6
forgive and forgiveness 6, 35, 36, 39, 40, 41, 143, 154, 159, 160; hopes for 61, 67, 70, 92; in crime narratives 174, 175, 182, 175, 182, 189, 190
Forman, Simon 79–80
fornication 38, 59, 138, 139, 141, 156, 200, 202; *see also* adultery; sexuality
Foundling Hospital, the 154–5
Fox, George 68–9, 71, 72
Foxe, John: *Actes and Monuments* 39–41
friendship 82, 83, 92, 94, 98, 110, 111, 118–24, 126, 129, 132, 186, 188

Galenic and humoral medicine 25, 28–31, 34, 202
gender and gendered 6, 11, 15, 27–31, 43, 78, 96, 183, 198, 201–2, 227, 230; and satire 208–9, 218, 219; changing attitudes 201–2; *see also* shame (feminine, masculine)
Goffman, Erving 13n14, 14n31, 232
gossip 2–3, 11, 140, 141, 142, 143, 160, 211, 219, 228
Griffin, Jane 176, 184
guilt 2, 8–9, 34–5, 38, 42, 52–3, 56, 58–66, 68, 84, 87–8, 93–6, 97, 100–1, 108, 116, 122–3, 127–9, 132–3, 143, 154, 159, 160, 173–5, 177, 179, 182, 187, 200, 213, 217, 220, 229, 233

Heywood, Thomas 34, 35
Hogarth, William 208, 209, 211
humanism 2, 20, 16, 21, 25–6, 32, 35, 82, 149, 202
humiliation 6, 9–10, 11, 17, 32, 33, 35, 78–81, 83, 90–2, 97, 99, 101, 107, 122, 128, 138–40, 141, 144–5,

148–9, 151–4, 157–9, 160–1, 196, 202, 205, 211–2, 216, 226, 229, 230, 231, 232, 233
humility 34, 40, 85, 99, 112, 149
honesty 20, 68, 105, 108, 114, 115, 127, 132, 133, 141, 185, 196, 212; *see also* dishonesty
honour and dishonour 7, 16–26, 32–4, 88–96, 111–17, 173, 212–17, 219–20, 230

idolatry 138, 156
illegitimate children 153–4, 161; *see also* bastard
imprisonment 155, 167, 174, 177, 178, 64, 71; for debts 133, 230; increase of 230, 232
infanticide 156, 169, 170, 177, 178, 183, 185, 187
insubordination 43, 132, 209–10; *see also* defiance
insult 9, 20, 78–9, 88, 89, 91, 92, 99, 109, 112, 113, 114–5, 132, 141, 143, 154, 160, 206, 213–14, 217, 220, 230; *see also* defamation

James, Mervin 2
Jonson, Ben 33, 35
June, John 209

Lawrence, Isaac 87, 107, 109, 110–11, 123, 127
letter-writing 77–8, 81–4, 89, 95, 99–100, 101, 226; by women 96–9
libels 140–1, 144–7, 160, 206
Locke, John 44, 80, 88, 202–4, 218, 231

Mandeville, Bernard 1, 214–15, 218, 219, 229
manners: *see* civility and incivility; politeness
Marlowe, Christopher 33
military and militarism 2, 25, 32, 212, 230, 232; cult of 220; discourse of 215–6; sports 26, 216–7
Mitford, Michael 107, 127
mockery 19, 33, 78, 139, 141, 142–6, 161, 194, 197, 206, 209–11, 227, 230; *see also* satire; ridicule
modesty 1, 23, 24, 27–8, 34, 89, 202
More, Thomas 32
Mulcaster, Richard 26, 28, 29
mutilation 33, 39, 139; *see also* shame and the body

networks 12, 77, 78, 100; commercial 105–33; kin and patronage 88–96, 99; *see also* friendship; obligations
newspapers 167, 190, 207, 208, 211, 229, 232
Norwood, Richard 54, 57–8, 60, 78–9, 80

obligations 6, 10–11, 138, 146, 169, 171, 185, 187–8, 196, 227; commercial 105, 106, 109, 114, 118–21, 124–32; among kin and friends 82, 90, 92, 94, 96, 100, 187; parent-child 81, 88, 99, 169
Oldbury, John 113, 119–20, 125–6, 130
Ordinary of Newgate: *Accounts* 168, 170–3, 175–8, 179–81, 183–88, 189

pamphlet literature: expansion of 38, 206–7; news and crime 38, 168, 169–70, 174–5, 177–9, 182–3; *see also* ballads, newspapers
pardon 35, 42, 91, 95, 116, 124, 158, 159, 160, 177, 184, 190, 194; royal 156, 174, 175, 177, 181
pardonable crimes 11, 157, 190, 228
passions (early modern uses of) 1, 15, 23, 25, 28, 212, 214–16, 219; *see also* emotions
patriarchy and patriarchal 4, 36, 78, 139, 160, 227
pauper letters 149–50, 154–5
Pelham, Thomas 88
penal reform 12, 194, 202, 204–5, 228–9, 232
penal system 11, 138, 155–60, 161, 168, 194–5, 217
Pepys, Samuel 88, 89–92
politeness and polite society 22, 31, 112, 195, 196–99, 206, 207, 209–11, 214–15, 216, 218, 220, 226, 228, 230; *see also* civility and incivility; shame (polite)
Poor Laws 11, 138, 147, 148, 153
poverty: attitudes towards 147–8, 160, 196–7; in crime narratives 184–5; and the penal system 156, 161; rising levels of 137, 230; and stigma 151, 154, 232; *see also* apprenticeship (pauper); badging; begging; illegitimate children; pauper letters; Poor Laws; prostitutes and prostitution; vagrancy; whores and whoredom; workhouses

Presbyterians 54, 55, 66, 200
pride 1, 7, 20, 29, 32–3, 36, 38, 39, 44, 52, 54, 68, 82, 92, 93, 110, 113, 114, 115, 116, 123, 132, 150, 152, 180, 184, 190, 204–5, 210, 212–17, 219, 229
Primaudaye, Pierre de la 12n2, 24, 25, 28
print market 5, 11, 12, 15, 62, 66, 140, 145, 168, 175, 190, 195, 206–22, 226, 227; *see also* ballads; pamphlet literature; newspapers
prostitutes and prostitution 131, 201, 202, 208, 210, 218; *see also* whores and whoredom
Protestantism 2, 3, 4, 8, 21, 31–2, 61, 70, 78, 127–8, 138, 160, 173, 180, 190, 199–200, 218, 226; notions of poverty 147–8; theology of sin 37–42, 43, 50–1; *see also* providentialism; puritans
providentialism 38–9, 42–3, 57, 70, 199, 217
public sphere 12, 220, 230, 233
puritans: amplification of shame 51–7; autobiographies 10, 50–1, 54–7, 61, 62, 66, 70; biblical models 52–3; diaries 10, 50–1, 51–4, 62, 66, 71, 200; dissenters 200, 217–8; life-cycle narratives 54–5; lists of sins 51–3; mitigating strategies 57–60; nonconformists 51, 67, 141, 138, 222; radicals 51, 66, 68–70, 72; spiritual oscillations 60–6; *see also* evangelical awakening; guilt; Presbyterians; self (self-examination); shame (punitive, redemptive)

Quakers
Quakers (Society of Friends) 68–70, 71, 128, 141, 186

rape 156, 202, 233
rebuke 9, 19, 39, 58–9, 81, 84, 87, 89, 92, 97, 99–100, 113, 116, 128, 131, 142, 157, 160, 203–4, 213, 228, 229; *see also* reproach
repentance 6, 34, 36, 37–42, 43, 51, 60, 61, 159, 160, 171, 173–8, 181, 186–7, 190, 227
reproach 27, 29, 32, 34, 38, 39, 58, 85, 92, 93–5, 99–100, 93–5, 99–100, 113, 120, 121, 122, 126, 127, 139, 145, 187, 196, 211, 219, 231; self-reproach 35, 53, 67; *see also* rebuke

reputation 23, 84, 90–1, 98, 106–12, 125, 130–2, 140–2, 150, 161, 171, 178, 185–6, 188, 204, 211, 212–13, 220, 227
resentment 80, 90–1, 153, 233; *see also* anger
ridicule 18, 20, 29, 30, 34, 79, 86, 140, 141, 143, 160, 178, 198, 205, 207–12; *see also* satire

satire 145, 147, 205–12, 219, 227, 230
Scattergood, John 107, 108, 113–15, 119
schools 16, 24, 78, 79, 80, 84, 172, 216–7, 220, 232; schoolboys 55, 79, 217; schoolmasters, 58, 78
scold 138, 139, 140, 142
Seager, Francis 16, 17, 19, 20–1
self: external 8, 15, 21, 22, 23, 44, 77, 112, 219, 228–9; inner and internal 3, 4, 5, 8, 11, 34–7, 43–4, 51, 59, 64, 69, 71, 77, 95, 97–9, 112–3, 132, 190, 200, 213, 219, 228–8, 233; multifaceted 190, 229; relational 5, 11, 44, 77, 101, 228, 233; self-awareness 5, 22, 36, 44, 77, 220, 229; self-esteem 1, 5, 9, 11, 23, 113, 132, 228–9; self-examination 6, 51–7, 72, 200; self-reflection 8, 23, 36, 101, 228; self-respect 11, 162, 181–9, 180, 229
servants 17, 30, 89, 91, 100, 152, 153–4; in crime narratives 176, 183, 184, 187, 188
sexuality and sexual 15, 29, 31, 33–4, 42, 138, 140–1, 145, 146, 156–7, 160, 161, 199, 200–2, 208, 210–12, 217–18, 229, 231, 232; *see also* shame (and sexuality)
Shakespeare, William 6, 33–5, 36, 44
shame punishments: branding 156, 158, 194–5; decline of 194, 205–6, 217, 229; hair shaving 139, 156, 158; persistence of 231; and penance 156–9, 161, 227; scold's bridle and branks 139, 140–2; *see also* ducking; executions; skimmington and charivari; stocks and pillory; whipping
shame and shaming: benign 51, 66–9, 148, 152, 195, 197, 219, 228; and the body 15, 16, 21, 25, 27–31, 33–8, 40, 42–3, 140, 155, 157–8, 159, 168–9, 174, 205, 208, 227, 232; bounded 11, 181–88, 190, 228;

British collective 233; concealed and hidden 6, 78, 86, 101, 131, 155; and conflict resolution 196, 229; and conformity 2, 3, 8, 137, 143, 160, 186, 209, 227, 232, 233; and conciliation 11, 133, 143, 159, 160, 174, 213, 214, 228; and damaged relations 99, 233; and deference 19–20, 83, 89, 96, 100, 147; and disputes (interpersonal) 84, 89, 99, 100, 105–6, 111, 117, 118, 125, 130, 131–2, 133, 141, 196, 213–14, 215, 220; early modern discourse of 1–2, 15–6; exclusionary 4, 6, 17, 19, 21, 34, 42, 99, 112, 131, 138, 159–161, 189, 199, 214, 218, 226–7, 232; external 6, 8, 15, 21–3, 44, 112, 219, 228–9; feminine 24–5; *see also* shamefastness; modesty; inclusive 4, 101, 143, 159, 190, 227–8; insinuated 6, 43, 57, 85, 90, 100, 130, 172, 227; integrative and re-integrative 6, 40, 43, 132, 159, 227–8; internal 3, 5, 8, 20–1, 23–7, 35–6, 37, 43–4, 97, 112, 200, 219, 228–9, 233; masculine 24–7, 33–4, 201, 204–17; and mental illness 56–7; as moral and social critique 11, 21, 43, 85, 96, 100–1, 146–7, 161, 206, 208–9, 211, 218; personalized 11, 78, 87, 90, 93–6, 100–1, 118–23, 132–3, 227; polite 81–3, 92, 96; punitive 4–5, 6, 11, 117–20, 36–9, 51–7, 60–5, 78, 83, 87–8, 92–3, 97, 132, 159–61, 168–72, 226–7; and race 6, 12, 195–9, 218, 227, 229–30, 232; redemptive 36–7, 40–1, 51, 60–6, 173–8; retributive 38, 173, 218, 231; and sexuality 29, 31, 199, 201–2; and social divisions 4, 11, 160, 197, 226; and solidarity 6, 39–40, 43, 98–9, 130, 158–9, 232–3; and stigma 6, 11, 145–6, 151–5, 158, 159, 161, 197, 199, 202, 231–2; transformations of 5, 194–220
shamefastness 23, 24–5, 33, 43; *see also* modesty
shameless 24, 34–5, 40, 42, 82, 109, 121, 157, 169, 179–80, 189
shamelessness 38, 109, 131, 180; *see also* defiance; shameless
sin and sins: amplification of 51–3, 54–7; original 31, 37, 70, 72, 172, 199–200, 203, 217–8; in spiritual guides 37–8; in sermons and providential stories 38–9; youthful 54–5, 58, 67, 70, 71, 82, 172, 200; *see also* guilt; repentance; shame (punitive, redemptive); transgressions
Sitwell, George 120, 123, 126–7, 130
skimmington and charivari 138–9, 139–40, 141, 142, 143, 206, 218
Skinner, Ephraim 113, 125–6, 127
slaves and slavery 140, 198, 199, 218, 219
Spenser, Edmund 197
stocks and pillory 41, 67, 146, 156, 157, 158, 159, 160, 194, 210
stuttering and stammering 19, 79
Steele, Richard: *The Tradesman's Calling* 112
sympathy 94, 95, 112, 120, 130, 142, 189, 190, 202; *see also* empathy
Symson, Joseph 85–8, 117, 118, 119, 121, 122, 125, 126, 128, 129

transgressions (moral, religious, social) 38, 52, 55, 66, 67, 92, 100, 109, 110, 128, 137, 156, 160
transportation (punishment) 180, 194
Trosse, George 55, 56, 57, 58, 60
trust 92, 95, 98–9, 101, 105–6, 107, 109, 111, 113–14, 115–18, 119–20, 129–31, 133
Turner, William 115–17, 133

vagrancy: beggars 144, 168, 197, 209; pauper migrants 150, 156, 161; vagabonds 30, 144, 197
Vesalius, Andreas 30–1

Wallington, Nehemiah 52, 53, 56, 57, 59, 62, 72, 92–6, 99
Ward, Samuel 52, 53, 59
Webster, John 33
whipping 80, 156–7, 159–60, 194–5, 217; of children 80–1, 203, 205
Williams, Philip 108, 109–10, 117, 121, 130
workhouses 151–3
whores and whoredom 24, 33, 98, 139, 141, 145, 146, 153, 173, 201, 202, 203, 208; *see also* prostitutes and prostitution

youth and youthful 16, 29, 53, 56–7, 58, 61, 142–3

Printed in the United States
by Baker & Taylor Publisher Services